Game-theoretic models of bargaining

Game-theoretic models of bargaining

Edited by
ALVIN E. ROTH
University of Pittsburgh

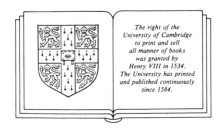

The right of the
University of Cambridge
to print and sell
all manner of books
was granted by
Henry VIII in 1534.
The University has printed
and published continuously
since 1584.

CAMBRIDGE UNIVERSITY PRESS

Cambridge
London   New York   New Rochelle
Melbourne   Sydney

Published by the Press Syndicate of the University of Cambridge
The Pitt Building, Trumpington Street, Cambridge CB2 1RP
32 East 57th Street, New York, NY 10022, USA
10 Stamford Road, Oakleigh, Melbourne 3166, Australia

© Cambridge University Press 1985

First published 1985

Printed in the United States of America

Library of Congress Cataloging in Publication Data

Main entry under title:

Game theoretic models of bargaining.

   1. Game theory – Congresses. 2. Negotiation –
Mathematical models – Congresses. I. Roth, Alvin E.,
1951-
HB144.G36   1985   302.3′0724   84-28516
ISBN 0-521-26757-9

Contents

v

Contributors

KEN BINMORE is Professor of Mathematics and Chairman of the Economic Theory Workshop at the London School of Economics, where he has taught since 1969. He has a Ph.D. in Mathematics from Imperial College, London, and is an Associate of the Royal College of Science.

KALYAN CHATTERJEE has been an Assistant Professor of Management Science at The Pennsylvania State University since 1979. He obtained a D.B.A. from Harvard University in 1979. Prior to that he studied at the Indian Institute of Management and at the University of Calcutta.

PETER C. CRAMTON is Assistant Professor at the Yale School of Organization and Management. He received his Ph.D. from Stanford University in 1984.

VINCENT P. CRAWFORD is Associate Professor of Economics at the University of California at San Diego, where he has taught since 1976, when he received his Ph.D. from the Massachusetts Institute of Technology.

DREW FUDENBERG is Assistant Professor of Economics at the University of California at Berkeley. He was awarded his Ph.D. from the Massachusetts Institute of Technology in 1981.

SERGIU HART is Associate Professor of Statistics in the School of Mathematical Sciences at Tel-Aviv University where he received his Ph.D. in 1976.

DAVID LEVINE is an Assistant Professor of Economics at the University of California at Los Angeles. He received his Ph.D. from the Massachusetts Institute of Technology in 1981.

ROGER B. MYERSON is Professor of Managerial Economics and Decision Sciences at Northwestern University, where he has taught since 1976, when he was granted his Ph.D. from Harvard University. He has been awarded a Guggenheim Fellowship and an Alfred P. Sloan Research Fellowship, and is a Fellow of the Econometric Society.

MARTIN J. OSBORNE is an Assistant Professor of Economics at Columbia University. He received his Ph.D. from Stanford University in 1979.

HANS PETERS teaches in the Economics Department of the University of Limburg, Maastricht, The Netherlands.

ROBERT W. ROSENTHAL was awarded the Ph.D. in Operations Research from Stanford University in 1971. He served on the faculty of the Department of Industrial Engineering and Management Sciences at Northwestern University from 1970 to 1976, on the technical staff at Bell Laboratories from 1976 to 1983, and on the faculty of the Department of Economics at Virginia Polytechnic Institute and State University from 1983 to 1984. He is currently a Professor of Economics at the State University of New York at Stony Brook.

ALVIN E. ROTH is the A. W. Mellon Professor of Economics at the University of Pittsburgh, where he has taught since 1982. He received a Ph.D. from Stanford University in 1974. He has been awarded the Founders' Prize of the Texas Instruments Foundation, a Guggenheim Fellowship, and an Alfred P. Sloan Research Fellowship. He is a Fellow of the Econometric Society.

ARIEL RUBINSTEIN is Senior Lecturer in the Department of Economics of the Hebrew University of Jerusalem, which granted him a Ph.D. in 1979.

WILLIAM SAMUELSON is Associate Professor of Economics at Boston University School of Management. He received a Ph.D. from Harvard University in 1978.

JOEL SOBEL is Associate Professor of Economics at the University of California at San Diego, where he has taught since 1978, when he was awarded his Ph.D. from the University of California at Berkeley.

WILLIAM THOMSON is Associate Professor of Economics at the University of Rochester, where he has taught since 1983. He received his Ph.D. from Stanford University in 1976.

STEF TIJS is Professor in Game Theory, Mathematical Economics, and Operations Research in the Department of Mathematics of the Catholic University in Nijmegen, The Netherlands, where he has taught since 1968. He received a Master's degree at the University of Utrecht in 1963, and wrote a Ph.D. dissertation in Nijmegen in 1975.

JEAN TIROLE has taught at Ecole Nationale des Ponts et Chaussees, Paris, since 1981. He received engineering degrees from Ecole Polytechnique (1976) and Ecole Nationale des Ponts et Chaussees (1978), a "Doctorat de 3eme cycle" in Decision Mathematics from University Paris 9 (1978), and a Ph.D. in Economics from the Massachussetts Institute of Technology (1981).

ROBERT WILSON is the Atholl McBean Professor of Decision Sciences at Stanford University, where he has taught since 1964. He received a D.B.A. from Harvard University in 1963. He has been awarded a Guggenheim Fellowship, and is a Fellow of the Econometric Society.

Preface

The readings in this volume are revised versions of papers presented at the Conference on Game-Theoretic Models of Bargaining held June 27–30, 1983, at the University of Pittsburgh. Support for the conference was provided by the National Science Foundation and by the University of Pittsburgh.

The conference would not have been possible without the support at the University of Pittsburgh of Chancellor Wesley Posvar, Dean Jerome Rosenberg, and my colleague Professor Mark Perlman. Michael Rothschild was instrumental in arranging the NSF support.

A. E. Roth

CHAPTER 1

Editor's introduction and overview

Alvin E. Roth
UNIVERSITY OF PITTSBURGH

There are two distinct reasons why the study of bargaining is of fundamental importance to economics. The first is that many aspects of economic activity are influenced directly by bargaining between and among individuals, firms, and nations. The second is that bargaining occupies an important place in economic *theory,* since the "pure bargaining problem" is at the opposite pole of economic phenomena from "perfect competition."

It is not surprising that economic theory has had less apparent success in studying bargaining than in studying perfect competition, since perfect competition represents the idealized case in which the *strategic* aspect of economic interaction is reduced to negligible proportions by the discipline of a market that allows each agent to behave as a solitary decision maker, whereas pure bargaining is the case of economic interaction in which the market plays no role other than to set the bounds of discussion, within which the final outcome is determined entirely by the strategic interaction of the bargainers. The fact that the outcome of bargaining depends on this strategic interaction has led many economists, at least since the time of Edgeworth (1881), to conclude that bargaining is characterized by the indeterminacy of its outcome. In this view, theories of bargaining cannot, even in principle, do more than specify a range in which an agreement may be found; to attempt to accomplish more would be to introduce arbitrary specificity.

The contrary view, of course, is that sufficient information about the attributes of the bargainers and about the detailed structure of the bargaining problem that these bargainers face will allow the range of indeterminacy to be narrowed, and perhaps eliminated. This view was illustrated in an article written by John Nash (1950*a*), making use of the properties of expected utility functions outlined by John von Neumann and Oskar Morgenstern in their book *Theory of Games and Economic Behavior* (1944).

Nash (1950*a*) developed what has come to be called an *axiomatic*

1

model of bargaining. (It is also sometimes called a *cooperative* model, since it models the bargaining process as a cooperative game.) He was interested in predicting a particular outcome for any given bargaining situation, and his approach was to propose a set of postulates, or axioms, about the relationship of the predicted outcome to the set of feasible outcomes, as represented in terms of the utility functions of the bargainers. In this way, he characterized a particular function that selects a unique outcome from a broad class of bargaining problems. By concentrating on the set of potential agreements, and abstracting away from the detailed procedures by which a particular set of negotiations might be conducted, Nash's approach offered the possibility of a theory of bargaining that would enjoy substantial generality. This was perhaps the first general model of bargaining to gain wide currency in the theoretical literature of economics.

Three years later, Nash (1953) published another article on bargaining, which extended his original analysis in several ways. Perhaps the most significant of these extensions was the proposal of a specific *strategic* model that supported the same conclusions as the general axiomatic model outlined earlier. His approach was to propose one very particular bargaining procedure embodied in a noncooperative game in extensive form. (The *extensive form* of a game specifies when each agent will make each of the choices facing him, and what information he will possess at that time. It thus allows close attention to be paid to the specific strategic questions that arise under a given set of bargaining rules.) Nash then argued that the predicted outcome of this noncooperative bargaining game would be the same as the outcome predicted by the axiomatic model. To show this, he called on the newly developing theory of noncooperative games, to which he had made the seminal contribution of proposing the notion of equilibrium (Nash 1950b) that today bears his name. Although the noncooperative game he proposed possessed a multitude (indeed, a continuum) of Nash equilibria, he argued that the one corresponding to the prediction of his axiomatic model had distinguishing characteristics.

In subsequent years, the axiomatic approach pioneered by Nash was developed widely. The particular model he proposed was studied and applied extensively, and other axiomatic models were explored. By contrast, there was much less successful development of the strategic approach. In 1979, when my monograph *Axiomatic Models of Bargaining* was published, most of the influential game-theoretic work on bargaining fit comfortably under that title. However, since then, there has been a renewed interest in the strategic approach, resulting in a number of striking developments in the theory of bargaining.

Recent progress in the strategic approach to the theory of bargaining has been due in large part to two developments in the general theory of noncooperative games. One of these developments, originating in the work of Harsanyi (1967, 1968a, 1968b), extends the theory to include games of "incomplete information," which allow more realistic modeling of bargaining situations in which a bargainer holds private information (e.g., information that only he knows, such as how much he values some potential agreement). The other development, originating in the work of Selten (1965, 1973, 1975) on "perfect equilibria," offers a technique for reducing the multiplicity of Nash equilibria found in many noncooperative games, by proposing criteria to identify a subset of equilibria that could credibly be expected to arise from certain kinds of rational play of the game. (An important reformulation of some of these ideas on credible equilibria, which makes explicit how certain kinds of behavior depend on agents' beliefs about one another's behavior, has been given by Kreps and Wilson (1982).)

Two articles that demonstrate how these two developments have separately contributed to the recent progress in the theory of bargaining are those by Rubinstein (1982) and Myerson and Satterthwaite (1983). The paper by Rubinstein develops a model of multiperiod bargaining under complete information, in which two agents alternate proposing how to divide some desirable commodity between them, until one of them accepts the other's proposal. When the agents discount future events, so that the value of the commodity diminishes over time, Rubinstein characterizes the agreements that could arise from perfect equilibria, and shows that the model typically predicts a unique agreement.

Myerson and Satterthwaite consider the range of bargaining procedures (or "mechanisms") that could be used to resolve single-period bargaining under incomplete information, in which two agents negotiate over whether, and at what price, one of them will buy some object from the other, when each agent knows his own value for the object and has a continuous probability distribution describing the other agent's value. They show that, when no outside subsidies are available from third parties, no bargaining procedure exists with equilibria that are ex post efficient, that is, with equilibria having the property that a trade is made if and only if the buyer values the object more than does the seller. The intuition underlying this is that a bargainer who behaves so that he *always* makes a trade when one is possible must, in most situations, be profiting less from the trade than he could be. Equilibrium behavior involves a tradeoff between the expected profitability of each trade and the probability of reaching an agreement on the terms of trade.

These and related results derived from strategic models have added a dimension to the game-theoretic treatment of bargaining that was not present when my book on axiomatic models appeared in 1979. In addition, there have been subsequent developments in the study of axiomatic models, and some encouraging progress at bridging the gap between these two approaches, as well as in identifying their limitations. It was for the purpose of permitting these developments to be discussed in a unified way that the Conference on Game-Theoretic Models of Bargaining, from which the readings in this volume come, was held at the University of Pittsburgh in June 1983. Together, these papers provide a good picture of some of the new directions being explored.

The first two selections, those by Chatterjee (Chapter 2) and by Wilson (Chapter 3), are surveys that put in context some of the theoretical developments that depend critically on the ability to model rational play of games under incomplete information. Chatterjee focuses on models that predict a positive probability of disagreement in bargaining, as a consequence of the demands of equilibrium behavior. Wilson focuses on the role of players' expectations and beliefs about one another in games and markets that have some degree of repeated interaction among agents. An agent's "reputation" is the belief that others have about those of his characteristics that are private information. In particular, Wilson discusses the role that agents' reputations, and the opportunities that agents have to influence their reputations, play in determining their equilibrium behavior.

The next reading, by Rosenthal (Chapter 4), discusses a rather different approach to the effects of reputation. In his models, Rosenthal views reputation as a summary statistic of an agent's past behavior, in bargaining against previous opponents. He considers how the reputations of the agents mediate the play of the game when the members of a large population of potential bargainers are paired randomly in each period.

The paper by Fudenberg, Levine, and Tirole (Chapter 5), and the paper by Rubinstein (Chapter 6), both define a multiperiod game of incomplete information that is sufficiently complex to allow a variety of bargaining phenomena to be exhibited at equilibrium. Both papers conclude that the beliefs that agents hold play an important part in determining equilibrium behavior, and both discuss some of the methodological and modeling issues that arise in studying bargaining in this way.

The readings by Myerson (Chapter 7) and Cramton (Chapter 8) each consider the problem of mechanism design for bargaining with incomplete information. Myerson examines some single-period bargaining models in terms of the comprehensively articulated approach to bargaining that he has explored elsewhere. Cramton addresses similar questions with respect to bargaining that takes place over time. The inefficiencies due to equilibrium behavior that appear as disagreements in single-period models appear in his model as delays in reaching agreement.

The next two papers, by Osborne (Chapter 9) and by Tijs and Peters (Chapter 10), address a different kind of question: the relationship between risk posture and bargaining ability. This question was first raised in the context of axiomatic models, when it was shown in Roth (1979) and Kihlstrom, Roth, and Schmeidler (1981) that a wide variety of these models predict that risk aversion is disadvantageous in bargaining when all of the potential agreements are deterministic. (The situation is a little more complicated when agreements can involve lotteries; see Roth and Rothblum (1982).) A similar result has now been shown to hold for the strategic model proposed by Rubinstein (1982) (see Roth (1985)). However, in his selection in this volume, Osborne explores a strategic model that yields more equivocal results. Tijs and Peters adopt the axiomatic approach and explore how various properties of a bargaining model are related to the predictions it makes about the influence of risk aversion.

The reading by Thomson (Chapter 11) presents a survey of a new direction in the axiomatic tradition. Thomson looks at axiomatic models defined over a domain of problems containing different numbers of agents, and interprets the problem as one of fair division, which is an orientation that reflects the close association between bargaining and arbitration. (The problems he considers can also be viewed as multiperson pure bargaining problems if the rules state that no coalition of agents other than the coalition of all the agents has any options that are not available to the agents acting individually.)

I am the author of the next reading (Chapter 12), which reviews some experimental results that point to limitations of the descriptive power of both axiomatic and strategic models as presently formulated. The paper suggests an approach that may hold promise for building descriptive game-theoretic models of bargaining, and suggests in particular that disagreement at equilibrium may have systematic components that cannot be modeled as being due to incomplete information.

The readings by Binmore (Chapter 13) and by Hart (Chapter 14) can both be viewed as extending bargaining models from the two-person case to the case of multiperson games (which differ from multiperson pure bargaining problems in that subsets of agents acting together typically have options not available to individuals). In his analysis of three-person games Binmore follows (as he has elsewhere) in the tradition proposed by Nash, of developing solution concepts for cooperative games from strategic considerations. Hart reviews some recent axiomatizations of solution concepts for general multiperson games. (Both papers have the potential to shed some light on the ongoing discussion that Binmore refers to as the

"Aumann–Roth debate" concerning the interpretation of the nontransferable utility, NTU, value.)

The final three selections attempt to bridge the gap between abstract models of bargaining and more institutionally oriented models of dispute resolution. Samuelson (Chapter 15) focuses on the consequences for efficiency of assigning property rights in cases involving externalities (e.g., the right to unpolluted air). Sobel (Chapter 16) considers the role played by assigning the burden of proof in a model of litigation in which a third party (a judge) is available to settle disputes. Crawford (Chapter 17) considers points of potential contact between the literature on mechanism design for bargaining under incomplete information and the literature on third-party arbitration. His paper makes clear both the necessity and the difficulty of establishing two-way contact between the abstract theoretical literature and the institutionally oriented applied literature in this area.

REFERENCES

Edgeworth, F. Y.: *Mathematical Psychics*. London: Kegan, Paul, 1881.

Harsanyi, John C.: Games with Incomplete Information Played by "Bayesian" Players I: The Basic Model. *Management Science,* 1967, 14, 159–82.

Games with Incomplete Information Played by "Bayesian" Players II: Bayesian Equilibrium Points. *Management Science,* 1968a, 14, 320–34.

Games with Incomplete Information Played by "Bayesian" Players III: The Basic Probability Distribution of the Game. *Management Science,* 1968b, 14, 486–502.

Kihlstrom, Richard E., Alvin E. Roth, and David Schmeidler: Risk Aversion and Solutions to Nash's Bargaining Problem. Pp. in *Game Theory and Mathematical Economics*. Amsterdam: North-Holland, 1981, 65–71.

Kreps, David M., and Robert Wilson: Sequential Equilibria. *Econometrica,* 1982, 50, 863–94.

Myerson, R. B., and M. A. Satterthwaite: Efficient Mechanisms for Bilateral Trading. *Journal of Economic Theory,* 1983, 29, 265–81.

Nash, John F.: The Bargaining Problem. *Econometrica,* 1950a, 18, 155–62.

Equilibrium Points in *n*-Person Games. *Proceedings of the National Academy of Science,* 1950b, 36, 48–9.

Two-Person Cooperative Games. *Econometrica,* 1953, 21, 128–40.

Roth, Alvin E.: *Axiomatic Models of Bargaining*. Berlin: Springer, 1979.

A Note on Risk Aversion in a Perfect Equilibrium Model of Bargaining. *Econometrica,* 1985, 53, 207–11.

Roth, Alvin E., and Uriel G. Rothblum: Risk Aversion and Nash's Solution for Bargaining Games with Risky Outcomes. *Econometrica,* 1982, 50, 639–47.

Rubinstein, Ariel: Perfect Equilibrium in a Bargaining Model. *Econometrica,* 1982, 50, 97–110.

Selten, Reinhard: Spieltheoretische Behandlung eines Oligopolmodells mit Nachfragetragheit. *Zeitschrift fur die gesamte Staatswissenschaft,* 1965, 121, 301–24 and 667–89.

A Simple Model of Imperfect Competition where 4 Are Few and 6 Are Many. *International Journal of Game Theory,* 1973, 2, 141–201.

Reexamination of the Perfectness Concept for Equilibrium Points in Extensive Games. *International Journal of Game Theory,* 1975, 4, 25–55.

von Neumann, John, and Oskar Morgenstern: *Theory of Games and Economic Behavior.* Princeton, N.J.: Princeton University Press, 1944.

CHAPTER 2

Disagreement in bargaining: Models with incomplete information

Kalyan Chatterjee
THE PENNSYLVANIA STATE UNIVERSITY

2.1 Introduction

This essay serves as an introduction to recent work on noncooperative game-theoretic models of two-player bargaining under incomplete information. The objective is to discuss some of the problems that motivated formulation of these models, as well as cover some of the issues that still need to be addressed. I have not set out to provide a detailed survey of all the existing models, and I have therefore discussed only certain specific aspects of the models that I believe to be especially important. The reader will find here, however, a guide to the relevant literature.

The title of this chapter was chosen to emphasize the phenomenon of disagreement in bargaining, which occurs almost as a natural consequence of rational behavior (i.e., equilibrium behavior) in some of these models and is difficult to explain on the basis of equilibrium behavior using the established framework of bargaining under complete information. Disagreement, of course, is only one reflection of the problem of inefficient bargaining processes. I also spend some time on the general question of efficiency and its attainment. Whereas in most models classical Pareto-efficiency is not attainable in equilibrium, it may be obtained by players who deviate from equilibrium, as will be shown.

The chapter is organized as follows. Section 2.2 lays out the problem and discusses the important modeling approaches available. Section 2.3 focuses on a particular group of models, each of which specifies a strategic (i.e., extensive) form of the bargaining process. Section 2.4 is concerned with studies in which the strategic form is not specified. The final section contains conclusions about the material covered.

I am grateful to Al Roth, Gary Lilien, and an anonymous referee for their valuable comments.

9

2.2 Problem context and modeling approaches

The process of resource allocation through bargaining between two parties who have some common interests and some opposing ones is widespread in the modern world. Examples include negotiations between an industrial buyer and a potential supplier (or, in general, between any buyer and any seller), between management and union representatives, and between nations. (Raiffa (1982) contains accounts of many different bargaining situations.)

In view of its importance, it is not surprising that bargaining has generated much theoretical interest, beginning with the classic work of Nash (1950, 1953) and Raiffa (1953). Until a few years ago, most of the theoretical work had assumed complete information; that is, the bargainers' utility functions, the set of feasible agreements, and the recourse options available if bargaining failed were all considered to be common knowledge. Any uncertainty present in the situation would be shared uncertainty, with both bargainers having the same information about the uncertain event.

Within this set of assumptions, the problem has been explored using one of three broad categories of theoretical endeavor. The first approach, present in Nash (1950, 1953) and Raiffa (1953) and extended and completed in recent work (see Roth (1979)), has not sought to describe the bargaining process explicitly through a specific extensive form. Rather, it has concentrated on formulating and exploring the implications of general principles that are compatible with possibly many different extensive forms. These principles can be interpreted as descriptive of actual bargaining but often have been regarded as normative rules.

The main theoretical results in this type of work lead to the specification of a rule for choosing an agreement (usually leading to a unique solution) that is characterized by a particular set of principles or axioms.

This approach is often described as "cooperative" since the jointly agreed-upon solution is implemented presumably by a binding agreement.

The second way of exploring the bargaining process specifies a bargaining game, whose equilibrium outcome then serves as a predictor of the actual bargaining process. For example, the Nash solution is an equilibrium (only one of many) of a simple one-stage demand game in which players make demands simultaneously, and the agreement occurs if the two demands can be met by a feasible agreement. (If the demands are not compatible in this way, a conflict occurs, and the "status-quo point" is the solution.) Work by Harsanyi (1956), Binmore (1981), and others has sought to explain why the equilibrium given by the Nash solution would, in fact, be the one chosen in the bargaining.

Note that the presence of multiple equilibria may explain why bargainers disagree, even under complete information. In Chapter 12 of this volume, Roth proposes a simple coordination game in which players use mixed strategies and thus may, with positive probability, not choose the same outcome.

The third approach to investigating bargaining, which will not be considered here, applies general theories to construct explanations for specific problems, for example the determination of the wage and the amount of labor used in management – union bargaining (e.g., see McDonald and Solow (1981)).

Each of the first two approaches has its strengths and weaknesses. Specifying an extensive form enables us to model (e.g., in the work under incomplete information) the strategic use of private information and, therefore, has implications that could prove useful for individual bargainers. However, an extensive form is bound to be arbitrary to some extent, and the axiomatic approach cuts through disputes about choice of extensive forms.

The focus of the remainder of this chapter is on models of bargaining under incomplete information. These models are concerned with situations wherein each party has private information (e.g., about preferences) that is unavailable to the other side. This relaxation of the assumptions made in the complete-information framework has crucial implications. The most interesting one for economists is the persistence of Pareto-inefficient outcomes in equilibrium, the most striking of which is the existence of disagreement even when mutually beneficial agreements exist. The bargaining research has also generated new notions of constrained efficiency that appear to be of general relevance in many different areas of economics.

As before in the case of complete information models, the theoretical studies under conditions of incomplete information have employed two somewhat different research strategies. The axiomatic approach was pioneered by Harsanyi and Selten (1972). The strategic approach is based on Harsanyi (1967, 1968), work that supplied the extension of the Nash-equilibrium concept essential to explaining games of incomplete information. The two basic contributions of this series of papers by Harsanyi were: (1) the specification of the consistency conditions on the probability distributions of the players' private information (or, to use Harsanyi's term, "types"); and (2) the specification that a player's strategy consisted of a mapping from his type to his action. A conjecture about an opponent's strategy combined with the underlying probability distribution of the opponent's type would generate a probability distribution over the opponent's actions. A player would maximize his conditional expected utility given his type and this conjectured probability distribution.

Table 2.1. *Strategic models of bargaining under incomplete information*

Models	Features							
	1	2	3	4	5	6	7	8
Binmore (1981)	✓		✓					
Chatterjee and Samuelson (1983)	✓	✓	✓					✓
Cramton (1983)	✓	✓		✓				✓
Crawford (1982)	✓	✓	✓					
Fudenberg and Tirole (1983)	✓[a]			✓				✓
Fudenberg, Levine, and Tirole (Chapter 5, this volume)		✓	✓[a]	✓				✓
Rubinstein (1983)			✓	✓				
Sobel and Takahashi (1983)		✓		✓				✓
Wilson (1982)	✓	✓	✓				✓	✓

Key to Features:
1 – Two-sided incomplete information
2 – Continuous probability distributions
3 – Both parties make offers
4 – Sequential-information transmission incorporated in model
5 – Bargaining on more than one dimension
6 – Explicit consideration of alternatives to current bargain
7 – Many buyers and sellers in market
8 – Bargainers uncertain before bargaining of the size of gains from trade
[a] This feature is included in some of the models proposed.

Selten (1975) and, more recently, Kreps and Wilson (1982*a*, 1982*b*) have proposed that an equilibrium pair of strategies should satisfy an additional requirement, that of "perfectness," or "sequential rationality," in order to be considered an adequate solution. This requirement entails that a player's equilibrium strategy should still be optimal for him at every stage of a multistage extensive-form game, given his beliefs about the future and current position in the game. For example, an equilibrium based on a threat strategy (e.g., to blow up the world) that would clearly not be in a player's best interest to implement would not be a perfect equilibrium.

The theoretical research in strategic models of bargaining is summarized in Table 2.1. This summary table is by no means an exhaustive list of all the features important to modeling the bargaining process. It does, however, contain some salient ones useful for comparing the different models.

Three explanatory notes are in order here. First, papers such as Crawford (1982) are written in terms of utility – possibility sets and therefore theoretically encompass bargaining on more than one dimension. However, players engaged in such bargaining will not find any strategic advice in these papers.

Second, feature 6 refers to determining explicitly what recourse players have in the event of disagreement – in other words, models of variable conflict outcomes. Crawford (1982) contains some pointers on developing such a model, although a scheme is not fully laid out.

Third, one area of analytical research is not included in Table 2.1. This area consists of the asymmetric decision-analytic models inspired by Raiffa (1982). In these models, no equilibrium conjectures are used to generate probability distributions of the other player's acts. Rather, such probability distributions are assessed directly, based either on subjective judgment or on empirical observation of the other player's past behavior. Although this approach is evidently incomplete as a formal theory of interaction, it has the advantage of being able to provide advice to bargainers faced with complex tasks. For example, in Chatterjee and Ulvila (1982), a start is made (in work by Ulvila) in analyzing multidimensional bargaining problems. In this study, bargainers possess additive linear utility functions over two attributes, with the relative importance accorded to each attribute being private information. The bargainers announce these weights, and the Nash solution conditional on these announcements is used to determine the attribute levels. The analysis is done for a given probability distribution of announcements by the opponent, and an optimal strategy, which proves to be discontinuous, is calculated.

Papers by Chatterjee (1982) and Myerson and Satterthwaite (1983) provide a bridge between the extensive forms of Table 2.1 and the full-fledged axiomatic approach of Myerson (1983, 1984). Essentially, these papers show the general Pareto-inefficiency of bargaining procedures under incomplete information and the tradeoffs needed to restore efficiency.

In the new cooperative theory developed by Myerson, there is explicit recognition of the constraints imposed by incomplete information. Not all binding contracts are possible; since players' strategies are unobservable, a requirement of any contract is that it is sustainable as an equilibrium of some extensive-form game. These recent papers by Chatterjee and by Myerson and Satterthwaite therefore constitute a synthesis of the two prevalent approaches.

Finally, bargaining is especially suited to controlled experimentation. Various carefully designed experiments involving conditions of complete information have been conducted by Roth (see Chapter 12 in this volume) and others. Somewhat more informal experimentation under incomplete information is reported in Chatterjee and Ulvila (1982) and Chatterjee and Lilien (1984). These latter articles cast some doubt on the validity of Bayesian equilibrium as a predictor of the outcome of bargaining under incomplete information.

2.3   Models of disagreement and incomplete information

In this section, models that seek to explain the inefficiency of actual bargaining as an equilibrium phenomenon are considered. The concept of efficiency used here is the familiar one of Pareto-efficiency (often called "full-information efficiency") – namely, trade takes place if and only if it is mutually advantageous for both bargainers to conclude a trade. The next section presents a discussion of the study of efficient procedures or mechanisms for bargaining (which could, in general, lead to inefficient outcomes).

The concept of equilibrium used is the Nash-equilibrium notion in the setting of incomplete information (developed by Harsanyi (1967, 1968) and called Bayesian equilibrium in the literature). Models that involve multistage extensive forms need, in addition, to consider whether commitments made at one stage would be rational to carry out in future stages. Some models accomplish this by explicitly using perfect equilibrium as the solution concept, whereas others use an implicit perfectness notion in the model formulation (see Chapter 3 in this volume for a more detailed discussion of the numerous papers in various fields of economics that could be completed by making an explicit perfectness argument).

All of the models presented here involve incomplete information, and some also include sequential offers (see Table 2.1). The main concern is that most of these models do not have equilibria that are full-information efficient, with finite-horizon models expressing this inefficiency through disagreement in the presence of gains from trade, and infinite-horizon ones through delayed agreement. However, there are incomplete-information models that exhibit efficient equilibria.

An example is Binmore (1981). I shall mention briefly some aspects of this model relevant to this chapter, although the main thrust of Binmore's work lies elsewhere.

The paper by Binmore considers the "divide-the-dollar" game with incomplete information. That is, there is some perfectly divisible commodity of a known amount that has to be divided between two players, I and II. Player I could be one of a finite set of types $i = 1, 2, \ldots, m$, with commonly known probabilities $\lambda_1, \lambda_2, \ldots, \lambda_m$, respectively. Player I knows his type, but player II knows only the probabilities of the various different types. Similarly, player II could be any one of types $j = 1, 2, \ldots, n$, with commonly known probabilities $\mu_1, \mu_2, \ldots, \mu_n$, respectively. Player II knows his own type, but player I knows only the probabilities. Each player has a von Neumann–Morgenstern utility function on the amount of the commodity that he obtains in the event of an agreement and on his payoff if there is no agreement. A player's utility function depends also on his type.

Binmore then considers a bargaining game in which players make demands in terms of amounts of the commodity desired. If the sum of the two demands is at most the amount of the commodity available, each player gets his demand. If not, each gets his conflict payoff. Note that the demands are firm commitments from which neither player is permitted to back down in the event of a disagreement.

It is clear that there exists a set of "just-compatible commitment" equilibria (using Crawford's (1982) terminology), with all types of player I demanding x_1 and all types of player II demanding x_2, where the sum of x_1 and x_2 equals the amount of the commodity available. Such equilibria are "nonrevealing" or "pooling," in that the demand is the same for all types of a given player. They are also efficient despite the incomplete knowledge of the players' payoffs involved in the model. On the other hand, it is possible, as Binmore shows, to obtain "revealing" or "separating" equilibria in such models, wherein the demand made by a player does depend on his type. Such separating equilibria could involve some probability of disagreement (even though both players are manifestly better off agreeing than not agreeing).

This brings us to the tricky question of which equilibrium, separating or pooling, will be the more accurate predictor in a given bargaining situation. Empirical data on this might be the best indicator. Another indicator might be the theoretical properties of the equilibrium itself. The efficiency of a nonrevealing equilibrium in this setting is an attractive feature, as is Binmore's demonstration that nonrevealing equilibria of a smoothed demand game approximate the Harsanyi–Selten generalized Nash bargaining solution (Harsanyi and Selten (1972)).

The key features of the Binmore example for the present discussion are that the efficient equilibrium outcome is not "responsive" to the types of the players (the same outcome is obtained for all types), and that the size of the total gains from trade is fixed.

Two points should be noted in passing. First, Binmore's model has already specialized the abstract Nash framework to bargaining over a single issue, as do most of the studies discussed here. Second, a version of the game discussed previously in which bargainers' nonnegative costs of disagreement were private information, would have the same just-compatible commitment equilibria because any agreement would be preferable to no agreement.

A natural extension of the Binmore approach might be to make the amount of the divisible commodity *variable* and dependent on the bargainers' private information. An article by Bill Samuelson and myself (Chatterjee and Samuelson (1983)) could be interpreted as providing this extension. Once again, the bargaining is on a single issue, namely, the price of an object owned by a seller who is willing to part with it for anything less than an amount v_1 (which we call the seller's "reservation price") and desired by a buyer who is unwilling to pay any more than v_2 (the buyer's reservation price). The size of the potential pie is then $v_2 - v_1$, if $v_2 > v_1$. However, in our model, each bargainer knows his own reservation price but not the other player's. Probability distributions on the reservation prices are commonly known and are, in the model, continuous. The bargaining game consists in each player making an offer or a demand. If the buyer's offer, a_2, is at least as great as the seller's offer, a_1, there is an agreement at a price between a_1 and a_2, perhaps midway between them. If not, there is no agreement, and the players obtain zero payoffs. Once again, therefore, irreversible commitments are assumed.

We looked for equilibrium strategies in this game that were revealing in that a player's offer would be strictly increasing in his type (or reservation price). A player would choose an offer to maximize his conditional expected return given his type and a probability distribution over the other player's offers. An optimal strategy would therefore be a Bayes' decision rule against the probability distribution of the other player's offers. In equilibrium, this probability distribution of offers would be identical to that generated by the other player's equilibrium strategy and the underlying probability distribution on that player's reservation price. (This Bayesian/Nash equilibrium therefore has a fulfilled-expectations property, not unexpectedly, as several authors have pointed out earlier.)

We found that if there were revealing strategies in equilibrium, we could characterize them as involving a positive difference between a player's reservation price and his offer, with the amount of the difference being dependent on the derived probability distribution of offers. Of course, this meant that the bargaining game was not full-information efficient and could lead to disagreement. This equilibrium was not unique. In particular, there were uninteresting (and inefficient) nonrevealing equilibria that would never lead to an agreement (e.g., offer something such that the probability of agreement is zero), and sometimes partially revealing equilibria.

We could not show, however, the existence of such revealing equilibria under general conditions. A weakening of the requirement to a revealing epsilon equilibrium might lead to more positive results.

Despite this problem, we believed that the revealing equilibrium studied would have considerable appeal to bargainers who would want their
offers to be strictly monotonic in their reservation prices. To some extent,
this belief was bolstered by the strategies obtained from classroom simula-
tion in Howard Raiffa's course at Harvard. Of the groups that played this
game with which I am familiar, very few chose nonrevealing strategies,
and those that did fared badly. (Some of these results are reported in
Chatterjee and Ulvila (1982) and in Raiffa (1982).)

As contrasted with Binmore's model, in this model the final outcome
was responsive to the types.

An alternative explanation for disagreement is offered by Crawford
(1982), who relaxes the requirement that commitments, once made, are
irreversible, and allows bargainers to reverse them at a cost. (The cost
could be private information to the individual bargainer, but a player
learns his costs only after the first-stage decisions have been made.) Crawford shows in his model that, in some instances, commitments to incompatible demands are in equilibrium. The intuition comes through clearly
in the section of the article where he assumes that players have constant
probabilities of not backing down in the second stage from incompatible
commitments made in the first stage. Thus, if incompatible commitments (or demands) are attempted in the first stage, there is a positive
probability of disagreement resulting from both bargainers holding firm.
Crawford then shows that when dominated options are removed, the
choice of demanding one's maximum utility level dominates that of not
making any commitments, and so ex ante one would expect a positive
probability of disagreement.

Crawford's model might be useful in developing a theory for negotiation between agents with principals exercising veto power on the final
agreement. An initial demand, once made, may be costly to back away
from, because some principals might lose by the concession. However, the
initial demand might be sufficiently high as to convince the principals that
the agent was bargaining honestly on their behalf.

The Crawford model also begins to address an issue that has been
developed further in several recent papers. The issue is the descriptive
relevance of a model that assumes irreversible commitments (or, to put it
another way, a one-stage bargaining game), possibly ending in disagreement even though both sides are aware after the fact (perhaps by inverting
the equilibrium strategies) that an agreement is possible.

Such an argument has been made in the recent literature on sequential
bargaining models (Cramton (1983), Fudenberg and Tirole (1983), Rubinstein (1983), Sobel and Takahashi (1983), and Chapter 5 of this volume). All of these models involve incomplete information, at least about
the buyer's reservation price, with Fudenberg and Tirole (1983) consider-

ing incomplete information about both sides' reservation prices for a discrete probability distribution, and Cramton (1983) extending the framework to continuous uniform distributions. Because these models are discussed elsewhere in this volume (see Chapter 3). I will not consider them in detail here. The essential difference with the one-stage and other finite-horizon models is that the bargaining inefficiency does not result from a lack of agreement when agreement is mutually beneficial but from a delay in the eventual agreement caused by information being revealed over time in the bargaining process. Of course, because of unequal time preferences, an agreement may not be beneficial at the time all the information is revealed (and therefore will not occur), even though it may have been beneficial in the first stage of the game. The models that involve one-sided incomplete information (e.g., Sobel and Takahashi (1983)) contain the intuitive feature that perfect equilibrium offers by the seller involve concessions over time. (In this model, the seller can commit to repeating the same offer before the bargaining begins, but this is not a credible commitment once the bargaining is in process.) The models involving two-sided incomplete information need not have an equilibrium with this structure.

Except for that proposed by Rubinstein (1983), who discusses bargaining over a pie of fixed size, these models all have one active player, who makes offers, and one passive player, who responds. Most of these models also use discounting to express time preference. This specification, rather than the use of stage costs and a quit option, is justified by Fudenberg, Levine, and Tirole (see Chapter 5 of this volume). However, casual observation does seem to indicate frequent real-world use of the quit option by bargainers whose expected value of continuing may be low. This may be due to real bargains being over a finite horizon (because the end of the universe is guaranteed in finite time), or due to use of a bargaining process different from the ones that have been modeled.

To summarize the contents of this section, the advent of noncooperative bargaining models with incomplete information has explained the occurrence of inefficient outcomes in equilibrium, both in single-stage games and in more realistic, multistage games. However, the presence of incomplete information does not automatically result in all equilibria being inefficient. In the examples discussed, this result seemed to have something to do with the nonresponsiveness of equilibrium outcomes to players' types.

The finding of inefficiency for type-responsive equilibria in bargaining runs somewhat counter to the positive results obtained by Bhattacharya (1982) in the context of signaling environments. In these environments, with only one-sided incomplete information, and with varying amounts

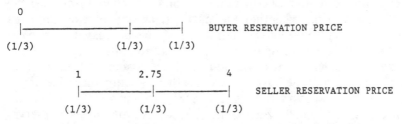

Figure 2.1 Example of an efficient bargaining procedure

of a commodity (rather than a fixed item of uncertain value) being traded, it is possible to design mechanisms that guarantee full-information efficiency. The role of two-sided incomplete information may therefore be crucial.

2.4 The efficiency question

Now that we know that bargaining under incomplete information generally leads to inefficient outcomes, we might explore the question of whether any bargaining procedure could be devised that would lead to efficient outcomes. If the answer to that question is no, we might think of searching for a procedure that is optimal in some sense, even though it is not full-information efficient. To these ends, we will discuss one of my papers (Chatterjee (1982)), and also a more general presentation by Myerson and Satterthwaite (1983).

The notion of efficiency is a difficult one in incomplete-information situations, especially if we conceive of a prebargaining game in which players try to reach an agreement on the procedure to use in the actual bargaining. Once the procedure is selected, the players could resolve the actual bargaining by playing their equilibrium strategies, conditional on the information received in the course of the choice of mechanism. In two recent papers, Myerson (1983, 1984) has provided important insights into these questions, and we shall consider them briefly.

In this section, I also mention some recent empirical work that could have some bearing on the issues discussed.

An example based on one given in Myerson and Satterthwaite's paper clarifies the nature of the problem. Suppose that the seller reservation price is 1, 2.75, or 4 with equal probabilities and that the buyer reservation price is 0, 2.5, or 3, also with equal probabilities (Figure 2.1). In addition, suppose that the bargaining procedure is as follows. The seller and the buyer announce their respective valuations simultaneously, with the buyer restricted to announcing at most 3 and the seller at least 1. If the buyer's valuation is greater than the seller's, an agreement takes place at a price $p = 2$ unless the seller's valuation is 2.75, in which case the price p is 2.85. If there is no agreement, payoffs are zero to both.

Consider a seller with reservation price 1 who assumes a truthful revelation on the part of the buyer. Does the seller have any incentive not to announce his valuation (i.e., reservation price) truthfully? If an announcement of 1 is made, agreements are realized with buyers of reservation price 2.5 and 3 at a price of 2. The expected payoff to the seller is then

$$(2 - 1)\left(\frac{1}{3} + \frac{1}{3}\right) = \frac{2}{3}.$$

Any announcement up to 2.5 will give the seller the same expected payoff. An announcement of 2.6 will lead to an expected payoff of $\frac{1}{3}$, because agreement takes place only with a buyer of reservation price 3. If the seller announces 2.75, his expected payoff is $(2.85 - 1)(\frac{1}{3})$, or .617, a number less than $\frac{2}{3}$. It is therefore optimal to announce 1. What about a seller of valuation 2.75? In this case, there is no reason to announce less since this leads to a negative payoff, and announcing 2.75 gives the seller a positive expected payoff of $(2.85 - 2.75)(\frac{1}{3})$. A seller of reservation price 4 will obviously never agree with any buyer.

What about a buyer who assumes a truthful seller? Would he announce truthfully? Since the buyer's announcement has no effect on the price but only on the probability of agreement, there is no incentive for the buyer to understate his reservation price. A buyer of reservation price 0 would prefer no agreement to one at price 2 and therefore has no incentive to overstate. A buyer of reservation price 2.5 would increase his probability of obtaining an agreement by overstating, but the only additional agreement he would get would be with the seller of reservation price 2.75, whose announcement would cause the agreed price to go to 2.85, causing a negative payoff. Therefore, the procedure is incentive compatible; that is, it induces truthful revelation and is efficient in the full-information sense – an agreement is obtained whenever it is mutually advantageous. It is also individually rational since neither player, whatever his reservation price, would ever receive a negative expected payoff. In general, these desirable properties are difficult to obtain simultaneously, and so it might be worth pointing out that the probability distributions are discrete and that the agreed price is not responsive to the announced valuations, except for one change when the seller's price becomes 2.75.

Now, suppose that we make the probability distributions continuous in the following way. For the probability density of the seller reservation price, we take the sum of three normal densities, normalized to be of mass

$\frac{1}{3}$ each, and centered around 1, 2.75, and 4, respectively, with arbitrary small standard deviation ϵ. We perform a like construction for the buyer reservation price. Suppose that we use a similar procedure, modified by making the agreed price 0 if the seller announces a value of less than $1 - 6\epsilon$ and 2.85 if the seller announces a value of more than $2.75 - 6\epsilon$.

It is easy to see that the procedure is no longer incentive compatible for the seller even if the buyer is assumed to be truthful. However, the deviations from incentive compatibility take place if the seller's valuation is far enough away from the three mass points. Such valuations occur with very low probability.

Thus, a procedure may be "almost" efficient in the sense of being incentive compatible for all but a small set of types. Similarly, there could be several different versions of individual rationality, namely, nonnegative expected payoff prior to learning one's reservation price, nonnegative expected payoff conditional on one's reservation price, nonnegative conditional expected payoff for almost all reservation prices, and nonnegative payoffs for all types.

The consensus among investigators of this issue seems to be that the appropriate version of individual rationality is the one that generates nonnegative conditional expected payoffs for *all* reservation prices. Using a stronger version of this assumption, assuming responsiveness of the final outcome to announcements, and considering only one-stage procedures, it is easy to see (refer to Chatterjee (1982)) that a full-information-efficient procedure is impossible. Note that the responsiveness assumption is violated by the bargaining procedure in the discrete example given, even the procedure that is almost incentive compatible under the continuous distributions of types.

Myerson and Satterthwaite (1983) begin their presentation by demonstrating that the restriction to one-stage games where players are asked to reveal their reservation prices is not a real restriction, since, for any equilibrium outcome of any procedure, there exists an equivalent incentive-compatible procedure in a one-stage revelation game. This is the "revelation principle" (Myerson (1979)) and is based essentially on the ability of the system designer to mimic the game playing of bargainers through a suitable outcome function mapping reservation prices to final payoffs (see also Chapter 7 in this volume).

They then show that full-information efficiency and individual rationality in the sense of nonnegative conditional expected payoffs for *all* values of reservation prices are incompatible provided the underlying reservation-price distributions are absolutely continuous, with positive densities everywhere on the respective domains. They do not need the responsiveness assumption because they limit themselves to such distributions.

Incidentally, if the individual rationality requirement is imposed in an ex ante sense prior to bargainers learning their reservation prices, and if the reservation prices are independently distributed, the simultaneous-offers procedure can be made full-information efficient with side payments. This result is based on the work of D'Aspremont and Gerard-Veret (1979) on public goods and is contained in Chatterjee (1982).

Full-information efficiency may also be obtained by the following bidding procedure, if players are naive in the sense of not taking into account the information revealed by winning the bid. In this procedure, the players bid for the right to make an offer. The winner then makes a single take-it or leave-it offer.

Given this general finding of inefficiency, Myerson and Satterthwaite proceed to the problem of characterizing efficient solutions. They show that, subject to incentive-compatibility and individual-rationality constraints, the ex ante expected gains from trade are maximized (for the case of [0,1] uniform distributions) by the simultaneous-revelation game studied in Chatterjee and Samuelson (1983). However, the mechanism that maximizes the expected sum of payoffs before bargainers know their private information may not seem very attractive *after* each player learns his reservation price. Myerson (1983, 1984) has formulated a theory on the choice of mechanism under such circumstances. He first restricts the mechanisms that can be chosen to "incentive-efficient" ones, that is, to procedures such that there is no other incentive-compatible procedure that does at least as well for every type (value of private information) of every player and strictly better for at least one. Myerson then shows that such mechanisms can be characterized as those that maximize the sum of "virtual utilities" for the players, where virtual utilities are, broadly speaking, actual utilities reduced by the cost of satisfying the incentive-compatibility constraints. Using an axiomatic structure that generalizes Nash's, Myerson arrives at a new cooperative-solution concept, which he calls a "neutral bargaining mechanism."

Although I am not sure that Myerson would agree, the story here seems to be that the players bargain cooperatively on the choice of mechanism and perhaps arrive at a neutral bargaining mechanism that implies a certain incentive-compatible, direct-revelation game, which the bargainers then play. Their choice of strategy in this cooperatively chosen direct-revelation game is not enforceable by any contract due to the constraints of information availability (i.e., because each person has some private information) and hence the requirement that the mechanism be incentive compatible (or, equivalently, that the strategies be in equilibrium so that no player has an incentive to deviate from his strategy). In other words, a player cannot be penalized for not revealing his private information, since this information is unobservable. It is possible, however, for the players to write down an enforceable contract prior to the game, restricting it to one stage. (Violations of such a contract could be observed and hence punished.)

Similarly, prior to knowing their reservation prices, the players could cooperatively commit themselves to the Myerson–Satterthwaite mechanism by writing a binding contract. It might be argued that this distinction between cooperative games where players are permitted to make binding contracts that can be enforced, and noncooperative games where players make the decisions to make and obey such contracts, is not valid, since all games are really noncooperative. If such an assertion is accepted, Cramton's (Chapter 8 in this volume) contribution to restricting the class of allowed bargaining mechanisms to those that are "sequentially rational" becomes relevant. Cramton contends that there could be direct-revelation mechanisms in the sense of Myerson and Satterthwaite that cannot be implemented as *perfect* (or sequential) equilibria of a suitably designed bargaining game, even though they could be equilibria of such a game. For example, the Chatterjee–Samuelson game that implements the Myerson–Satterthwaite ex ante optimal mechanism in the uniform-distribution example is not permissible in Cramton's theory because bargainers walk away even when it is common knowledge that gains from trade are possible. Of course, given the one-stage extensive form, this equilibrium is perfect, but Cramton appears to be criticizing nonsequential extensive forms. Instead of defining an outcome function as an expected payment to the seller and a probability of agreement contingent on the revealed private information, Cramton defines a sequential bargaining mechanism outcome as an expected payment and a time that the agreement is to be reached. (This time is infinity if an agreement is never reached.) Whereas a positive probability of disagreement is needed to keep players honest in the Myerson–Satterthwaite game, a delayed time of agreement performs a similar role in Cramton's discussion. It is not clear, however, what extensive form would implement a "sequential bargaining mechanism."

In concluding this section, we might pause to consider the relevance of the discussion of inefficiency and disagreement contained in the literature. In equilibrium in incomplete-information games, such inefficiency occurs either because of disagreement or because of delayed agreement. How serious is the phenomenon in the real world, and what is the source of inefficiency – incomplete information, an inability to make commitments, or some less complicated mechanism?

In simulated games with student players, "good" solutions are reached with high frequency, especially in multistage games. The inefficiency question is clearly an important conceptual issue in the design of better bargaining processes. In practice, however, where nonequilibrium behavior may occur or players may bring in longer-term considerations, the actual inefficiency due to incomplete information may not be as great as might be predicted by equilibrium behavior in simply specified games. Perhaps future modeling activity could be based on exploring weaker rationality requirements or a different solution concept. The efficiency problem might also be alleviated if reservation prices were verifiable ex post with some probability, and contingent agreements were possible. Recent empirical work (Chatterjee and Lilien (1984)) seems to indicate that unsophisticated bargainers, such as most people in real life, behave less strategically and reveal more information than our equilibrium calculations would indicate. Paradoxically, when confronted with a stylized "no-tomorrow" game such as that in the Chatterjee–Samuelson article, these bargainers react by being more aggressive than they are in equilibrium.

2.5   Conclusions

In the last few sections, I have reviewed the recent work on bargaining under incomplete information that seems to have potential as a beginning of a descriptive theory. This work has explained disagreement and inefficiency as results of equilibrium behavior and has offered a rationale for concession strategies in multistage games. It has also made clear the limits of designing better mechanisms for bargaining, as well as provided a way of choosing among efficient mechanisms.

I think that empirical work is needed to demonstrate whether or not the theories hold up when real-world bargainers confront each other. Perhaps attempts should be made to involve business decision makers in addition to students in order to strengthen the experimental results.

In addition, theoretical work might concern itself with more explicit models in an attempt to fill in Table 2.1, and to use the new theories in applied contexts, such as wage bargaining. We might also try to see if our negative conclusions on efficiency are sustained by alternative solution concepts.

I also believe that the field of bargaining is sufficiently developed to warrant an attempt at synthesizing it with other areas in the economics of information and uncertainty. This might give us more insight into how exactly to resolve the general problems of inefficiency caused in different contexts by incomplete information. An example of such work, noted in Table 2.1 but not discussed here in detail, is Wilson's (1982) work on double auctions. Wilson generalizes the Chatterjee–Samuelson trading framework to many buyers and sellers, each of whom submits a sealed price offer. The trading rule specifies the resulting price, and it is shown that, for large numbers of traders, such a trading rule is incentive efficient in the sense of Myerson.

REFERENCES

Bhattacharya, Sudipto (1982): Signalling Environments, Efficiency, Sequential Equilibria, and Myerson's Conjecture. Mimeo, Stanford University.

Binmore, K. G. (1981): *Nash Bargaining and Incomplete Information.* Department of Applied Economics, Cambridge University.

Chatterjee, Kalyan (1982): Incentive Compatibility in Bargaining under Uncertainty. *Quarterly Journal of Economics,* Vol. 96, pp. 717–26.

Chatterjee, Kalyan, and Gary L. Lilien (1984): Efficiency of Alternative Bargaining Procedures: An Experimental Study. Vol. 28, pp. 270–295. *Journal of Conflict Resolution,* June.

Chatterjee, Kalyan, and William F. Samuelson (1983): Bargaining under Incomplete Information. *Operations Research,* Vol. 31, pp. 835–51.

Chatterjee, Kalyan, and Jacob W. Ulvila (1982): Bargaining with Shared Information. *Decision Sciences,* Vol. 13, pp. 380–404.

Cramton, Peter (1983): *Bargaining with Incomplete Information: An Infinite-Horizon Model with Continuous Uncertainty.* Graduate School of Business, Stanford University.

Crawford, Vincent P. (1982): A Theory of Disagreement in Bargaining. *Econometrica,* Vol. 50, pp. 607–38.

D'Aspremont, Claude, and L. A. Gerard-Varet (1979): Incentives and Incomplete Information. *Journal of Public Economics,* Vol. 11, pp. 25–45.

Fudenberg, Drew, and Jean Tirole (1983): Sequential Bargaining with Incomplete Information. *Review of Economic Studies,* April, pp. 221–248.

Harsanyi, John C. (1956): Approaches to the Bargaining Problem before and after the Theory of Games. *Econometrica,* Vol. 24, pp. 144–57.

(1967, 1968): Games of Incomplete Information Played by "Bayesian" Players. *Management Science,* Vol. 14, pp. 159–83, 320–34, 486–502.

Harsanyi, John C., and Reinhard Selten (1972). A Generalized Nash Solution for Two Person Bargaining Games with Incomplete Information. *Management Science,* Vol. 18, pp. 80–106.

Kreps, David, and Robert B. Wilson (1982a): Sequential Equilibria. *Econometrica,* Vol. 50, pp. 863–94.

(1982b): Reputation and Imperfect Information. *Journal of Economic Theory,* Vol. 27, pp. 253–79.

McDonald, I. M., and Robert M. Solow (1981): Wage Bargaining and Employment. *American Economic Review,* Vol. 71, pp. 896–908.

Myerson, Roger B. (1979): Incentive Compatibility and the Bargaining Problem. *Econometrica,* Vol. 47, pp. 61–73.

(1983): Mechanism Design by an Informed Principal. *Econometrica,* Vol. 51, pp. 1767–97.

(1984): Two-Person Bargaining Problems with Incomplete Information. *Econometrica,* Vol. 52, pp. 461–88.

Myerson, Roger, and Mark Satterthwaite (1983): Efficient Mechanisms for Bilateral Trading. *Journal of Economic Theory,* Vol. 29, pp. 265–81.
Nash, John F. (1950): The Bargaining Problem. *Econometrica,* Vol. 18, pp. 155–62.
    (1953): Two-Person Cooperative Games. *Econometrica,* Vol. 21, pp. 128–40.
Raiffa, Howard (1953): Arbitration Schemes for Generalized Two-Person Games. Pp. 361–87 in H. W. Kuhn and A. W. Tucker (eds.), *Contributions to the Theory of Games II.* Annals of Mathematics Studies No. 28, Princeton University Press.
    (1982): *The Art and Science of Negotiation.* The Belknap Press of Harvard University Press.
Roth, Alvin E. (1979): *Axiomatic Models of Bargaining.* Springer-Verlag.
Rubinstein, Ariel (1983): A Bargaining Model with Incomplete Information. Mimeo, Hebrew University of Jerusalem.
Selten, Reinhard (1975): Reexamination of the Perfectness Concept For Equilibrium Points in Extensive Games. *International Journal of Game Theory,* Vol. 4, pp. 25–55.
Sobel, Joel, and Ichiro Takahashi (1983): A Multistage Model of Bargaining. *Review of Economic Studies,* July, pp. 411–26.
Wilson, Robert B. (1982): Double Auctions. Mimeo, Graduate School of Business, Stanford University.

CHAPTER 3

Reputations in games and markets

Robert Wilson
STANFORD UNIVERSITY

3.1 Introduction

The notion of reputation found in common usage represents a concept
that plays a central role in the analysis of games and markets with dynamic features. The purpose of this exposition is to describe how mathematical constructs roughly interpretable as reputations arise naturally as
part of the specification of equilibria of sequential games and markets. In
addition, several examples will be sketched, and a few of the economic
applications surveyed.

The main theme here is that reputations account for strong intertemporal linkages along a sequence of otherwise independent situations.
Moreover, from examples one sees that these linkages can produce strategic and market behavior quite different from that predicted from analyses
of the situations in isolation. The economic applications, for instance,
indicate that a firm's reputation is an important asset that can be built,
maintained, or "milked," and that reputational considerations can be
major determinants of the choices among alternative decisions.

The key idea is that one's reputation is a state variable affecting future
opportunities; moreover, the evolution of this state variable depends on
the history of one's actions. Hence, current decisions must optimize the
tradeoffs between short-term consequences and the longer-run effects on
one's reputation. As the discussion proceeds, this general idea will be
shown to have a concrete formulation derived from the analysis of sequential games.

Semantics

In common usage, reputation is a characteristic or attribute ascribed to
one person (firm, industry, etc.) by another (e.g., "*A* has a reputation for

Research support for this presentation came from a Guggenheim Fellowship,
NSF grants SES-81-08226 and 83-08723, and Office of Naval Research contract
ONR-N00014-79-C-0685.

courtesy"). Operationally, this is usually represented as a prediction about likely future behavior (e.g., "*A* is likely to be courteous"). It is, however, primarily an empirical statement (e.g., "*A* has been observed in the past to be courteous"). Its predictive power depends on the supposition that past behavior is indicative of future behavior.

This semantic tangle can be unraveled by the application of game theory. In a sequential game, a player's strategy is a function that assigns the action to be taken in each situation (i.e., each possible information condition) in which he might make a choice. If the player has some private information (e.g., his preferences), then the choices of actions may depend on this information. In this case, others can interpret his past actions (or noisy observations that embody information about his past actions) as signals about what his private information might have been. More specifically, they can use Bayes' rule to infer from the history of his observed actions, and from a supposition about what his strategy is, a conditional probability assessment about what it is that he knows. Further, if the information concerns something that persists over time, then these inferences about the private information can be used to improve predictions of his future behavior.

In a narrow sense, the player's reputation is the history of his previously observed actions. The relevant summary, however, is simply the derived probability assessment whenever this is a sufficient statistic. The operational use of this probability assessment is to predict the player's future actions; the probability distribution of his actions in a future circumstance is the one induced from his supposed strategy, regarded as a function of his private information.

The sketch just described has important ramifications for the behavior of the player. To be optimal, the player's strategy must take into consideration the following chain of reasoning. First, his current reputation affects others' predictions of his current behavior and thereby affects their current actions; so he must take account of his own current reputation to anticipate their current actions and therefore to determine his best response. Second, if he is likely to have choices to make in the future, then he must realize that whatever are the immediate consequences of his current decision, there will also be longer-term consequences due to the effect of his current decision on his future reputation, and others' anticipation that he will take these longer-term consequences into account affects their current actions as well.

The role of reputations in the calculation of optimal strategies is rather complex, more so than the simple language of common usage might indicate. Moreover, the effects are subtle and, from a practical empirical viewpoint, discouragingly ephemeral. An outside observer may have no way to measure a player's reputation, since in substance it exists only as probability assessments entertained by other participants. Without some structure imposed on the unobserved state variable hypothesized to explain the actions observed, nearly any history of play in a game could be interpreted as being consistent with the hypothesis that reputations have an explanatory role. It is important, therefore, to study reputational effects within tightly specified models. We shall see that in well-specified models, reputational effects can explain behavior that has often been construed as inexplicable with any other hypothesis.[1]

Ingredients

At least four ingredients are necessary to enable a role for reputations. (1) There must be several players in the game, and (2) at least one player has some private information that persists over time. This player (3) is likely to take several actions in sequence, and (4) is unable to commit in advance to the sequence of actions he will take. The last ingredient requires explanation. The essential requirement for a player's reputation to matter for his current choice of action is his anticipation that his later decisions will be conditioned by his later reputation. That is, he must anticipate that when a later choice arrives, he will look at the matter anew and take an action that is part of an optimal strategy for the portion of the game that remains. On that later occasion, he will, in effect, reinitialize the subgame that remains by taking his reputation and the reputations of others as the initializing probability assessments that complete the specification of the subgame. It is this anticipation that brings into play the tradeoffs between the short-term consequences and the long-term reputational effects of the action he takes on an earlier occasion. Thus, the player's strategy is the solution to a dynamic programming problem in which his and the others' reputations are among the state variables that link successive stages of the game. This aspect of the calculation of strategies will be illustrated in the examples that follow.

The argument just outlined has an explicit formulation that occupies a central role in the analysis of sequential games. Game theory can be construed as the analysis of multiperson decision problems in which the participants share a base of common knowledge. That is, there exists a body of information that is known to all, that each knows is known to all, that each knows that each knows is known to all, ad infinitum. The common knowledge comprises the "rules of the game." The strategies available to a participant consist of those functions that specify for each circumstance in which he might choose an action (depending, for example, on his private information and the observations he has made of his and others' actions[2]), the action he will take among those available. Contained in the common knowledge, since it is a logical implication of the rules of the game, is the specification of those combinations of strategies for the players that are Nash equilibria; that is, each player's strategy is an optimal response to the others' strategies. Among the Nash equilibria, moreover, are sequential equilibria (Kreps and Wilson (1982a)); in each circumstance, a player's strategy for the remainder of the game is an optimal response to the others' strategies, conditional on the prior history of the game.[3] An assumption in the following discussion is that the players make common suppositions about which sequential equilibrium is selected.

Sequential equilibria invoke the criterion of sequential rationality. In each circumstance, a player chooses an action that is part of an optimal strategy for the remainder of the game. Thus, optimality (i.e., rationality) is tested repeatedly as the game proceeds; or in reverse, the strategy is computed by backward recursion using the technique of dynamic programming. Part of this computation is the construction in each circumstance of a probability assessment for those events about which the player is uncertain. One of the implications of optimality is that this probability assessment is a conditional probability satisfying Bayes' rule whenever the conditioning event (i.e., the circumstance in which the player finds himself) has nonzero probability according to the supposed strategies of the other players.

Among the sequential equilibria are the perfect equilibria (Selten (1975)).[4] Say that a strategy combination is positive if each player in every circumstance takes each feasible action with positive probability. A particular strategy combination is a perfect equilibrium if there exists a sequence of positive combinations converging to it such that each player's designated strategy is an optimal response to each member of the sequence. The motivation for this definition is the requirement that the equilibrium strategies be robust best responses, in the sense that they remain optimal even for some small probabilities that the others will err. An important implication of this specification is that a perfect equilibrium entails well-specified probability assessments for the players in each circumstance. (To demonstrate this, let $\sigma = (\sigma_1, \ldots, \sigma_n)$ represent a combination of strategies for the n players. If this is a positive combination, then Bayes' rule is surely applicable in each circumstance to compute for the player taking an action a conditional probability assessment over those events he does not know; let $\pi[\sigma] = (\pi_1, \ldots, \pi_n)$ represent these. Then, a sequence σ^k of positive strategies converging as $k \to \infty$ to a perfect equilibrium σ includes a subsequence for which $\pi[\sigma^k]$ converges to a combination $\pi[\sigma]$ of probability assessments associated with the perfect equilibrium σ. One can verify, moreover, that the probability assessments $\pi[\sigma]$ justify the sequential rationality of σ, in the sense that with these probability assessments, each player's strategy solves the associated dynamic programming problem that confirms that it meets the requirements for a sequential equilibrium.[5])

Examples

The following examples will help to clarify the ideas presented.

Sequential bargaining. Consider a model of sequential bargaining over price between a seller and a buyer, studied in various versions by Cramton (1983a, 1983b), Fudenberg and Tirole (1983a), and Sobel and Takahashi (1980). In its simplest form, the seller makes repeated offers until the buyer accepts. All features are common knowledge except the buyer's valuation of the item offered, which he knows privately. Both players are assumed to be impatient for a trade; payoffs are discounted according to the time a trade is concluded. A sequential equilibrium entails a decreasing sequence of offers by the seller and, for the buyer, a maximum price at which he will accept that is an increasing function of his valuation.[6] Before each offer, the buyer's reputation, that is, the seller's probability assessment for his valuation, is conditioned on the history of past rejections. Hence, it is obtained by truncating the original probability assessment at the upper end at that valuation beyond which the seller anticipated acceptance from his previous offer. The buyer's reputation affects his behavior since, rather than accepting a favorable offer, he might defer and obtain a later, lower offer that would be the seller's optimal one to offer given his later (perhaps false) reputation that his valuation is lower than it is. The equilibrium offer sequence and acceptance rule are computed to take full account of these considerations.[7]

The chain-store game. Consider the chain-store game studied by Selten (1978), Easley, Masson, and Reynolds (1981), Rosenthal (1981), Kreps and Wilson (1982b), and Milgrom and Roberts (1982b). In the simplest version, a firm (the "store") plays in sequence against n opponents (the "entrants") the following stage game with simultaneous moves that are observed by all players. The entrant chooses to be "*out,*" obtaining an assured payoff of zero, or "*in,*" obtaining a payoff of 1 or -1 depending on whether the store chooses to be "*soft*" or "*tough.*" The store's payoff is zero if (*in,soft*) is played, and it costs 1 to be *tough,* whereas *out* yields a benefit of 2. Each entrant maximizes its expected payoff; the store maximizes the sum of its expected payoffs over the n stage games. It is obviou that the only equilibrium has (*in,soft*) played at every stage, since *soft* is a dominant strategy for the store in each stage game and *in* is the entrant's best response.

Now, suppose that the entrants initially assign a probability $\delta > 0$ that *tough* is the store's only feasible action; that is, that the store is "*strong*" rather than "*weak*." In this case, a sequential equilibrium is the following. Let p_t be the entrants' probability assessment that the store is *strong* when t stages remain; that is, $p_n = \delta$. Then, the *weak* store plays *tough* if $p_t \geq .5^{t-1}$, and otherwise it plays *tough* with a probability determined by the condition that p_{t-1} will be $.5^{t-1}$ if the entrant plays *tough* (and zero if he plays *soft*). Note that necessarily $p_{t-1} = p_t$ if $p_t \geq .5^{t-1}$, since both the *strong* and *weak* stores play *tough* in this case. The entrant plays *out* if $p_t > .5^t$, plays *in* if $p_t < .5^t$, and randomizes equally if $p_t = .5^t$. (The details of these calculations are described in Kreps and Wilson (1982*b*).)

Of course, it is p_t that one interprets as the store's reputation. This equilibrium will be used to illustrate how reputational considerations affect the players' choices of actions. An entrant prefers *out* if he assigns the store's choice of *tough* a probability exceeding .5; this is certainly the case if $p_t \geq .5^{t-1}$, since both the *strong* and the *weak* stores then play *tough*. Otherwise, the marginal probability of *tough* is determined by the condition (from Bayes' rule) that the ratio of p_t and this probability must be the posterior probability $.5^{t-1}$; hence, the marginal probability is $p_t/.5^{t-1}$, and we see that the entrant prefers *out* if $p_t > .5^t$, as specified in the equilibrium. The *weak* store's expected payoff when t stages remain, assuming the preceding strategies, is 0, 1, or $2 + t - \tau(p_t)$ according as $p_t <, =,$ or $> .5^t$, where $\tau(p_t) = \inf\{\tau \mid p_t > .5^\tau\}$. Hence, if $p_t > .5^{t-1}$, the entrant could save 1 now by playing *soft*, but it would cost more than that in the long run, since it would reveal that he is *weak*, that is, $p_{t-1} = 0$ after *soft* is observed by subsequent entrants; whereas, if $p_t \leq .5^{t-1}$, then the savings of 1 from playing *soft* is offset exactly by the long-term effect, and so the entrant is indifferent and the randomized strategy is among the optimal ones. Note that the preceding analysis of the *weak* store's decision problem amounts to a verification that the entrant's strategy solves the associated dynamic programming problem, given the way in which the reputation evolves according to Bayes' rule.

We observe here the gist of reputational effects. If the *weak* store's reputation for possibly being *strong* is sufficiently large compared to the number of stages remaining, the *weak* store prefers to imitate the behavior of the *strong* store so as to deter later entrants from choosing *in*. The store's reputation is an asset that it acts to maintain, even if doing so is costly in the short term, so as to reap the benefits in subsequent stages of the game. Indeed, if the number n of stages is very large (i.e., $\tau(\delta)$ is small compared to *n*), then the *weak* store obtains an expected payoff per stage of nearly 1, whereas if it were to reveal itself by playing *soft,* its payoff would be 0 thereafter.

Another version of the chain-store game, with a more detailed modeling of the economic structure, is presented in Benoit (1983).

Beliefs

The preceding examples illustrate the role of reputational effects in sequential games with incomplete information. The key ingredient is that a player can adopt actions that sustain the probability assessments made by other participants that yield favorable long-term consequences. Whenever it is feasible to imitate the behavior one would adopt if one's private information were different than it is, and this would affect others' actions favorably, there is a potential role for reputational effects.[8] The operative mechanism is the process of inference by which observed actions are taken as signals of private information. Behavior that in common usage is interpreted as bluffing, imitation, dissembling, or the like, can all be considered as designed to affect others' responses by sustaining or altering their beliefs. Nor need this behavior have a role only in competitive contexts; as we shall see later, it can be an important factor in cooperative behavior.

Milgrom and Roberts (1982*b*) emphasize that these ingredients are available whenever any of the players has information that is not common knowledge among all of them. It may be, in fact, that they have the same immediate perceptions but this fact is not common knowledge.

3.2 Concepts

This section contains a description of some of the key ideas obtained from analyses of reputational effects in sequential games. The intention is to indicate those concepts that have validity in circumstances more general than the examples with which they are illustrated.

Disequilibrium

One of the strengths of game theory is the precision and completeness with which it describes and analyzes multiperson decision problems. For example, the rules of the game are completely specified, and a strategy indicates what to do in every possible circumstance; in particular, an equilibrium predicts not only what is expected to happen (i.e., those sequences of actions and events having positive probability using the equilibrium strategies – we call these the equilibrium paths), but also the anticipated consequences of any deviation from the optimal strategies of the players. In the case of reputations, the game-theoretic analysis reveals that the anticipated equilibrium behavior depends sensitively on the players' interpretations of the significance of disequilibrium actions (Rubinstein (1983*b*)). This feature derives from the fact that after an unanticipated action by one player, the other players cannot use Bayes' rule to obtain a conditional probability assessment for the player's private information. Yet, the equilibrium is sustained by the player's expectation of what assessments they will make and thus what responses they will be led to choose. In the chain-store game described previously, this feature did not arise since the action *soft* was conclusive evidence that the store was *weak,* for the reason that the *strong* store was incapable of that action. The equilibrium remains unchanged, however, if we allow that the *strong* store could choose *soft* but that this action is dominated by the action *tough.* In this case, the equilibrium depends critically on the supposition that the entrants interpret the action *soft* as conclusive evidence that the store is *weak.* Other suppositions are possible, and some of these lead to equilibria that are qualitatively different. We find, therefore, that sequential equilibria are sustained by suppositions about what beliefs (i.e., probability assessments) will be entertained off the equilibrium paths. Technically, the disequilibrium beliefs are determined by the sequence $(\sigma^k, \pi[\sigma^k])$ whose limit justifies the equilibrium pair (σ, π) of strategies and beliefs (compare with "Ingredients" in Section 3.1). From a practical point of view, this amounts to saying that the beliefs are determined by a supposition as to which types (i.e., the private information) of a player are more likely to deviate or err. In the chain-store game, the salient supposition is that the *weak* store is more likely to play *soft,* since in the stage game it is dominant for the *weak* store and dominated for the *strong* store. In general, considerations of this kind would seem to be crucial ingredients of a fully predictive theory as to which sequential equilibrium will be found in practice.

Imitation

In the chain-store game, the *weak* store chooses *tough* if $p_t \geq .5^{t-1}$, even though this action is costly whether the entrant chooses *in* or *out.* As was indicated, a plausible interpretation of this strategy is that imitating the dominant behavior of the *strong* store yields the future benefit of deterring later entrants by sustaining their belief that the store might be *strong.* Imitation in this case has a competitive advantage for the *weak* store, and it is disadvantageous for the entrants; were there no possibility of imitation (e.g., $\delta = 0$), the payoffs to the store and the entrant would be reversed.

Imitation may, however, confer joint advantages, and indeed it can be the foundation for mutual cooperation. The following example illustrates this possibility.

The prisoners' dilemma game. Consider the finitely repeated version of the symmetric prisoners' dilemma studied by Kreps, Milgrom, Roberts, and Wilson (1982). In each stage, the two players move simultaneously, choosing either to cooperate or to not cooperate, and each then observes the other's choice. If neither cooperates, their payoffs are zero, and each gains 3 from the other's cooperation but it costs the other 1 to cooperate. Each seeks to maximize the sum of his payoffs over n repetitions of the stage game. The only equilibrium of this game has both players choosing not to cooperate every time, regardless of the number of repetitions. At the final stage, cooperation is disadvantageous for both players; at the penultimate stage, therefore, there is no chance that cooperation will be reciprocated in the next stage and so again cooperation is disadvantageous; and so on ad infinitum.

Suppose, however, that player A entertains a positive probability δ, possibly very small, that player B is addicted to the strategy TIT-FOR-TAT, that is, that B will cooperate unless A does not, in which case his following action will be to not cooperate.[9] In this case, there is a sequential equilibrium in which they both cooperate for all but a relatively few stages. The lengthy derivation of this result invokes the following argument, which is stated intuitively and somewhat imprecisely here.

Suppose that B is not addicted to TIT-FOR-TAT. We argue that for most of the game, B will want to imitate TIT-FOR-TAT. The first part is trivial: He surely must punish any noncooperative behavior by A since this yields a short-term advantage and does not alter his reputation. The key, therefore, is to establish that B will reciprocate A's cooperation if many stages remain. The argument uses the following inequalities, in which $A(r,s)$ and $B(r,s)$ represent A's and B's expected payoffs if they use strategies r and s, respectively. Also, let t represent B's TIT-FOR-TAT strategy, and let $(r°,s°)$ be a sequential equilibrium.

1. $B(r°,s°) \geq B(r°,t)$, since $s°$ is B's optimal response to $r°$.
2. $B(r°,t) \geq A(r°,t) - 4$, since by using TIT-FOR-TAT, B is assured of a payoff within $1 + 3$ of A's payoff, regardless of which strategy A uses. Moreover, when B uses the strategy TIT-FOR-TAT, B's expected payoff is the same as the contingent payoff depending on B's type, since both types use TIT-FOR-TAT.
3. $A(r°,t) \geq A(r°,s°)$, since B's use of TIT-FOR-TAT can only benefit A.

This is based on the fact that $s°$ punishes A for noncooperation just as TIT-FOR-TAT does, but possibly $s°$ does not reciprocate cooperation to the degree that TIT-FOR-TAT does.

4. $A(r°,s°) \geq 2\delta(n-1) - 2$. If A previously cooperated, then by continuing cooperation until B does not, A's payoff is at least $2n$ if B is addicted to TIT-FOR-TAT, and it is at least -1 otherwise. Similarly, if A previously did not cooperate, then B is sure to not cooperate, and so with this strategy A gets -1 immediately by cooperating plus a continuation value that is at least the corresponding amounts given: $2(n-1)$, or -1. Either way, the expected payoff, using the initial probability assessment, is at least the stated amount.

Combining these results, we see that B's expected payoff is at least $2\delta(n-1) - 6$ when his reputation is δ and n stages remain. Consequently, when B considers whether to reciprocate cooperation, he calculates as follows. He can choose to not cooperate, yielding an immediate payoff of at most 3 but zero thereafter (since his type is revealed, the only equilibrium path thereafter has no cooperation). Or he can cooperate, yielding at least -1 immediately and at least $2\delta(n-2) - 6$ in the remaining $n-1$ stages (which he will begin with a reputation that is at least δ if he reciprocates cooperation). Thus, if n and δ satisfy $-1 + 2\delta(n-2) - 6 > 3$, then B's best choice is to reciprocate cooperation.

This result can be strengthened further to provide a bound, independent of the length of the game, on the number of noncooperative episodes. Thus, we see that cooperative behavior (from both players) prevails for all but a relatively few stages of a long game.

This equilibrium stems from the basic observation that each player prefers to play with another who uses TIT-FOR-TAT, will respond in kind if the actions taken are consistent with TIT-FOR-TAT, and will initiate TIT-FOR-TAT if there is some chance that the other player will play TIT-FOR-TAT and there are sufficiently many stages remaining. What is needed to bootstrap the equilibrium is A's assessment that B might be addicted to TIT-FOR-TAT, in which case A is willing to cooperate until it is not reciprocated; in turn, B wants to maintain this belief in A's mind by imitating addiction and thus reaping the long-term rewards of cooperation. The first time that B fails to follow TIT-FOR-TAT, he ruins the prospects for further cooperation, whereas as long as there is a chance that B is addicted, so that even if he is not addicted he will imitate addiction, A's optimal response is to cooperate until it is not reciprocated.

A striking aspect of this game is that a little private information is good for both parties. Even before B knows his type, both players prefer that this information not be revealed once it is known to B. For example, A prefers that B has an opportunity to imitate an addiction to TIT-FOR-TAT.

Monopoly power. Imitation can be an intrinsic ingredient of monopoly power. This is indicated obliquely by the chain-store game described earlier in which the *weak* store's *tough* actions until near the end of the game deter entrants from entering. An example in the classical mode is derived from studies of durable-good monopoly. Consider Picasso's problem as rendered by Moorthy (1980). During his lifetime, the artist Picasso can command a price for his work that depends on the total supply that will exist when he dies; collectors who purchase from Picasso realize that the resale value later will be high or low depending on whether he produces few or many paintings during his lifetime. Naturally, Picasso would like to select an optimal quantity to produce during his lifetime, say, to maximize his lifetime income. This strategy is not credible, however, since collectors realize that, regardless of what he produced previously, each year Picasso will reconsider the problem and again attempt to maximize his income for the remainder of his life. In doing so, Picasso will regard his previous production as a shift in the demand function for his paintings. Anticipating this, collectors expect him to increase his output rate as he ages until he nearly exhausts the demand before he dies; thus, even when he is young, they are willing to pay only the low price corresponding to his large lifetime output. Thus, Picasso's monopoly power evaporates, due essentially to the ramifications of sequential rationality.

Suppose, on the other hand, that collectors are uncertain whether Picasso's maximum output rate is high or low, and that initially they assign probability $\delta > 0$ that it is low. In this case, there is a sequential equilibrium rather like the one for the chain-store game: For all but the last few years of his life, Picasso's output rate is low. If he actually has a high output rate, then late in life he randomizes between a high and a low production rate, until the first time he produces at a high rate collectors realize that this is possible, and thereafter he produces at a high rate. With this strategy, Picasso realizes a substantial portion of his monopoly power. Without the uncertainty about his production rate, Picasso is unable to capture these monopoly profits if his output rate is actually high. (As it happens, after their deaths, both Pablo Picasso and Norman Rockwell were discovered to have numerous paintings in storage that were not previously known to collectors.)

General theorems. The chain-store game, the finitely repeated prisoners' dilemma, and Picasso's problem as analyzed here are all examples of a general theory of finitely repeated games with incomplete information that has been developed by Maskin and Fudenberg (1983). In a two-player, one-stage game, say that a vector of payoffs for the players is attainable if there are strategies the players could use that yield these payoffs, and for each player the payoff exceeds what the player could guarantee (using his max-min strategy); if there are more than two players, require further that each player's payoff exceeds what he gets in some Nash equilibrium. Their theorem states that for each attainable vector of payoffs and each $\epsilon > 0$, there exists an integer n and a corresponding repeated game of incomplete information with the following properties. First, each player has probability $1 - \epsilon$ of having the preferences specified in the stage game, and a complementary probability, ϵ, of having preferences that lead him to play differently, as will be specified later. Second, there exists a sequential equilibrium such that for all but the last n stages (or fewer), the equilibrium specifies actions that result in the specified attainable vector of payoffs. Thus, if the number of repetitions is large, then the attainable vector is realized for most of the history of the game, the exceptions occurring only near the end of the game. The construction that makes this result possible specifies that with probability ϵ, a player has preferences (not further specified) that lead him to play the following strategy: He will use the action required to obtain the attainable vector for as long as the other player(s) do the same, after which for the remainder of the game he will play the max-min strategy (if there are two players) or the Nash equilibrium strategy for the stage game. This construction is somewhat different than the ones employed in the previous examples, but the gist of the result is the same. It shows that a small dose of incomplete information, and a long repetition of a stage game, are sufficient to induce equilibrium strategies that yield any attainable vector of payoffs, except near the end of the game.

Adverse selection and self-selection

Imitation is not the only mode in which reputational features operate. This section focuses on two other possibilities. One is that other uncertainties in the situation are sufficient to make imitation unnecessary, and yet, as we shall see, the effects of reputations can continue to be substantial. The other is the possibility that a player's goal in the situation is to make sure he is identified correctly, so that the unfortunate consequences of a false identification do not result.

Repeated auctions. Bikhchandani (1982) has pursued a preliminary study of the following repeated auction affected by the "winner's curse." Consider a sequence of auctions in which each prize is awarded to the bidder submitting the highest bid, at the price equal to the second highest bid. It suffices to consider just two bidders and suppose that they submit bids for every prize, each seeking to maximize the expectation of the sum of the values of the prizes he wins net of the prices paid for them. The values of the prizes are the same to the two bidders but unobservable until the game is over; instead, each bidder has some sample information about the value of each prize. Assume that the values of the prizes are distributed independently and identically, and that conditional on each prize's value, the two samples observed by the bidders are independently and identically distributed. It is clear that with this setup, the bidders will treat the auctions as independent, and in each one a bidder will bid an amount that depends on his sample observation.

A key fact here is that an optimal bid must take account of the observation that in order to win, the bid must exceed the opponent's bid, and this in turn implies that the opponent's sample observation was sufficiently small. That is, winning an auction is an informative event, since it tells the winner something about the samples observed by other bidders, and thereby it adds further information about the value of the prize.

Now, suppose that bidder A assigns a small probability $\delta > 0$ to the possibility that bidder B obtains a payoff from each prize he wins that is $1 more than its value to bidder A. Bidder B is assumed to know whether prizes are worth $1 more to him, and of course all of this is common knowledge. In this case, the auctions obviously are not independent, since A may use his observations of B's bids to infer information about his type. Because the sampling process adds so much noise to the inferential process, B may have little incentive to modify his bids directly either to hide or to advertise his type. There is, however, an indirect effect that should be emphasized. Bidder A realizes that the implications of winning are more severe than before: If A wins, his bid was sufficient to beat out the B bidder of the ordinary type, but now there is the added possibility that it was also sufficient to beat out the B bidder who values the prize more, which implies that B observed an even lower sample than before. Thus, bidder A will select a lower bid than previously. Realizing this, bidder B of the ordinary type sees that winning implies that bidder A's sample may have been higher than previously allowed; hence, the ordinary bidder B is inclined to raise his bid. However, this rebounds to reinforce A's conclusion, and therefore B's conclusion. Thus, we see that the ultimate effect of A's incomplete information is to lower A's bids and to raise the ordinary B's bids until a new equilibrium is reached. The result of this, of course, is that bidder B *of either type* is more likely to win auctions, although obviously the high-value B will win more often than the ordinary B. If many auctions remain, the ordinary B may be in danger of detection by A, which may motivate him to raise his bid further to match the bids by the high-value bidder B. This has been verified in one numerical example studied by Bikhchandani.

As this example illustrates, reputational effects can interact with and reinforce other informational effects in a sequential game. Here, B's reputation that he might value prizes more accentuates the adverse-selection problem faced by A, and this rebounds to affect B's bids as well.

Limit pricing.   The preceding examples reflect the fact that reputational features are associated most often with "pooling equilibria," in which a player's type cannot be inferred completely from his actions. There is, however, a related feature that arises in "screening equilibria," in which a player's actions completely reveal his type. A prime example is found in the models of limit pricing formulated by Milgrom and Roberts (1982*a*), Saloner (1982), and Matthews and Mirman (1983). A monopolist firm operates in two periods, and in the second of these periods there is the possibility that a potential entrant will choose to enter. Assume that the monopolist acquieces to entry; even so, the entrant's anticipated profits depend on its estimate of the monopolist's costs, since these affect the monopolist's price or output decisions in a duopoly. Assuming that the entrant incurs fixed costs to enter, its decision will be influenced by its observation of what the monopolist does in the first period, since that can be interpreted as a signal about what the monopolist's costs are. In some models of this sort, there is no other source of uncertainty, and so the entrant can determine from observable market data what price or output decisions the monopolist selected. Then, from this and a supposition about the monopolist's strategy, the entrant can calculate exactly what the monopolist's costs are, if the strategy specifies a one-to-one relationship between costs and first-period actions. Consequently, the entrant's decision about whether to enter is based on a correct assessment of the monopolist's costs. In most cases, the monopolist's best strategy necessarily involves actions that depend on its costs; consequently, the one-to-one relationship is inevitable, and it follows that the entrant will act with a perfect inference about the monopolist's true costs.

Since the sequential-equilibrium strategy does not deter entry (the entrant enters under precisely the circumstances it would if it had perfect information from the beginning), it appears that the monopolist's first-period action is fruitless in deterring entry, and therefore that the monopolist should adopt ordinary monopoly practices in the first period – revealing its costs by doing so but reaping maximum profits in the interim. What appears to be true is not, however; in fact, the firm's actions in the first period imply prices lower than monopoly prices. The explanation for this is that the firm must price low enough (as specified by the equilibrium) to signal its costs correctly, so that higher prices (e.g., monopoly prices) are not interpreted as a sign that its costs are high and thus encourage excessive entry. It is certainly clear that the equilibrium cannot entail ordinary monopoly pricing in the first period, since if the prospective entrant assumed such pricing in the first period, then the monopolist would have an incentive to set its price somewhat lower so as to realize some of the tradeoffs between first-period profit and diminishing the chance of subsequent entry.

It is evident from this analysis that in some cases, a player must work hard to establish an accurate reputation, signaling his type via his actions, in order to avoid incorrect inferences by others. As in most signaling and "rat-race" models (Spence (1974)), the result tends to be a heavy investment in the signal. In the present example, the investment in the signal manifests itself as limit pricing. First-period prices are below the monopoly price, but they limit or deter entry only to the extent that they prevent inferences that the monopolist's costs are higher than they actually are. Indeed, in Saloner's (1982) multistage model with noisy observations, the amount of entry exceeds that which would occur with complete information, because there is the chance that entrants enter early and mistakenly due to exceptionally optimistic observations that, in fact, reflect only noise.

Bargaining language

A standard view of bargaining asserts that one can say anything but what counts are the actions taken. What, then, is the language of negotiation by which accords are reached? From the game-theoretic viewpoint, bargaining is a sequential game in which the actions selected by the parties determine the outcome. The informational content of the process, that is, the semantic content of the negotiation, comprises the inferences each party makes about the other's preferences and other relevant information from the actions taken. These inferences depend, of course, on suppositions the players make about each other's equilibrium strategy. The following examples are presented to illustrate this interpretation. They are all quite simple in that the language is limited to two alternatives; either to continue the negotiation or to stop. For this reason, a participant's strategy takes the form of a stopping rule.

Litigation.   Consider the model of pretrial negotiations studied by Ordover and Rubinstein (1983). Parties A and B are negotiating a pretrial settlement of a dispute that will be settled in favor of either one or the other. If they fail to agree within T periods, the matter will be settled at trial. Party A knows privately the information that will be revealed at trial and therefore knows the outcome of the trial, whereas party B initially assigns probability δ that it will be settled in his favor. In each of the first T

periods, first A and then B has an opportunity to concede. Therefore, a strategy specifies (in the case of A, depending on his private information) at each time the probability that he will concede if the other has not done so previously. Assume that player i's payoff if player j wins in period t is $u_i(j)\theta^t$, where $u_i(j) \geq 0, 0 < \theta < 1; u_i(i) > u_i(j)$, if $i \neq j$; and $u_A(A)\theta^T > u_A(B)$. In particular, the latter implies that if A knows that the trial will yield a judgment in his favor (i.e., A is *strong*), then he will never concede. Let (x_t) and (y_t) be the strategies of A if *weak* and of B in a sequential equilibrium, respectively. Associated with these is the posterior probability p_t at time t when B moves that A is *weak* if he has not previously conceded; of course, $p_0 = \delta$, and according to Bayes' rule,

$$p_{t+1} = \frac{p_t(1 - x_{t+1})}{p_t(1 - x_{t+1}) + (1 - p_t) \cdot 1},$$

provided the denominator of this expression is not zero (i.e., $p_t x_{t+1} < 1$). Let $\alpha_t = p_{t-1} x_t$ and $\beta_t = y_t$ be the marginal probabilities that A and B, respectively, concede in period t. Ordover and Rubinstein construct a sequential equilibrium in which these marginal probabilities are determined by the condition that in each period each player is indifferent to whether he concedes or does not; that is, α_t and β_t are determined independently of t by the conditions that

$$u_A(B) = \beta_t u_A(A) + (1 - \beta_t)u_A(B)\theta$$

$$u_B(A) = \alpha_t u_B(B)\theta + (1 - \alpha_t)u_B(A)\theta.$$

Thus, in each period a player's value of continuation is the same as the value of concession. These conditions determine the equilibrium except in the case when δ is initially so small that A does not concede and B does concede in the first period.

A summary description of this equilibrium is that each player picks a random stopping time at which he will concede. As periods pass without a concession being made, the uniformed player B updates his probability assessment that he will win in a trial, and indeed his prospects will appear less favorable as time passes. Alternatively, one can say that A's reputation that he is likely to win in trial grows the longer he refuses to concede. In each period, he faces the choice between conceding immediately and holding out to build his reputation further. Improving his reputation enhances his prospects that B will concede first. B's inferential process, or equally A's continued insistence on going to trial, constitutes the informational content of the negotiations.

Attrition.   The archetype for many of the studies of bargaining is the classical war of attrition. The original context was the study of evolutionary biologists of competition between animals of the same species for prey or a mate, but of course such contests have an analog in economic competition. In the simplest case, suppose that two players are battling for a prize of value 1. Each player i incurs a cost c_i per unit time for continuing the fight. These costs are privately known, but it is common knowledge that they are independently and identically distributed according to the distribution function F having the positive density f on an interval of positive costs. A strategy in this case is a function $T(c)$ that specifies that if the player's cost is c, then he will continue to fight for at most a duration $T(c)$. A symmetric equilibrium in which T is a smooth declining function can be characterized simply in terms of the inverse function $C(t)$ that identifies the cost of a player who quits when a duration t has passed. Note that $F(C(t))$ is the probability that a player will last for a duration exceeding t, and that conditional on this event, the probability density that he will expire in the next small interval dt is $[1 - F(C(t))]'/F(C(t))\, dt$. This, then, is the probability that the other player will win the prize of value 1 by incurring the cost $c\, dt$, and so he will want to stop when the marginal cost equals the expected marginal benefit:

$$c = \frac{[1 - F(C(t))]'}{F(C(t))};$$

that is, at the time $t = T(c)$. Making this substitution yields the following differential equation characterizing the symmetric-equilibrium strategy:

$$T'(c) = \frac{-f(c)}{cF(c)},$$

together with the boundary condition that $T(c^*) = 0$ if $F(c^*) = 1$. For example, if each player's cost is uniformly distributed between zero and 1, then $T(c) = 1/c - 1$. The gist of the matter is that after a duration t in which a player has continued fighting, the other player assesses a distribution function $F(c)/F(C(t))$ for his cost c. This process of continuously truncating the cost distribution conveniently summarizes the evolution of the player's reputation that he possibly has the lower cost of continuing to fight.

In a similar vein, economic competition among firms is often implicitly a negotiation over prices or market shares in which the language is the sequence of competitive actions that are taken by the participants. Typically, these actions are costly in the short run but they sustain the credibility of the players' claims for more market share.

Consider the game between a monopolist and an entrant studied by Kreps and Wilson (1982b). This is the same as the chain-store game described earlier, except that there is a single entrant against whom the monopolist plays repeatedly. As was the case before, the entrant initially assesses probability $\delta > 0$ that the monopolist is *strong;* in addition, it is assumed that the monopolist initially assesses probability $\gamma > 0$ that the entrant's stage-game payoff if he enters (chooses *in*) is positive whether the monopolist plays *soft* or *tough;* that is, γ is the initial probability that the entrant is *strong.*

A sequential equilibrium for this game has the following features. Of course, the *strong* monopolist always plays *tough* and the *strong* entrant always plays *in.* If the monopolist ever plays *soft,* the entrant concludes that the monopolist is *weak,* and thereafter the entrant (of either type) plays *in*; similarly, if the entrant ever plays *out,* the monopolist concludes that the entrant is *weak,* and thereafter the monopolist plays *tough* until (if he is *weak*) the last few periods – as described previously. The *weak* monopolist and the *weak* entrant each pick (random) stopping times that specify how long they will play *tough* and *in,* respectively, if the other has not stopped previously. When the time remaining is t, the prior history of the game is summarized by the triplet $(p_t, q_t; t)$, where p_t is the entrant's assessed probability that the monopolist is *strong* and q_t is the monopolist's assessed probability that the entrant is *strong;* initially, of course, this triplet is $(\delta, \gamma; n)$. As time progresses with the players continuing to play *tough* and *in,* p_t and q_t increase (following the evolution prescribed by Bayes' rule and the hypothesized equilibrium strategies), and either p_t or q_t reaches 1 only if the corresponding player is actually *strong.* At each stage, the conditional probabilities that the *weak* players will continue to imitate *strong* players are functions solely of this state variable.

As in the previous example, the nature of this negotiation is that the *weak* monopolist accedes to the entrant and allows a continuing duopoly, rather than force him out of the market, only if the entrant persists for a longer time than the monopolist persists with his aggressive response to entry – thereby establishing the entrant's credibility that he is likely to be *strong.* Similarly, the *weak* entrant is increasingly likely to back out as the monopolist's reputation that he is likely to be *strong* increases with a continuing history of *tough* play. Price wars, labor – management contract negotiations (or strikes), and other games of attrition among competing economic actors often seem to follow this scenario. For purposes of the present discussion, the key feature is that the informational content of the negotiation is contained in the sequence of actions taken, which provides the language from which inferences are made by the participants.

A similar model with a more detailed economic structure has been studied by Fudenberg and Tirole (1983*b*), who consider the war of attrition between two firms in a market that is a natural monopoly. Each firm's fixed cost of maintaining a presence in the market is known privately. As in the previous model, each firm picks a stopping time (depending on its fixed cost) after which it will exit if the other has not left previously. The model involves continuous time and is sufficiently general to encompass technologies and market conditions that vary with time, such as a growing or declining industry.

All of the models addressed here allow only two actions for each player (essentially either "*in*" or "*out*"), and this accounts for the fact that the strategies take the form of stopping times. Generally, the passage of time produces a truncation of each player's probability assessment about the other's possible types. Models with richer languages of communication remain to be studied in detail.

General theory. Hart (1982) has developed a complete theory of the communication that transpires in the course of equilibrium play in infinitely repeated games (without any discounting of future payoffs) with incomplete information. His results are described here only briefly. In the absence of discounting, a player's long-run average payoff does not depend on any finite history; consequently, during an initial finite phase of the game, the players can use their actions solely for the purpose of communication and bargaining over the strategies that they will use thereafter for the remaining (infinite) portion of the game. These strategies must, of course, amount to a contract that is self-enforcing due to the threat of reprisal from the injured party if the other fails to sustain his role agreed to in the initial phase. Moreover, the terms of the contract depend on the information revealed in the initial phase. Anticipating this, the players, during the initial phase, reveal information gradually through their choices of actions, which constitute an alphabet for communication. Hart shows that the equilibrium strategies in the initial phase are characterized by an implicit set of rules about the informational content of actions (i.e., the relationship between the player's private information and the action he will choose) and the subsequent revision of probability assessments (using Bayes' rule) to take account of this information.

In summary, an equilibrium consists of a family of possible communication sequences, each terminating in a self-enforcing agreement that is sustained for the remainder of the game. Each communication sequence corresponds to a particular configuration of the players' private information, which is partially revealed over time as the sequence evolves. Along the sequence, each player's actions are optimal responses to the other's strategy and the information so far revealed by the history of previous communication.

Of course, in finite-horizon games, or in games with discounting, this convenient separation between the communication phase and the subsequent agreement phase is not likely to occur. Nevertheless, the characterization reveals the essential role of the communication process in the early stages of a long game with incomplete information.

Expectations. Roth and Schoumaker (1983) have devised an experiment that illustrates the role of reputational effects in bargaining. The intention is to show that if both parties have experienced, and have reputations for, only one way to divide a prize, and therefore presumably expect to divide it in this way, then in fact that will be the experimental result. A subject is engaged in a series of negotiations with different opponents. In each negotiation, the subject and his opponent either agree on the division of a prize or forfeit it; each first states a proposed division, and then in a second stage each can either repeat his proposal or accept the other's. Unknown to the subject, the first part of the series is a "training" phase in which the subject is allowed to claim a fixed fraction of each prize from opponents acting under the experimentors' instructions. Following the training phase, the subject encounters as opponents other subjects, who have been "trained" to accept the complementary fraction of each prize. Moreover, each subject is provided a history of the opponent's choices in recent bargaining sessions. The striking result is that most subjects continue to bargain for and accept the divisions for which they were trained.[10]

This result accords well with a prediction based on reputational effects: The histories of prior actions and observations affect expectations and thereby influence current actions.

One can, of course, imagine a similar scenario in more complex negotiations. The subject is initially uncertain whether opponents view his arguments for a division of the prize in his favor as more or less pursuasive (deserving, meritorious, convincing, threatening etc.); that is, he is uncertain about the effectiveness of his skills as a negotiator or about the appeal of his claims. After a history of bargains concluded in his favor, he assesses a high probability that he is extraordinarily effective, and the reverse if he consistently fails to get more than a small share. In subsequent negotiations, if he encounters an opponent with a reputation that confirms his own, then he bargains for and accepts the share he expects.

Credibility

Direct information transmission (e.g., via natural language) from one individual to another is especially susceptible to the hazard of deception if their motivations differ. What, then, determines the reliability that the receiver assigns to the message from the sender? Since ultimately the role of information is encompassed entirely by its effect on decisions, this issue must be studied in the context of the game between the sender and the receiver. First, an important result for the static case is considered.

The sender–receiver game. Consider the game studied by Crawford and Sobel (1982) in which the sender first receives superior information (a real-valued signal $s \in [0,1]$ having a positive density) and then sends a message ($\hat{s}$) to the receiver, who in turn takes an action (a real number x) that affects the payoffs to both players. Assume that each player's preferred choice of x is a continuous increasing function of s, but that their preferred choices differ. In all of the sequential equilibria of this game, the receiver takes only a finite number of different actions. One interpretation of these equilibria is that the sender selects among a finite set of messages, which have the effect of informing the receiver as to which element of a finite partition of the domain [0,1] of signals contains the signal observed by the sender. Alternatively, the equilibria can allow randomization, in which case the sender can be construed as randomizing as to which message in the same element of the partition as the signal he will send. Interestingly, these equilibria are ordered by the Pareto-criterion: The finest partition admitting an equilibrium is the one that is best for both players. It is clear that this finest partition cannot induce a continuum of responses by the receiver, since if that were true, the sender could induce his preferred action, whereas it is assumed that their preferences differ. We see from this analysis that the reliability of an information channel is endogenously determined by the sequential equilibrium of the game between the sender and the receiver if their preferences differ. This conclusion has obvious implications for bargaining processes in which information is transmitted verbally.

The George Smiley game. A dynamic version of the sender–receiver game has been studied by Sobel (1982). A spymaster (George) and his spy repeatedly play a stage game in which the spy observes a signal and then transmits a message to George, who in turn takes one of two actions. After making his decision, George observes the signal originally observed by his spy. The players' stage-game payoffs depend on the signal, the action, and another variable (the "importance" of the decision) that scales the payoffs (not necessarily proportionately) and is observed by both players. Each player seeks to maximize the expectation of the sum of his stage-game payoffs over n repetitions in which the signal and the scaling variable are independently and identically distributed. Assume that George initially assigns a probability $1 - \delta$ that the spy shares his preferences, that is, that they are a team; and a probability $\delta > 0$ that the spy's preferences are diametrically opposed (as in a zero-sum game), that is, that the spy is a double agent. A sequential equilibrium of this game has the feature that if George ever discovers that the spy has lied to him, then he concludes that their interests are opposed and thereafter adopts his minimax strategy in the zero-sum game – in effect, ignoring any further messages from the double agent. Until that happens, the spy of either type sends truthful messages, and so (according to Bayes' rule) George continues to assess probability at most δ that the spy is a double agent, and this affects George's selection of his action. If the spy is a double agent, then the spy waits until the importance of the decision is large enough (declining as the number of stages remaining declines, and depending on the signal) to execute his double cross, deceiving George by sending a false message that leads him to take the wrong action. Because the equilibrium may in some circumstances entail the double agent randomizing between double crossing or not, his reputation that he might be loyal may in fact increase as episodes pass in which there was some chance that a double agent would have lied. This example illustrates in stark form the importance to the double agent of maintaining his reputation that he is likely to be loyal, so that he can wait for an opportune time to deceive George.

Auditing.   In Wilson (1983), I have discussed informally the application of these ideas to the study of the auditing industry. A public accounting firm charges fees that reflect its reputation for accuracy (as well as fairness, independence, etc.) in verifying client firms' financial statements distributed to potential investors. The firm whose statements are verified is the auditor's client, but the auditor's reputation resides with investors. In effect, the firm "rents" the reputation of the auditor to lend credibility to the statements of assets, liabilities, and earnings. Credibility might be lacking in the judgments of potential investors if the firm were to offer unverified statements (due to the "moral hazard" that present investors might stand to gain from deceptive statements). Because an auditor can rent its reputation frequently, there are economies of specialization realized by an auditor that can not be obtained by a firm that is new or that issues financial instruments infrequently. The auditor's strategic problem can be viewed as the choice of a balance between acceding to the interests of the client (either to acquire the account or to keep it) and the long-term maintenance of its reputation among investors. The auditor that caters to clients to acquire business in the short term is likely to find that, as investors subsequently discover favoritism in the statements it has certified, the rental value of its reputation will decline among future clients. We see here that a reputation for veracity in the reporting of information has an asset value (the capitalized value of the auditor's goodwill) that reflects past actions and that influences the selection of subsequent strategy. The strategy can build or maintain the reputation, or the reputation can be "milked" for short-term gains. This scenario does not seem to depend greatly on what the auditor's reputation is about. One possibility is that the investors assess the likelihood that the auditor has enough clients, sufficient financial resources of its own, and sufficient foresight and patience to be uninterested in catering to clients; another is that they assess the probability that the auditor is addicted to scrupulously ethical conduct. In any case, one can conjecture that in a well-formulated sequential equilibrium, even an unscrupulous auditor will find it in his best interest to imitate ethical behavior.

The auditing context has a nearly exact parallel in the case of legal firms that prepare legal opinions. Somewhat different is the physician – patient relationship studied by Dranove (1983). The purpose of the analysis is to elucidate the factors that temper the physician's opportunities to "induce" demand. That is, the physician's superior information about the significance of symptoms observed by the patient enables the physician to recommend more or fewer procedures (e.g., surgery), which the physician then supplies. The argument is that the physician's ability to recommend excessive procedures is limited by the fact that the patient's choice of physician and willingness to follow a prescription for treatment depend on the physician's reputation – the history of his other recommendations and their ultimate consequences as observed by the community generally. Consequently, the physician's optimal strategy if his motives were to maximize revenues would balance the short-term gains from induced demand and the long-term effects on his reputation. This scenario fits a small community better than a metropolis, but it has implications for the latter as well when one considers the medical profession's standards for treatment and the maintenance of norms of conduct.

Beliefs and expectations

Reputations in the customary sense reflect the evolution of players' probability assessments as a game progresses. Even at the beginning of a game, however, players' expectations are important determinants of the initial choices. In some cases, these initial assessments are subject to the same kinds of considerations examined earlier, to the extent that it is plausible to interpret any game as a subgame of some larger game. In such cases, expectations play a key role in the selection among equilibria of the subgame, and in the attainment of coordination between the players.

Presumptive reputations.   Some one-shot situations are affected by reputations the parties bring to the encounter. For example, an economist might favor the simplistic definition of predatory practices (by a monopolist against an entrant) that accepts as sufficient evidence that the monopolist could have adopted other practices that would be more profitable in the long run *if* the entrant stays in the market. Thus, in a trial the prosecution must offer evidence that it could have done a better job than the firm's management. If jurors presume that management is more likely than are outside lawyers to know what actions are optimal in the long run, then convictions may be difficult to obtain. In this case, the professional histories of the disputants support the presumption that one is better informed or has better managerial skills than the other.

A somewhat different presumption is applicable in other instances noted by Kreps and Wilson (1982*a*) and studied by Kohlberg and Mertens (1982). In these cases, there is a presumption about the *connection* between a player's past and future equilibrium actions. Abstracting away from other features, suppose that *A* and *B* are playing a (sub)game that has multiple equilibria, only one of which gives a positive payoff to *A*. If *B* knows that *A* entered this game voluntarily, forsaking a zero payoff elsewhere, shouldn't *B* presume that *A* will play the strategy that is part of the equilibrium in which he can expect a positive payoff? A presumption of this kind is tied closely to reputational features since it identifies the probability assessments that each player must make to sustain the distinguished equilibrium. A typical example is the following.

> Firm *B* reads in a trade journal that firm *A* has formed a subsidiary, obviously preparing to enter the market for a certain low-volume technical product. Firm *B*, which is already in the market, awaits *A*'s entry but is unsure whether *A*'s intent is to move quickly or slowly to bring out an advanced design that has recently become technologically feasible. *B* knows that whichever firm is first to market the new design will profit and the other will lose, and that they will both fail to recover their investments if they split the market at the same time. *B* wonders whether to initiate an accelerated research program.

In an example such as this, one presumes that *A*'s reputation, namely *B*'s probability assessment as to the chances that *A* has already initiated an accelerated program, is that indeed such a program is already underway (and *B* should plan to bow out, having missed its chance to be first). Otherwise, *A* would never have wanted to enter the market. Similarly, one presumes that *B*'s reputation is that it is not considering an accelerated program and that it will exit the market when *A* enters it.

We see here that reputations about actions undertaken privately without the opportunity for observation by other players may be formed presumptively on the basis of intertemporal consistency with prior actions that were observable. A firm's reputation for the quality of the product offered currently (observable by a buyer after some delay or experience using the product) may be assessed presumptively by customers on the grounds that it is consistent with the quality the firm has provided previously. That is, for example, the firm would not previously have incurred the cost of providing high quality if it did not intend to recoup those costs in the future, enjoying high prices for as long as it continues to provide high-quality products. A model that incorporates these features will be examined later in the Chapter, when market models of product quality are considered.

Expectations and coordination. An alternative view of Roth and Schoumaker's experimental results, and of bargaining in general, is that the game ordinarily has multiple equilibria and therefore the players face an initial task of focusing on one equilibrium. Experience with one equilibrium could be the basis for a player's expectation that it will be repeated in subsequent encounters.

A formal development of this view is given by Rosenthal and Landau (1979).[11] These investigators consider the steady state associated with the infinitely repeated version of a stage game played among randomly matched players from a large population. The stage game allows each pair of players to divide a prize if at least one "yields" to the other (if only one yields, he gets less than the other), and otherwise they get nothing. The key feature is that each player is identified to his opponent by his reputation, which in this case is a finite-valued integer label that reflects his past actions. In one variant, the label is (approximately) the player's percentile ranking in the population with respect to how frequently he has refused to yield to opponents. Different equilibrium steady states are associated with different specifications of the reputations, and with how these are used by the players to coordinate their play of a particular stage-game equilibrium. One such coordinating custom is: A player is expected to yield to another player with a higher reputation, and not to one with a lower reputation (C1). Another is: A player is expected to yield to another player with a lower reputation, and not to one with a higher reputation (C2). For both of these customs, players with equal reputations adopt randomized strategies, and therefore there is a chance of no agreement, as there is in the corresponding symmetric randomized equilibrium of the stage game corresponding to: Ignore the reputations (C3). In the example studied, these customs all sustain equilibrium steady states. Moreover, the coordination is successful to the extent that the frequency of impasses is less with C1 and C2 than with C3; somewhat surprising is the fact that C2 has fewer impasses than C1.

These results illustrate the general principle that reputations, or any labels or identifiers from the past, can be used to coordinate selections of equilibria, and in particular to favor those that are more efficient. There is also the possibility that reputations will allow behavior to be sustained in equilibrium steady states that cannot otherwise be expected.

This view is developed in more general terms by Rosenthal (1979). As before, members of a large population of players are randomly matched on each of many occasions to play a stage game. Each player knows his own reputation and observes the reputation of his current opponent. In this case, the player's reputation is a history (of fixed finite length) of his recent moves. An equilibrium steady state is specified by the probability distribution of reputations that will exist, and by the probability distribution of the actions taken by each reputational class (possibly depending on private information of the individuals); and to be in equilibrium, these specifications must be confirmed by the players' optimal responses to these hypotheses. Refer to Chapter 4 in this volume for more information on this approach.

3.3   Market models

We turn now to an examination of the role of reputations in markets. Necessarily, the opportunity for such a role depends on the market being imperfectly competitive or lacking complete contingent contracts, and it arises most clearly when these features stem from informational asymmetries. Of the many possible applications, the focus here is on product and factor markets with unobserved quality attributes and on implicit contracts that are sustained by reputational effects. Unfortunately, most of the work on these topics does not make explicit the source of the reputational effects; rather, it simply presumes that they are present.

Product quality

A firm's reputation for the quality of its product is an important determinant of demand whenever quality is unobservable at the time of purchase (although observable later) and contingent contracts (warranties, service contracts, etc.) are not offered, presumably because of the moral hazard that defects and careless usage cannot be distinguished. The central issue in the theory of this topic is to account for the higher quality that higher-priced products provide; the resolution is found in the seller's incentive to maintain or build its reputation. In particular, a seller earns a rent on its reputation, which repays the cost of building and maintaining it.

A simple model. The following is the model developed by Shapiro (1985). Consider a market with free entry and exit by firms that at each time can offer one unit of the product with any quality $q \geq 0$ at a cost $c(q)$ that is an increasing and strictly convex function of the actual quality q, which is observed by consumers after a lag of one period. Assume the existence of a price schedule $p(\hat{q})$ anticipated by consumers. It suffices to suppose here that at time t, consumers anticipate $\hat{q}_t = q_{t-1}$ if the firm sold in the previous period. Any market equilibrium in which firms maintain quality must have the property that

$$\frac{1}{1 - \rho} (p(q) - c(q)) \geq p(q) - c(0),$$

where $\rho < 1$ is the factor by which firms discount future profits, since otherwise the present value of the profits from maintaining quality would be less than the immediate profit from offering the least quality, zero, at the price $p(q)$ and then exiting the market. This must be an equality at $q = 0$, and therefore $p(0) = c(0)$, since firms insist on $p(0) \geq c(0)$, and if this inequality were strict, then an entrant could make a positive profit by offering quality 0. On the other hand, if an entrant initially obtains a price p_0, then the equilibrium condition that no entry be profitable yields the condition that

$$p_0 - c(q) + \frac{\rho}{1 - \rho} (p(q) - c(q)) \leq 0,$$

since otherwise it would be profitable to enter and supply quality q thereafter. The equilibrium must entail $p_0 = c(0)$, since if $p_0 > c(0)$, then an entrant could profitably enter for one period, and the reverse inequality implies that a firm offering quality 0 takes an initial loss that cannot be recovered. Combining these results yields $p(q) = c(q) + r(c(q) - c(0))$, where $r = (1/\rho) - 1$ is the interest rate. To show that this equilibrium price schedule sustains quality maintenance by firms, observe that a firm's problem of choosing its sequence of qualities q_t to maximize its discounted profit,

$$\max_{\{q_t\}} \sum_{t=0}^{\infty} \rho^t (p(\hat{q}_t) - c(q_t)),$$

subject to the constraint $\hat{q}_t = q_{t-1}$, has the necessary condition $p'(q_t) = (1 + r)c'(q_t)$. Because this condition is satisfied identically for the equilibrium price schedule, the firm's optimal strategy is to maintain the reputation $\hat{q}_0$ it starts with. The value of the maximand is computed to be $(c(\hat{q}_0) - c(0))/\rho$, which is precisely the capitalized value of the extra cost the firm incurred to establish the reputation $\hat{q}_0$. Similarly, the price schedule allows the firm a premium of $r(c(\hat{q}_0) - c(0))$ over the actual cost $c(\hat{q}_0)$, which is the return on this capitalized value of the reputation at the interest rate r. We see from this example that a firm can build and maintain a reputation for product quality, and charge prices sufficient to earn the required return on its investment in its reputation that it incurred when initially it offered high quality at the entrant's price $p_0 = c(0)$ corresponding to the lowest quality. A dynamic version of Shapiro's model is studied by Salant (1983). A model in which consumers have imperfect information initially and make imperfect observations about product quality is developed by Rogerson (1982b); in this case, reputation effects derive from probability assessments.

Labor effort

Labor inputs to production are especially subject to reputational effects. An employer may be unable to observe the quantity or quality of work provided, or to monitor an individual's output exactly. In such instances, long-term employment relationships enable better monitoring and permit intertemporal incentives that sustain more efficient production. The incentives can take the form of remuneration that depends in each period on the history of observations the employer has made; thus, the worker in each period takes account of the effect of his actions on his current wage and its effect on his subsequent wages. This is the kind of system that will be considered shortly. A somewhat different form is one in which a wage is paid until evidence accumulates that the required work has not been performed; see Radner (1981) for a study of this.

Managers' careers.   Holmström (1982) studies a model in which a manager's measurable effect on output in each period is the sum of three effects: a fixed component, a component chosen by the manager, and a random noise term. Interpreting the fixed component as talent, ability, or skill pertinent to the managerial task in the firm, and the second as a measure of the intensity of effort or work, assume that the manager incurs disutility from effort (and, of course, utility from consumption out of wages). The fixed component is assumed to move over time as a random walk. At all times, the manager knows his effort contribution to output, whereas the owner of the firm cannot distinguish between effort and talent from his (noisy) observations of output. Assume that the manager does not know his talent except as he infers it from his observations of output and the effort he supplies. In a competitive market, neutral to risk, the manager's wage is equal to his expected contribution to output. In this case, it is the sum of his expected contributions from ability and effort, where ability is the mean of the owner's current probability assessment for the fixed component conditional on past observations of output (i.e., the manager's reputation), and effort is the manager's optimal effort given his reputation. A market equilibrium requires fulfilled expectations; the wage is based on a supposed effort contribution that is, in fact, the optimal one for the manager to provide, taking account of both the immediate disutility and the subsequent effect on his reputation. The situation is again rather like a "rat race," in that the manager must provide sufficient effort to prevent the owner from inferring that his ability contribution is low. For a class of models, Holmström shows that a stationary equilibrium induces a supply of effort that is close to the efficient one to the degree that the manager's interest rate is near zero, and the variance of ability's random walk is large relative to the variance of the noise term.

This model illustrates a general feature about the role of reputations in providing incentives in labor markets. To the extent that quality, quantity, and output are substitutes and unobservable, long-term contracts with remuneration contingent on the history of measured performance provide incentives for workers to invest effort (quantity) in building a reputation for quality that will sustain wages and productivity near optimal levels.

An empirical study by Wolfson (1983) measures the returns to reputation earned by general partners of oil-drilling ventures. Provisions in the tax code create an incentive for general partners to complete fewer wells than the limited partners prefer. In addition, the skill of a general partner is an important factor of production that is not directly observed and is inferred only imperfectly from the record of past performance. New partnerships are formed repeatedly, and with each new venture, investors judge the skill of the general partner from the disclosures in the prospectus, including the general partner's record in previous ventures. (Prospectuses discuss incentive problems with candor and often include explicit promises that the general partner will not take certain actions that benefit the general partner at the expense of the limited partners who invest in the venture.) To build and maintain a reputation as a skillful operator, the general partner can complete more wells than he would choose based on his private information and personal incentives were he not dependent on obtaining funds from investors in subsequent ventures. This strategy improves performance from the perspective of the investors, but at a considerable private expense to the general partner. The general partner's motivation to follow this strategy is the prospect that his current "investment" can be recovered in subsequent partnerships through better profit-sharing arrangements that he can command if he has a reputation as a skillful operator. Wolfson finds statistically significant evidence that a general partner's reputation is effectively priced in the market. He also finds statistically significant evidence, however, that residual incentive problems remain and that these also are priced by the market for limited partners' shares.

Repeated contracting. Rogerson (1982*a*) studies a model of repeated contracting with a supplier who has superior information about the buyer's benefits from each project and recommends its purchase to the buyer. The buyer and supplier face a known sequence of projects, each of which may either succeed or fail, and the supplier has superior information about the chances of failure. The strategies studied have the form that the buyer contracts for those projects recommended by the supplier, paying a cost plus fixed fee, so long as the number of failures experienced previously is less than a fixed bound. The key result is that the supplier reveals truthfully his private information about the chances for success only if he has no more than a certain critical number of failures left in his quota. If the supplier is initially given a larger quota than this critical number, then he will distort his recommendations in order to be hired more often, until he exhausts his excess opportunities for failure and then returns to truthful reports. Thus, the relationship must surely end even if the supplier is being truthful; the buyer can induce truthful revelation only by limiting the supplier's number of chances for projects to fail.

This model does not invoke reputational effects of the sort discussed previously, since the supplier has no private information that persists from one project to another. Nevertheless, the supplier's reputation in another sense – his history of failed projects that were recommended – plays the key role. The supplier entertains the hypothesis that the supplier's recommendation is truthful only if the residual quota does not exceed the critical number that ensures a sufficient incentive to recommend accurately.

Implicit contracts

A legal enforceable contract between two parties modifies the sequential game they play by altering the payoffs. That is, noncompliance (i.e., failure to take the actions prescribed by the contract) results in penalties sufficiently severe to make compliance the best strategy. It is also useful, however, to interpret a contract as altering the requirements for sequential rationality in the choice of actions. In other words, if a contract is in force, then in each circumstance in which the contract specifies a prescribed action for one party, that party chooses that action if for *either* party it is part of an optimal strategy for the remainder of the game. In particular, one party takes the prescribed action if the other party finds it in his interest to enforce the terms of the contract.

In the case of an implicit contract, penalties based on restitution or damages are not explicitly available. Nevertheless, if noncompliance would result in responses that are sufficient to deter offenders, then the contract is effectively enforceable. The theory of this subject typically omits an explicit description of the responses that deter noncompliance. Nevertheless, in some cases it is fairly clear that the operative effect is that the offender loses the reputation that is necessary in the future to reap gains from such agreements. Market models with this feature characteristically require that there be multiple equilibria in order that noncompliance can be punished compared to compliance.

Firing shirkers. A typical example of this genre is the model of a labor market studied by Shapiro and Stiglitz (1981). There are many identical workers, each of whom has an exogenously specified quit rate. There is also an exogenous rate at which new jobs open up, so at all times there is a pool of unemployed workers. Employed workers can work or shirk, and shirking is detected by employers with a specified probability. The employment contract calls for firing a worker caught shirking. If a fired worker's expected time in the pool of unemployed is long enough and the unemployment benefits, if any, are sufficiently less than the wage, then this contract deters shirking.

Such a contract is presumably implicit. Moreover, its enforcement is problematic, since neither the worker nor the employer has an immediate incentive to carry it out; knowing that the workers are identical, the employer gains nothing by replacing the worker. To understand this equilibrium, it is helpful to consider an equilibrium in which there are two kinds of firms: those that workers expect to enforce the no-shirking provision and those that offer a lower wage in anticipation of shirking. Such an equilibrium is sustained by its disequilibrium features. A firm that fails to enforce the no-shirking rule loses its credibility, perhaps only temporarily; to first establish or subsequently regain credibility, the firm must pay high wages to workers who expect to be allowed to shirk. This cost of establishing a reputation for enforcement is an investment (as in Shapiro's (1985) product-quality model, examined in Section 3.3) that ultimately the firms recover through the wage. Once a reputation is established, the firm's incentive is to maintain it. Apparently, any proportion of the firms might have reputations in an equilibrium; the one in the previous paragraph is simply the extreme case where the proportion is 100 percent.

Credit markets. A complex example of implicit contracts is the model of credit markets studied by Stiglitz and Weiss (1983). These authors assume overlapping generations of identical borrowers, each of whom lives two periods. Borrowers seek money from banks to invest in risky projects, although the banks cannot observe the riskiness of the projects selected. The key feature is a loan contract that specifies that borrowers who default in the first half of life are denied loans in the second half, whereas those who repay are given loans at less than the market rate of interest. Thus, a project that succeeds enables a borrower to obtain a prize in the form of a profitable loan to finance another project in the second half of life. The prize for repayment is sufficient to deter young borrowers from investing in excessively risky projects (which otherwise they would do since the bank bears the risk of default). Of course, this two-period loan contract is not the only one possible, and another equilibrium exists in which all loan contracts are for one period only. In this second equilibrium, credit is not rationed, and borrowers, except lucky old ones, undertake projects that are more risky than before. Because this risk is borne by the lenders, who compete for the funds of savers, the end result is that the second equilibrium transfers income from savers to borrowers.

The features of the second equilibrium explain why banks enforce the terms of the two-period contract in the first equilibrium. The banks have no immediate incentive to deny credit to the unlucky old and award prizes to the lucky (although the lucky ones have an incentive to claim their prizes). However, if they were to fail to maintain a reputation for carrying through the original understanding, then the contractual relationship with borrowers would degenerate to that associated with the equilibrium of one-period contracts. A bank cannot afford to do this, since it competes for loanable funds, and it can offer the highest rate to savers only if it uses the two-period contract form.

One could, of course, imagine an alternative setup in which banks compete mainly for loans rather than deposits; in this case, it would be more plausible that the equilibrium involves only one-period contracts.

This result is not unique to market models. Whenever the stage game for a repeated game has multiple equilibria, a player may aim to develop a reputation for playing the equilibrium he prefers.

3.4   Conclusion

The purpose of this survey has been to illustrate the many ways that reputational considerations arise in games and markets with dynamic features and informational differences among the participants. More-over, several examples have been offered in which reputational features account for behavior that is precluded in static- or complete-information versions of the same model.

The key idea has been that differences in the information available to participants make their strategies acutely sensitive to their beliefs and expectations. This in turn affects the behavior not only of the uninformed person, but also of the informed one, who realizes that his current actions affect others' later beliefs, their expectations about his subsequent behav-ior, and ultimately their choice of actions. Knowing that this chain of events will occur, the informed person has an incentive to trade off the immediate consequences of his current decision against the long-term effects on his reputation.

The examples provided emphasized mainly the role of one's private information about preferences, feasible actions, or environmental condi-tions; however, in some cases the private information is simply that one knows one's recent action and others do not. Reputational features were said to appear most clearly in models admitting pooling equilibria (so that imitation is possible), but that screening equilibria (in which self-selection is the dominant motive) include such features implicitly. In negotiations, the informational content of the actions taken comprises the inferences drawn from these actions about the motives of the parties; thus, in a sense negotiations are the evolution of the parties' reputations. In the case of direct information transmission, the imputed reliability of the informa-tion channel from one person to another is determined endogenously within the sequential game they play, and depends on the degree to which, or the likelihood that, their preferences are aligned. Cooperative behavior in the finitely repeated prisoners' dilemma game depends in a fragile way on the small chance that one player is committed to cooperation, in which case he will imitate this behavior even if he is not committed, and the other player will reciprocate. The same kind of reasoning, however, im-plies aggressively competitive behavior in the chain-store game and its many variants, including the hiding of productive capacity as in the Picasso scenario. All told, there are myriad sorts of behavior that reputa-tional considerations can make into optimal behavior as part of a sequen-tial equilibrium.

The discussion of the market models emphasized that reputations are assets that, like any other asset, are subject to economic analysis, and that in some cases (e.g. auditing, product quality) they account for the promi-nent features observed in practice. In the case of implicit contracts, repu-tational considerations are likely the glue that sustains the incentives for compliance.

The final words of this chapter are ones of encouragement and caution.

Reputations can explain many behaviors – perhaps too many. It is too easy to suppose that there is an unobserved state variable called reputation that explains all that happens. The better approach is to develop a well-specified model in which the effects of reputations are delineated, and that circumscribes the observations that an outside observer might make.

NOTES

1. References are provided for the formulations and analyses of models that are described here only briefly.
2. It is sufficient to assume that each player's information, whether private or not, includes his preferences. The game is assumed to have perfect recall; that is, no player ever forgets what he knew or did previously. Randomized actions are interpreted as depending on the private observation of an independent random variable.
3. The discussion will subsequently clarify what this conditioning entails.
4. Actually, the perfect equilibria are generically the same as the sequential equilibria; compare Kreps and Wilson (1982a).
5. In the general case, one specifies that (σ, π) is a sequential equilibrium if it is in the closure of the set of pairs $(\sigma', \pi[\sigma'])$ for which σ' is positive, and using π the dynamic programming problems for the players are solved by σ.
6. This description applies along the equilibrium path, that is, as long as the seller adheres to the equilibrium sequence of offers. If the seller deviates, the buyer's acceptance price may depend on the history of the seller's offers.
7. See Chapters 5 and 8 in this volume.
8. Reputations need not be sustained via a "pooling" equilibrium in which one's actions are independent of one's private information. So long as one's action does not fully reveal one's information, reputational effects are possible. Moreover, the role of reputational features even in screening equilibria will be considered later on.
9. That is, using TIT-FOR-TAT, B initially cooperates and thereafter plays whatever A played on the previous round.
10. This experiment is conducted by using lottery tickets as the prize; moreover, there are two kinds of subjects, each of which gets a different monetary prize from the lottery. This scheme makes it possible to train the subjects either to divide the tickets equally or to divide the expected monetary value equally.
11. See also Chapter 4 in this volume.

REFERENCES

Benoit, Jean-Pierre (1983): *Entry with Exit: An Extensive-Form Treatment of Predation with Financial Constraints.* Technical Report 405, Institute for Mathematical Studies in the Social Sciences, Stanford University, May.

Bikhchandani, Sushil (1982): Repeated Auctions with Reputations. Unpublished, Graduate School of Business, Stanford University.

Cramton, Peter C. (1983a): *Bargaining with Incomplete Information: A Two-Period Model with Continuous Uncertainty.* Research Paper 652, Graduate School of Business, Stanford University, February.

(1983*b*): *Bargaining with Incomplete Information: An Infinite-Horizon Model with Continuous Uncertainty.* Research Paper 680, Graduate School of Business, Stanford University, March.

Crawford, Vincent P., and Joel Sobel (1982): Strategic Information Transmission. *Econometrica, 50,* 1431–51.

Dranove, David (1983): An Economic Model of the Physician–Patient Relationship. Ph.D. thesis, Graduate School of Business, Stanford University.

Dybvig, Phillip, and Chester Spatt (1980): *Does It Pay To Maintain a Reputation?* Technical Report 32, Financial Research Center, Princeton University.

Easley, David; Robert Masson; and R. J. Reynolds (1981): A Dynamic Analysis of Predatory Pricing with Rational Expectations. Unpublished, Cornell University.

Fudenberg, Drew, and Jean Tirole (1983*a*): Sequential Bargaining with Incomplete Information. *Review of Economic Studies, 50,* 221–47.

(1983*b*): *A Theory of Exit in Oligopoly.* Technical Report 429, Institute for Mathematical Studies in the Social Sciences, Stanford University, July.

Hart, Sergiu (1982): *Non-Zero-Sum Two-Person Repeated Games with Incomplete Information.* Technical Report 367, Institute for Mathematical Studies in the Social Sciences, Stanford University, February.

Holmström, Bengt (1982): Managerial Incentive Problems: A Dynamic Perspective Pp. 209–30, in *Essays in Economics and Management in Honour of Lars Wahlbeck.* Helsinki: Swedish School of Economics.

Kohlberg, Elon, and Jean-Francois Mertens (1982): *On the Strategic Stability of Equilibria.* Technical Report 8248, CORE, Université Catholique de Louvain, Belgium, November.

Kreps, David M., and Robert B. Wilson (1982*a*): Sequential Equilibria. *Econometrica, 50,* 863–94.

(1982*b*): Reputation and Imperfect Information. *Journal of Economic Theory, 27,* 253–79.

Kreps, David M.; Paul Milgrom; John Roberts; and Robert Wilson (1982): Rational Cooperation in the Finitely Repeated Prisoners' Dilemma. *Journal of Economic Theory, 27,* 245–52.

Maskin, Eric, and Drew Fudenberg (1983): Folk Theorems for Repeated Games with Discounting and Incomplete Information. Working Paper 310, Massachusetts Institute of Technology, August; forthcoming in *Econometrica.*

Matthews, Steven, and Leonard Mirman (1983): Equilibrium Limit Pricing: The Effects of Private Information and Stochastic Demand. *Econometrica, 51,* 981–996.

Milgrom, Paul, and D. John Roberts (1982*a*): Limit Pricing and Entry under Incomplete Information: An Equilibrium Analysis. *Econometrica, 50,* 443–59.

(1982*b*): Predation, Reputation, and Entry Deterrence. *Journal of Economic Theory, 27,* 280–312.

Moorthy, K. Sridhar (1980): *The Pablo Picasso Problem.* Working Paper, Graduate School of Business, Stanford University.

Ordover, Janusz A., and Ariel Rubinstein (1983): *On Bargaining, Settling, and Litigating: A Problem in Multistage Games with Imperfect Information.* Technical Report 83-07, New York University, April.

Radner, Roy (1981): Monitoring Cooperative Agreements in a Repeated Principal–Agent Relationship. *Econometrica, 49,* 1127–48.

Rogerson, William (1982*a*): *The Role of Reputation in a Repeated Agency Problem Involving Information Transmission.* Technical Report 377, Institute for Mathematical Studies in the Social Sciences, Stanford University, May.
(1982*b*): *Reputation and Product Quality.* Technical Report 384, Institute for Mathematical Studies in the Social Sciences, Stanford University, October.
Rosenthal, Robert W. (1979): Sequences of Games with Varying Opponents. *Econometrica, 47,* 1353–66.
(1981): Games of Perfect Information, Predatory Pricing, and the Chain-Store Paradox. *Journal of Economic Theory, 25,* 92–100.
Rosenthal, Robert W., and Henry J. Landau (1979): A Game-Theoretic Analysis of Bargaining with Reputations. *Journal of Mathematical Psychology, 20,* 233–255.
Roth, Alvin E., and Françoise Schoumaker (1983): Expectations and Reputations in Bargaining: An Experimental Study. *American Economic Review, 73,* 362–372.
Rubinstein, Ariel (1983*a*): A Bargaining Model with Incomplete Information about Time Preferences. Unpublished, Hebrew University, Jerusalem. Forthcoming in *Econometrica.*
(1983*b*): The Choice of Conjectures in a Bargaining Game with Incomplete Information. Unpublished, Institute for International Economic Studies, University of Stockholm.
Salant, Stephen W. (1983): Analysis of the Dynamic Competitive Equilibrium in Shapiro's Model of Reputation Building. Unpublished, The RAND Corporation.
Saloner, Garth (1982): Essays on Information Transmission under Uncertainty. Ph.D. thesis, Graduate School of Business, Stanford University.
Selten, Reinhard (1975): Re-Examination of the Perfectness Concept for Equilibrium Points in Extensive Games. *International Journal of Game Theory, 4,* 25–55.
(1978): The Chain-Store Paradox. *Theory and Decision, 9,* 127–59.
Shapiro, Carl (1982): Consumer Information, Product Quality, and Seller Reputation. *Bell Journal of Economics, 13,* 20–35.
(1985): Premiums for High-Quality Products as Rents for Reputation. *Quarterly Journal of Economics, 1985,* in press.
Shapiro, Carl, and Joseph E. Stiglitz (1981): Equilibrium Unemployment as a Worker Discipline Device. Unpublished, Woodrow Wilson School, Princeton University.
Sobel, Joel (1982): *A Theory of Credibility.* Technical Report 82-33, University of California at San Diego, September.
Sobel, Joel, and Ichiro Takahashi (1980): *A Multi-Stage Model of Bargaining.* Technical Report 80-25, University of California at San Diego, October.
Spence, A. Michael (1974): *Market Signalling.* Cambridge, Mass.: Harvard University Press.
Stiglitz, Joseph E., and Andrew Weiss (1983): Incentive Effects of Terminations: Applications to the Credit and Labor Markets. *American Economic Review, 73,* pp. 912–27.
Wilson, Robert B. (1983): Auditing: Perspectives from Multiperson Decision Theory. *Accounting Review, 58,* 305–18.
Wolfson, Mark A. (1983): *Empirical Evidence of Incentive Problems and Their Mitigation in Oil and Gas Tax Shelter Programs.* Technical Report, Graduate School of Business, Stanford University, June.

CHAPTER 4

An approach to some noncooperative game situations with special attention to bargaining

Robert W. Rosenthal
STATE UNIVERSITY OF NEW YORK AT STONY BROOK

4.1 Introduction

In this paper, I consider an approach to modeling certain kinds of game situations that is somewhat different from the standard noncooperative-game approach. Roughly speaking, the situations have the following features in common: (1) a large number of players; (2) repeated partitioning of the player set over time into small, randomly selected groups; (3) gamelike interaction of the members of each group over a brief span of time; and (4) extensive knowledge by each player about the past history of actions taken by aggregates from the population, but limited information about the past history of actions taken by identifiable individuals in the populations. I have already applied this approach to an election model (Rosenthal (1982)) and, jointly with Henry Landau, to two bargaining models (Rosenthal and Landau (1979, 1981)). (In addition, Shefrin (1981) has worked on a related approach, with a view toward economic applications. An early version of this paper antedated and stimulated my work in this general area.) My goals in this chapter are to describe the approach (first spelled out in Rosenthal (1979)), its applicability, its advantages and disadvantages relative to alternative approaches, and also to discuss some side issues. In keeping with the spirit of this volume, however, I concentrate on the bargaining models.

Because the actions of individuals in the situations under consideration have little influence on the population aggregates, the approach assumes implicitly that individuals neglect this influence in making their

I am greatly indebted to Henry Landau, who collaborated on much of what is described here, but who should not necessarily be presumed to agree with all of the opinions expressed. This presumption extends to Bell Laboratories, which provided financial support.

decisions. And, because individuals in these situations are usually anonymous as well, the approach similarly assumes that individuals do not admit the possibility that their present actions can affect the way others perceive and interact with them in the future, except insofar as their actions move them from one aggregated class within the population to another. In these two respects, the approach deviates from the pervasive rationality normally assumed in game-thoretic modeling. However, these two behavioral assumptions, together with an assumed stationary structure in the partitioning process, permit use of a model of a stationary stochastic process in which calculations are greatly simplified. The benefits of simplicity to the user of any model are obvious; in the present case, these benefits also accrue to the individuals being modeled, whose (less than completely rational) simple calculations might be interpreted as having been discovered (in some unspecified, transient part of the process) even when the underlying structure of the situation might not be known by the individuals. The approach is therefore responsive to the criticism of game-theoretic modeling that holds that assuming excessive rationality limits the applicability of models, since real-world players may have neither the abilities nor the resources to do the required calculations. On the other hand, the assumptions underlying the models directly limit the situations to which the models may usefully be applied.

In the next two sections, I describe informally the models and results from Rosenthal and Landau (1979, 1981). Following that will be a more general discussion of bargaining and other potential applications. With the two bargaining models having served as illustrations of the approach, I return in the final section to a discussion of the general philosophy underlying the approach, and contrast it with the philosophies underlying more conventional approaches.

4.2   A model of bargaining with reputations

In this section, I summarize the model and results of Rosenthal and Landau (1979). The motivation for that paper is that individuals are faced repeatedly with bargaining games over time. In such games, the opponents are not always the same, and information about the opponents' past behaviors may be fragmentary. It seems desirable, therefore, to expose the temporal linkages between the games in some simple way.

For purposes of the present discussion, a particularly simplistic view of the one-shot bargaining games is taken: They are all two-person noncooperative games, as pictured here.

	Y	$\overline{Y}$
Y	2,2	1,3
$\overline{Y}$	3,1	0,0

Each player in each of these games either yields (Y) or does not yield ($\overline{Y}$).
If at least one player yields, a total of four units of von Neumann–
Morgenstern utility is divided as indicated; if neither yields, the outcome
is (0,0). (Think of the situation where neither yields as being the noncooperative analog of the disagreement outcome in the Nash bargaining
model.) The one-shot game depicted here has three Nash equilibria: the
two off-diagonal, pure-strategy combinations and the mixed-strategy
combination in which both individuals play $\frac{1}{2} - \frac{1}{2}$ and receive $\frac{3}{2}$ in expectation.

Let us suppose that each individual expects to play this game repeatedly against a succession of randomly drawn opponents, about each of
whose pasts the individual will have only a single piece of information,
which represents the opponent's reputation. Let us also assume: that the
individual discounts the future with the factor σ ($0 \leq \sigma < 1$); that both his
and the opponents' reputations are always elements from the finite set
$\{1, \ldots, n\}$; that these reputations change in the same known, but not
necessarily deterministic, way at each time as a function of current-period
reputations and actions of the population; and that the population of
players is in a steady state with reputation frequency vector $\pi =
(\pi_1, \ldots, \pi_n)$ and with action frequencies p_{ij} and $(1 - p_{ij})$, denoting the
probabilities with which a randomly drawn player chooses Y and $\overline{Y}$,
respectively, whenever he has reputation i and his opponent has reputation j. (Let p denote $\{p_{ij} : 1 \leq i, j \leq n\}$.) With such a view, the individual
does not consider himself to be a player in a game in the usual sense;
rather, he considers himself to be facing a Markovian decision problem
(e.g., Derman (1970)) in which the state space is a pair of reputations (the
individual's and his current opponent's), the discount factor is σ, the
single-period rewards are expected payoffs from the bargaining game (if
the state is (i,j), the reward for Y is $2p_{ji} + (1 - p_{ji})$ and the reward for $\overline{Y}$ is
$3p_{ji}$), and the transition probabilities are the relevant functions of π, p, and
the individual's own action. A steady-state equilibrium consists of particular values for the vectors π and p such that p is itself an optimal solution
to the Markovian decision problem (i.e., an individual cannot increase his
expected payoff beyond what he gets by randomizing with probabilities
$(p_{ij}, 1 - p_{ij})$ whenever he has reputation i and his opponent has reputation

j) and such that π is an invariant distribution for the Markov chain describing an individual's reputation when the individual behaves according to p and the rest of the population's (including his opponents') reputations and actions from i.i.d. sequences generated by π and p.

In Rosenthal and Landau (1979), two variants of this model are explored corresponding to two particular examples of rules whereby reputations are updated. Essentially, both of these rules admit the interpretation that plays of Y tend to lower reputation and plays of $\overline{Y}$ tend to raise reputation. Three classes of possible steady-state equilibria are considered for each of the two rules. The first class, C1, arises from what might be called the social custom that if two players with unequal reputations are matched, then the player with the higher reputation plays $\overline{Y}$ and the player with the lower reputation plays Y; that is, the class C1 is the set of (π,p) satisfying the restrictions that

$$p_{ij} = 0 \text{ whenever } i > j \quad \text{and} \quad p_{ij} = 1 \text{ whenever } i < j.$$

A steady-state equilibrium from class C1 would seem to agree with the intuition that individuals with relatively weak reputations yield and individuals with relatively strong reputations do not yield. If the population adopts reputation as a coordinating device to reduce the frequency of conflict, a C1 steady-state equilibrium seems to be an intuitively plausible way for the society to organize itself (albeit noncooperatively). On the other hand, if some (π,p) from C1 can be a steady-state equilibrium, why not also some (π,p) from the (counterintuitive?) class C2, for which

$$p_{ij} = 1 \text{ whenever } i > j \quad \text{and} \quad p_{ij} = 0 \text{ whenever } i < j?$$

Finally, we also consider the class C3, which admits only one value for p, namely,

$$p_{ij} = \tfrac{1}{2} \text{ for all } i,j.$$

In class C3, all individuals ignore reputations and always play the mixed equilibrium for the one-shot game. It is obvious that there is always a steady-state equilibrium from C3 no matter what σ or the rules for updating reputation are.

So much for a general description of the setup in Rosenthal and Landau (1979). We had initially hoped that results about the nature of steady-state equilibria would not be sensitive to variations in the reputation-update rules so long as the theme was maintained that plays of $\overline{Y}$ tend to increase reputation whereas plays of Y tend to decrease it. Furthermore, we were interested in evaluating steady-state equilibria from the various classes to see whether one class or another would be best for the population as a whole, in the sense that in the steady state, the incidence of the

conflict outcome $(\overline{Y},\overline{Y})$ would be minimized. In particular, we specu-
lated that the intuitive appeal of C1 might be related, in some social-
Darwinian sense, to the evolutionary success of societies in the real world
with C1 steady-state equilibria. However, we found that the results generally were sensitive to the exact nature of the reputation-update rule. For
one of the rules, we were able to show only that with σ fixed, both C1 and
C2 steady-state equilibria exist when n is sufficiently large (unboundedly
large as σ approaches 1). For the other rule, the size of n played no role in
the existence results, and we could prove existence of both C1 and C2
steady-state equilibria only when $\sigma \leq \frac{1}{3}$. For the latter rule and $n \geq 6$, the
C1 equilibrium dominates the C2 equilibrium, which in turn dominates
the C3 equilibrium, in the sense of minimizing the incidence of conflict
(as our intuition suggested). For the former rule, however, the social
preference between C1 and C2 is reversed.

Although the results from this study are far from significant in either a
normative or a positive sense, the fact that it was possible for us to generate
detailed comparisons encourages me that further explorations into the
particular questions addressed about bargaining in the presence of reputations using this general approach may prove to be fruitful.

4.3 Repeated bargaining with opportunities for learning

In this section, I summarize the model and results of Rosenthal and
Landau (1981). Our intention in this paper was to incorporate into a
model of bargaining what seems to be a significant feature of many bargaining situations – the possibility of information acquisition. In this presentation, individuals are repeatedly matched to play a bargaining game
similar to the one considered in the preceding section, except that there is
some uncertainty about the stength of individual preferences regarding
the conflict outcome $(\overline{Y},\overline{Y})$. The game that is played by any pair at any
time may be described as

	Y	$\overline{Y}$
Y	2,2	1,3
$\overline{Y}$	3,1	x_R, x_C

,

where x_R is a number characteristic of the specific row player and x_C is
specific to the column player. No player ever knows his opponent's value
of x; and each player initially is ignorant of his own number as well,
learning it only after the outcome $(\overline{Y},\overline{Y})$ occurs in one of his bargaining

games for the first time (after which he continues to remember it.) It is common knowledge among the members of the population that the x's are all drawn from some common distribution with probability density f (the support of f is assumed to lie within $(-\infty, 1)$ to rule out uninteresting complications), and each player assumes that his draw and that of each of his opponents form an independent sequence. So that ignorance will be a recurring feature of this model, it is assumed that a fixed proportion $(1 - \beta)$ of the population (randomly chosen) dies after each period and is replaced by an equal-sized cohort of ignorant individuals. The conditional survival probability $\beta(<1)$ is taken to be also the discount factor in the individual Markovian decision problems. In this model, individuals receive no information about their opponents. A state of the individual's Markovian decision problem is here simply a possible value of his information about himself; that is, the state space is the support of f together with the state of ignorance. If individuals believe that their opponents' actions are independent draws from some distribution $(h, 1 - h)$ on $\{Y, \overline{Y}\}$, then a steady-state equilibrium is such an h and a stationary Markovian decision rule (function from the state space to distributions on $\{Y, \overline{Y}\}$), which, if used by the entire population, reproduces h.

It is easy to see that any optimal stationary Markovian decision rule may be characterized by a probability p that Y is played in the state of ignorance and a value $\hat{x} \in (\text{supp} f)$ above which the individual plays $\overline{Y}$ and below which the individual plays Y.

The main result of this work by Rosenthal and Landau is that for any given f and β, there exists a unique steady-state equilibrium. This steady-state equilibrium is characterized fairly extensively. In particular, the characterization enables us to examine the effect of changes in β on the steady-state equilibrium that are not apparent a priori.

The results indicate that it is possible to generate detailed testable hypotheses from our general approach. Furthermore, the analysis demonstrates that our approach can deal (at least in one example) with the important bargaining issue of information acquisition, even though the approach is essentially a picture of a stationary game-playing process. The information-acquisition possibilities modeled are, of course, quite specific and serve only to illustrate an application of the general approach.

4.4   General discussion of applications

Despite the enormous body of literature based on Nash's fixed-threat bargaining model and its extensions (e.g., Roth (1979) and references therein), and despite the increasing popularity of Nash's model in recent applied work (e.g., McDonald and Solow (1981) and Crawford (1982)), I believe that this model contains too little detail to be of much practical use for either positive or normative purposes. Instead of the considerations represented by the axioms typical of that literature as being what determine the choice of outcomes in bargaining situations, I suggest that in the real world, it is certain other factors in bargaining situations (e.g., sociological and psychological factors), not accounted for in Nash's model, that turn out to be decisive. (I would interpet some of the experimental results in Roth and Malouf (1979), for example, as supporting this view.) The models I have described illustrate one way of incorporating such factors. In Rosenthal and Landau (1979), it is the availability of reputations that allows individuals in a population to reduce the incidence of bargaining impasse. In Rosenthal and Landau (1981), the presence of uncertainty about utilities and the possibility that individuals may learn through experience are explicitly accounted for, again in a model of self-interested bargaining. Of course, the approach of those papers is limited to situations in which the bargaining games arise from independent matchings in a large population; hence, the sociological and psychological factors must themselves be well modeled by some stationary process. Nevertheless, it seems to me that some such large-population factors are to some extent present in some interesting bargaining situations. (The motivations behind this approach should not be confused with those of other recent noncooperative bargaining models [e.g., Harsanyi and Selten (1972) and Rubinstein (1982)], which aim more at exposing how bargaining outcomes are affected by the specific dynamic features present in individual bargaining situations.)

The results about bargaining presented in the papers described in the preceding sections are not definitive for any purpose; rather, these papers are intended as illustrations of the types of questions that might be addressed with the approach being advocated. It seems to me that if someone wanted to study, say, the long-run relationship between a firm and a labor union in which periodic negotiations over short-run contracts were the interesting points of interaction between the two organizations, the approach described in the present paper might generally be inappropriate for viewing the overall situation; but it might be effective as a way of focusing on specific aspects of the relationship (e.g., informational asymmetries between the firm and the union or between the union's leadership and its membership; the role of reputations of the negotiators, the firm's executives, and the union's leaders; the effect of the availability or imposition of third-party mediation or arbitration; and the motivations resulting from the procedures used by the firm to select its executives and the union to elect its leaders).

Turning briefly to the question of the applicability of this approach outside the specific context of bargaining, it seems to me that the approach is potentially useful in economic situations in which questions about the effects of institutional and informational details on individual market transactions are of interest. In such situations, however, the random matching of players seems a limiting feature (although random-matching assumptions already play key roles in some of this literature (e.g., see Butters (n.d.) and Diamond and Maskin (1979)); for instance, shoppers typically choose stores for specific reasons, such as: reputation for quality, proximity, exposure to advertising, and knowledge about prices. (On the other hand, the random-matching assumption in a simple model may not be especially unrealistic as a description of how a shopper limits the set from which further nonrandom selection is to be made.)

As noted earlier, I have also worked on an application of the approach in an election model (Rosenthal (1982)). There, politicians are randomly matched in sequences of elections. The link between the elections arises from the assumptions that the outcome of a specific election is influenced by the relative positions of the specific candidates on issues and that an individual cannot make a major change in his position in any single election campaign. Although this work may not by itself be of major interest to political scientists, I hope it indicates how certain dynamic questions resulting from spatial political models can be addressed.

4.5   General remarks about the approach

The approach of this paper is related to that of stochastic games, in which much of the interest focuses on equilibria composed of stationary, Markovian strategies. In such an equilibrium, each player chooses optimally in some Markovian decision problem, just as here, but the way in which the different players' decision problems tie together in equilibrium is quite different. There are also connections between the approach of this paper and that of rational expectations, which has been popular in recent years among economists (e.g., Grossman (1981)). Roughly speaking, the approach of rational expectations is that the individual actors in a model develop hypotheses about their environment that turn out to be consistent with their experiences (compare with the present approach of stationary processes of opponents' states and actions, which in steady-state equilibria are consistent with individual optimizing actions for the entire population).

One interesting question is whether the steady-state equilibria of the approach presented here bear some relationship to ordinary Nash equilibria of the associated dynamic game played by a large player set in which the roles of the matching process and information restrictions about opponents are appropriate analogs. It might be expected, for example, that as the player set in that game becomes large, some subset of the Nash equilibria converges in some sense to the steady-state equilibria of the present approach. Although I have not explored that particular question, there is a related result in Rosenthal (1979), which, roughly speaking, is (for the model of that paper): As the player set becomes large, if each individual plays his part of the steady-state equilibrium, then the error that each individual makes by solving the Markovian decision problem, instead of the non-Markovian problem resulting when the individual includes the extra information acquired through his past interactions, becomes vanishingly small.

Existence results for steady-state equilibria in the approach of this chapter are routine (e.g., theorem 1 in Rosenthal (1979)); the usual fixed-point approach is applicable. Questions about stability and non-steady-state behavior are intriguing, however. How might individuals learn about population averages? How important is it that an individual understand the stochastic matching process? Shefrin (1979) has made a start on answering some such questions in a related model.

REFERENCES

Butters, G.: Equilibrium Price Distributions in a Random Meetings Market. Mimeo, n.d.
Crawford, V.: Long-Term Relationships Governed by Short-Term Contracts. Discussion Paper 926, Harvard Institute of Economic Research, November 1982.
Derman, C.: *Finite State Markovian Decision Process.* New York: Academic Press, 1970.
Diamond, P., and E. Maskin: An Equilibrium Analysis of Search and Breach of Contract I. Steady States. *Bell J. Econ.* **10** (1979), pp. 282–316.
Grossman, S.: An Introduction to the Theory of Rational Expectations under Asymmetric Information. *Rev. Econ. Studies* **48** (1981), pp. 541–59.
Harsanyi, J., and R. Selten: A Generalized Nash Solution for Two-Person Bargaining Games with Incomplete Information. *Man. Sci.* **18** (1972), pp. P80–P106.
McDonald, I., and R. Solow: Wage Bargaining and Unemployment. *Amer. Econ. Rev.* **71** (1981), pp. 896–908.
Rosenthal, R.: Sequences of Games with Varying Opponents. *Econometrica* **47** (1979), pp. 1353–66.
    A Model of Far-Sighted Electoral Competition. *Math. Soc. Sci.* **2** (1982), pp. 289–97.
Rosenthal, R., and H. Landau: A Game-Theoretic Analysis of Bargaining with Reputations. *J. Math. Psych.* **20** (1979), pp. 233–55.
    Repeated Bargaining with Opportunities for Learning. *J. Math. Soc.* **8** (1981), pp. 61–74.
Roth, A.: *Axiomatic Models of Bargaining.* Berlin: Springer-Verlag, 1979.

Roth, A., and M. Malouf: Game-Theoretic Models and the Role of Information in Bargaining. *Psych. Rev.* **86** (1979), pp. 574–94.

Rubinstein, A.: Perfect Equilibrium in a Bargaining Model. *Econometrica* **50** (1982), pp. 97–109.

Shefrin, H.: Bayesian Learning, Convergence, and Information Equilibrium. Mimeo, 1979.

  Games with Self-Generating Distributions. *Rev. Econ. Studies* **48** (1981), pp. 511–19.

CHAPTER 5

Infinite-horizon models of bargaining with one-sided incomplete information

Drew Fudenberg
UNIVERSITY OF CALIFORNIA AT BERKELEY

David Levine
UNIVERSITY OF CALIFORNIA AT LOS ANGELES

Jean Tirole
ECOLE NATIONALE DES PONTS ET CHAUSSEES

5.1 Introduction

Bargaining occurs whenever two or more parties can share a surplus if an agreement can be reached on how the surplus should be shared, with a status-quo point that will prevail in the event of disagreement. Until recently, bargaining has been analyzed using the cooperative approach, which typically consists of specifying a set of axioms that the bargaining outcome should satisfy, and then proving that a solution satisfying these axioms exists and is unique. More recently, a second approach has emerged, which relies on the theory of noncooperative games. The typical paper of this type specifies a particular extensive form for the bargaining process, and solves for the noncooperative equilibria. Thus, the noncooperative approach replaces the axioms of the cooperative approach with the need to specify a particular extensive form.

Although this chapter is based on the noncooperative approach, which we believe has considerable power, we should point out that the reliance of the noncooperative approach on particular extensive forms poses two problems. First, because the results depend on the extensive form, one needs to argue that the chosen specification is reasonable – that it is a good approximation to the extensive forms actually played. Second, even if one particular extensive form were used in almost all bargaining, the analysis is incomplete because it has not, at least to-date, begun to address the question of why that extensive form is used. This chapter will consider

We thank Peter Cramton for his helpful comments. Research support from NSF grant SES 82-07925 is gratefully acknowledged.

the first point of extending the class of bargaining games for which we have solutions. The second and harder problem, we will leave unresolved.

Fudenberg and Tirole (1983) analyzed the simplest model of noncooperative bargaining that captures bargaining's two key aspects: Bargaining involves a succession of steps, and the bargainers do not know the value to others of reaching an agreement. Their model had only two periods, and only two possible valuations for each player. In each period, one player (the "seller") makes an offer, which the other player (the "buyer") can either accept or reject. Each player is impatient and prefers an agreement today to the same agreement tomorrow. The simplicity of the model permitted a complete characterization of the equilibria. Several common perceptions about the effects of parameter changes on bargaining outcomes were found to be suspect.

However, finite-horizon models are inevitably contrived: Why should negotiations be constrained to end after a fixed number of periods? Moreover, the specification of two-point distributions for the valuations of the bargainers is special. Finally, the assumption that the seller makes all the offers can also be questioned. The present chapter investigates the effect of relaxing the first two assumptions, and discusses relaxing the third, in the case of one-sided incomplete information. The seller's valuation is common knowledge, and only the buyer's valuation is private information.

We find that, as long as the seller makes all of the offers, the conclusions of Fudenberg and Tirole for the one-sided case are essentially unchanged by allowing an infinite bargaining horizon and general distributions: An equilibrium exists and is essentially unique, and the offers decline over time. Although many infinite-horizon games have multiple equilibria, this uniqueness result should not be surprising, since (1) if an agreement occurs, it occurs in finite time; and (2) the seller's offers convey no information because the seller's valuation is common knowledge. "Supergame"-type "punishment strategies" are not equilibria in bargaining games, because a bargainer cannot be punished for accepting the "wrong" offer. Once an offer is accepted, the game ends. The fact that offers decrease over time is similarly intuitive. The seller becomes increasingly pessimistic as each offer is refused. However, neither uniqueness nor decreasing offers holds with two-sided incomplete information, as Fudenberg and Tirole demonstrated in a two-period model. With two-sided incomplete information, the buyer's beliefs about the seller depend on the seller's offers. In particular, we must specify what the buyer infers from an offer to which the equilibrium strategies assign zero probability. In such circumstances, Bayes' rule is inapplicable, and many different inferences can be specified. This leeway in choosing the buyer's "conjectures" generates many equilibria.

The conclusions of noncooperative models of bargaining depend not only on the extensive form chosen but also, of course, on the specification of the payoffs. In particular, models of sequential bargaining assume some sort of impatience on the part of the players. Although most work has modeled these costs as arising from discounting future payoffs, a few studies have modeled impatience as fixed per-period bargaining costs. We examine the fixed per-period cost specification, and explain why that specification may lead to implausible equilibria.

The chapter is organized in the following manner. Section 5.2 reviews some previous work on infinite-horizon bargaining with incomplete information. Section 5.3 proves that if the seller makes all of the offers, an equilibrium exists, and is unique if it is common knowledge that the buyer's valuation strictly exceeds the seller's. This section also investigates the existence of differentiable equilibria. Section 5.4 discusses the case in which the buyer and the seller alternate making offers, and Section 5.5 discusses the specification of the costs of bargaining. Sections 6 and 7 offer some brief thoughts about the choice of the extensive form and the specification of uncertainty.

5.2   Infinite-horizon bargaining under incomplete information: The state of the art

Here, we review briefly the models of Cramton (1983a), Sobel and Takahashi (1983), and Rubinstein (1985). (Perry (1982a) will be discussed in Section 5.5.) Very schematically, we can distinguish the following steps involved in building these models.

Specification of an extensive form.   Cramton (1983a) and Sobel and Takahashi (1983) assume that the seller makes all of the offers, at the rate of one per period. Bargaining stops only when the buyer accepts the current offer, then trade takes place at the agreed-upon price. Rubinstein (1985), on the other hand, assumes that the traders take turns making offers. These two representations have a number of features in common. First, the extensive form is given from the outside. As indicated earlier, we have little to say about this assumption. Second, traders are not allowed to bargain with other traders; or, equivalently, bargaining with a given trader is not affected by the potential of bargaining with another trader. Actually, in the three contributions mentioned, traders will never quit the bargaining process. Not only are they prevented from bargaining with other parties, but their costs of bargaining take the form of discounting, and so they have no incentive to stop bargaining with their (unique) partner.

Specification of the payoff structure.   We just mentioned that in the three models, the cost of disagreement comes from discounting. Let δ_B and δ_S denote the buyer's and the seller's discount factors, respectively. Typically, if the buyer has valuation b for the object and the seller has valuation or production cost s, agreement at price p at time t yields utilities $\delta_B^t(b - p)$ to the buyer and $\delta_S^t(p - s)$ to the seller (Cramton). This framework is rich enough to include two interesting cases: (1) the production cost is already incurred (the seller owns the object before bargaining, that is, $s = 0$ (Sobel and Takahashi)); and (2) the traders bargain on how to divide a pie of a given size (Rubinstein). However, it does not formalize the cases in which bargaining may stop because of disagreement; for example, if $V_S(t,s)$ denotes time-t valuation of a seller with cost s when he quits the bargaining process at time $(t - 1)$ to start bargaining with someone else at time t, the seller's payoff is $\delta_S^t V_S(t,s)$.

Specification of the prior information structure.   Sobel and Takahashi assume that the asymmetric information concerns the buyer's valuation, which is known only to the buyer. All the rest is common knowledge. Rubinstein assumes instead that one of the traders' discount factors is unknown. Cramton considers two-sided incomplete information: Both the buyer and the seller have incomplete information about the other party's valuation (or production cost).

Solution.   The three papers look for special types of equilibria instead of characterizing the equilibrium set. We give only a very brief description of the restrictions used because these are clearly detailed by the authors and they differ greatly. Sobel and Takahashi look for an equilibrium that is the limit of finite-horizon equilibria.

To this purpose, they compute explicitly a sequence of finite-horizon equilibria in a simple case, and derive a limit. Rubinstein imposes some monotonicity conditions on off-the-equilibrium-path conjectures; he also rules out mixed strategies despite using a two-point distribution for the private information. And Cramton looks for equilibria in which the seller at some point of time reveals his information so that the bargaining game becomes a one-sided incomplete-information game, for which he takes the Sobel–Takahashi solution.

5.3   Seller makes the offers

We now consider a model in which the seller makes all of the offers and has incomplete information about the buyer's valuation. The seller has production cost $s = 0$ (the object has already been produced and the seller is not allowed to bargain with any other buyer). He has discount factor δ_S, which is common knowledge. The buyer's valuation, b, is known only to him. The seller has a smooth prior cumulative-distribution function $F(b)$, with bounded density $f(b)$, with $0 < \underline{f} \le f(b) \le \bar{f}$, concentrated on the interval $[\underline{b}, \bar{b}]$, where $\underline{b} \ge 0$. The buyer's discount factor, δ_B, is common knowledge. A *perfect Bayesian equilibrium* is a history-contingent sequence of the seller's offers (p_t), of the buyer's acceptances or refusals of the offers, and of updated beliefs about the buyer's valuation satisfying the usual consistency conditions (i.e., the actions must be optimal given the beliefs, and the beliefs must be derived from the actions by Bayes' rule).

The general case

We will show that an equilibrium exists and that it is unique if $\underline{b}$ *strictly* exceeds s. We begin with two lemmas that hold in either case.

Lemma 1 (Successive skimming).   In equilibrium and at any instant, the seller's posterior about the buyer's valuation is the prior truncated at some value b^e: $F(b)/F(b^e)$ for $b \le b^e$, 1 for $b \ge b^e$.

Proof.   Lemma 1 follows from the fact that for any time τ less than or equal to t, if a buyer with valuation b is willing to accept an offer p_τ, then a buyer with valuation $b' > b$ accepts the offer with probability 1. To prove the latter fact, notice that since b accepts p_τ,

$$b - p_\tau \ge \delta_B V_B(b, H_\tau),$$

where $V_B(b, H_\tau)$ is the time-$(\tau + 1)$ valuation of a buyer with valuation b when the history of the game up to and including τ is H_τ. Let us show that

$$b' - p_\tau > \delta_B V_B(b', H_\tau),$$

so that a buyer with valuation b' accepts p_τ with probability 1. Since from time $(\tau + 1)$ on, buyer b can always adopt the optimal strategy of buyer b', that is, accept exactly when buyer b' accepts, then

$$V_B(b', H_\tau) - V_B(b, H_\tau) \le \sum_{u=0}^{\infty} \delta_B^u \alpha_{\tau+1+u}(b', H_\tau)(b' - b),$$

where u is the index of time periods and $\alpha_{\tau+1+u}(b', H_\tau)$ is the probability conditional on H_τ that agreement is reached at time $(\tau + 1 + u)$ and the buyer uses buyer b'''s optimal strategy from time $(\tau + 1)$ on. Therefore,

$$V_B(b',H_\tau) - V_B(b,H_\tau) \le b' - b,$$

and the conclusion follows by a simple computation.

Lemma 1 implies that the seller's posterior at any instant can be characterized by a unique number, the buyer's highest possible valuation b^e. By abuse of terminology, we will call b^e the posterior.

Lemma 2.   The seller never (i.e., in no subgame) charges a price below $\underline{b}$.

Proof.   We know that the seller's equilibrium valuation must be nonnegative, and that expected equilibrium surplus cannot exceed $\bar{b}$, so that the expectation over all possible types of the buyer's equilibrium valuation cannot exceed $\bar{b}$. Moreover, following the proof of lemma 1, we can show that the buyer's equilibrium valuation is nondecreasing and has modulus of continuity no greater than 1; that is, if $b' > b$, then

$$V_B(b') \le V_B(b) + b' - b$$

(because the buyer of type b can always play as though he were type b'). Since the buyer's equilibrium valuation is nondecreasing and does not exceed $\bar{b}$ in expected value, it must be that $V_B(\underline{b}) \le \bar{b}$, and so $V(\bar{b}) \le 2\bar{b} - \underline{b}$. This implies that all buyers accept any price below $(\underline{b} - \bar{b})$, and therefore the seller would never charge such prices. Knowing that the lowest possible price is $(\underline{b} - \bar{b})$, all buyers accept prices such that $\underline{b} - p \ge \delta_B[\underline{b} - (\underline{b} - \bar{b})]$, or $p \le \underline{b} - \delta_B\bar{b}$. Proceeding as before, this implies that for every positive n, all prices below $\underline{b} - \delta_B^n\bar{b}$ are accepted by all buyers, and thus the seller never charges less than $\underline{b}$.

Now we specialize to the case $\underline{b} > 0$. The next lemma shows that if the posterior is sufficiently low the seller charges $\underline{b}$, and uses this fact to establish that the rate at which the seller's posterior decreases is uniformly bounded below over all subgames.

Lemma 3.   If $\underline{b} > 0$, there exists N^* such that in all equilibria with probability 1, an offer is accepted in or before period $(N^* + 1)$.

Proof.   First, we show that there exists a b^* such that if the seller's posterior is below b^*, he charges $\underline{b}$. We do this by demonstrating that such a b^* exists if the buyer plays myopically and accepts all prices less than his valuation. If a seller chooses to jump down to $\underline{b}$ against a myopic buyer, he will do so against a nonmyopic one, since nonmyopic buyers are less likely to accept prices above $\underline{b}$ but just as likely to accept $\underline{b}$ (because no lower price is ever charged).

Thus, we consider the maximization problem of a seller facing a myopic buyer, when the seller's posterior is b^e. The seller's return to charging price p is at most

$$M(p) = \left[(F(b^e) - F(p))p + \delta_S \int\limits_{\underline{b}}^p sf(s)\,ds \right] \Big/ F(b^e).$$

Taking the derivative with respect to p, we have

$$M'(p) \propto F(b^e) - F(p) + pf(p)(\delta_S - 1).$$

As $f(p)$ is bounded below, for b^e sufficiently near $\underline{b}$, $M'(p)$ is negative for all p between b^e and $\underline{b}$. Quantity $M(p)$ overstates the "continuation" payoff if p is refused, and so when b^e is sufficiently small, a seller with posterior b^e would charge $\underline{b}$ if the buyer was myopic, and a fortiori would do so against nonmyopic buyers. This establishes the existence of the desired b^*.

Next, we show that there exists N^* such that all equilibria end in $(N^* + 1)$ periods. We do this by showing that in N^* periods, the seller's posterior drops below b^*. We claim that there are constants k and w such that for all initial beliefs $b^e > b^*$, the seller's posterior is no higher than $\max\{\underline{b}, b^e - w\}$ after k additional periods. Assume not – then

$$V_S \leq \bar{b} \left[\frac{\bar{f}w}{F(b^*)} \right] + \delta_S^k \bar{b},$$

where V_S is the seller's valuation and the term in brackets is an upper bound on the probability that an offer is accepted in the first k periods. But for w sufficiently small and k sufficiently large, the right-hand side of this equation is less than $\underline{b}$. Thus, we can define N^* as

$$\left[\left[\frac{k(\bar{b} - b^*)}{w} \right]_{\text{int}} + 1 \right],$$

and all equilibria must end in $(N^* + 1)$ periods.

The proof of lemma 3 makes clear the importance of our assumption that $\underline{b} > 0$. With $\underline{b} > 0$, the potential surplus the seller might hope to extract eventually becomes insignificant compared to the "sure thing" of $\underline{b}$, and thus when the posterior is less than b^*, the seller settles for $\underline{b}$. The second part of the lemma in turn relies crucially on the first: Without the "termination condition" at b^*, the rate at which the seller's posterior fell would not be uniformly bounded below, but would instead decrease with the seller's posterior. When $\underline{b}$ is zero, the equilibria will clearly not be of bounded length, because the seller will never charge zero. This explains why we prove uniqueness only for $\underline{b} > 0$; existence will not be a problem.

Now, we can characterize the unique equilibrium when $\underline{b} > 0$. Let $\beta(p_t, H_{t-1})$ be the least (inf) value of any buyer to buy in period t. An equilibrium is called "weak-Markov" if $\beta(p_t, H_{t-1})$ depends only on p_t (which implies that $V_S(b, H_{t-1})$ depends only on b). Let $\sigma(b^e, H_{t-1})$ be the seller's probability distribution over prices in period t. An equilibrium will be called "strong-Markov" if it is weak-Markov and in addition σ depends only on b^e. In a strong-Markov equilibrium, players' actions depend solely on the "relevant" part of the history, namely, the seller's beliefs and the current offer.

Strong-Markov equilibria do not necessarily exist, as was discovered by Fudenberg and Tirole (1983) in a two-period model with a discrete distribution over the buyer's valuation, and by Kreps and Wilson (1982a) in their treatment of the chain-store paradox. The same forces lead to nonexistence here. Strong-Markov equilibria fail to exist in general, because it may be necessary for the probability of acceptance, $\beta(p)$, to be constant over some interval. The seller's posterior will be the same after any offer in such an interval is refused, but in order for $\beta(p)$ to be constant, the seller's next price will have to depend on the current one. As this discussion suggests, a necessary and sufficient condition for a weak-Markov equilibrium to be strong-Markov is that β be strictly increasing.

We will show that if $\underline{b} > 0$, the unique equilibrium is weak-Markov. The weak-Markov property is unsurprising given that the game ends in finite time and that the seller's offers convey no information. When $\underline{b} = 0$, bargaining can continue indefinitely and we have not been able to show that equilibria must be weak-Markov.

Our proof of uniqueness proceeds inductively. We start by solving what we will call the "one-period" game, in which we impose the constraint that the seller charge $\underline{b}$. Recall from the proof of lemma 3 that if the seller's posterior is sufficiently low (less than b^*), then this constraint is not binding because the seller chooses $\underline{b}$ when he is sufficiently pessimistic. In fact, there exists b^2 that is the largest value of b^e such that the seller charges $\underline{b}$ when his posterior falls below b^2. We then proceed to "work backward" on both the number of "periods remaining" and the seller's posterior simultaneously. Let p_1 be the highest price that buyer b^2 will accept if he expects the price to be $\underline{b}$ next period. In the "two-period" game, the seller is constrained not to charge prices above p_1, and thus the game indeed ends in two periods. Then, we solve for the seller's optimal action in the two-period game. The key to the proof is that if $b^e \leq b^2$, the seller will choose to charge $\underline{b}$ in the two-period game, and indeed in <u>any</u> equilibrium the seller must charge $\underline{b}$ when $b^e \leq b^2$. We then proceed to the "three-period" game, and so on. Because we know that all equilibria end with probability 1 by time $(N^* + 1)$, we need only work backward $(N^* + 1)$ steps. At that point, we will have worked out unique strategies such that (1) the buyer's decisions are best responses to the strategy of the seller, (2) the seller's strategy is an optimal response under the constraint that the seller's first-period price be less than p^{N^*}, and (3) the game ends by $(N^* + 1)$. This immediately implies that at most one equilibrium exists. We claim that it also establishes existence. The only way that the computed strategies could fail to be an equilibrium would be if the first-period constraint on the seller's action were binding. Holding the buyer's strategy fixed, let us consider the seller's optimization. The seller's choice set is compact (in the product topology) and his expected payoff is continuous; therefore, an optimal choice exists. The argument of lemma 3 shows that the seller's optimal choice must terminate the game by $(N^* + 1)$, and so the first-period constraint cannot bind.

After this lengthy overview, we now state and prove our main result. The statement is only generic, since the seller may have several optimal first-period offers.

Proposition 1. If $\underline{b} > 0$, an equilibrium exists and is generically unique. The equilibrium is weak-Markov; it is strong-Markov if and only if the buyer's reservation function $\beta(p)$ is strictly increasing.

Proof. See Appendix 1.

We now assume that there is "enough concavity" in the problem that the seller's optimal action at each instant is unique, in order to give a simpler proof of uniqueness. Moreover, we can show that the equilibrium is (strong-)Markov. The single-valuedness assumption permits us to use a simple dominance argument to show that when the seller's posterior is below b^n, his price is low enough that next period his posterior will be below b^{n-1}.

To state the single-valuedness assumption, (S), we need the following notation:

$$\beta^2(p) \equiv \frac{p - \delta_B \underline{b}}{1 - \delta_B}$$

$$W_S^2(b^e) \equiv \max_p \{[F(b^e) - F(\beta^2(p))]p + \delta_S F(\beta^2(p))\underline{b}\},$$

where $\beta^2(p)$ is the value of the buyer who is indifferent between paying p now or paying $\underline{b}$ next period, and $W_S^2(b^e)$ is the seller's maximal payoff when he is constrained to change $\underline{b}$ next period multiplied by the probability that the seller's posterior is below b^e. In other words, we work with "unconditional probabilities" rather than conditional ones. This is a re-normalization and does not change the seller's behavior.

Let $\sigma^2(b^e)$ denote the arg max, which we assume to be unique. Note that σ^2 increases with b^e, and let b^2 be uniquely defined by

$$b^2 = \max\{b^e \leq \bar{b} \mid W_S^2(b^e) = F(b^e)\underline{b}\}.$$

Quantity b^2 is the highest posterior for which the seller would choose to charge $\underline{b}$ now, given that $\underline{b}$ will be charged next period.

Let $\beta^n(p)$ be such that

$$\beta^n(p) - p = \delta_B[\beta^n(p) - \sigma^{n-1}(\beta^n(p))].$$

$\beta^n(p)$ is well defined and unique if σ^{n-1} is an increasing function. Consider

$$W_S^n(b^e) \equiv \max_p\{[F(b^e) - F(\beta^n(p))]p + \delta_S W_S^{n-1}(\beta^n(p))\}.$$

Let $\sigma^n(b^e)$ denote the arg max, which we assume to be unique. This is assumption (S).

Assumption (S).   For all n, $\sigma^n(b^e)$ is single valued.

We have verified that assumption (S) is satisfied for a uniform distribution. The assumption is quite strong; we use it only to be able to provide a simpler proof of our result.

Under (S), $\sigma^n(b^e)$ is an increasing function of b^e. Then, b^n is uniquely defined by

$$b^n = \max\{b^e \leq \bar{b} \mid W_S^n(b^e) = W_S^{n-1}(b^e)\}.$$

Proposition 1'.   Under (S), the equilibrium is generically unique and is (strong-)Markov.

Proof.   Lemma 3 proved that there exists b^* close to $\underline{b}$ such that if the posterior b^e belongs to $[\underline{b},b^*]$, the seller charges $\underline{b}$ whatever the history. We now proceed by upward induction on b^e.

Lemma 4.   If $b_t^e \in [\underline{b},b^2)$, then $\sigma_t(H_t) = \underline{b}$.

Proof.   Choose ϵ_1 sufficiently small such that for every $b \in [b^*,b^2]$,

$$(F(b + \epsilon_1) - F(b))(b + \epsilon_1) + \delta_S F(b)\underline{b} < F(b + \epsilon_1)\underline{b}$$

and

$$b^* + \epsilon_1 < b^2.$$

We claim that if at time t, for some history, b_t^e belongs to $(b^*,b^* + \epsilon_1]$, the seller charges $\underline{b}$. He can guarantee himself $\underline{b}$ by offering $\underline{b}$.

Assume that b_{t+1}^e belongs to $(\underline{b},b^*]$. Then, $p_{t+1} = \underline{b}$, and the buyer accepts p_t if and only if his valuation exceeds $\beta^2(p_t)$. Since the seller will change to b next period and $b^e \le b^2$, the seller charges b this period from the definition of b^2. More generally, the seller will never offer a price leading to $b_{t+\tau}^e$ in $(\underline{b},b^*]$. Alternatively, by offering prices leading to posteriors in $(b^*,b^* + \epsilon_1]$, he obtains at most

$$(F(b^* + \epsilon_1) - F(b^*))(b^* + \epsilon_1) + \delta_S F(b^*)\underline{b} < F(b^* + \epsilon_1)\underline{b}.$$

Therefore, for any history at time t such that $b_t^e \in (\underline{b},b^* + \epsilon_1]$, $p_t = \underline{b}$, $\beta^t = \beta^2$, and $W_S(b_t^e) = W_S^1(b_t^e)$. The same is true by induction for any $b_t^e \in [\underline{b},b^2)$.

Lemma 5. If $b_t^e \in (b^2,b^3)$, then $\sigma_t(H_t) = \sigma^2(b_t^e)$.

Proof. Assume that $b_t^e \in (b^2,b^3)$, and define $\epsilon_2 > 0$ sufficiently small that for every $b \in (b^2,b^3]$,

$$(F(b + \epsilon_2) - F(b))(b + \epsilon_2) + \delta_S W_S^2(b + \epsilon_2) < W_S^2(b + \epsilon_2)$$

and

$$b^2 + \epsilon_2 < b^3.$$

We claim that if at time t, for some history, b_t^e belongs to $(b^2,b^2 + \epsilon_2]$, the seller charges $\sigma^2(b_t^e)$. The seller can guarantee himself $W_S^2(b_t^e)$, as buyers with valuation exceeding $\beta^2(p_t)$ accept p_t since they will never face a better offer than $\underline{b}$. Can the seller do better? If he charges p_t such that $b_{t+1}^e < b^2$, then only buyers with valuations exceeding $\beta^2(p_t)$ accept the offer since they expect $\underline{b}$ at time $(t + 1)$.

More generally, if $p_{t+\tau}$ is accepted by buyers with a valuation less than b^2, the seller obtains at most $W_S^2(b_{t+\tau}^e)$. Therefore, an upper bound on what he obtains when his offer leads to a posterior $b_{t+1}^e \ge b^2$ is $(F(b_t^e) - F(b^2))b_t^e + \delta_S W_S^2(b_t^e)$, and hence the seller will not make an offer such that $b_{t+1}^e \ge b^2$. We conclude that if $b_t^e \in (b^2,b^2 + \epsilon_2]$, $p_t = \sigma^2(b_t^e)$, $b_e^{t+1} = \beta^2(p_t)$, and $W_S(b_t^e) = W_S^2(b_t^e)$ on the equilibrium path. The same reasoning applies for $b_t^e \in (b^2 + \epsilon_2, b^2 + 2\epsilon_2]$, and so on, until $b_t^e = b^3$.

Let us now choose ϵ_3 such that for every $b \in (b^3,b^4]$,

$$(F(b + \epsilon_3) - F(b))(b + \epsilon_3) + \delta_S W_S^3(b + \epsilon_3) < W_S^3(b + \epsilon_3)$$

and

$$b^3 + \epsilon_3 < b^4.$$

The proof that the seller charges $\sigma^3(b_t^e)$ when $b_t^e \in (b^3,b^4]$ is the same as the previous one. That the seller can guarantee himself $W_S^3(b_t^e)$ is slightly more complicated to demonstrate. It suffices to show that when the seller charges $p_t = \sigma^3(b_t^e)$, a buyer with valuation $\beta^3(p_t)$ accepts it. Imagine that this buyer refuses. Then, $b_{t+1}^e > \beta^3(p_t)$, which implies that $p_{t+1} \geq \sigma^2(b_{t+1}^e) > \sigma^2(\beta^3(p_t))$. Hence, buyer $\beta^3(p_t)$ will not buy at time $(t+1)$, since $\beta^3(p_t) - p_t < \delta_B(\beta^3(p_t) - p_{t+1})$ would contradict the definition of β^3. Similarly, he would not buy later on, and hence he accepts p_t now.

The rest of the proof is by induction on n. Lemma 3 guarantees that this induction takes at most $(N^* + 1)$ steps. Finally, the equilibrium is (strong)-Markov since, by construction, p_t depends only on the posterior b_t^e.

We would prefer not to invoke the restriction that $\underline{b} > 0 = s$. One might expect that the buyer's valuation could sometimes be less than s and that such buyers would not enter the bargaining game, but any buyer whose valuation exceeds s would enter, and thus effectively $\underline{b} = s$. For this case, we can prove that an equilibrium exists by considering a sequence of games with $\underline{b}^n \to s$, showing that there is a limit point of the associated equilibria, and further that this limit is an equilibrium. With $\underline{b} = s$, the seller will never choose to offer price $\underline{b}$, and so bargaining can continue indefinitely. This lack of an "endpoint" has prevented us from establishing uniqueness for this case.

Proposition 2. When $\underline{b} = 0$, a weak-Markov equilibrium exists.

Proof. See Appendix 2.

Smooth-Markov equilibria

Another approach to solving infinite-horizon bargaining games is to assume that a smooth, (strong)-Markov equilibrium exists, and to try to compute it from the differential equation resulting from the first-order conditions for the seller's maximization.

Let $W_S(b^e)$ be the seller's valuation when his posterior is b^e, multiplied by $F(b^e)$. Define

$$J(p, b^e, \beta(\cdot), W_S(\cdot)) = [F(b^e) - F(\beta(p))]p + \delta_S W_S(\beta(p)).$$

Then, $\sigma(b^e)$ must be an arg max of J, and $W_S(b^e)$ the maximized value. As in our previous discussion, we see that σ is strictly increasing if β is strictly increasing. When β has "flat spots," the induced σ will not be strictly increasing and a smooth-Markov equilibrium need not exist.

Differentiating J with respect to b^e and using the envelope theorem, we find that

$$\frac{dW_S}{db^e} = f(b^e)\sigma(b^e).$$

Maximizing J with respect to p, we then find the first-order condition

$$F(b^e) - F[\beta(\sigma(b^e))]$$
$$- \beta'(\sigma(b))f[\beta(\sigma(b^e))]\{\sigma(b^e) - \delta_S\sigma[\beta(\sigma(b^e))]\} = 0. \quad (5.1)$$

In case the second-order condition is also satisfied, (5.1) and its associated $\beta(p)$ characterize a Markov equilibrium. One such instance occurs when $F(b) = (b/\bar{b})^m$ for $0 \le b \le \bar{b}$ and $m > 0$. In this case, $F(\beta)/F(b)$ has the same functional form as F, and we can find a smooth-Markov equilibrium, with the linear form $\beta(b) = \beta p$ and $\sigma(b) = \sigma b$. It can be verified that the second-order condition corresponding to (5.1) is satisfied, and the constants σ and β may then be computed to be the unique solution of

$$(\beta\sigma)^{-m} + \delta_S m(\beta\sigma) = 1 + m$$

$$\beta = \frac{1 - \delta_B(\beta\sigma)}{1 - \delta_B}, \quad (5.2)$$

from which it follows that $\beta > 1$ and $\beta\sigma < 1$. This is the solution obtained as a limit of finite-horizon games by Sobel and Takahashi (1983), which was known to be an equilibrium from Fudenberg and Levine (1983). We have just provided a simpler derivation.

We now comment on a number of features of equilibrium in this model. First, in all cases $\sigma(\cdot)$ is nondecreasing so that equilibrium involves gradual *concessions*. How general a result this is remains to be seen. Fudenberg and Tirole (1983) show that in a finite-horizon model with two-sided incomplete information, prices may rise over time. Whether this can occur in infinite-horizon models is as yet unknown but seems likely.

It can be shown that when the buyer's and the seller's discount factors converge to 1, the seller's payoff converges to zero. In other words, the seller loses all ability to price discriminate when the time period goes to zero (since then both δ_S and δ_B approach 1). This result was obtained by Sobel and Takahashi and is similar to results of Kreps and Wilson (1982a) in the chain-store paradox and of Bulow (1982) and Stokey (1980) in work on durable-goods monopoly. Let us give a rough intuition. The incentive to bargain is due to the destruction of the pie by discounting. By making offers, the seller makes the buyer responsible for destroying the pie if he rejects the offer. The seller uses this leverage to extort the buyer's surplus and, when there is incomplete information, price discriminate. With short time periods, higher-valuation buyers are more willing to free ride on lower-valuation buyers. The seller consequently loses his ability to price discriminate.

Finally, note that if $V_S(b^e) = W_S(b^e)/F(b^e)$,

$$\lim_{m \to \infty} \lim_{\delta_S, \delta_B \to 1} V_S(\bar{b}) = 0 < \lim_{\delta_S, \delta_B \to 1} \lim_{m \to \infty} V_S(\bar{b}) = \bar{b}.$$

Here, $m \to \infty$ means that the seller is nearly certain that the buyer has valuation $\bar{b}$. Thus, in the infinite horizon, it makes a difference what order we pass to the limit.

5.4   Alternating offers

Thus far, we have assumed that the seller makes all of the offers, that is, that the buyer is not allowed to make counter offers but can only accept or reject offers of the seller. This assumption is far from innocuous, especially coupled with our assumption that only the buyer's valuation is private information, which as we suggested seems a good approximation if the seller owns the object before the bargaining starts, and values the object only for its eventual sale. If the seller makes all of the offers and the seller's valuation is known, the offers reveal no information. If the buyer is allowed to make counteroffers, in equilibrium the seller must update his posterior to reflect the information thereby transferred. In particular, we must specify how the seller revises his beliefs if the buyer makes an offer that according to the equilibrium strategies is not made by any type of buyer. Bayes' rule places no restrictions on such inferences, nor does Kreps and Wilson's (1982b) more restrictive concept of a sequential equilibrium. This leeway can be used to support a multiplicity of equilibria. If only the seller can make offers, the only zero-probability event that does not terminate the game immediately is if the buyer refuses a price below $\underline{b}$; however, as lemma 2 illustrated, the seller would never charge such a price in *any* equilibrium, and thus what the seller infers from this event is irrelevant. In contrast, when the buyer can make counteroffers, the seller's inferences can change the set of actions that occur in equilibria.

Let us illustrate this point with an example, which has the additional virtue of providing a form of justification for our seller-makes-the-offers specification. Specifically, we will describe an equilibrium in which, although the buyer does make counteroffers, these counteroffers are always rejected by the seller, so that the equilibrium is "observationally equivalent" to one in which the seller makes all of the offers but the time period is twice as long.

Before we present this equilibrium, recall that Rubinstein (1982) proved that for the corresponding complete-information game, there exists a unique equilibrium. The seller always offers $b(1 - \delta_B)/(1 - \delta_S\delta_B)$, the buyer offers $\delta_S[b(1 - \delta_B)/(1 - \delta_S\delta_B)]$, and these offers are accepted.

Our example is a "pooling equilibrium," in that all types of the buyer make the same offers, so that the buyer's offer conveys no information. All types of the buyer always offer price zero, which the seller always refuses. Were the buyer to offer a price other than zero, the seller would believe that the buyer has type $K\bar{b}$, where K is some large number (such beliefs are not consistent with the spirit of sequential equilibrium, because they put weight on types outside the initial support of the buyer's valuation. Such beliefs can be understood as resulting from trembles by nature as opposed to the trembles by players which are considered in sequential equilibrium.) The seller's offers are made as with one-sided offers, discussed in Section 5.3, except that the discount factors are δ_S^2 and δ_B^2. The periods in which the buyer makes offers do not count, and play evolves as though the seller made all of the offers and the period length is equal to twice that of the alternating-offers game.

For this to be an equilibrium, it is necessary and sufficient that no type of buyer wish to charge a price other than zero. However, any unexpected price causes the seller to believe that the buyer's valuation is $K\bar{b}$, and thus the seller refuses p unless $p \geq [K\bar{b}(1 - \delta_B)/(1 - \delta_S\delta_B)]$. Clearly, for K sufficiently large, this will require $p \geq \bar{b}$, which no buyer would offer.

There certainly are many other equilibria. Grossman-Perry (1985) have shown how to embed the one-sided offer equilibrium into the two-sided offer structure using beliefs which assign weight only to types in the interval support of the buyer's calculation.

5.5   Specification of the costs of bargaining

The models that we have discussed so far have modeled the costs of prolonged negotiations as the discounting of future outcomes. This section contrasts that form of the costs with two others; fixed per-period bargaining costs and costs of changing offers.

The assumption of fixed per-period costs is that agreement at price p in period t yields utilities $(b - p - c_Bt)$ and $(p - s - c_St)$, respectively. Fixed per-period costs were included in Rubinstein's (1982) complete-information bargaining model; in equilibrium, the player with lower cost captured the entire surplus. However, as pointed out in Fishburn and Rubinstein (1982), per-period costs are inconsistent with the existence of a "zero agreement," for which the trader has no impatience. Fishburn and Rubinstein show that any preferences at bargaining outcomes that are monotonic, impatient, continuous, and stationary can be represented by discounting if such a zero agreement is possible. Thus, the existence of a zero agreement is of primary importance in choosing a functional form for time preference.

In the absence of a zero agreement, there are outcomes that are inferior to "leaving the game," even when there are known to be gains from trade. Thus, to avoid violating (ex ante) individual rationality, an "exit option" must be included in the specification of the extensive form. With discounting, the exit option is superfluous in a model with only two traders: The value of the outside opportunity is normalized to be zero (and, therefore, even a greatly postponed agreement is preferred to none at all). Rubinstein's (1982) paper did not allow an exit option, so that the lower-cost trader could inflict "infinite damage" on his opponent "relatively" cheaply. This may partially explain his troublesome conclusions in the fixed-cost case. Perry's (1982a) model of bargaining with many sellers similarly assumes that the buyer cannot leave the game; and thus its conclusions may be similarly misleading.

The obvious alternative to requiring the players to potentially suffer arbitrarily large bargaining costs is to allow for the possibility of exit, which ensures the (current) reservation value. Although such an option can sensibly be added to bargaining models with complete information, with incomplete information the possibility of exit combined with fixed costs of continuing yields a trivial equilibrium, as was pointed out in Fudenberg and Tirole (1983). The equilibrium is trivial because, when an agent chooses not to exit, he signals that his expected value to continuing, and in particular his valuation, exceeds the sum of the per-period cost and his surplus in the eventual agreement. Consider, for example, the model of Fudenberg and Tirole (1983), with the addition that the buyer decides at the end of the first period whether or not to exit. Let $\underline{b}(c_B)$ denote the type of buyer that is just indifferent between exiting and paying cost c_B to continue. Clearly, the seller will never offer a price below $\underline{b}(c_B)$ in the second period, and so there is no equilibrium in which buyers choose to continue. Perry (1982b) analyzes an infinite-horizon, alternating-offers model, and obtains the same result. The only equilibrium in any subgame that begins with the buyer making an exit decision is the trivial one that all buyers leave immediately. Thus, if the seller makes the first move, the equilibrium is simply that of the one-period game, because everyone knows that all valuations of buyer will leave at the end of the first period. If the buyer pays a fee in order to play, the seller will charge a high enough price that the buyer who had been indifferent about staying in will regret having done so. Thus, in the presence of incomplete information, the specification of fixed bargaining costs results in a trivial outcome in which no bargaining in fact occurs. This is highly reminiscent of Diamond's (1971) observation about the effect of fixed search costs, which allowed firms to charge the monopoly price and thus precluded search.

Fixed bargaining costs are formally similar to entry fees to participate; yet entry fees have been shown to be optimal in the theory of optimal auctions (Maskin and Riley (1980)). The difference is that in auction theory, unlike bargaining, the seller is allowed to precommit to future actions, and thus to "promise" a nonnegative expected return to those who choose to pay the fee. Note that one way out of the dilemma in bargaining may be to modify the extensive form to allow such payments, so that the seller can pay the continuation fee.

The second alternative specification of bargaining costs that we wish to discuss is one in which it is costly to change offers. Such costs were introduced to the bargaining literature by Crawford (1981), who assumed that having made initial demands, bargainers could "back down" at a cost. More recently, Anderson (1983) studied repeated games with costs of adjustment. Although costs of adjustment may seem artificial and ad hoc in the context of bargaining between individuals, they are perhaps more plausible if the bargainers are agents for others, as in union–management negotiations.

These are the main alternatives to the discounting formulation that we have employed. Still other formulations may emerge with the continued development of the empirical literature on sequential bargaining.

5.6 Why should we study sequential processes? The thorny question of the extensive form

Here, we offer a few thoughts on the nature of the extensive form. It should be clear that these thoughts are incomplete. Their only purpose is to raise some questions we deem important for bargaining theory.

Myerson and Satterthwaite (1983) have studied the optimal negotiation mechanisms between a buyer and a seller. This work has been extended to situations with multiple buyers and sellers (double auctions) by Wilson (1982). According to the revelation principle, the optimal negotiation is a revelation game in which the buyer(s) and the seller(s) announce their characteristics simultaneously. Therefore, it seems that one could as well restrict attention to static revelation games and never be interested in sequential bargaining. A number of considerations actually go against this first intuition.

For one thing, real-world bargaining is almost always sequential. Myerson–Satterthwaite-type revelation games are not played. Thus, it seems that there is scope for sequential bargaining theory. Students of bargaining theory cannot content themselves with this proof-of-the-pudding argument. One must ask why such revelation games are not played, and when the Myerson–Satterthwaite model is internally consistent.

Imagine that two parties meet and want to discuss freely the possibility of a trade that might be advantageous. Their using the Myerson–Satterthwaite mechanism requires two fundamental assumptions: (1) the traders agree to bargain this way, and (2) the traders can commit themselves to not ever reopen the bargaining process in case of disagreement. It is immediately evident that these two conditions are likely not to be satisfied in real-world conditions, for the following reasons.

1. Most of the time, the traders have at least some of their private information before meeting. Depending on his information, a trader may want to use a bargaining mechanism that differs from the revelation game. One could object to this reasoning by noticing that, because the revelation game is the most efficient game, there could be transfers inducing the traders to play that game. However, this neglects the fact that choosing a bargaining mechanism itself conveys information and changes the outcome of the subsequent bargaining game. In particular, accepting the revelation game is not neutral: It says something about the trader. We are aware that we are raising a deep question without bringing any element of answer.

2. It is well known that any bargaining mechanism under asymmetric information and individual rationality constraints implies inefficiency. Traders may quit without realizing gains from trade. This is especially characteristic of the Myerson–Satterthwaite mechanism. Thus, there is an incentive to renegotiate later. This point is addressed in greater detail in Cramton (1983b).

What, then, is left of the Myerson–Satterthwaite analysis? We think that this mechanism is of interest for two reasons:

1. From a normative point of view, it gives a lower bound on the inefficiency associated with voluntary bargaining.
2. From a positive point of view, it may be applied to some special cases. Imagine, for example, that the parties meet when they have symmetric information. They know that later on they will acquire private information (value of a project, its cost), and that they will have to make a decision (production) on this basis. In this case, they decide to bargain according to the Myerson–Satterthwaite mechanism if they have a means of enforcing the absence of renegotiation in case of disagreement. One could think of reputation as an incentive not to renegotiate.

5.7 Specification of the information structure

The literature on sequential bargaining has up to now assumed that the random variables on which there is asymmetric information are uncorrelated. This may be a reasonable assumption in a number of cases. For example, the seller's production cost and the buyer's valuation for the object can be assumed to be independant. Similarly, costs of bargaining are likely to be uncorrelated between them and with the previous variables. However, there are two channels through which a trader can learn about his own valuation.

1. *Correlated values.* Imagine, for example, that the seller owns a used car, and knows its quality. His willingness to sell the car depends on this quality. In addition, the buyer's willingness to buy the car would depend on this parameter if he knew it. In this case, the valuations are correlated and the buyer is eager to learn about the seller's information not only to discover his bargaining power but also to assess the value of a deal.
2. *Learning from an unknown distribution.* Imagine that there are several sellers, whose production costs are drawn from a probability distribution that is unknown to the buyer. Imagine further that the buyer can switch sellers. When the buyer bargains with a given seller, he learns not only the specific characteristics of this seller (and therefore about his bargaining power), but also about the other sellers' characteristics. Therefore, the buyer learns about his expected profit if he switches to another seller. Even though the buyer and the seller's characteristics may be uncorrelated, the buyer learns about more than his bargaining power. Another possibility leading to the same effect is the correlation of production costs between sellers. Indeed, the case of independent draws from a distribution that is unknown to the buyer is processed like that of correlated draws by the buyer.

An interesting example that combines items (1) and (2) can be found in the work of Ordover and Rubinstein (1983) on litigation. In their paper, one of the bargaining parties knows who will win if the dispute is resolved in court, that is, if disagreement occurs. On the one hand, the parties are interested in their valuations after disagreement, and they can learn something about them before disagreement as outlined in item (2). On the other hand, the valuations after disagreement are correlated.

Whereas in the independent-draws model, the only purpose of learning is to discover one's bargaining power, when draws are correlated between traders the parties learn about their positions *after* bargaining with the current partner whether there is agreement or disagreement. Consequently, during the bargaining process the parties must take into account two kinds of "curses":

1. *The celebrated winner's curse in case of agreement.* For example, the fact that the seller of the used car accepts the buyer's offer may be a bad signal about the quality of the car.
2. *The "bargaining curse."* The seller's making a low offer may not be good news to the buyer if the seller knows the quality of the car. In the unknown-distribution framework, the seller's making a high offer may signal that the production costs of the other potential sellers are likely to

be high as well. On the other hand, such learning may not be a curse, but good news. For instance, in the used car example the seller's turning down the buyer's offer may signal a high quality. Such transmission of information can easily be embodied in bargaining models. Although we will not pursue this topic here, it is clear that some new insight can be gained from it.

5.8   Conclusion

As we stated in Section 5.3, the outcome of bargaining with one-sided information is fairly easy to characterize if the player whose valuation is known makes all of the offers. In this case, the price must decrease over time, and things are generally "well behaved." With alternating offers, however, there are multiple equilibria, which are qualitatively very dissimilar. Thus, the problem of the choice of extensive form is fairly severe, even when only one-sided incomplete information is being considered. If both player's valuations are private information, the situation is even more complex. We fear that in this case, few generalizations will be possible, and that even for convenient specifications of the functional form of the distributions over the valuations, the problem of characterizing the equilibria will be quite difficult. Cramton (1983a) is a start in this direction.

Throughout this paper, because the bargaining costs took the form of discounting and players had no other opportunities to trade, players had no incentive to stop bargaining. If traders have alternative bargaining partners, we would expect them to switch to a new partner whenever they become sufficiently pessimistic about the valuation of the party with whom they are currently negotiating. Thus, the length of bargaining between any pair of traders could be endogenously determined by the outside opportunities. Shaked and Sutton (1984) have modeled bargaining with several sellers under complete information. Because the sellers are known to have the same valuation in equilibrium, traders never quit bargaining without an agreement if there exist gains from trade. Thus, the Shaked–Sutton model again predicts that traders will never stop negotiating. In a forthcoming paper, we analyze bargaining with many traders and incomplete information to study the effect of outside opportunities on equilibrium prices and on the length of negotiations.

The noncooperative approach to bargaining theory is still in its infancy. Although much remains to be done, substantial progress has been made in the past few years. Solving a wider variety of extensive forms may permit some generalizations to emerge. The problem of the choice of extensive forms by the players remains open.

APPENDIX 1
Proof of Proposition 1

We proceed by induction on n. For each n, we construct p^n, the highest price the seller is allowed to charge. The index n will keep track of the number of periods remaining: When $p < p^n$, the game will be shown to end in at most n periods. For $n = 1$, set

$$p^1 = \underline{b}, \qquad W_S^1(b^e) = F(b^e)\underline{b}, \qquad \beta^2(p) = \frac{p - \delta_B \underline{b}}{1 - \delta_B},$$

$$\sigma^1(b^e) = \overline{\sigma}^1(b^e \,|\, p) = \underline{b}, \qquad \text{and} \qquad b^1 = \underline{b},$$

Here, $p^1 = \underline{b}$ is the price the seller is required to charge to guarantee that the game ends immediately, and $W_S^1(b^e)$ is the seller's payoff to charging $\underline{b}$ multiplied by the probability that the posterior is below b^e. In other words, we work with "unconditional probabilities" instead of conditional ones; the conditional probability of a sale at $\underline{b}$ is 1, but the unconditional probabilities prove simpler to work with. Note that this renormalization does not affect the seller's optimal behavior. Quantity $\beta^2(p)$ is the reservation value of the buyer who is just indifferent between p in this period and $\underline{b}$ in the next one. Because the seller's offers will be nonincreasing and no less than $\underline{b}$, if the seller charges $\underline{b}$ in this period, buyers must expect $\underline{b}$ in subsequent periods. The term $\beta^{n+1}(p)$ will be the lowest reservation value of a buyer who accepts p when there will be n *subsequent* periods, that is, in the $(n + 1)$-period game. Observe that W_S^1 and β^1 are continuous and nondecreasing. If $p \leq p^1$, the game is over; if $p > p^1$, it (with some probability) lasts at least one more period. Value $\sigma^n(b^e)$ is the correspondence that yields the seller's optimal choices in the n-period game when he is constrained to charge no more than p^n (when $n = 1$, this constraint forces σ^1 to be single valued). Quantity $\overline{\sigma}^1(b^e \,|\, p)$ is the expected value of the seller's price if the last price was p. And b^1 is a dummy, which will not be used; for larger n, b^n will be a bound on b^e that guarantees that the seller charges no more than p^{n-1} in the next period.

In the n-period game, the seller is constrained to not charge more than p^n, where p^n is chosen such that if p^n is charged, the buyer's reservation value is at most b^n; so the next period's price is below p^{n-1} and, by inductive hypothesis, the game ends in $(n - 1)$ additional periods.

We will now define $W_S^n(b^e)$, $\beta^{n+1}(p)$, p^n, $\sigma^n(b^e)$, and $\overline{\sigma}^n(b^e, p)$ recursively, and prove by induction that

1. W_S^n and β^{n+1} are continuous and nondecreasing, and that β^n is the unique solution of $p \in (1 - \delta_B)\beta^n(p) + \delta_B \hat{\sigma}^n(\beta^n(p))$, where $\hat{\sigma}^n$ is the convexification of σ^n;

2. When a price $p \leq p^n$ is charged, the game lasts n or fewer periods, and so for $p \leq p^n$, $\beta^{n+1}(p) = \beta^n(p)$;
3. When $b^e \leq b^n$, the seller charges a price less than p^{n-1};
4. $\sigma^n(b^e) < b^e$, where σ^n is nonempty, nondecreasing, and has a compact graph;
5. In the $(n + 1)$-period game, the buyer with valuation $\beta^{n+1}(p)$ is just indifferent between paying p now and waiting one period, and strictly prefers buying next period to waiting longer;
6. The expected price that the seller charges in period n, $\bar{\sigma}^n(b^e \mid p)$, is uniquely determined, given b^e and the price p charged in previous period;
7. In any equilibrium, the buyer must play according to β^{N^*+1}, and the seller's initial price belongs to $\sigma^{N^*+1}(\bar{b})$.

Having by inductive hypothesis proved claims (1) through (5) for the $(n - 1)$-period game, let us extend them to the n-period game. First, we solve for W_S^n and σ^n. Let $c \geq \underline{b}$ be a given constant. Define the maximization problem, denoted $J(p, b^e, \beta, W_S, c)$, as follows:

$$\max_p \{ p[F(b^e) - F(\beta(p))] + \delta_S W_s(\beta(p)) \}$$

subject to $\underline{b} \leq p \leq \min\{b^e, c\}$.

Since, by inductive hypothesis, β and W_S will be continuous, and the constraint set is compact, the arg max correspondence has a nonempty image and a compact graph. Moreover, the correspondence is nondecreasing, since increasing b^e strictly increases the gradient of the objective function. (The correspondence is strictly increasing whenever the objective is continuously differentiable, but it may be flat if not.)

Let σ denote the arg max correspondence, $\bar{\sigma}$ the expected price charged by the seller, and $\hat{\sigma}$ the correspondence whose image is the convex hull of the image σ. Note that $\hat{\sigma}$ is continuous, is convex valued, and contains $\bar{\sigma}$. Finally, note that $\sigma(\underline{b}) = \underline{b}$, whereas for $b > \underline{b}$, $\sigma(b) < b$.

Now, we can find W_S^n, p^n, and β^{n+1}. Consider first $J(p, b^e, \beta^n, W_S^{n-1}, \bar{b})$. Associated with this are $\sigma^n(b^e, \bar{b})$ and $\hat{\sigma}^n(b^e, \bar{b})$. Define b^n to be the largest value of b^e for which $p^{n-1} \in \hat{\sigma}^n$. The key is that when $b^e \leq b^n$, we can without loss restrict the seller to not charge more than p^{n-1}; that is, $J(p, b^e, \beta^n, W_S^{n-1}, \bar{b}) = J(p, b^e, \beta^n, W_S^{n-1}, p^{n-1})$. However, by inductive hypothesis, when $p \leq p^{n-1}$, the game ends in $(n - 1)$ periods, and so $\beta^n(p) = \beta^{n-1}(p)$ and $\beta^{n-1}(p) \leq b^{n-1}$ (from the definition of b^{n-1}), implying that $W_S^{n-1}(\beta^n(p)) = W_S^{n-2}(\beta^{n-1}(p))$. Thus, when $b^e \leq b^n$, the n-period game in fact ends in at most $(n - 1)$ periods, and the behavior we previously determined for the $(n - 1)$-stage game must still apply. We conclude that for $b^e \leq b^n$, $\sigma^n(b^e, \bar{b}) = \sigma^{n-1}(b^e, \bar{b}) = \sigma^{n-1}(b^e)$. This argument holds only for $n > 2$; for $n = 2$, $p^{n-1} = \underline{b}$, and the result is trivial.

Next, we must define p^n, the bound on the seller's price that ensures that next period's price is less than p^{n-1} and therefore that the game ends in n periods. This situation is complicated slightly by the possible discontinuity of σ. Let $\underline{p}^{n-1}$ be the largest value in $\sigma^{n-1}(b^n)$ less than or equal to p^{n-1}, and define $\overline{p}^n = (1 - \delta_B)b^n + \delta_B \underline{p}^{n-1}$. We claim that if $p \leq p^n$ in the n-period game, then the next-period price will be less than $\underline{p}^{n-1}$ and the game in fact ends in n periods. Assume not – then the seller's posterior next period, $\beta^n(p)$, must exceed b^n. From the definition of p^n, this implies that $(1 - \delta_B)\beta^n(p) > p^n - \delta_B \underline{p}^{n-1}$. Since $\beta^n(p) < p \leq p^n$, $\sigma^{n-1}(\beta^n(p)) \leq \sigma^{n-1}(p^n) \leq \sigma^{n-1}(b^n) \leq p^{n-1}$. Yet, by inductive hypothesis, β^n satisfies $p \in (1 - \delta_B)\beta^n(p) + \delta_B \hat{\sigma}^{n-1}(\beta^n(p))$, and so $(1 - \delta_B)\beta^n(p) \geq p - \delta_B \underline{p}^{n-1}$, which is a contradiction. This means that imposing the constraint $p \leq p^n$ guarantees that the n-period game in fact ends in n periods. Later, we will show that if $p \leq p^n$, the $(n + 1)$-stage game ends in n periods as well.

Given p^n, we consider the optimization problem $J(p, b^e, \beta^n, W_S^{n-1}, p^n)$. The solution to this problem is $\sigma^n(b^e)$, with convex null $\hat{\sigma}^n(b^e)$. As shown above, we know that for $b^e \leq b^n, W_S^n(b^e) = W_S^{n-1}(b^e)$, and $\sigma^n(b^e, \overline{b}) = \sigma^n(b^e) = \sigma^{n-1}(b^e)$; therefore, behavior below b^n is not changed by increasing the number of periods.

Next, we work backward one period to show that $\beta^{n+1}(p)$ is uniquely defined by the assumed equation. The valuation of the buyer who is just indifferent between paying p in period $(n + 1)$ and waiting must satisfy

$$(\beta^{n+1}(p) - p) \in \delta_B[\beta^{n+1}(p) - \hat{\sigma}^n(\beta^{n+1}(p))]$$

or

$$p \in (1 - \delta_B)\beta^{n+1}(p) + \delta_B \hat{\sigma}^n(\beta^{n+1}(p)). \tag{A.1}$$

The right-hand side of (A.1) is a continuous, convex-valued, strictly increasing correspondence, and thus has a unique inverse function $\beta^{n+1}(p)$, which is nondecreasing and has modulus of continuity smaller than $1/(1 - \delta_B)$.

Note that since $\max\{\hat{\sigma}^n(\beta^{n+1}(p))\} < \beta^{n+1}(p)$, the choice of buyer $\beta^{n+1}(p)$ whether to accept p in period $(n + 1)$ or to wait one period and then buy is unaffected if we replace the anticipated next-period probability distribution over elements of $\sigma^n(\beta^{n+1}(p))$ by its expected value $\overline{\sigma}^n$. Because $\overline{\sigma}^n$ must lie in $\hat{\sigma}^n$, equation (A.1) defining β^{n+1} ensures that the buyer of valuation $\beta^{n+1}(p)$ is indifferent between paying p in period $(n + 1)$ and waiting to face $\overline{\sigma}^n$ next period. If buyer $\beta^{n+1}(p)$ were willing to wait more than one period, then all buyers with lower valuations would strictly prefer to wait, and there would be no sales in period n. This would contradict the behavior that we derived for the n-period game.

Thus, we have verified the inductive hypotheses for $k = n$. Because we know that all equilibria end in at most $(N^* + 1)$ periods, we know that after $(N^* + 1)$ steps, we will have $b^{N^*+1} = \bar{b}$, and the induction is complete. Thus, the first price charged must (1) be an element of $\sigma^{N^*+1}(\bar{b})$ and, moreover, (2) be less than or equal to p^{N^*+1}, and that thereafter equilibrium play is uniquely determined. Thus, if an equilibrium exists, it is unique up to the seller's choice of an initial price (or any probability distribution over $\sigma^{N^*+1}(\bar{b})$). The argument given before the statement of proposition 1 shows that an equilibrium does in fact exist, because given the functions $\beta^n(p)$, the seller will choose to end the game in no more than $(N^* + 1)$ periods.

APPENDIX 2
Proof of Proposition 2

To proceed, we need the following lemma.

Lemma 6.   The functions $\beta(p)$ and $W(b^e)$ derived in the proof of proposition 1 are equicontinuous.

Proof.   We observed earlier that the modulus of continuity of $\beta(p)$ is no greater than $1/(1 - \delta_B)$. Recall the definition of $W(b^e)$:

$$W(b^e) = \max_p \{[F(b^e) - F(\beta(p))]p + \delta W(\beta(p))\}.$$

Now, consider $W(b_1^e) - W(b_2^e)$, where $b_1^e > b_2^e$. Let p_1 and p_2 be the respective maximizing prices. We claim that

$$W(b_1^e) - W(b_2^e) \le (F(b_1^e) - F(b_2^e))p_1,$$

because the seller could always choose to offer price p_1 when his beliefs were b_2^e, and so we have used a lower bound on $W(b_2^e)$. However, since the density, $f(b)$, is bounded by $\bar{f}$, we have

$$W(b_1^e) - W(b_2^e) \le \bar{b}\bar{f}|b_1^e - b_2^e|.$$

Proof of proposition 2.   Consider the sequence of games with buyer valuation densities

$$f^n(b) = \begin{cases} \dfrac{f(b)}{1 - F(\underline{b}^n)} & \text{if } b \ge \underline{b}^n, \\ 0 & \text{if } b < \underline{b}^n, \end{cases}$$

where $\underline{b}^n \to 0$ as $n \to \infty$. Each of these games has a unique weak-Markov equilibrium (β^n, W^n, σ^n). Since the family of functions (β^n, W^n) is equicontinuous, it has a uniformly convergent subsequence converging to continuous (nondecreasing) functions (β, W). For notational simplicity, assume that (β^n, W^n) actually converge to (β, W). There are now two distinct concepts of the limiting σ. First, there is σ, which is the arg max correspondence for the seller's optimization problem $J(p, b, \beta, W, \bar{b})$; this is monotonic and piecewise continuous, as always. Furthermore, since each J^n is Lipschitz continuous in β^n and W^n (in the uniform topology), J^n converges uniformly to J, and from the theorem of the maximum, the limit points of σ^n are contained in σ. Thus, at continuity points of σ, σ^n converges to σ.

Second, there is the $\hat{\sigma}$ correspondence, defined uniquely as the solution of

$$\hat{\sigma}(b) = \frac{\beta^{-1}(b) - (1 - \delta_B)b}{\delta_B},$$

where equality is the equality of sets.

Let us show that limit points of $\hat{\sigma}^n$ are in $\hat{\sigma}$. Suppose, in fact, that for some b, $s^n \in \hat{\sigma}^n(b) \to p$. This is true if and only if $g^n \equiv \delta_B(s^n + (1 - \delta_B)b) \to \delta_B(p + (1 - \delta_B)b) \equiv g$. From the definition of $\hat{\sigma}$ given previously, $p \in \hat{\sigma}(b)$ if and only if $g \in \beta^{-1}(b)$. Consider the sequence $\beta(g^n)$. Since $b = \beta^n(g^n)$ and the β^n converge uniformly, then $\beta(g^n)$ converges to b. Since $g^n \to g$ and β is continuous, $\beta(g^n) \to \beta(g)$, and so $b = \beta(g)$, or $g \in \beta^{-1}(b)$. Thus, we can conclude that at continuity points of $\hat{\sigma}$, $\hat{\sigma}^n$ converges to $\hat{\sigma}$, and since $\hat{\sigma}^n$ is the convex hull of σ^n, that $\hat{\sigma}$ and σ agree wherever they are continuous. Finally, since σ and $\hat{\sigma}$ are monotonic, they are continuous except at countably many points, and thus $\hat{\sigma}$ is the convex hull of σ. Therefore, the optimal seller behavior given β and W (i.e., σ) is consistent with playing the mixed strategies in $\hat{\sigma}$, which in turn induce the desired behavior from the buyer, and we indeed have an equilibrium.

REFERENCES

Anderson, R. (1983): Quick-Response Equilibria. Mimeo, University of California at Berkeley.
Bulow, J. (1982): Durable-Goods Monopolists. *Journal of Political Economy*, 90, 314–32.
Cramton, P. (1982): *Bargaining with Incomplete Information: A Two-Period Model with Continuous Uncertainty.* Research Paper 652, Graduate School of Business, Stanford University.
    (1983a): *Bargaining with Incomplete Information: An Infinite-Horizon Model with Continuous Uncertainty.* Research Paper 680, Graduate School of Business, Stanford University.
    (1983b): *Sequential Bargaining Mechanisms.* Research Paper 688, Graduate School of Business, Stanford University.

Crawford, V. (1981): A Theory of Disagreement in Bargaining. *Econometrica,* 50, 607–38.

Diamond, P. (1971): A Model of Price Adjustment. *Journal of Economic Theory,* 3, 156–68.

Fishburn, P., and A. Rubinstein (1982): Time Preference. *International Economic Review,* 23, 677–94.

Fudenberg, D., and D. Levine (1983): Subgame-Perfect Equilibria of Finite- and Infinite-Horizon Games. *Journal of Economic Theory,* 31, 251–68.

Fudenberg, D., and J. Tirole (1983): Sequential Bargaining under Incomplete Information. *Review of Economic Studies,* 50, 221–47.

Grossman, S., and M. Perry (1985): "Sequential Bargaining under Asymmetric Information." Mimeo.

Kreps, D., and R. Wilson (1982a): Reputation and Imperfect Information. *Journal of Economic Theory,* 27, 253–79.

    (1982b): Sequential Equilibria. *Econometrica,* 50, 863–94.

Maskin, E., and J. Riley (1980): *Auctioning an Indivisible Object.* Discussion Paper #87D. Kennedy School of Government.

Myerson, R., and M. Satterthwaite (1983): Efficient Mechanisms for Bilateral Trading. *Journal of Economic Theory,* 29, 265–81.

Ordover, J., and A. Rubinstein (1983): On Bargaining, Settling, and Litigating: A Problem in Multistage Games with Imperfect Information. Mimeo, New York University.

Perry, M. (1982a): A Theory of Search. Mimeo, Princeton University.

    (1982b): Who Has the Last Word: A Bargaining Model with Incomplete Information. Mimeo, Princeton University.

Rubinstein, A. (1982): Perfect Equilibrium in a Bargaining Model. *Econometrica,* 50, 97–109.

    (1985): *Choice of Conjectures in a Bargaining Game with Incomplete Information.* Chapter 6 in this book.

Shaked, A., and J. Sutton (1984): Involuntary Unemployment as Perfect Equilibrium in a Bargaining Model. *Econometrica,* 52, 1351–1364.

Sobel, J., and I. Takahashi (1983): A Multi-Stage Model of Bargaining. *Review of Economic Studies,* 50, 411–26.

Stokey, N. (1980): Rational Expectations and Durable Goods Pricing. *Bell Journal of Economics,* Spring, 11, 112–28.

Wilson, R. (1982): Double Auctions. Technical Report 391, Institute for Mathematical Studies in the Social Sciences, Stanford University.

CHAPTER 6

Choice of conjectures in a bargaining game with incomplete information

Ariel Rubinstein
THE HEBREW UNIVERSITY, JERUSALEM

6.1 Introduction

The axiomatic approach to bargaining may be viewed as an attempt to predict the outcome of a bargaining situation solely on the basis of the set of pairs of utilities that corresponds to the set of possible agreements and to the nonagreement point.

The strategic approach extends the description of a bargaining situation. The rules of bargaining are assumed to be exogenous, and the solution is a function not only of the possible agreements but also of the procedural rules and the parties' time preferences.

The aim of this chapter is to show that in the case of incomplete information about the time preferences of the parties, the bargaining solution depends on additional elements, namely, the players' methods of making inferences when they reach a node in the extensive form of the game that is off the equilibrium path.

The solution concept commonly used in the literature on sequential bargaining models with incomplete information is one of sequential equilibrium (see Kreps and Wilson (1982)). Essentially, this concept requires that the players' strategies remain best responses at every node of decision in the extensive form of the game, including nodes that are not expected to be reached. The test of whether a player's strategy is a best response depends on his updated estimation of the likelihood of the uncertain elements in the model. For nodes of the game tree that are reachable, it is plausible to assume that the players use the Bayesian formula. Off the equilibrium path, the Bayesian formula is not applicable. The formulation of a game with incomplete information does not provide the description of how the players modify their beliefs when a "zero-probability"

I would like to thank Al Roth and Asher Wolinsky for valuable comments, and Margret Eisenstaedt, who drew the diagrams.

event has occurred. (A zero-probability event occurs when the players reach a node in the extensive form of the game that is off the equilibrium path.) The concept of sequential equilibrium requires that the *solution* specifies the players' new beliefs after a zero-probability event occurs. The new beliefs that a player adopts after a zero-probability event is called a *conjecture*. The sequential-equilibrium concept also requires that a conjecture be the basis for continuing the updating of the player's beliefs unless another zero-probability event occurs, in which case the player must choose another conjecture.

Although we have great freedom to select conjectures to support strategies to be best responses, ideally the sequential-equilibrium concept should enable selection of a unique outcome out of the set of sequential-equilibrium outcomes. Indeed, several sequential bargaining models reach uniqueness of the sequential equilibrium (see Sobel and Takahashi (1983), Ordover and Rubinstein (1983), and Perry (1985)). The uniqueness of sequential-equilibrium outcomes in sequential bargaining models is not robust to changes in the procedural bargaining rules or the informational structure. Even in simple models such as Fudenberg and Tirole's (1983) two-period seller–buyer bargaining game, where only the seller makes offers, the incomplete information about the seller's reservation price makes a multiplicity of equilibria possible.

In the current paper, I argue that the multiplicity of equilibria is not a drawback either of the model or of the solution concept, but rather an outcome of the arbitrariness of the choice of conjectures. Specification of rules that the players use to choose conjectures enables us to restrict the set of outcomes of the sequential equilibria. A comparison between the set of sequential-equilibrium outcomes under various assumptions about the properties of the choice of conjectures, clarifies the connection between the choice of conjectures and the outcome of the game.

To present a more concrete discussion of the conjectures problem, I analyze a special case of the model for bargaining over a partition of a dollar that I presented earlier (Rubinstein (1982)). In the present version of the model, each bargainer bears a constant cost per period of negotiation. One of the players has incomplete information about the bargaining cost of his opponent, which may be higher or lower than his own. The inferences that the player with the incomplete information makes about his opponent's bargaining cost lie at the center of the following discussion.

6.2   The model

The basic model used here is a subcase of the model analyzed in Rubinstein (1982). Two players, 1 and 2, are bargaining on the partition of one dollar. Each player in turn makes an offer; his opponent may agree to the offer (Y) or reject it (N). Acceptance of an offer terminates the game. Rejection ends a period, and the rejecting player makes a counteroffer, and so on without any given time limit.

Let $S = [0,1]$. A partition of the dollar is identified with a number s in S by interpreting s as the proportion of the dollar that player 1 receives.

A strategy specifies the offer that a player makes whenever it is his turn to do so, and his reaction to any offer made by his opponent. Let F be the set of all strategies available to a player who starts the bargaining. Formally, F is the set of all sequences of functions $f = \{f^t\}_{t=1}^{\infty}$, where

$$\text{For } t \text{ odd}, f^t\colon S^{t-1} \to S,$$

$$\text{For } t \text{ even}, f^t\colon S^t \to \{Y,N\},$$

where S^t is the set of all sequences of length t of elements of S. (In what follows, G is the set of all strategies for a player whose first move is a response to the other player's offer.)

A typical outcome of the game is a pair (s,t), which is interpreted as agreement on partition s in period t. Perpetual disagreement is denoted by $(0,\infty)$.

The outcome function of the game $P(f,g)$ takes the value (s,t) if two players who adopt strategies f and g reach an agreement s at period t, and the value $(0,\infty)$ if they do not reach an agreement. The players are assumed to bear a fixed cost per period. Player 1's utility of the outcome (s,t) is $s - c_1 t$, and player 2's utility of the outcome (s,t) is $1 - s - c_2 t$. The number c_i is player i's bargaining cost per period. The outcome $(0,\infty)$ is assumed to be the worst outcome (utility $-\infty$). It is assumed that the players maximize their expected utility.

Assume one-sided incomplete information. Player 1's cost, $c_1 = c$, is common knowledge. Player 2's cost might be either c_w or c_s, where $c_w > c > c_s > 0$. Assume that ω_0 is player 1's subjective probability that player 2's cost is c_w, and that $1 - \omega_0$ is his probability that player 2's cost is c_s. If player 2's cost is c_w, it is said that he is of type 2_w, or the "weaker" type; if player 2's cost is c_s, it is said that he is of type 2_s, or the "stronger" type. Consider these numbers to be small; specifically, assume that $1 > c_w + c + c_s$.

It was shown in Rubinstein (1982) that if it is common knowledge that player 2 is of type 2_w, then the only perfect equilibrium is for player 1 to demand and receive the entire one dollar in the first period. If player 1 knows he is playing against 2_s, the only perfect equilibrium is for him to demand and receive c_s in the first period.

The game just described is one with incomplete information. Let

$(f,g,h) \in F \times G \times G$ be a triple of strategies for player 1, player 2_w, and player 2_s, respectively. The outcome of the play of (f,g,h) is

$$P(f,g,h) = \langle P(f,g), P(f,h) \rangle,$$

that is, a pair of outcomes for the cases of player 2 actually being type 2_w or 2_s.

The set of Nash equilibria in this model is very large. In particular, for every partition s, the pair $\langle (s,1),(s,1) \rangle$ is an outcome of a Nash equilibrium (see Rubinstein (1985)).

We turn now to the definition of sequential equilibrium. Define a belief system to be a sequence $\omega = (\omega^t)_{t=0,2,4,\ldots}$, such that $\omega^0 = \omega_0$ and ω^t: $S^t \to [0,1]$. The term $\omega^t(s^1, \ldots, s^t)$ is player 1's subjective probability that player 2 is 2_w after the sequence of offers and rejections $s^1, \ldots, s^{t-1}$, after player 2 has made the offer s^t and just before player 1 has to react to the offer s^t.

A sequential equilibrium is a four-tuple $\langle f,g,h,\omega \rangle$ satisfying the requirement that after any history, a player's residual strategy is a best response against his opponent's residual strategy. The belief system is required to satisfy several conditions: It has to be consistent with the Bayesian formula; a deviation by player 1 does not change his own belief; after an unexpected move by player 2, player 1 chooses a new conjecture regarding player 2's type, which he holds and updates at least until player 2 makes another unexpected move.

So far, the choice of new conjectures is arbitrary. In Section 6.4, several possible restrictions on the choice of new conjectures are presented. The study of these restrictions is the central issue of the present paper.

6.3   Review of the complete-information model

In this section, the characterization of the perfect-equilibrium outcomes in the complete-information model (where the bargaining costs are common knowledge) is reviewed.

Proposition 1 (Conclusion 1 in Rubinstein (1982)).   Assume that c_1 and c_2 are common knowledge. If $c_1 < c_2$, the outcome $(1,1)$ (i.e., player 1 gets the whole dollar in the first period) is the only perfect-equilibrium outcome, and if $c_1 > c_2$, the outcome $(c_2,1)$ (i.e., player 2 gets $1 - c_2$ in the first period) is the only perfect-equilibrium outcome.

Remark.   The asymmetry is due to the procedure of the bargaining. If the size of the costs is "small," the dependence of the bargaining outcome on the bargaining order is negligible.

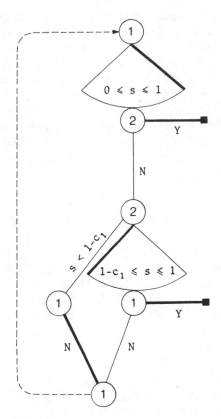

Figure 6.1

Proof.

ASSERTION 1A.   If $c_1 < c_2$, the outcome $(1,1)$ is a perfect-equilibrium outcome.

PROOF.   Define a pair of strategies $(\hat{f}, \hat{g})$, such that

For t odd, $\hat{f}^t \equiv 1$ and $\hat{g}^t \equiv Y$,

For t even, $\hat{g}^t \equiv 1 - c_1$,

and

$$\hat{f}^t \equiv \begin{cases} Y & \text{if } s^t \geq 1 - c_1, \\ N & \text{otherwise.} \end{cases}$$

The procedure for checking that $(\hat{f}, \hat{g})$ is a perfect equilibrium is straightforward and is illustrated diagrammatically in Figure 6.1. The circled numbers in the diagram are the "names" of the players who must move at the corresponding node of the game. The edges correspond to moves in the game. Heavy edges correspond to moves planned by the pair of strategies $(\hat{f},\hat{g})$. Light edges are deviations. Whenever the continuation of the strategies is the same for a range of moves, one of two types of notation is used. A light edge with a formula like $s < 1 - c_1$ means that the continuation is the same for every offer s satisfying the formula $s < 1 - c_1$. An arch with a formula like $0 \leq s \leq 1$ means that the continuation of the strategies is the same for every offer s satisfying the formula $0 \leq s \leq 1$. The heavy edge of the segment corresponds to the only offer in the range that is the planned offer. The small solid squares designate terminal points of the game.

ASSERTION 1B.   If $c_1 < c_2$, the outcome $(1,1)$ is the only perfect-equilibrium outcome.

PROOF.   Let U^1 be the set of all $u = s - c_1(t - 1)$, where (s,t) is a perfect-equilibrium outcome in a subgame starting with player 1's offer. Let U^2 be the set of all $u = s - c_1(t - 1)$, where (s,t) is a perfect-equilibrium outcome of a subgame starting with player 2's offer. By assertion 1A, $1 \in U^1$ and $1 - c_1 \in U^2$. Since player 1 always accepts an offer $s \geq 1 - c_1$, then $1 - c_1 = \max U^2$.

Next, it is proved that $\inf U^2 \geq \inf U^1 - c_1$. Assume that $\inf U^1 - c_1 > \inf U^2$. Pick $u \in U^2$, such that $u < \inf U^1 - c_1$, and select a perfect equilibrium that corresponds to this u. It must be that player 2's first offer in this perfect equilibrium is u and that player 1 accepts it; otherwise, $u - c_1 \in U^1$. However, player 1 gains if he deviates and rejects this offer, since then he receives at least $\inf U^1$, and $\inf U^1 - c_1 > u$.

Assume that $\inf U^1 < 1$. Let $u \in U^1$, $u < 1$, and $\epsilon > 0$. Pick a perfect equilibrium that corresponds to this u. Player 2 must reject a demand by player 1 of $u + \epsilon$. Thus, for every $\epsilon > 0$, $\inf U^2 \leq u + \epsilon - c_2$, and therefore $\inf U^2 \leq \inf U^1 - c_2$, which contradicts $\inf U^2 \geq \inf U^1 - c_1$. Consequently, in $U^1 = 1$ and $U^1 = \{1\}$.

The rest of proposition 1 is proved in similar fashion.

The players' dilemma is now clearer. If it is common knowledge that player 2 is type 2_w, then player 1 gets the entire dollar. If it is common knowledge that player 2 is type 2_s, then player 1 gets only c_s. These are the two extreme possible outcomes of the bargaining. Here, player 1 does not know player 2's identity, and the solution is likely to depend on ω_0. In the rest of the chapter, we study possible ways in which the bargaining outcome depends on player 1's initial beliefs.

6.4 Conjectures

The sequential-equilibrium concept allows the free choice of an arbitrary new conjecture when a zero-probability event occurs. It seems reasonable that adopting new conjectures is not an arbitrary process. In this section, several possible consistency requirements for the choice of conjectures are described.

(C-1) Optimistic conjectures

The conjectures of $\langle f,g,h,\omega \rangle$ are said to be *optimistic conjectures* if, whenever a zero-probability event occurs, player 1 concludes that he is playing against type 2_w (i.e., the weaker type). Thus, a player whose conjectures are optimistic has the prejudgment that a deviator is type 2_w. Such conjectures serve as a threat to player 2. Any deviation by player 2 will make player 1 "play tough." It is shown in Section 6.6 that optimistic conjectures support many sequential-equilibrium outcomes. In the complete-information game, the (subgame) perfectness notion eliminates many unreasonable threats. In the incomplete-information game, many of these threats are possible, being supported by the optimistic conjectures. Optimistic conjectures have often been used in bargaining literature (see Cramton (1982), Fudenberg and Tirole (1983), and Perry (1985)). They are very useful in supporting equilibrium outcomes because they serve as the best deterring conjectures.

(C-2) Pessimistic conjectures

The conjectures of $\langle f,g,h,\omega \rangle$ are said to be *pessimistic conjectures* if, whenever a zero-probability event occurs, player 1 concludes that he is playing against type 2_s (i.e., the stronger type).

In what follows, denote by $\gtrsim_1$, $\gtrsim_w$, and $\gtrsim_s$ the preferences of players 1, 2_w, and 2_s on the set of all lotteries of outcomes.

(C-3) Rationalizing conjectures

The conjectures of $\langle f,g,h,\omega \rangle$ are said to be *rationalizing conjectures* if

1. Whenever $\omega^{t-2}(s^{t-2}) \neq 1$, $(s^t,1) \gtrsim_s (s^{t-1},0)$, and $(s^{t-1},0) >_w (s^t,1)$, then $\omega^t(s^t) = 0$, and,
2. In any other zero-probability event, $\omega^t(s^t) = w^{t-2}(s^{t-2})$.

In order to understand condition (1), imagine that player 1 makes the offer s^{t-1}, and player 2 rejects it and offers s^t, which satisfies that

$(s^t,1) \succsim_s (s^{t-1},0)$ and $(s^{t-1},0) >_w (s^t,1)$. That is, player 2 presents a counteroffer that is better for type 2_s and worse for type 2_w than the original offer, s^{t-1}. Then, player 1 concludes that he is playing against type 2_s.

The rationalizing conjectures enable player 2_s to sort himself out by rejecting s^{t-1} and demanding an additional sum of money that is greater than c_s but less than c_w.

The underlying assumption here is that a player makes an offer hoping that his opponent will accept it. Thus, making an offer s^t, where $(s^{t-1},0) >_w (s^t,1)$ and $(s^t,1) \succsim_s (s^{t-1},0)$, is not rational for type 2_w, and is rational for type 2_s. Therefore, player 1 adopts a new conjecture that rationalizes player 2's behavior.

By condition (2), in the case of any other unexpected move made by player 2, player 1 does not change his prior.

The analysis of a weaker version of the rationalizing requirement for a more general framework of the bargaining game with incomplete information is the issue of a previous paper (Rubinstein (1985)).

There are many reasonable requirements on conjectures that are not discussed here. Let me briefly mention three other requirements found in the literature.

(C-4) Passive conjectures

The conjectures of $\langle f,g,h,\omega \rangle$ are *passive* if $\omega^t(\underline{s}^t) = \omega^{t-2}(\underline{s}^{t-2})$ whenever neither type 2_w nor type 2_s plans to reject s^{t-1} and to offer s^t after the history $\underline{s}^{t-2}$ and after player 1 offered the partition s^{t-1}. In other words, unless the Bayesian formula is applicable, player 1 does not change his beliefs.

It should be noted that in complete-information game-theoretic models, it is usually assumed that players react passively about the basic conjecture, that is, that all of the players behave rationally. Even when a player makes a move that is strongly dominated by another move, all of the other players continue to believe that he is a rational player.

(C-5) Monotonic conjectures

The conjectures of $\langle f,g,h,\omega \rangle$ are said to be *monotonic* if, for every $s^1, \ldots, s^{t-1}$ and $x < y$ (t even), $\omega^t(s^1, \ldots, s^{t-1},y) \geq \omega^t(s^1, \ldots, s^{t-1},x)$. In other words, the lower player 2's offer, the greater player 1's probability that he is playing against type 2_s.

(C-6) Continuous conjectures

The belief system ω is said to be *continuous* if, for every t, $\omega^t(s^1, \ldots, s^t)$ is a continuous function.

Note that although the preceding consistency requirements are defined in terms of the present bargaining game, the definitions may be naturally extended to a wider class of games. In particular, it is easy to define the analogs of these properties for seller–buyer games in which the buyer's or the seller's reservation price is unknown.

6.5   Several properties of sequential equilibrium in this model

The following several properties of sequential equilibrium in this model are valid without further assumptions about the choice of conjectures.

Proposition 2.   In any sequential equilibrium,

1. Whenever it is player 2's turn to make an offer, players 2_w and 2_s make the same offer (although they might respond differently to player 1's previous offer);
2. If player 1 makes an offer and player 2_s accepts it, then player 2_w also accepts the offer;
3. If player 1 makes an offer, x, that player 2_w accepts and player 2_s rejects, then player 2_s makes a counteroffer, y, which is accepted by player 1 where $x - c_s \geq y \geq x - c_w$.

Outline of the proof (For a full proof, see Rubinstein (1985)).

1. Assume that there is a history after which players 2_w and 2_s make two different offers, y and z, respectively. After player 2 makes the offer, player 1 identifies player 2's type. Player 1 accepts z because otherwise he gets only c_s in the next period. If in the sequential equilibrium player 1 rejects the offer y, then he would get the whole dollar in the next period and player 2_w does better by offering z. If player 1 accepts both offers, y and z, the type that is supposed to make the higher offer (the worst for player 2) deviates to the lower offer and gains.
2. Note that if player 2_s accepts player 1's offer and player 2_w rejects it, then player 2_w reveals his identity and player 1 receives the whole dollar in the next period. Player 2_w gains by accepting player 1's offer.
3. If player 2_w accepts x and player 2_s offers y, player 1 identifies player 2_s and accepts y. Thus, if $y < x - c_w$, player 2_w does better by rejecting x; and if $y > x - c_s$, player 2_s does better by accepting x.

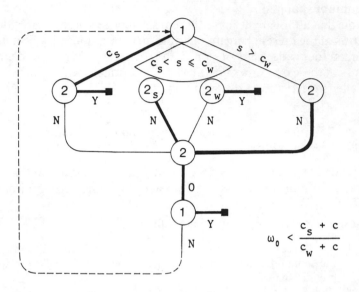

$$\omega_0 < \frac{c_s + c}{c_w + c}$$

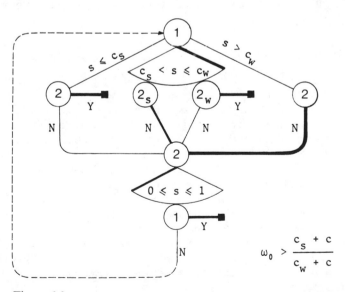

$$\omega_0 > \frac{c_s + c}{c_w + c}$$

Figure 6.2

6.6 Pessimistic and optimistic conjectures

The following two propositions show how dramatically the equilibrium outcomes vary under different methods of choosing conjectures.

Proposition 3. In any sequential equilibrium with pessimistic conjectures, the outcome is

$$\langle (c_s,1),(c_s,1)\rangle \text{ if } \omega_0 < \frac{c_s + c}{c_w + c},$$

$$\langle (c_w,1),(0,2)\rangle \text{ if } \frac{2C}{C_w + C} > \omega_0 > \frac{c_s + c}{c_w + c}.$$

Proof. Figure 6.2 illustrates sequential equilibrium with pessimistic conjectures in both cases. By proposition 2, both types of player 2, 2_w and 2_s, always make the same offer. In sequential equilibrium with pessimistic conjectures, the offer must be 0 and has to be accepted by player 1; otherwise, player 2 would deviate, offering some small positive ϵ. This persuades player 1 that player 2 is type 2_s, and player 1 accepts the offer. Since player 1 accepts the offer of 0 in the second round, the only two possible outcomes of a sequential equilibrium are $\langle (c_w,1),(0,2)\rangle$ and $\langle (c_s,1),(c_s,1)\rangle$. The exact outcome is determined by the relationship between ω_0 and $(c_s + c)/(c_w + c)$.

Proposition 4.

1. If $\omega_0 \leq 2c/(c + c_w)$, then, for every $1 - c + c_s \geq x^* \geq c$, $\langle (x^*,1),(x^*,1)\rangle$ is a sequential-equilibrium outcome with optimistic conjectures.
2. If $\omega_0 > (c_s + c)/(c_w + c)$, then for every $1 - c + c_s \geq x^* \geq c_w$, $\langle (x^*,1),(x^* - c_w,2)\rangle$ is a sequential-equilibrium outcome with optimistic conjectures.

Proof.

1. Figure 6.3 is a diagrammatic description of a sequential equilibrium with optimistic conjectures whose outcome is $\langle (x^*,1),(x^*,1)\rangle$. The symbol $1 \Leftrightarrow 2_w$ stands for the continuation of the equilibrium as in the complete-information game with players 1 and 2_w. Note that a deviation by player 1, by demanding more than x^*, is not profitable since the most that he can hope for from a deviation is

$$\omega_0(x^* - c + c_w) + (1 - \omega_0)(x^* - 2c) = x^* + \omega_0 c_w - c(2 - \omega_0) \leq x^*.$$

The restriction $x^* \leq 1 - c + c_s$ is needed for assuming that player 2_s will not prefer to reject the offer x^*.

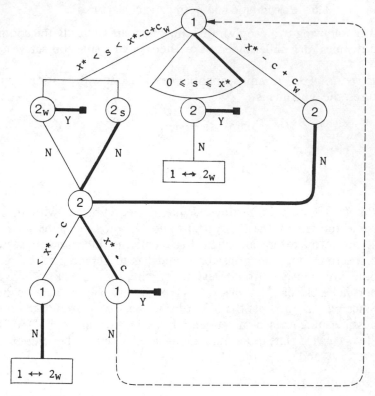

Figure 6.3

2. Figure 6.4 is an illustration of a sequential equilibrium with optimistic conjectures whose outcome is $\langle (x^*,1),(x^* - c_w,2)\rangle$. Note that if player 1 demands only $x^* - c_w + c_s$, he does not gain, since if $(c + c_s)/(c + c_w) < \omega_0$,

$$x^* - c_w + c_s < \omega_0 x^* + (1 - \omega_0)(x^* - c_w - c).$$

We have shown that optimistic conjectures turn almost every outcome into a sequential-equilibrium outcome. A very small ω_0 is sufficient to support a sequential equilibrium in which player 1 receives almost as much of the dollar as he would receive had he known with certainty that he was playing against player 2_w. On the other hand, pessimistic conjectures shrink the set of sequential equilibrium outcomes such that player 1 receives virtually nothing, since player 2 is always able to persuade him that he is type 2_s.

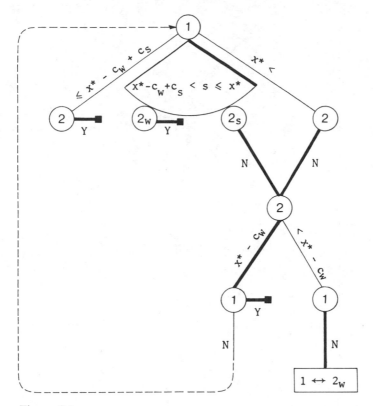

Figure 6.4

The sharp differences between the set of sequential-equilibrium outcomes under pessimistic and optimistic conjectures is no coincidence. It points to a sensible connection between conjectures and the bargaining outcome: Optimism strengthens player 1's position by limiting player 2's prospects of deviation.

6.7 Rationalizing conjectures

The next proposition states that for almost all ω_0, there is a unique (C-3) sequential-equilibrium outcome. If ω_0 is small enough (under a certain cutting point, ω^*), player 1 receives almost nothing. If ω_0 is high enough (above ω^*), player 1 receives almost the entire dollar.

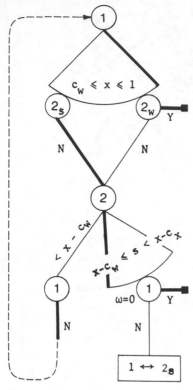

Figure 6.5

Proposition 5.   For any sequential equilibrium with rationalizing conjectures,

1. If $\omega_0 > 2c/(c + c_w)$, its outcome is $\langle(1,1),(1 - c_w,2)\rangle$;
2. If $2c/(c + c_w) > \omega_0 > (c + c_s)/(c + c_w)$, its outcome is $\langle(c_w,1),(0,2)\rangle$;
3. If $(c + c_s)/(c + c_w) > \omega_0$, its outcome is $\langle(c_s,1),(c_s,1)\rangle$.

The proof of this proposition follows the basic logic of the main theorem in Rubinstein (1985). Here, many simplifications are possible because the time preferences are very simple. In this review, I will settle for presenting a sequential equilibrium with the outcome $\langle(1,1),(1 - c_w,2)\rangle$ for the case where $\omega_0 > 2c/(c + c_w)$. Figure 6.5 describes this sequential equilibrium.

Player 1 offers the partition 1, player 2_w accepts the offer, and player 2_s rejects it and offers $1 - c_w$. The offer $1 - c_w$ persuades player 1 that he is playing against type 2_s, and he accepts the offer. Even if player 1 demands $x < 1$, player 2_s rejects the offer x (unless $x \le c_s$) and makes the offer $\max\{0, x - c_s\}$, which persuades player 1 that player 2 is type 2_s. If player 2 offers player 1 less than $x - c_w$, then player 1 rejects it without changing his subjective probability, ω_0. The rejection is optimal for player 1 because $\omega_0(1 - c) + (1 - \omega_0)(1 - 2c - c_w) > 1 - c_w$, since $\omega_0 > 2c/(c + c_w)$.

Remark. The characterization of sequential equilibrium remains valid when we replace (C-3,b) with a weaker condition, (C-3,b*).

(C-3,b) Monotonicity with respect to insistence*

The conjectures of $\langle f, g, h, \omega \rangle$ are said to be *monotonic with respect to insistence* if, whenever $\omega^{t-2}(s^{t-2}) \neq 1$, and player 2 rejects an offer s^{t-1} and offers the partition s^t satisfying that for both types, $(s^t, 1)$ is better than $(s^{t-1}, 0)$ (i.e., $s^t \le s^{t-1} - c_w$), then $\omega^t(s^t) \le \omega^{t-2}(s^{t-2})$.

The role of condition (C-3,b*) is to prevent player 1 from "threatening" player 2 that insistence will increase player 1's probability that he is playing against player 2_w.

Remark: I have little to say about sequential equilibrium with passive conjectures. However, the following partial observations indicate a strengthening in player 1's position relative to sequential equilibrium with rationalizing conjectures. This occurs because, with rationalizing conjectures, player 2_s could identify himself only by rejecting an offer x and making a new offer $x - c_w$. With passive conjectures, it might also be that in equilibrium, player 2_s identifies himself by rejecting x and offering a certain y_0 satisfying $x - c_s > y_0 > x - c_w$.

Proposition 6. The following are possible outcomes of sequential equilibrium with passive conjectures:

1. If $\omega_0 \ge c/c_w$, $\langle (1,1), (1 - \epsilon, 2) \rangle$ is a sequential-equilibrium outcome for $c/\omega_0 \ge \epsilon \ge c_w$.
2. If $\omega_0 \le 2c/(c + c_w)$, either $\langle (c_w, 1), (0, 2) \rangle$ or $\langle (c_s, 1), (c_s, 1) \rangle$ is a sequential-equilibrium outcome.

The proof is omitted since it repeats ideas that appear in the construction of equilibria in previous proofs.

6.8   Final remarks

The results in Sections 6.6 and 6.7 reveal systematic differences between bargaining outcomes due to systematic differences in the choice of conjectures. What has been done here is partial in many ways:

1. The informational structure is very special: one-sided uncertainty and only two possible types.
2. A special class of time preferences (fixed bargaining costs) is used.
3. A special bargaining problem is studied: partition of a dollar.
4. Only three sets of conjectures are analyzed.

However, I believe that the results indicate the spirit of more general results pertaining to the influence of the choice of conjectures on the bargaining outcome.

It seems that the next important task in extending the analysis is a systematic study of the choice of conjectures. Interesting partial orderings on conjectures–choice methods are likely to derive interesting comparative static results.

REFERENCES

Cramton, P. C. (1982): A Bargaining Model with Incomplete Information. Graduate School of Business, Stanford University, Research Paper 652.
Fudenberg, D., and J. Tirole (1983): Sequential Bargaining under Incomplete Information. *Review of Economic Studies* 50, pp. 221–48.
Kreps, D. M., and R. Wilson (1982): Sequential Equilibria. *Econometrica* 50, pp. 863–94.
Ordover, J., and A. Rubinstein (1983): On Bargaining, Settling, and Litigating: A Problem in Multistage Games with Imperfect Information. Mimeo, New York University.
Perry, M. (1985): A Theory of Price Formation in Bilateral Situations. *Econometrica* (forthcoming).
Rubinstein, A. (1982): Perfect Equilibrium in a Bargaining Model. *Econometrica* 50, pp. 97–109.
    (1985): A Bargaining Model with Incomplete Information about Time Preferences. *Econometrica* (forthcoming).
Sobel, J., and I. Takahashi (1983): A Multi-Stage Model of Bargaining. *Review of Economic Studies* 50, pp. 411–26.

CHAPTER 7

Analysis of two bargaining problems with incomplete information

Roger B. Myerson
NORTHWESTERN UNIVERSITY

7.1 Introduction

In analyzing a cooperative game with incomplete information, three kinds of solution concepts should be considered. First, we should characterize the set of coordination mechanisms or decision rules that are *feasible* for the players when they cooperate, taking account of the incentive constraints that arise because the players cannot always trust each other. Second, we should characterize the mechanisms that are *efficient* within this feasible set. Efficiency criteria for games with incomplete information have been discussed in detail by Holmström and Myerson (1983). Third, we should try to identify *equitable* mechanisms on the efficient frontier that are likely to actually be implemented by the players if they are sophisticated negotiators with equal bargaining ability. (We might also want to consider cases where one player has more bargaining ability than the others, as in principal – agent problems.) For this analysis, a concept of *neutral bargaining solution* has been axiomatically derived by Myerson (1983, 1984).

In this chapter, two bilateral trading problems with incomplete information are analyzed in terms of these three solution concepts. Sections 7.2 through 7.4 consider the *symmetric uniform trading problem,* a simple problem in which the buyer and seller each have private information about how much the object being traded is worth to him. This problem was first studied by Chatterjee and Samuelson (1983), and was also considered by Myerson and Satterthwaite (1983). Sections 7.5 and 7.6 contain a discussion of the *lemon problem,* in which only the seller has private information, but the value of the object to the buyer may depend on this information. Akerlof (1970) first studied a version of the lemon problem, in a market context, and Samuelson (1984) characterized the seller's ex ante optimal mechanisms. Section 7.7 contains the more technical proofs relating to the neutral bargaining solutions. Readers who are not familiar with the earlier papers on this subject may prefer to omit this final section.

7.2   The symmetric uniform trading problem: Feasibility

In this section and the next two, a bargaining problem is considered in which there is only one seller (trader 1) and one potential buyer (trader 2) for a single indivisible object. Both buyer and seller have risk-neutral utility for money. We let $\tilde{V}_1$ denote the value of the object to the seller and $\tilde{V}_2$ denote the value to the buyer. We assume that $\tilde{V}_1$ and $\tilde{V}_2$ are independent random variables, and that each is uniformly distributed over the interval from 0 to 1 (in some monetary scale). Thus, the bargaining situation may be termed the *symmetric uniform trading problem.*

We assume that each trader i knows his own valuation $\tilde{V}_i$ at the time of bargaining, but that he considers the other's valuation as a random variable. Furthermore, neither trader can observe directly the other's valuation. The traders can communicate with each other, but each would be free to lie about the value of the object to him, if he expected to get a better price by doing so.

A *direct trading mechanism* is one in which each trader simultaneously reports his valuation to a mediator or broker, who then determines whether the object is transferred from seller to buyer and how much the buyer must pay the seller. A direct mechanism is thus characterized by two *outcome functions,* denoted by $p(\,\cdot\,,\cdot\,)$ and $x(\,\cdot\,,\cdot\,)$, where $p(v_1,v_2)$ is the probability that the object is transferred to the buyer and $x(v_1,v_2)$ is the expected payment to the seller, if v_1 and v_2 are the reported valuations of the seller and buyer, respectively. A direct mechanism is *(Bayesian) incentive compatible* if honest reporting forms a Bayesian/Nash equilibrium. That is, in an incentive-compatible mechanism, each trader can maximize his expected utility by reporting his true valuation, given that the other trader is expected to report honestly.

We can, without loss of generality, restrict our attention to incentive-compatible direct mechanisms. This is possible because, for any Bayesian equilibrium of any bargaining game, there is an equivalent incentive-compatible direct mechanism that always yields the same outcomes (when the honest equilibrium is played). This result, which is well known and very general, is called the *revelation principle.* The essential idea is that, given any equilibrium of any bargaining game, we can construct an equivalent incentive-compatible direct mechanism as follows. First, we ask the buyer and seller each to confidentially report his valuation. Then, we compute what each would have done in the given equilibrium strategies with these valuations. Finally, we implement the outcome (i.e., transfers of money and the object) as in the given game for this computed behavior. If either individual had any incentive to lie to us in this direct mechanism, then he would have had an incentive to lie to himself in the original game, which is a contradiction of the premise that he was in equilibrium in the original game. (For more on this revelation principle, see Myerson (1979).)

Given a direct mechanism with outcome functions (p,x), we define the following quantities:

$$\bar{x}_1(v_1) = \int_0^1 x(v_1,t_2)\, dt_2, \qquad \bar{x}_2(v_2) = \int_0^1 x(t_1,v_2)\, dt_1,$$

$$\bar{p}_1(v_1) = \int_0^1 p(v_1,t_2)\, dt_2, \qquad \bar{p}_2(v_2) = \int_0^1 p(t_1,v_2)\, dt_1,$$

$$U_1(v_1,p,x) = \bar{x}_1(v_1) - v_1 \bar{p}_1(v_1), \; U_2(v_2,p,x) = v_2 \bar{p}_2(v_2) - \bar{x}_2(v_2).$$

Thus, $U_1(v_1,p,x)$ represents the expected profits or gains from trade for the seller if his valuation is v_1, since $\bar{x}_1(v_1)$ is his expected revenue and $\bar{p}_1(v_1)$ is his probability of losing the object given $\tilde{V}_1 = v_1$. Similarly, $U_2(v_2,p,x)$ is the expected gains from trade for the buyer, $\bar{x}_2(v_2)$ is the buyer's expected payment, and $\bar{p}_2(v_2)$ is the buyer's probability of getting the object, if his valuation is v_2.

In this formal notation, (p,x) is *incentive compatible* if and only if

$$U_1(v_1,p,x) \geq \bar{x}_1(t_1) - v_1 \bar{p}_1(t_1) \qquad \text{and} \qquad U_2(v_2,p,x) \geq v_2 \bar{p}_2(t_2) - \bar{x}_2(t_2)$$

for every v_1, v_2, t_1, and t_2 between 0 and 1. These two inequalities assert that neither trader should expect to gain in the mechanism by reporting valuation t_i when v_i is his true valuation.

We say that a mechanism (p,x) is *individually rational* if and only if each trader gets nonnegative expected gains from trade given any valuation, that is,

$$U_1(v_1,p,x) \geq 0 \qquad \text{and} \qquad U_2(v_2,p,x) \geq 0$$

for every v_1 and v_2 between 0 and 1. Since each individual already knows his valuation when he enters the bargaining process and neither individual can be forced to trade, a feasible mechanism should be individually rational in this sense, as well as incentive compatible. We say that a mechanism is *feasible* if and only if it is both individually rational and incentive compatible.

Many bargaining games satisfy a stronger individual-rationality condition: that neither individual ever consents to a trade that leaves him worse off ex post. Formally, this condition is given as

$$x(v_1,v_2) - v_1 p(v_1,v_2) \geq 0 \quad \text{and} \quad v_2 p(v_1,v_2) - x(v_1,v_2) \geq 0$$

for every v_1 and v_2. If (p,x) satisfies this condition, then we must have

$$U_1(1,p,x) = 0 \quad \text{and} \quad U_2(0,p,x) = 0.$$

That is, the seller expects no gains from trade if $\tilde{V}_1 = 1$, since he knows that the buyer's valuation is lower; and, similarly, the buyer expects no gains from trade if $\tilde{V}_2 = 0$. We may say that a feasible mechanism (p,x) is *normal* if and only if $U_1(1,p,x) = 0 = U_2(0,p,x)$.

The following proposition characterizes completely the set of feasible mechanisms for the symmetric uniform trading problem.

Proposition 1. Given any function p: $[0,1]\times[0,1] \to [0,1]$, there exists some function $x(\cdot,\cdot)$ such that (p,x) is a feasible mechanism for the symmetric uniform trading problem if and only if $\bar{p}_1(\cdot)$ is a weakly decreasing function, $\bar{p}_2(\cdot)$ is a weakly increasing function, and

$$0 \leq \int_0^1 \int_0^1 (v_2 - v_1 - .5)p(v_1,v_2)\, dv_1\, dv_2. \tag{7.1}$$

Furthermore, x can be constructed so that (p,x) is normal if and only if (7.1) is satisfied with equality. In general, for any incentive-compatible mechanism (p,x),

$$U_1(1,p,x) + U_2(0,p,x) = 2 \int_0^1 \int_0^1 (v_2 - v_1 - .5)p(v_1,v_2)\, dv_1\, dv_2 \tag{7.2}$$

and, for every v_1 and v_2,

$$U_1(v_1,p,x) = U_1(1,p,x) + \int_{v_1}^1 \bar{p}_1(s_1)\, ds_1, \tag{7.3}$$

$$U_2(v_2,p,x) = U_2(0,p,x) + \int_0^{v_2} \bar{p}_2(s_2)\, ds_2. \tag{7.4}$$

Proof. This proposition is a special case of theorem 1 of Myerson and Satterthwaite (1983).

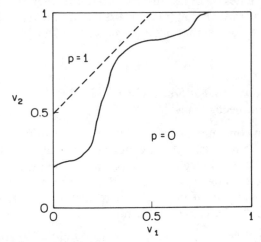

Figure 7.1

It is straightforward to check that

$$\int\limits_{0}^{1} \int\limits_{0}^{v_2} \left(v_2 - v_1 - \frac{1}{3} \right) dv_1 \, dv_2 = 0.$$

Thus, conditional on the event that $\tilde{V}_2 \geq \tilde{V}_1$ (so that the individuals have something to gain from trading), the expected value of $(\tilde{V}_2 - \tilde{V}_1)$ equals $\frac{1}{3}$. However, condition (7.1) asserts that, conditional on the event that a trade actually occurs, the expected value of $(\tilde{V}_2 - \tilde{V}_1)$ must be at least $\frac{1}{2}$, for any feasible mechanism. Thus, it is not possible to construct a feasible mechanism in which trade occurs if and only if $\tilde{V}_2 \geq \tilde{V}_1$.

Condition (7.1) has experimentally testable implications. If we observe many instances of the symmetric uniform trading problem, with $\tilde{V}_1$ and $\tilde{V}_2$ chosen independently each time, and with each buyer and seller facing each other at most once (to avoid the complications of a repeated game), then the average difference $(\tilde{V}_2 - \tilde{V}_1)$ in those instances where trade occurs should be close to $\frac{1}{2}$. This prediction holds no matter what social conventions regulate the negotiation process. We need to assume only that buyer and seller in each instance are playing some Bayesian/Nash equilibrium of some bargaining game in which neither individual ever has to trade at a loss.

To interpret proposition 1 geometrically, consider Figure 7.1. The dashed line represents the set of points where $v_2 = v_1 + \frac{1}{2}$. If we draw any increasing curve in the unit square such that the center of gravity of the region above the curve lies on or above the dashed line, then there exists some feasible mechanism such that trade occurs if and only if $(\tilde{V}_1, \tilde{V}_2)$ lies above the curve. For a normal mechanism, the center of gravity must be *on* the dashed line.

7.3   The symmetric uniform trading problem: Efficient mechanisms

If two individuals can communicate effectively in a bargaining problem, then we may expect them to use a trading mechanism that is efficient, in the sense that there is no other incentive-compatible mechanism that they both would surely prefer. That is, we may say that an incentive-compatible mechanism (p,x) is *efficient* if and only if there does not exist any other incentive-compatible mechanism $(\hat{p}, \hat{x})$ such that

$$U_1(v_1, \hat{p}, \hat{x}) > U_1(v_1, p, x) \quad \text{and} \quad U_2(v_1, \hat{p}, \hat{x}) > U_2(v_2, p, x)$$

for every v_1 and v_2 between 0 and 1. In the terminology of Holmström and Myerson (1983), this concept of efficiency corresponds to a weak form of *interim incentive efficiency*.

Using a standard separation argument, we can show that this definition is equivalent to the following, more tractable characterization. A given incentive-compatible mechanism is efficient if and only if there exist two weakly increasing functions $L_1: [0,1] \to [0,1]$ and $L_2: [0,1] \to [0,1]$, with $L_1(0) = L_2(0) = 0$ and $L_1(1) = L_2(1) = 1$, such that the given mechanism maximizes

$$\int_0^1 U_1(v_1, p, x) \, dL_1(v_1) + \int_0^1 U_2(v_2, p, x) \, dL_2(v_2) \tag{7.5}$$

over all incentive-compatible mechanisms (p,x). (It can be easily shown that $L_1(1) - L_1(0)$ must equal $L_2(1) - L_2(0)$, because otherwise a lump-sum transfer of money could make (7.5) arbitrarily large.) If L_1 and L_2 are differentiable, with $L_i' = \ell_i$, then the Riemann–Stieltjes integrals in (7.5) may be rewritten as

$$\int_0^1 U_1(v_1, p, x)\ell_1(v_1) \, dv_1 + \int_0^1 U_1(v_2, p, x)\ell_2(v_2) \, dv_2.$$

The following proposition gives us a direct computational procedure for verifying efficiency of a mechanism.

Proposition 2.   Suppose that (p,x) is an incentive-compatible mechanism for the symmetric uniform trading problem and that $L_1(\cdot)$ and $L_2(\cdot)$ are weakly increasing functions such that $L_1(0) = L_2(0) = 0$ and $L_1(1) = L_2(1) = 1$. Suppose also that, for every v_1 and v_2 between 0 and 1,

$$p(v_1,v_2) = \begin{cases} 1 & \text{if } 2v_1 - L_1(v_1) < 2v_2 - L_2(v_2), \\ 0 & \text{if } 2v_1 - L_1(v_1) > 2v_2 - L_2(v_2). \end{cases}$$

Then, (p,x) is efficient.

Proof: By proposition 1, if (p,x) is incentive compatible, then

$$\int_0^1 U_1(v_1,p,x)\, dL_1(v_1) + \int_0^1 U_1(v_2,p,x)\, dL_2(v_2)$$

$$= U_1(1,p,x) + \int_0^1 \int_{v_1}^1 \bar{p}_1(s_1)ds_1\, dL_1(v_1) + U_2(0,p,x)$$

$$+ \int_0^1 \int_0^{v_2} \bar{p}_2(s_2)\, ds_2\, dL_2(v_2)$$

$$= U_1(1,p,x) + U_2(0,p,x) + \int_0^1 L_1(s_1)\bar{p}_2(s_1)\, ds_1 + \int_0^1 (1 - L_2(s_2))\bar{p}_2(s_2)\, ds_2$$

$$= \int_0^1 \int_0^1 (2v_1 - 2v_1 - 1)p(v_1,v_2)\, dv_1\, dv_2 + \int_0^1 \int_0^1 (L_1(s_1)$$

$$+ 1 - L_2(s_2))p(s_1,s_2)\, ds_1\, ds_2$$

$$= \int_0^1 \int_0^1 [(2v_2 - L_2(v_2)) - (2v_1 - L_1(v_1))]\, p(v_1,v_2)\, dv_1,\, dv_2.$$

The conditions in proposition 2 imply that p maximizes this double integral over all functions from $[0,1] \times [0,1]$ to $[0,1]$.

Let us now consider three specific mechanisms that were studied by Chatterjee and Samuelson (1983). The first mechanism corresponds to a game in which the seller has the authority to demand any price for his object, and then the buyer can either take it or leave it. The seller's optimal

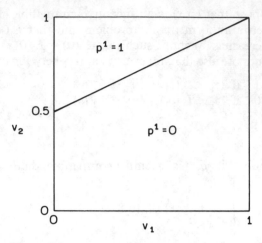

Figure 7.2

price in this game is $q_1 = (1 + \tilde{V}_1)/2$, which maximizes his expected profit $(1 - q_1)(q_1 - \tilde{V}_1)$. Thus, this mechanism is represented by (p^1, x^1), where

$$p^1(v_1, v_2) = \begin{cases} 1 & \text{if } v_2 \geq \dfrac{1 + v_1}{2}, \\ 0 & \text{if } v_2 < \dfrac{1 + v_1}{2}; \end{cases}$$

$$x^1(v_1, v_2) = \begin{cases} \dfrac{1 + v_1}{2} & \text{if } v_2 \geq \dfrac{1 + v_1}{2}, \\ 0 & \text{if } v_2 < \dfrac{1 + v_1}{2}; \end{cases}$$

It is straightforward to verify that (p^1, x^1) is efficient, using proposition 2 with

$$L_1(v_1) = v_1 \quad \text{and} \quad L_2(v_2) = \begin{cases} 0 & \text{if } v_2 = 0, \\ 1 & \text{if } v_2 > 0. \end{cases}$$

Figure 7.2 shows the trading region for this mechanism (p^1, x^1).

The second mechanism corresponds to a game in which the buyer can commit himself to any offer price for the object, and then the seller can only accept it or reject it. The buyer's optimal price in this game is $q_2 = \tilde{V}_2/2$, which maximizes his expected profit $q_2(\tilde{V}_2 - q_2)$. Thus, this

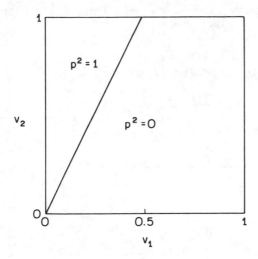

Figure 7.3

mechanism is represented by (p^2, x^2), where

$$p^2(v_1, v_2) = \begin{cases} 1 & \text{if } \dfrac{v_2}{2} \geq v_1, \\[2mm] 0 & \text{if } \dfrac{v_2}{2} < v_1; \end{cases}$$

$$x^1(v_1, v_2) = \begin{cases} \dfrac{v_2}{2} & \text{if } \dfrac{v_2}{2} \geq v_1, \\[2mm] 0 & \text{if } \dfrac{v_2}{2} < v_1. \end{cases}$$

To verify that (p^2, x^2) is efficient, use proposition 2 with

$$L_2(v_2) = v_2 \quad \text{and} \quad L_1(v_1) = \begin{cases} 0 & \text{if } v_1 < 1, \\ 1 & \text{if } v_1 = 1. \end{cases}$$

Figure 7.3 shows the trading region for (p^2, x^2).

The third mechanism corresponds to a game in which the seller and buyer announce a bid price simultaneously. If the seller's bid is lower than the buyer's bid, then the buyer gets the object for the average of the two bids. On the other hand, if the seller's bid is higher than the buyer's bid, then there is no trade. Chatterjee and Samuelson (1983) have shown that the equilibrium bids for this game are $q_1 = \frac{2}{3}\tilde{V}_1 + \frac{1}{4}$ and $q_2 = \frac{2}{3}\tilde{V}_2 + \frac{1}{12}$.

Note that $q_1 \geq q_2$ if and only if $\tilde{V}_2 \geq \tilde{V}_1 + \frac{1}{4}$. Thus, this mechanism is represented by (p^3, x^3), where

$$p^3(v_1, v_2) = \begin{cases} 1 & \text{if } v_2 \geq v_1 + \frac{1}{4}, \\ 0 & \text{if } v_2 < v_1 + \frac{1}{4}, \end{cases}$$

$$x^3(v_1, v_2) = \begin{cases} \dfrac{v_1 + v_2 + \frac{1}{2}}{3} & \text{if } v_2 \geq v_1 + \frac{1}{4}, \\ 0 & \text{if } v_2 < v_1 + \frac{1}{4}. \end{cases}$$

To verify that (p^3, x^3) is efficient, use proposition 2 with

$$L_1(v_1) = \begin{cases} \frac{2}{3}v_1 & \text{if } v_1 < 1, \\ 1 & \text{if } v_1 = 1; \end{cases}$$

$$L_2(v_2) = \begin{cases} 0 & \text{if } v_2 = 0, \\ \frac{2}{3}v_2 + \frac{1}{3} & \text{if } v_2 > 0. \end{cases}$$

Figure 7.4 shows the trading region for (p^3, x^3).

Myerson and Satterthwaite (1983) showed that (p^3, x^3) maximizes the expected sum of the two traders' profits over all feasible mechanisms. To verify this, let L_1 and L_2 be as in the preceding paragraph, and observe that

$$\int_0^1 U_1(v_1, p, x)\, dL_1(v_1) + \int_0^1 U_2(v_2, p, x)\, dL_2(v_2)$$

$$= \frac{2}{3}\left[\int_0^1 U_1(v_1, p, x)\, dv_1 + \int_0^1 U_2(v_2, p, x)\, dv_2 \right.$$

$$\left. + \frac{1}{2} U_1(1, p, x) + \frac{1}{2} U_2(0, p, x) \right].$$

The expression in brackets may be interpreted as the Lagrangian function for the problem of maximizing the expected sum of the traders' profits, when we give a shadow price of $\frac{1}{2}$ to each of the individual-rationality constraints $U_1(1, p, x) \geq 0$ and $U_2(0, p, x) \geq 0$. Since (p^3, x^3) maximizes this expression over all incentive-compatible mechanisms (by the proof of proposition 2) and satisfies these two individual-rationality constraints with equality, it maximizes the expected sum of profits over all feasible mechanisms.

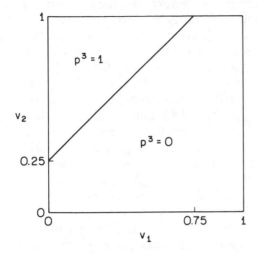

Figure 7.4

7.4   The symmetric uniform trading problem: Neutral solutions

Let us suppose now that the seller and buyer in the symmetric uniform trading problem can negotiate face to face (perhaps with some time limit) to try to determine a mutually acceptable price for the object. In a real-world setting, such negotiations would be much more complicated than the three simple games discussed in the preceding section. In real negotiations, each trader's strategy is a plan for making a sequence of demands, offers, and arguments, which may be chosen from the infinite richness of human language. Obviously, we have no simple mathematical model of the traders' strategy sets in such face-to-face negotiations. However, if one could construct a realistic model of face-to-face negotiations as a noncooperative game in strategic form, any equilibrium of the model would still correspond to some feasible mechanism, by the revelation principle. Thus, instead of trying to model the negotiation process as a game in strategic form, we may try to model it as a direct mechanism. That is, by analyzing the various incentive-compatible mechanisms, we may find one that is a realistic description of face-to-face negotiations.

A concept of *neutral bargaining solutions* has been defined by Myerson (1984) for general bargaining problems with incomplete information. This solution concept generalizes Nash's (1950) bargaining solution, and is based on axioms of equity, efficiency, and independence of irrelevant alternatives. For the symmetric uniform trading problem, this solution concept identifies a new efficient mechanism, different from the three mechanisms that were discussed in the preceding section. However, before we consider this mechanism and argue why it may be a good model of face-to-face negotiations for this symmetric uniform trading problem, let us reconsider the mechanism (p^3, x^3) discussed in the preceding section.

At first glance, (p^3, x^3) seems to have many good properties to recommend it as a bargaining solution for symmetric uniform trading. As we have seen, (p^3, x^3) is efficient. It treats the two traders symmetrically. It is also *ex ante efficient*, in the sense that, among all feasible mechanisms for the symmetric uniform problem, (p^3, x^3) maximizes the sum of the two traders' ex ante expected gains from trade. Thus, if the traders could commit themselves to a mechanism before either learns his own valuation $\tilde{V}_i$, then the best symmetric mechanism for both would be (p^3, x^3).

However, each trader already knows his actual valuation $\tilde{V}_i$ when he negotiates, and this is not assumed to be a repeated game. Therefore, each trader cares only about his conditionally expected gains given his actual valuation. Ex ante expected gains are not relevant to the actual traders during negotiations, so ex ante efficiency should be irrelevant to our theory of negotiations. In fact, if the seller's valuation is higher than .75, then the mechanism (p^3, x^3) is among the seller's least preferred mechanisms, since $U_1(v_1, p^3, x^3) = 0$ for all $v_1 \geq .75$.

Suppose, for example, that the seller's valuation is $\tilde{V}_1 = .8$, and that he is negotiating with a buyer who wants to play the simultaneous-bid split-the-difference game with the equilibrium that is equivalent to (p^3, x^3). The seller knows that he has nothing to gain by playing this game, since the buyer will never bid above .75. Thus, the seller has nothing to lose by refusing to play by its rules, and instead trying to make a nonnegotiable first-and-final offer to sell at price .9. The buyer may be antagonized by such an arrogant "Boulware" strategy, but if $\tilde{V}_2 \geq .9$, there should be at least some positive probability that the buyer would accept. Thus, the seller would be strictly better off than in the mechanism (p^3, x^3).

Similarly, $U_2(v_2, p^3, x^3) = 0$ if $v_2 \leq .25$, and so the buyer would have nothing to lose by refusing to participate in the (p^3, x^3) mechanism and instead trying to make a nonnegotiable first-and-final offer to buy at some low price. Thus, the mechanism that accurately describes the real negotiation process should have more trade occurring when $\tilde{V}_1 \geq .75$ or $\tilde{V}_2 \leq .25$ than in the (p^3, x^3) mechanism. To satisfy the "center-of-gravity" condition (7.1) of proposition 1, the mechanism must also have less trade than (p^3, x^3) under some other circumstances, when $\tilde{V}_1$ and $\tilde{V}_2$ are in the middle of their range.

The following mechanism (p^4, x^4) satisfies the conditions for a neutral

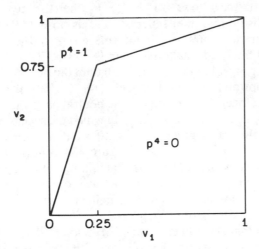

Figure 7.5

bargaining solution from Myerson (1984), and it differs qualitatively from (p^3, x^3) exactly as described previously:

$$p^4(v_1, v_2) = \begin{cases} 1 & \text{if } v_2 \geq 3v_1 \text{ or } 3v_2 - 2 \geq v_1, \\ 0 & \text{if } v_2 < 3v_1 \text{ and } 3v_2 - 2 < v_1; \end{cases}$$

$$x^4(v_1, v_2) = \begin{cases} \dfrac{p^4(v_1, v_2)v_2}{2} & \text{if } v_2 \leq 1 - v_1, \\[2mm] \dfrac{p^4(v_1, v_2)(1 + v_1)}{2} & \text{if } v_2 > 1 - v_1. \end{cases}$$

Figure 7.5 shows the trading region for (p^4, x^4). (The kink in the boundary of the trading region is at $(.25, .75)$.)

It is straightforward to check that this neutral mechanism (p^4, x^4) is incentive compatible and individually rational. To verify that (p^4, x^4) is efficient, use proposition 2 with

$$\begin{aligned} L_1(v_1) &= \begin{cases} 0 & \text{if } v_1 < \tfrac{1}{4}, \\ \tfrac{4}{3}v_1 - \tfrac{1}{3} & \text{if } v_1 \geq \tfrac{1}{4}; \end{cases} \\[2mm] L_2(v_2) &= \begin{cases} \tfrac{4}{3}v_2 & \text{if } v_2 \leq \tfrac{3}{4}, \\ 1 & \text{if } v_2 > \tfrac{3}{4}. \end{cases} \end{aligned} \tag{7.6}$$

We say that the seller is in a *strong* bargaining position if $\tilde{V}_1$ is close to 1, since he has very little to lose by not trading. Similarly, we say that the buyer is in a strong bargaining position if $\tilde{V}_2$ is close to 0. The formula for

x^4 can then be interpreted as follows. If $\tilde{V}_2 < 1 - \tilde{V}_1$, then the buyer is in a stronger bargaining position than the seller (since $\tilde{V}_2$ is closer to 0 than $\tilde{V}_1$ is to 1). In this case, if trade occurs, then it takes place at price $\tilde{V}_2/2$, which is the buyer's optimal first-and-final offer, as in (p^2, x^2). If $\tilde{V}_2 > 1 - \tilde{V}_1$, then the seller is in a stronger bargaining position than the buyer, and any trade is at the seller's optimal first-and-final offer $(1 + \tilde{V}_1)/2$, as in (p^1, x^1). Thus, if the seller is stronger than the buyer, the neutral bargaining solution (p^4, x^4) resembles the mechanism (p^1, x^1), in which the seller controls the price, except that the trading region is slightly smaller (compare the upper wedge in Figure 7.5 with the form of Figure 7.2). Similarly, if the buyer is stronger than the seller, the neutral bargaining solution (p^4, x^4) resembles the mechanism (p^2, x^2), in which the buyer controls the price, except that the trading region is again slightly smaller (compare the lower wedge in Figure 7.5 with the form of Figure 7.3).

The neutral bargaining-solution concept of Myerson (1984) is meant to be applied to two-person bargaining problems with incomplete information in which the two players have equal bargaining ability. Here, *bargaining ability* means the ability to argue articulately and persuasively in the negotiation process. Myerson (1983) defined a theory of solutions for cooperative games with incomplete information in which one individual has all of the bargaining ability. In the terminology of that paper, if the seller had all of the bargaining ability, then (p^1, x^1) would be the seller's *neutral optimum* (because it is undominated for the seller and is safe, in the sense that it would be incentive compatible and individually rational even if the buyer knew the seller's valuation). Similarly, (p^2, x^2) would be the buyer's neutral optimum if he had all of the bargaining ability.

Thus, the neutral bargaining solution (p^4, x^4) is a first illustration of the following important property, which we may call *arrogance of strength*. If two individuals of symmetric bargaining ability negotiate with each other, but one individual has a surprisingly strong bargaining position (i.e., the range of agreements that would be better for him than the disagreement outcome is smaller than the other individual expects), then the outcome of the neutral bargaining solution tends to be similar to what would have been the outcome if the strong individual had had all of the bargaining ability, except that the probability of disagreement (no trade) is higher.

The proof that (p^4, x^4) is a neutral bargaining solution for the symmetric uniform trading problem is given in Section 7.7. However, it may be helpful to discuss here the essential properties of (p^4, x^4) that identify it as a bargaining solution. The neutral bargaining solutions were defined by Myerson (1984) using axioms that generalize the axioms of Nash's (1950) bargaining solution. Then, in a theorem, it was shown that these neutral bargaining solutions can also be characterized by two properties: efficiency and *virtual equity*. The efficiency property has already been discussed, but the virtual-equity property needs more explanation.

Given any L_1 and L_2 as in proposition 2, we define functions W_1 and W_2, respectively, by

$$W_1(v_1) = 2v_1 - L_1(v_1) \qquad \text{and} \qquad W_2(v_2) = 2v_2 - L_2(v_2).$$

We call $W_i(v_i)$ the *virtual valuation* of the object to trader i if v_i is his true valuation. For L_1 and L_2 as in (7.6), the virtual valuations are

$$W_1(v_1) = \begin{cases} 2v_1 & \text{if } v_1 < \frac{1}{4}, \\ \dfrac{2v_1 + 1}{3} & \text{if } v_1 \geq \frac{1}{4}; \end{cases} \tag{7.7}$$

$$W_2(v_2) = \begin{cases} \frac{2}{3}v_2 & \text{if } v_2 \leq \frac{3}{4}, \\ 2v_2 - 1 & \text{if } v_2 > \frac{3}{4}. \end{cases}$$

By proposition 1, for any feasible mechanism there must be a positive probability of negotiations ending without a trade when the object is worth more to the buyer than to the seller. Such a conclusion may seem paradoxical if the traders have the option to continue negotiating. Why should they stop negotiating when they know that there is still a possibility of mutual gains from trade? One possible explanation is that each trader i deliberately distorts his preferences in bargaining, in response to the other's distrust, and acts as if the object were worth the virtual valuation $W_i(\tilde{V}_i)$ to him, instead of the actual valuation $\tilde{V}_i$. (In (7.7), $W_1(v_1) \geq v_1$ and $W_2(v_2) \leq v_2$, and so the seller is overstating and the buyer is understating the object's value.) The mechanism (p^4, x^4) has trade occurring if and only if $W_2(\tilde{V}_2) \geq W_1(\tilde{V}_1)$; thus, there is no possibility of further virtual gains from trade after (p^4, x^4).

Of course, any efficient mechanism that satisfies proposition 2 would satisfy a similar property (which we may call *virtual ex-post efficiency*) in terms of some other virtual valuation function. However, (p^4, x^4) is also virtually equitable, in terms of the same virtual valuations (7.7) that make it virtually ex post efficient. To see this, consider any $v_1 \geq \frac{1}{4}$. If the seller's true valuation is v_1, then his conditionally expected virtual gains in (p^4, x^4) are

$$\int_0^1 (x^4(v_1, v_2) - W_1(v_1)p^4(v_1, v_2))\, dv_2 = \int_{(v_1+2)/3}^1 \left(\frac{1 + v_1}{2} - \frac{2v_1 + 1}{3} \right) dv_2$$

$$= \frac{(1 - v_1)^2}{18},$$

which is equal to his conditional expectation of the buyer's virtual gains in (p^4, x^4):

$$\int_0^1 (W_2(v_2)p^4(v_1,v_2) - x^4(v_1,v_2))\, dv_2 = \int_{(v_1+2)/3}^1 \left(\frac{(2v_2-1)-1+v_1}{2}\right) dv_2$$

$$= \frac{(1-v_1)^2}{18}.$$

Similarly, if $\tilde{V}_2 = v_2 \le \frac{3}{4}$, then the buyer's conditional expectation of his own virtual gains in (p^4, x^4),

$$\int_0^{v_2/3} \left(\frac{2v_2}{3} - \frac{v_2}{2}\right) dv_1 = \frac{(v_2)^2}{18},$$

is equal to his conditional expectation of the seller's virtual gains,

$$\int_0^{v_2/3} \left(\frac{v_2}{2} - 2v_1\right) dv_1 = \frac{(v_2)^2}{18}.$$

For $v_1 \le \frac{1}{4}$ or $v_2 \ge \frac{3}{4}$, these equalities do not hold, but L_1 and L_2 from (7.6) are constant over these intervals, so that the corresponding objective function (7.5) puts no weight on these valuations. Thus, with respect to the virtual valuations in (7.7), (p^4, x^4) is both virtually ex post efficient and virtually equitable, except for some weak types that get no weight in the corresponding objective function. These are necessary conditions for a neutral bargaining solution derived in Myerson (1984). However, more important, they demonstrate that (p^4, x^4) can be justified as both efficient and equitable, in a newly recognized sense.

7.5 The lemon problem: Feasibility and efficiency

Let us now consider some trading problems in which the seller has private information related to the quality of the object being sold, so that the value of the object to the buyer is a function of the seller's valuation. To keep the problem tractable, let us assume that the seller knows this function and the buyer has no private information. We may call this the *lemon problem,* after Akerlof's (1970) seminal paper "The Market for Lemons," which studied a special case of this problem, in a market context. (In colloquial American, a bad used car is a "lemon.")

Again, let trader 1 be the only seller and trader 2 be the only potential buyer of a single indivisible object. Both have risk-neutral utility for money. The quality of the object, which is known only to the seller, is measured by the random variable $\tilde{V}_1$, which is the value of the object to the seller. The buyer has a probability distribution for $\tilde{V}_1$ with cumulative distribution $F(v_1) = \text{Prob}(\tilde{V}_1 \leq v_1)$, and with a continuous density $f(v_1) = F'(v_1)$ that is positive over a bounded interval $0 \leq v_1 \leq M$. The value of the object to the buyer is $g(\tilde{V}_1)$, where $g: [0,M] \rightarrow \mathbb{R}$ is a continuous function.

A direct trading mechanism for the lemon problem is characterized by two outcome functions, $p: [0,M] \rightarrow [0,1]$ and $x: [0,M] \rightarrow \mathbb{R}$, where $p(v_1)$ is the probability of trade occurring and $x(v_1)$ is the expected revenue to the seller, if the seller's valuation equals v_1. The expected gain to the buyer from (p,x) is

$$U_2(p,x) = \int_0^M (g(v_1)p(v_1) - x(v_1))\, dF(v_1).$$

The expected gain to the seller from (p,x) if his valuation equals v_1 is

$$U_1(v_1,p,x) = x(v_1) - v_1 p(v_1).$$

In this context, mechanism (p,x) is incentive compatible if and only if, for every v_1 and t_1 in $[0,M]$,

$$U_1(v_1,p,x) \geq x(t_1) - v_1 p(t_1).$$

Mechanism (p,x) is individually rational if and only if $U_2(p,x) \geq 0$ and, for every v_1 in $[0,M]$, $U_1(v_1,p,x) \geq 0$. As before, a mechanism is feasible if and only if it is incentive compatible and individually rational.

(In this formulation, we are assuming that the terms of trade cannot be made conditional on the actual quality of the object, only on the seller's report of it. Presumably, the buyer will eventually learn the quality of the object if he buys it, but too late to renegotiate the price.)

The following proposition characterizes the set of feasible mechanisms.

Proposition 3. Given any function $p: [0,M] \rightarrow [0,1]$, there exists some function $x(\cdot)$ such that (p,x) is a feasible mechanism for the lemon problem if and only if $p(\cdot)$ is a weakly decreasing function and

$$\int_0^M \left(g(v_1) - v_1 - \frac{F(v_1)}{f(v_1)} \right) p(v_1) f(v_1)\, dv_1 \geq 0.$$

In general, for any incentive-compatible mechanism (p,x), $p(\cdot)$ is weakly decreasing,

$$U_1(M,p,x) + U_2(p,x) = \int_0^M \left(g(v_1) - v_1 - \frac{F(v_1)}{f(v_1)} \right) p(v_1) f(v_1) \, dv_1$$

and, for every v_1 in $[0,M]$,

$$U_1(v_1,p,x) = U_1(M,p,x) + \int_{v_1}^M p(s) \, ds.$$

Proof. The proof of the equation for $U_1(v_1,p,x)$ and of p decreasing is exactly as in the proof of theorem 1 of Myerson and Satterthwaite (1983). The equation for $U_1(M,p,x) + U_2(p,x)$ is derived from the following chain of equalities:

$$\int_0^M (g(v_1) - v_1) p(v_1) f(v_1) \, dv_1 = \int_0^M U_1(v_1,p,x) f(v_1) \, dv_1 + U_2(p,x)$$

$$= \int_0^M \int_{v_1}^M p(s) \, ds \, f(v_1) \, dv_1 + U_1(M,p,x) + U_2(p,x)$$

$$= \int_0^M F(v_1) p(v_1) \, dv_1 + U_1(M,p,x) + U_2(p,x).$$

Finally, if p is weakly decreasing and satisfies the inequality in proposition 3, then we can construct a feasible mechanism by using

$$x(v_1) = v_1 p(v_1) + \int_{v_1}^M p(s) \, ds,$$

which is straightforward to check.

As in the symmetric uniform example, our next task is to characterize the efficient mechanisms for the lemon problem. Again, we use the term *efficient* in the sense of weak interim incentive efficiency; that is, (p,x) is efficient if and only if there exists no other incentive-compatible mechanism $(\hat{p},\hat{x})$ such that $U_2(\hat{p},\hat{x}) > U_2(p,x)$ and, for every v_1, $U_1(v_1\hat{p},\hat{x}) > U_1(v_1,p,x)$.

For any number s between 0 and M, let $(p^{(s)}, x^{(s)})$ denote the mechanism

$$p^{(s)}(v_1) = \begin{cases} 1 & \text{if } v_1 \leq s, \\ 0 & \text{if } v_1 > s; \end{cases}$$

$$x^{(s)}(v_1) = \begin{cases} s & \text{if } v_1 \leq s, \\ 0 & \text{if } v_1 > s. \end{cases}$$

We may refer to any such mechanism $(x^{(s)}, p^{(s)})$ as a *simple mechanism*, since there are only two possible outcomes: Either the object is sold for s dollars (if $\tilde{V}_1 \leq s$) or it is not sold at all. These simple mechanisms are important because they represent the extreme points of the set of incentive-compatible mechanisms for the lemon problem, up to addition of a lump-sum transfer between buyer and seller. To understand why, note that any incentive-compatible mechanism differs by a lump-sum transfer (i.e., a constant added to $x(\cdot)$) from an incentive-compatible mechanism with $U_1(M, p, x) = 0$. By proposition 3, any such mechanism is then characterized completely by the weakly decreasing function p; and both $U_1(v_1)$ and U_2 are linear functions of p. However, any weakly decreasing function from $[0, M]$ into $[0, 1]$ can be approximated arbitrarily closely (except possibly on a countable set) by a convex combination of the step functions $\{p^{(s)}\}$. Since we are assuming that F is a continuous distribution, changing p on a countable set would not change any of the expected payoffs in proposition 3. (Without this continuity assumption, we would have to distinguish $(p^{(s)}, x^{(s)})$ from the mechanism in which the object is sold for s dollars if and only if $\tilde{V}_1 < s$, and we also would add such mechanisms to the list of extreme points.)

A mechanism is efficient for the lemon problem if and only if it maximizes some linear functional of the form

$$\int_0^M U_1(v_1, p, x) \, dL_1(v_1) + U_2(p, x) \tag{7.8}$$

over the set of all incentive-compatible mechanisms, where $L_1(\cdot)$ is weakly increasing, $L_1(0) = 0$, and $L_1(M) = 1$. However, the maximum of any such linear functional must be attained at some simple mechanism $(p^{(s)}, x^{(s)})$, because these are the extreme points. (Similarly, the maximum of any linear functional subject to one linear constraint can always be attained at a simple mechanism or a linear combination of two simple mechanisms. Thus, as Samuelson [1984] has shown, the seller's ex ante optimum, subject to nonnegative expected utility for the buyer, can always be attained at a mechanism with a one-step or two-step p function.)

To characterize the set of efficient mechanisms for the lemon problem, we need some additional definitions. Let $Y(s)$ denote the expected gain to the buyer from mechanism $(p^{(s)}, x^{(s)})$; that is,

$$Y(s) = U_2(p^{(s)}, x^{(s)}) = \int_0^s (g(v_1) - s)f(v_1)\, dv_1.$$

Let $\overline{Y}: [0,M] \to \mathbb{R}$ be the lowest concave function that is greater than or equal to $Y(\cdot)$ and has a slope between 0 and -1 everywhere. That is, $\overline{Y}$ differs from the concave hull of Y only in that $\overline{Y}$ is constant over the interval where the concave hull is increasing, and $\overline{Y}$ has slope -1 over any interval where the concave hull is decreasing at a steeper slope than -1. Finally, let $L_1^*: [0,M] \to [0,1]$ be defined such that $L_1^*(0) = 0$, $L_1^*(M) = 1$, and

$$L_1^*(v_1) = -\overline{Y}'(v_1)$$

at every v_1 in $(0,M)$ where the derivative $\overline{Y}'$ is defined. (Define L_1^* by left continuity when $\overline{Y}'$ jumps.) Notice that L_1^* is an increasing function, since $\overline{Y}$ is concave. Note also that $\overline{Y}(0) = \max_{s \in [0,M]} Y(s)$.

The set of efficient mechanisms for the lemon problem has a remarkably simple structure: It is a flat set contained in a hyperplane. That is, given any two efficient mechanisms, their convex combination is also efficient. The function L_1^* gives us the normal to this flat efficient set, as is shown in the following proposition.

Proposition 4. Let (p,x) be any incentive-compatible mechanism for the lemon problem. Then, (p,x) is efficient if and only if

$$\int_0^M U_1(v_1', p, x)\, dL_1^*(v_1) + U_2(p,x) = \overline{Y}(0). \tag{7.9}$$

Equivalently, (p,x) is efficient if and only if p satisfies the following three conditions: $p(0) = 1$ if $\overline{Y}(0) > 0$, $p(M) = 0$ if $\overline{Y}(M) > Y(M)$, and

$$\int_0^M (\overline{Y}(v_1) - Y(v_1))\, dp(v_1) = 0,$$

so that p must be constant over any interval in which $\overline{Y} > Y$.

Proof. Notice first that, from the definition of Y,

$$Y(0) = 0 \quad \text{and} \quad Y'(v_1) = (g(v_1) - v_1)f(v_1) - F(v_1).$$

Now, using proposition 3, for any incentive-compatible mechanism (p,x),

$$\int_0^M U_1(v_1,p,x)\, dL_1^*(v_1) + U_2(p,x)$$

$$= \int_0^M \int_{v_1}^M p(s)\, ds\, dL_1^*(v_1) + U_1(M,p,x) + U_2(p,x)$$

$$= \int_0^M L_1^*(v_1)p(v_1)\, dv_1 + \int_0^M ((g(v_1) - v_1)f(v_1) - F(v_1))p(v_1)\, dv_1$$

$$= \int_0^M (Y'(v_1) - \overline{Y}'(v_1))p(v_1)\, dv_1$$

$$= \overline{Y}(0)p(0) - (\overline{Y}(M) - Y(M))p(1) + \int_0^M (\overline{Y}(v_1) - Y(v_1))\, dp(v_1).$$

Since $\overline{Y}(v_1) \geq Y(v_1)$ for all v_1, the decreasing function p that maximizes the last expression must have $p(0) = 1$ if $\overline{Y}(0) > 0$, $p(M) = 0$ if $\overline{Y}(M) > Y(M)$, and must be constant over any interval in which $\overline{Y} > Y$. (Note that the integral is not positive, because p is decreasing.) Such a function p does exist and gives the maximum value $\overline{Y}(0)$. Thus, p is efficient if it satisfies (7.9).

Let r_1 be the lowest number in $[0,M]$ such that $\overline{Y}(r_1) = Y(r_1)$, and let r_2 be the highest such number (see Figure 7.6). Now, consider any simple mechanism $(p^{(s)},x^{(s)})$ that does not satisfy (7.9). Then,

$$\overline{Y}(0) > \int_0^M U_1(v_1,p^{(s)},x^{(s)})\, dL_1^*(v_1) + U_2(p^{(s)},x^{(s)}) = \overline{Y}(0) - (\overline{Y}(s) - Y(s)),$$

and so $\overline{Y}(s) > Y(s)$. We will show that $(p^{(s)},x^{(s)})$ is not efficient. There are three cases to consider: $s < r_1$, $s > r_2$, and $r_1 < s < r_2$.

If $s < r_1$, then $Y(s) < Y(r_1) = \overline{Y}(0)$. Therefore, the buyer would strictly prefer $(p^{(r_1)},x^{(r_1)})$ to $(p^{(s)},x^{(s)})$. The seller also prefers $(p^{(r_1)},x^{(r_1)})$ to $(p^{(s)},x^{(s)})$, since

$$U_1(v_1,p^{(s)},x^{(s)}) = \max\{0,s - v_1\}$$

is increasing in s. Thus, $(p^{(s)},x^{(s)})$ is not efficient.

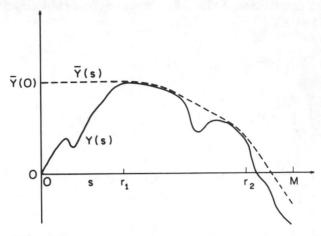

Figure 7.6

If $s > r_2$, then $Y(s) < Y(r_2) + (r_2 - s)$, since the slope of $\overline{Y}$ is -1 for all $v_1 > r_2$. Thus, the buyer would strictly prefer to pay $s - r_2$ as a lump-sum transfer and then implement $(p^{(r_2)}, x^{(r_2)})$. It is easy to see that the seller would also prefer this change, and so $(p^{(s)}, x^{(s)})$ is not efficient.

If $r_1 < s < r_2$, then there exist numbers s_1, s_2, and λ such that $s = \lambda s_1 + (1 - \lambda)s_2$, $0 \leq \lambda \leq 1$, and $Y(s) < \lambda Y(s_1) + (1 - \lambda)Y(s_2)$. Therefore, the buyer would strictly prefer to randomize between $(p^{(s_1)}, x^{(s_1)})$ with probability λ and $(p^{(s_2)}, x^{(s_2)})$ with probability $1 - \lambda$, rather than use $(p^{(s)}, x^{(s)})$. Since $U_1(v_1, p^{(s)}, x^{(s)})$ is a convex function of s, the seller would also prefer this randomization. Thus, $(p^{(s)}, x^{(s)})$ is not efficient if it violates (7.9).

Any efficient mechanism must be equal to some convex combination of efficient simple mechanisms plus a lump-sum transfer. Thus, any efficient mechanism must satisfy condition (7.9) of proposition 4.

Furthermore, if $g(v_1) \geq v_1$ for every v_1 between 0 and M, then $L_1^*(v_1) \leq F(v_1)$ for every v_1 between 0 and M. That is, if the object is always worth more to the buyer than to the seller, then L_1^* puts more weight on the higher valuations of the seller than F does, in the sense of first-order stochastic dominance. To verify this fact, observe that if $L_1^*(v_1) > 0$, then there exists some w_1 such that $w_1 \leq v_1$ and

$$L_1^*(v_1) = -\overline{Y}'(v_1) = -Y'(w_1) = F(w_1) - (g(w_1) - w_1) \leq F(w_1) \leq F(v_1).$$

To illustrate these results, consider first the example studied by Akerlof (1970), in which $M = 2$, $F(v_1) = .5v_1$, and $g(v_1) = 1.5v_1$. That is, the seller's valuation is uniformly distributed over [0,2], and the object would always be worth 50 percent more to the buyer, if he knew the seller's valuation. For this example,

$$g(v_1) - v_1 - F(v_1)/f(v_1) = -.5v_1 < 0.$$

So, by proposition 3, there does not exist for Akerlof's example any feasible mechanism with a positive probability of trade.

For a second example, let $M = 1$, $F(v_1) = v_1$, and $g(v_1) = v_1 + \alpha$, where $0 < \alpha < 1$. We may call this the *uniform additive* lemon problem. For this example, there are many feasible mechanisms (e.g., $(p^{(s)}, x^{(s)})$ for every $s \le 2\alpha$). To apply proposition 4,

$$Y(s) = \int_0^s (v_1 + \alpha - s)\, dv_1 = \alpha s - .5s^2,$$

and so

$$\overline{Y}(s) = \begin{cases} \alpha s - .5s^2 = Y(s) & \text{if } \alpha \le s \le 1, \\ .5\alpha^2 > Y(s) & \text{if } s < \alpha. \end{cases}$$

Thus, an incentive-compatible mechanism (p,x) is efficient if and only if $p(v_1) = 1$ for every v_1 such that $0 \le v_1 < \alpha$.

7.6   The uniform additive lemon problem: Neutral solutions

As in Section 7.4, let us now try to make some prediction as to which efficient mechanism may actually be implemented by the seller and buyer in the lemon problem if they negotiate face to face. To simplify the analysis, we will consider only one specific case: the uniform additive case with $\alpha = .4$. That is, the seller knows his valuation $\tilde{V}_1$, which is a uniform random variable on [0,1], and if the buyer gets the object, then it will be ultimately worth $\tilde{V}_1 + .4$ to him. The seller is free to make statements to the buyer about $\tilde{V}_1$, but there is no way for the buyer to verify whether these claims are true or false until after the negotiations end and the terms of trade are fixed.

For simplicity, let us begin with the assumption that the buyer has all of the bargaining ability, perhaps because he is much more articulate and persuasive in negotiations than the seller. The best feasible mechanism for the buyer is the simple mechanism $(p^{(.4)}, x^{(.4)})$. That is, if the buyer can control the negotiations, he wants to make a nonnegotiable first-and-final offer to buy the object for a price of .4. To verify that this mechanism is optimal, note that

$$Y(s) = \int\limits_0^s (v_1 + .4 - s) \, dv_1 = .4s - .5s^2,$$

which is maximized at $s = .4$. The buyer's expected gain from his optimal mechanism is $Y(.4) = .08$.

Now, let us assume that the seller has all of the bargaining ability. The problem of determining which mechanism he should implement is a problem of mechanism design by an informed principal, as studied in Myerson (1983).

Among the simple mechanisms, $U_1(v_1, p^{(s)}, x^{(s)})$ is increasing in s, and $U_2(p^{(s)}, x^{(s)}) \geq 0$ if and only if $s \leq .8$. That is, for any price s that is higher than .8, the expected value of the object to the buyer conditional on $\tilde{V}_1 \leq s$ is $.5s + .4$, which is less than s, and so the buyer expects to lose. Thus, if the seller were to implement a simple mechanism, his best choice would be $(p^{(.8)}, x^{(.8)})$. (Even though the object is always worth more to the buyer than to the seller, there is no feasible mechanism in which the buyer always gets the object, because the inequality in proposition 3 would fail if $p(v_1) = 1$ for all v_1.)

The mechanism $(p^{(.8)}, x^{(.8)})$ maximizes both the probability of trade and the seller's ex ante expected gains $(\int_0^1 U_1(v_1, p, x) \, dv_1)$ over all feasible mechanisms for this example. Thus, if the seller could have selected any feasible mechanism before he learned $\tilde{V}_1$, he would certainly have selected $(p^{(.8)}, x^{(.8)})$. However, this argument is not necessarily relevant to our analysis of negotiations, because we are assuming that the seller knows $\tilde{V}_1$ when the negotiations begin, and this is not a repeated game.

There exist other mechanisms that the seller would prefer to $(p^{(.8)}, x^{(.8)})$ if $\tilde{V}_1$ were relatively high. (Observe that $U_1(v_1, p^{(.8)}, x^{(.8)}) = 0$ if $v_1 \geq .8$.) For example, consider $(\hat{p}, \hat{x})$ defined by

$$\hat{p}(v_1) = e^{-v_1/.4} \quad \text{and} \quad \hat{x}(v_1) = (v_1 + .4)\hat{p}(v_1).$$

That is, the seller demands that the buyer pay the full value $q = \tilde{V}_1 + .4$, and the buyer accepts with probability $e^{-(q-.4)/.4}$. It is straightforward to check that $(\hat{p}, \hat{x})$ is individually rational and incentive compatible. If the seller demanded a higher price, the decrease in probability of acceptance would be just enough to prevent him from gaining more. Among all of the mechanisms in which the buyer never loses ex post (*safe mechanisms*, in the terminology of Myerson (1983)), $(\hat{p}, \hat{x})$ is the best for the seller. If $\tilde{V}_1 \geq .74$, then the seller would prefer $(\hat{p}, \hat{x})$ over $(p^{(.8)}, x^{(.8)})$ ($.4e^{-.74/.4} > .8 - .74$).

One theory of negotiations that *cannot* be valid is to suggest that the seller would implement $(p^{(.8)},x^{(.8)})$ if $\tilde{V}_1 < .74$ and would implement $(\hat{p},\hat{x})$ if $\tilde{V}_1 \geq .74$. The buyer would refuse to buy the object for .8 if he believed that the seller would make this demand only when $\tilde{V}_1 < .74$, because the conditionally expected value of the object to him would be only $.74/2 + .4 = .77$. On the other hand, the buyer would never expect losses in $(\hat{p},\hat{x})$, even if he inferred that $\tilde{V}_1 \geq .74$. Therefore, $(p^{(.8)},x^{(.8)})$ is blocked for the seller by $(\hat{p},\hat{x})$, since the buyer knows that $(p^{(.8)},x^{(.8)})$ would be implemented by the seller only if $\tilde{V}_1$ were in $[0,.74]$, where the buyer expects to lose on average.

However, $(\hat{p},\hat{x})$ is not an efficient mechanism, because any efficient mechanism must have $p(v_1) = 1$ for all v_1 in the interval $[0,.4)$ (where $\overline{Y}(v_1) > Y(v_1)$), as was shown at the end of Section 7.5. For example, $(\hat{p},\hat{x})$ is dominated by the mechanism (p^*,x^*) defined by

$$p^*(v_1) = \begin{cases} 1 & \text{if } v_1 < .4, \\ .5e^{-(v_1 - .4)/.4} & \text{if } v_1 \geq .4; \end{cases}$$

$$x^*(v_1) = \begin{cases} .6 & \text{if } v_1 < .4, \\ (v_1 + .4)p(v_1) & \text{if } v_1 \geq .4. \end{cases}$$

It is straightforward to verify that (p^*,x^*) is incentive compatible, that $U_2(p^*,x^*) = U_2(\hat{p},\hat{x}) = 0$, and that $U_1(v_1,p^*,x^*) > U_1(v_1,\hat{p},\hat{x})$ for all v_1. Also, (p^*,x^*) is efficient because a sale will always occur if $0 \leq V_1 < .4$. If $\tilde{V}_1 \geq .4$, then the seller insists on getting the buyer's reservation price $\tilde{V}_1 + .4$, and the buyer's probability of acceptance decreases in the price in such a way as to keep the seller honest. It can be shown (see Section 7.7) that this mechanism (p^*,x^*) is a neutral optimum for the seller, in the sense of Myerson (1983).

Thus, we predict that the outcome of negotiations would be as in $(p^{(.4)},x^{(.4)})$ if the buyer had all of the bargaining ability, and would be as in (p^*,x^*) if the seller had all of the bargaining ability.

Let us now assume that the buyer and seller have equal bargaining ability. In this case, the solution theory of Myerson (1984) identifies the average of these mechanisms, $(p^{\circ},x^{\circ}) = .5(p^{(.4)},x^{(.4)}) + .5(p^*,x^*)$, as a neutral bargaining solution. That is, the neutral bargaining solution is

$$p^{\circ}(v_1) = \begin{cases} 1 & \text{if } v_1 < .4, \\ .25e^{-(v_1 - .4)/.4} & \text{if } v_1 \geq ,4; \end{cases}$$

$$x^{\circ}(v_1) = \begin{cases} .5 & \text{if } v_1 < .4, \\ (v_1 + .4)p^{\circ}(v_1) & \text{if } v_1 \geq .4. \end{cases}$$

Notice that if $\tilde{V}_1 \geq .4$, the seller fully exploits the buyer in (p°,x°) by charging him $\tilde{V}_1 + .4$ when trade occurs, just as in (p^*,x^*). However, the probability of trade occurring when $\tilde{V}_1 \geq .4$ in $(p°,x°)$ is half of what it is in (p^*,x^*). Thus, the neutral bargaining solution $(p°,x°)$ has the property of arrogance of strength, defined in Section 7.4. That is, if the traders have equal bargaining ability but the seller is in a surprisingly strong bargaining position, then the outcome is the same as when the seller has all of the bargaining ability, except that the probability of disagreement is higher.

The mechanism $(p°,x°)$ may seem more equitable when we look at virtual-utility payoffs. For this example, the function L_1^*, which supports all efficient mechanisms (as stated in proposition 4), is

$$L_1^*(v_1) = -\overline{Y}'(v_1) = \begin{cases} 0 & \text{if } v_1 < .4, \\ v_1 - .4 & \text{if } .4 \leq v_1 < 1, \\ 1 & \text{if } v_1 = 1. \end{cases}$$

Because the seller's valuation is uniformly distributed over $[0,1]$, his virtual valuation is $2\tilde{V}_1 - L_1^*(\tilde{V}_1)$ (as in the symmetric uniform trading problem), which equals $\tilde{V}_1 + .4$ if $\tilde{V}_1 \geq .4$ (except at the endpoint $\tilde{V}_1 = 1$, which has zero probability). Thus, when $\tilde{V}_1 \geq .4$, the seller's virtual valuation equals the buyer's valuation, and so $\tilde{V}_1 + .4$ is the only virtually equitable price. (Since the buyer has no private information in this example, his virtual and real valuations are equal.) When $\tilde{V}_1$ is in the interval $[0,.4)$, the seller's average virtual valuation (i.e., $2\tilde{V}_1$) is .4, and the buyer's average valuation (i.e., $\tilde{V}_1 + .4$) is .6; thus, the price .5 in $(p°,x°)$ is virtually equitable on average.

7.7   Derivation of the neutral solutions

To show how the solution concepts of Myerson (1983, 1984) are applied to the examples of this chapter, let us first consider a discrete approximation to the lemon problem. That is, let δ be a small number, and let $T_1 = \{0, \delta, 2\delta, 3\delta, \ldots, M\}$ be the set of possible seller's valuations for the object. Let $f(v_1)\delta = F(v_1) - F(v_1 - \delta)$ be the probability that $\tilde{V}_1 = v_1$ for any v_1 that is a multiple of δ. Given an increasing function L_1 as in (7.8), let $\ell(v_1) = (L_1(v_1) - L_1(v_1 - \delta))/\delta$. Thus, the discrete analog of (7.8) is

$$\sum_{v_1 \in T_1} ((x(v_1) - v_1 p(v_1))\ell(v_1)\delta + (g(v_1)p(v_1) - x(v_1))f(v_1)\delta). \tag{7.10}$$

It can be shown that, for the discrete lemon problem, local incentive compatibility implies global incentive compatibility. (That is, if for every v_1, the seller with valuation v_1 could not gain by reporting $v_1 + \delta$ for $v_1 - \delta$, then the seller cannot gain by any lie.) Furthermore, in most cases the binding incentive constraint for the seller is the one in the upward direction, that is, that the seller should not gain by reporting $v_1 + \delta$ when his valuation is v_1. So, let $A(v_1)$ denote the shadow price of this incentive constraint in the problem of maximizing (7.10) among all incentive-compatible mechanisms. Then, the Lagrangian function for this problem can be written

$$\sum_{v_1 \in T_1} ((x(v_1) - v_1 p(v_1))\ell(v_1)\delta + (g(v_1)p(v_1) - x(v_1))f(v_1)\delta$$

$$+ A(v_1)((x(v_1) - v_1 p(v_1)) - (x(v_1 + \delta) - v_1 p(v_1 + \delta))))$$

$$= \sum_{v_1 \in T_1} ([(\ell(v_1)\delta + A(v_1))(x(v_1) - v_1 p(v_1)) - A(v_1 - \delta)(x(v_1)$$

$$- (v_1 - \delta)p(v_1))] + (g(v_1)p(v_1) - x(v_1))f(v_1)\delta). \tag{7.11}$$

The coefficient of $x(v_1)$ in this Lagrangian formula must be zero, since $x(v_1)$ is an unconstrained variable. Thus, we must have, for all v_1,

$$A(v_1) - A(v_1 - \delta) = f(v_1)\delta - \ell(v_1)\delta,$$

and so

$$A(v_1) = F(v_1) - L_1(v_1).$$

The seller's *virtual utility* is defined in Myerson (1984) as the bracketed expression in (7.11) divided by the probability $f(v_1)\delta$. That is, if the seller's valuation is v_1, if his expected revenue is $y = x(v_1)$, and if his probability of sale is $q = p(v_1)$, then his *virtual-utility payoff* $z_1(v_1)$ is defined as

$$z_1(v_1) = \frac{(\ell(v_1)\delta + A(v_1))(y - v_1 q) - A(v_1 - \delta)(y - (v_1 - \delta)q)}{f(v_1)\delta}$$

$$= y + \left(v_1 + \frac{F(v_1 - \delta) - L_1(v_1 - \delta)}{f(v_1)} \right) q.$$

Equivalently, if we let $u_1(v_1) = y - v_1 q$ denote the seller's actual-utility payoff when his valuation is v_1 (and let $u(v_1 - \delta) = y - (v_1 - \delta)q$), then the seller's virtual-utility payoff can be rewritten

$$z_1(v_1) = u_1(v_1) + \left(\frac{F(v_1 - \delta) - L_1(v_1 - \delta)}{f(v_1)} \right) \left(\frac{u_1(v_1) - u_1(v_1 - \delta)}{\delta} \right).$$

At the maximum of (7.10), the product of incentive constraint times shadow price is always zero, by complementary slackness, and so (7.11) implies that

$$\sum_{v_1 \in T_1} (x(v_1) - v_1 p(v_1))\ell(v_1)\delta = \sum_{v_1 \in T_1} z_1(v_1)f(v_1)\delta.$$

Now, letting δ go to zero, let us return to the continuous version of the lemon problem. The immediately preceding three equations become

$$z_1(v_1) = x(v_1) + \left[v_1 + \left(\frac{F(v_1) - L_1(v_1^-)}{f(v_1)} \right) \right] p(v_1), \qquad (7.12)$$

$$z_1(v_1) = u_1(v_1) + \left(\frac{F(v_1) - L_1(v_1^-)}{f(v_1)} \right) u_1'(v_1), \qquad (7.13)$$

$$\int_0^M u_1(v_1) \, dL_1(v_1) = \int_0^M z_1(v_1) f(v_1) \, dv_1, \qquad (7.14)$$

respectively, where

$$L_1(v_1^-) = \lim_{\delta \to 0^+} L_1(v_1 - \delta).$$

The seller's virtual valuation for the object is, from (7.12),

$$W_1(v_1) = v_1 + \frac{F(v_1) - L_1(v_1^-)}{f(v_1)}. \qquad (7.15)$$

In the uniform case with $F(v_1) = v_1$ on $[0,1]$, when L_1 is continuous this virtual valuation is simply $W_1(v_1) = 2v_1 - L_1(v_1)$, as in Section 7.4.

Since the buyer has no private information in the lemon problem and gets a weight of 1 in the objective functions (7.8) and (7.10), the buyer's virtual utility is the same as his real utility.

We are now ready to verify that (p°, x°) is the neutral bargaining solution for the uniform additive lemon problem with $g(v_1) = v_1 + .4$. To prove this, we must apply theorem 4 of Myerson (1984), which gives necessary and sufficient conditions for a neutral bargaining solution. This theorem requires us to consider a sequence of virtual-utility scales, each of which is generated by an objective function that puts positive weight on all types of all players. (For the lemon problem, this means that L_1 must be strictly increasing over the whole range of possible valuations.) For each virtual-utility scale, we must first compute the *virtually equitable allocations,* in which the traders plan to divide the available virtual gains equally among themselves in every state. Then, we must solve equations (7.13) and (7.14) to find which allocations of real utility would correspond to the equitable allocations of virtual utility. The corresponding allocations of real utility are called the *warranted claims* of the seller and the buyer. If the limit of these warranted claims (over the sequence of virtual-utility scales) does not exceed the actual expected utility generated by our mechanism for any type, then that mechanism is a neutral bargaining solution.

The sequence of objectives that supports $(p°,x°)$ is

$$L_1^\epsilon(v_1) = \begin{cases} \epsilon v_1 & \text{if } 0 \le v_1 < \dfrac{.4}{1-\epsilon}, \\ v_1 - .4 & \text{if } \dfrac{.4}{1-\epsilon} \le v_1 < 1, \\ 1 & \text{if } v_1 = 1, \end{cases}$$

where the index ϵ is positive and converging to zero. Notice that each L_1^ϵ is strictly increasing over $[0,1]$ and converges to L_1^* of Section 7.6 as ϵ goes to zero.

With respect to $L_1 = L_1^\epsilon$, if the seller's actual valuation is v_1, then his virtual valuation (from (7.15)) is

$$W_1(v_1) = \begin{cases} (2 - \epsilon)v_1 & \text{if } 0 \le v_1 < \dfrac{.4}{1-\epsilon}, \\ v_1 + .4 & \text{if } \dfrac{.4}{1-\epsilon} \le v_1 \le 1, \end{cases}$$

and so the total available virtual gains from trade are

$$g(v_1) - W_1(v_1) = \begin{cases} .4 - (1 - \epsilon)v_1 & \text{if } 0 \le v_1 < \dfrac{.4}{1-\epsilon}, \\ 0 & \text{if } \dfrac{.4}{1-\epsilon} \le v_1 \le 1. \end{cases}$$

The virtually equitable allocation with respect to L_1^ϵ would give the seller half of these virtual gains; that is, he would get

$$z_1(v_1) = \begin{cases} .2 - .5(1 - \epsilon)v_1 & \text{if } 0 \le v_1 < \dfrac{.4}{1-\epsilon}, \\ 0 & \text{if } \dfrac{.4}{1-\epsilon} \le v_1 \le 1 \end{cases}$$

in virtual utility when his valuation is v_1. The seller's warranted claims with respect to L_1^ϵ are the values of $u_1(v_1)$ that satisfy (7.13) and (7.14) for this z_1 function. That is, u_1 must satisfy

$$.2 - .5(1 - \epsilon)v_1 = u_1(v_1) + (1 - \epsilon)v_1u_1'(v_1)$$
$$\text{if } 0 \leq v_1 < .4/(1 - \epsilon),$$

$$0 = u_1(v_1) + .4u_1'(v_1) \quad \text{if } .4/(1 - \epsilon) \leq v_1 \leq 1,$$

$$\int_0^1 (.2 - .5(1 - \epsilon)v_1)\, dv_1 = \int_0^{.4/(1-\epsilon)} u_1(v_1)\epsilon\, dv_1$$
$$+ \int_{.4/(1-\epsilon)}^1 u_1(v_1)\, dv_1 + .4u_1(1).$$

(The term $.4u_1(1)$ comes from the jump in L_1^ϵ at $v_1 = 1$.) The unique solution to these equations is

$$u_1(v_1) = \begin{cases} .2 - .5\left(\dfrac{1 - \epsilon}{2 - \epsilon}\right)v_1 & \text{if } 0 \leq v_1 < \dfrac{.4}{1 - \epsilon}, \\[2ex] .2\left(\dfrac{1 - \epsilon}{2 - \epsilon}\right)e^{(1/(1-\epsilon)-v_1/.4)} & \text{if } \dfrac{.4}{1 - \epsilon} \leq v_1 \leq 1. \end{cases}$$

As ϵ goes to zero, these warranted claims converge to

$$u_1(v_1) = \begin{cases} .2 - \dfrac{v_1}{4} & \text{if } 0 \leq v_1 < .4, \\[2ex] .1e^{-(v_1-.4)/.4} & \text{if } .4 \leq v_1 \leq 1. \end{cases}$$

The seller's actual payoff from the mechanism $(p°, x°)$ is

$$U_1(v_1, p°, x°) = \begin{cases} .5 - v_1 & \text{if } 0 \leq v_1 < .4, \\ .1e^{-(v_1-.4)/.4} & \text{if } .4 \leq v_1 \leq 1, \end{cases}$$

and so $U_1(v_1, p°, x°) \geq u_1(v_1)$ for all v_1 in $[0,1]$.

Since the buyer has only one possible type in this problem, his warranted claim with respect to L_1^ϵ is simply half of the expected virtual gains from trade:

$$u_1 = \int_0^{.4} (.2 - .5(1 - \epsilon)v_1)\, dv_1 = .04(1 + \epsilon).$$

As ϵ goes to zero, this expression converges to $.04 = U_2(p°, x°)$.

So the mechanism $(p°, x°)$ fulfills all of the limiting warranted claims, and therefore is a neutral bargaining solution, by theorem 4 of Myerson (1984).

If the seller had all of the bargaining ability, then his warranted claims for each type would be computed in the same way, except that he would get all of the virtual gains from trade, instead of half. This would simply double the values of z_1 and u_1 throughout the preceding derivation. Since $U_1(v_1,p^*,x^*) = 2U_1(v_1,p^\circ,x^\circ)$ for all v_1, (p^*,x^*) satisfies the conditions for a seller's neutral optimum, given in theorem 7 of Myerson (1983).

Let us now consider the symmetric uniform trading problem and show that (p^4,x^4) is a neutral bargaining solution, as was claimed in Section 7.5. The formulas for the seller's virtual utility, (7.12) through (7.15), can be derived for the symmetric uniform trading problem exactly as in the lemon problem. (Now, $M = 1$, $F(v_1) = v_1$, and $f(v_1) = 1$.) Analogous formulas define virtual utility for the buyer, who now also has private information.

For any small $\epsilon > 0$, we let

$$
L_1^\epsilon(v_1) = \begin{cases} \epsilon v_1 & \text{if } 0 \le v_1 < \dfrac{1}{4 - 2\epsilon}, \\[2ex] \left(\dfrac{4 - 3\epsilon}{3 - 2\epsilon}\right) v_1 - \dfrac{1 - \epsilon}{3 - 2\epsilon} & \text{if } \dfrac{1}{4 - 2\epsilon} \le v_1 \le 1; \end{cases}
$$

$$
L_2^\epsilon(v_2) = \begin{cases} \left(\dfrac{4 - 3\epsilon}{3 - 2\epsilon}\right) v_2 & \text{if } 0 \le v_2 \le \dfrac{3 - 2\epsilon}{4 - 2\epsilon}, \\[2ex] \epsilon v_2 + (1 - \epsilon) & \text{if } \dfrac{3 - 2\epsilon}{4 - 2\epsilon} < v_2 \le 1. \end{cases}
$$

Notice that each L_i^ϵ is strictly increasing over $[0,1]$, and converges to L_i of equation (7.6) as ϵ goes to zero.

The seller's warranted claims with respect to L_1^ϵ and L_2^ϵ are determined by the following equations:

$$
u_1(v_1) + (v_1 - L_1^\epsilon(v_1))u_1'(v_1) = z_1(v_1),
$$

$$
\int_0^1 u_1(v_1) \, dL_1^\epsilon(v_1) = \int_0^1 z_1(v_1) \, dv_1,
$$

where

$$
z_1(v_1) = .5 \int_0^1 \max\{0, W_2(v_2) - W_1(v_1)\} \, dv_2,
$$

$$
W_1(v_1) = 2v_1 - L_1^\epsilon(v_1),
$$

$$
W_2(v_2) = 2v_2 - L_2^\epsilon(v_2).
$$

It can be shown (somewhat tediously) that the unique solution to these equations is

$$u_1(v_1) = \begin{cases} \dfrac{3-\epsilon}{16-8\epsilon} - .5v_1 + \left(\dfrac{2-\epsilon}{4}\right)(v_1)^2 & \text{if } 0 \le v_1 < \dfrac{1}{4-2\epsilon}, \\[3mm] \left(\dfrac{2-\epsilon}{12-8\epsilon}\right)(1-v_1)^2 & \text{if } \dfrac{1}{4-2\epsilon} \le v_1 \le 1. \end{cases}$$

As ϵ converges to zero, these warranted claims converge to

$$u_1(v_1) = \begin{cases} \dfrac{3-8v_1+8(v_1)^2}{16} & \text{if } 0 \le v_1 < .25, \\[3mm] \dfrac{(1-v_1)^2}{6} & \text{if } .25 \le v_1 \le 1. \end{cases}$$

If the seller's valuation is v_1, then his actual expected utility from the mechanism (p^4, x^4) is

$$U_1(v_1, p^4, x^4) = \begin{cases} \dfrac{6-15v_1+12(v_1)^2}{32} & \text{if } 0 \le v_1 < .25, \\[3mm] \dfrac{(1-v_1)^2}{6} & \text{if } .25 \le v_1 \le 1. \end{cases}$$

It is straightforward to check that $U_1(v_1, p^4, x^4) \ge u_1(v_1)$ for every v_1, and thus (p^4, x^4) fulfills all of the seller's limiting warranted claims. A symmetric argument shows that (p^4, x^4) satisfies the buyer's limiting warranted claims for every v_2 as well. Thus, (p^4, x^4) satisfies the conditions for a neutral bargaining solution.

A final remark about the uniqueness of these solutions is in order. The general conditions for a neutral bargaining solution are well determined, in the sense of giving us as many equations as unknowns (see theorem 5 of Myerson (1984)), but there is no general uniqueness theorem. For the symmetric uniform trading problem, some inessential nonuniqueness is known. There exist other functions x such that (p^4, x) is a feasible mechanism, and all of these mechanisms are neutral bargaining solutions giving the same expected utility allocations as (p^4, x^4). Apart from this nonuniqueness in x, it is my unproven belief that (p^4, x^4) is probably the unique neutral bargaining solution for the symmetric uniform trading problem, and that (p°, x°) is the unique neutral bargaining solution for the uniform additive lemon problem considered in Section 7.6.

REFERENCES

Akerlof, G. (1970): The Market for Lemons: Qualitative Uncertainty and the Market Mechanism. *Quarterly Journal of Economics 84*, 488–500.

Chatterjee, K., and W. Samuelson (1983): Bargaining under Incomplete Information. *Operations Research 31*, 835–51.

Holmström, B., and R. B. Myerson (1983): "Efficient and Durable Decision Rules with Incomplete Information. *Econometrica 53*, 1799–1819.

Myerson, R. B. (1979): Incentive Compatibility and the Bargaining Problem. *Econometrica 47*, 61–73.

——— (1983): Mechanism Design by an Informed Principal. *Econometrica 53*, 1767–97.

——— (1984): Two-Person Bargaining Problems with Incomplete Information, *Econometrica 52*, 461–87.

Myerson, R. B., and M. A. Satterthwaite (1983): "Efficient Mechanisms for Bilateral Trading. *Journal of Economic Theory 29*, 265–81.

Nash, J. F. (1950): The Bargaining Problem. *Econometrica 18*, 155–162.

Samuelson, W. (1984): Bargaining under Asymmetric Information. *Econometrica 52*, 995–1005.

CHAPTER 8

Sequential bargaining mechanisms

Peter C. Cramton
YALE UNIVERSITY

8.1 Introduction

A fundamental problem in economics is determining how agreements are reached in situations where the parties have some market power. Of particular interest are questions of efficiency and distribution:

- How efficient is the agreement?
- How can efficiency be improved?
- How are the gains from agreement divided among the parties?

Here, I explore these questions in the context of bilateral monopoly, in which a buyer and a seller are bargaining over the price of an object.

Two features of my analysis, which are important in any bargaining setting, are information and impatience. The bargainers typically have private information about their preferences and will suffer some delay costs if agreement is postponed. Information asymmetries between bargainers will often lead to inefficiencies: The bargainers will be forced to delay agreement in order to communicate their preferences. Impatience will tend to encourage an early agreement and will make the parties' communication meaningful. Bargainers with high delay costs will accept inferior terms of trade in order to conclude agreement early, whereas patient bargainers will choose to wait for more appealing terms of trade.

Some authors have examined the bargaining problem in a static context, focusing solely on the role of incomplete information and ignoring the sequential aspects of bargaining. Myerson and Satterthwaite (1983) analyze bargaining as a direct revelation game. In this game, the players agree to a pair of outcome functions: one that maps the players' statements of their types into an expected payment from buyer to seller, and one that maps the players' statements into a probability of trade. These outcome functions are chosen in such a way that truthful reporting is an

I am indebted to Robert Wilson for his encouragement and inspiration. My thanks to Drew Fudenberg for his helpful comments.

149

equilibrium strategy for the players. An important feature of this game is that it is static: Outcome functions are selected, the players report their true types, and then dice are rolled to determine the payment and whether or not trade occurs. To ensure that the players have the proper incentives for truthful reporting, the game will end with positive probability in disagreement even when there are substantial gains from trade. Thus, in the event that the randomization device calls for disagreement, the players may find themselves in a situation in which it is common knowledge that there are gains from trade.

Chatterjee and Samuelson (1983) analyze a strategic game in which both players make offers simultaneously, and trade occurs at a price between the two offers if the seller's offer is less than the buyer's offer. This game is closely related to the direct revelation game, in that it is static. Moreover, it can be shown that for a particular class of examples, the simultaneous-offers game implements the direct revelation game in which the outcome functions are chosen to maximize the players' ex ante utility. As in the direct revelation game, this game ends with positive probability in a state in which both bargainers know that gains are possible (since their respective reservation prices have been revealed), and yet they are forced to walk away from the bargaining table. Thus, the bargaining game assumes implicitly that the players are able to commit to walking away without trading, after it has been revealed that substantial gains from trade exist.

In situations where the bargainers are unable to make binding agreements, it is unrealistic to use a bargaining mechanism that forces them to walk away from known positive gains from trade. Such mechanisms violate a broad interpretation of *sequential rationality* as discussed by Selten (1976) (in terms of subgame perfection), and later by Kreps and Wilson (1982), if one applies sequential rationality not only to the hypothesized game, but to the game form as well. In particular, one should restrict attention to mechanisms that satisfy sequential rationality: It must never be common knowledge that the mechanism induced at any point in time is dominated by an alternative mechanism.

When there is uncertainty about whether or not gains from trade exist, any static game will violate sequential rationality. The players must have time to learn through each other's actions whether gains are possible. In a sequential game, the players communicate their preferences by exhibiting their willingness to delay agreement. Bargainers who anticipate large gains from trade (low-cost sellers and high-valuation buyers) will be unwilling to delay agreement, and so will propose attractive terms of trade that the other is likely to accept early in the bargaining process. On the other hand, high-cost sellers and low-valuation buyers will prefer to wait for better terms of trade. Static games must use a positive probability of disagreement to ensure incentive compatibility, where the probability of disagreement increases as the gains from trade shrink. The advantage of delaying agreement rather than forbidding agreement is that mechanisms can be constructed in which negotiations continue so long as each bargainer expects positive gains. Thus, the bargaining will not end in a state in which it is common knowledge that the players want to renege on their agreed-upon outcome.

Two approaches can be taken in the analysis of perfect bargaining games. The first approach is to examine specific extensive-form games, which determine the set of actions available to the players over time. Intrinsic to any bargaining process is the notion of offers and replies: Bargaining consists of a sequence of offers and decisions to accept or reject these offers. Who makes the offers; the time between offers, responses, and counteroffers; and the possibilities for commitment are determined by the underlying communication technology present in the bargaining setting. This communication technology will imply, in part, a particular bargaining game in extensive form. Cramton (1984), Sobel and Takahashi (1983), and Fudenberg, Levine, and Tirole (Chapter 5 in this volume) illustrate the analysis of particular extensive forms that are perfect bargaining games.

The second approach, and the one adopted in this chapter, is to analyze a general direct revelation game, which maps the players' beliefs into bargaining outcomes. An important distinction between direct revelation games and strategic games is that the direct revelation game does not explicitly model the *process* of bargaining. The sequence of offers and replies that eventually leads to an outcome is not studied in the direct revelation game as it is in strategic games. However, embedded in each sequential bargaining mechanism is a particular form of learning behavior, which can be analyzed. In addition, much can be learned about how information and impatience influence the efficiency of the bargaining outcome and the allocation of gains between players. Thus, even though bargainers will not play direct revelation games in practice, analysis of these games is a useful tool to determine how well the bargainers can hope to do by adopting an appropriate strategic game.

The difference between the static direct revelation game analyzed by Myerson and Satterthwaite (1983) and the sequential direct revelation game considered here is that in the sequential game, the outcome functions not only determine the probability and terms of trade, but also dictate *when* trade is to take place. In the static game trade may occur only at time zero whereas in the sequential game trade may occur at different times depending on the players' reports of their private information.

Thus, by analyzing sequential bargaining mechanisms, one is able to infer what the players' learning process is over time. Furthermore, by analyzing mechanisms that are sequentially rational, one can study what bargaining outcomes are possible when the bargainers are unable to make binding agreements.

The introductory discussion presented in this chapter considers the simplest type of sequential bargaining games in which the players' time preferences are described by known and fixed discount rates. I begin by characterizing the class of perfect bargaining mechanisms, which satisfy the desirable properties of incentive compatibility (i.e., each player reports his type truthfully), individual rationality (i.e., every potential player wishes to play the game), and sequential rationality (i.e., it is never common knowledge that the mechanism induced over time is dominated by an alternative mechanism). It is shown that ex post efficiency is unobtainable by any incentive-compatible and individually rational mechanism when the bargainers are uncertain about whether or not they should trade immediately. I conclude by finding those mechanisms that maximize the players' ex ante utility, and show that such mechanisms violate sequential rationality. Thus, the bargainers would be better off ex ante if they could commit to a mechanism before they knew their private information. In terms of their ex ante payoffs, if the seller's delay costs are higher than those of the buyer, then the bargainers are better off adopting a sequential bargaining game rather than a static mechanism; however, when the buyer's delay costs are higher, then a static mechanism is optimal.

The methodology of this paper is based on Myerson and Satterthwaite (1983). I have freely borrowed from their insightful work in much of my analysis. Complete proofs for each proposition, even though many are only slightly different from the proofs found in Myerson and Satterthwaite, are given as an aid to the reader.

8.2   Formulation

Two parties, a buyer and a seller, are bargaining over the price of an object that can be produced by the seller at a cost s and is worth b to the buyer. The seller's cost s and the buyer's valuation b are also called their *reservation prices,* since they represent, respectively, the minimum and maximum price at which each party would agree to trade. Both the buyer and the seller have costs of delaying the bargaining process. Specifically, the value of the object is discounted in the future according to the positive discount rates ρ for the seller and σ for the buyer. Thus, the payoffs, if the bargainers agree to trade at the discounted price x at time t, are $x - se^{-\rho t}$

for the seller and $be^{-\sigma t} - x$ for the buyer. Should the players fail to reach agreement, both of their payoffs are zero. Implicit in this formulation is the assumption that the bargainers discount future money at the same rate, so that at any time t the discounted payment by the buyer equals the discounted revenue to the seller. Without this assumption, it would be possible for the players to achieve an infinite payoff by having the player with the lower discount rate lend an arbitrarily large amount of money to the other player.

The buyer, although aware of his own valuation b, does not know the seller's cost of production s, but assesses this cost to be distributed according to the distribution $F(s)$, with a positive density $f(s)$ on $[\underline{s}, \bar{s}]$. Similarly, the seller knows his cost s, but only assess the buyer's valuation to be distributed according to the distribution $G(b)$, with a positive density $g(b)$ on $[\underline{b}, \bar{b}]$. Their discount rates and the distributions of the potential buyers and sellers are common knowledge. In addition, it is assumed that both the buyer and the seller are interested solely in maximizing their expected monetary gain.

To summarize, let $\langle F, G, \rho, \sigma \rangle$ be a sequential direct revelation game, where

$F = $ the distribution of the seller's cost s on $[\underline{s}, \bar{s}]$,
$G = $ the distribution of the buyer's valuation b on $[\underline{b}, \bar{b}]$,
$\rho = $ the seller's discount rate for the object,
$\sigma = $ the buyer's discount rate for the object.

In the revelation game, the players' actions consist of reports of their types, which are mapped into the bargaining outcome by the bargaining mechanism. Thus, the seller s reports that his cost is $s' \in [\underline{s}, \bar{s}]$, and the buyer b reports that his valuation is $b' \in [\underline{b}, \bar{b}]$. The revelation game is said to be *direct* if the equilibrium strategies of the players involve truthful reporting, that is, $(s', b') = (s, b)$. The important role of direct revelation games stems from the fact that one can, without loss of generality, restrict attention to direct mechanisms. For any Nash equilibrium of any bargaining game, there is an equivalent direct mechanism that always yields the same outcomes. This well-known result is called the *revelation principle*. Given any mechanism M that maps reports into outcomes, and a set of equilibrium strategies x that maps true types into reported types, then the composition $\hat{M} = M \circ x$ is a direct mechanism that achieves the same outcomes as the mechanism M.

For the revelation game $\langle F, G, \rho, \sigma \rangle$, a *sequential bargaining mechanism* is the pair of outcome functions $\mathcal{T}(\cdot | \cdot, \cdot)$ and $x(\cdot, \cdot)$, where $\mathcal{T}(t | s, b)$ is the probability distribution that the object will be transferred to the buyer at time t, and $x(s, b)$ is the discounted expected payment from the buyer to the seller, given that the seller and buyer report the reservation prices s and b, respectively.

Typically, randomization of the outcomes over time is not necessary. Without randomization, the outcome function $\mathcal{T}$ can be replaced by the function $t(\cdot,\cdot)$, which determines the time of trade given the players' reports. A sequential bargaining mechanism, then, is the set of outcome functions $\langle t,x \rangle$ where $t(s,b)$ is the time of trade and $x(s,b)$ is the discounted expected payment, given that the seller reports s and the buyer reports b. Most bargaining mechanisms seen in practice require that the exchange of money and goods take place at the same time. Such a requirement is not restrictive in this model, because there is no benefit to be gained by exchanging money at a different time from the exchange of the good, since both players have identical time preferences for money. For reasons of tractability, I will frequently restrict attention to the simplified mechanism $\langle t,x \rangle$.

8.3   Perfect bargaining mechanisms

The weakest requirements one would wish to impose on the bargaining mechanism $\langle \mathcal{T},x \rangle$ in the direct revelation game are (1) individual rationality, that is, that everyone wishes to play the game, and (2) incentive compatibility, that is, that the mechanism induces truth telling. In addition, when the bargainers are unable to make binding commitments, one needs the further restriction of sequential rationality: It must never be common knowledge that the mechanism induced over time is dominated by an alternative mechanism. Bargaining schemes that satisfy incentive compatibility, individual rationality, and sequential rationality are called *perfect bargaining mechanisms*. The adjective *perfect* is adopted because of the close relationship between perfect bargaining mechanisms in the direct revelation game and perfect (or sequential) equilibria in an infinite-horizon extensive-form game. It remains to be proven that a sequential bargaining mechanism is perfect if and only if it is a perfect equilibrium for some infinite-horizon extensive-form game. This issue will be addressed in future research.

In this section, I derive necessary and sufficient conditions for the sequential bargaining mechanism to be perfect. The incentive-compatibility and individual-rationality conditions were first established in Myerson and Satterthwaite (1983), and later extended to the case of multiple buyers and sellers by Wilson (1982) and Gresik and Satterthwaite (1983). It is important to realize that these properties are actually necessary and sufficient conditions for any Nash equilibrium of any bargaining game, since every Nash equilibrium induces a direct revelation mechanism, as mentioned in Section 8.2.

Incentive compatibility

In order to define and determine the implications of incentive compatibility on the sequential bargaining mechanism $\langle \mathcal{T}, x \rangle$, it is convenient to divide each player's expected payoff into two components as follows. Let

$$S(s) = \int_{\underline{b}}^{\bar{b}} x(s,b) g(b) \, db, \qquad P(s) = \int_{\underline{b}}^{\bar{b}} \int_{0}^{\infty} e^{-\rho t} \, d\mathcal{T}(t \mid s,b) \, g(b) \, db,$$

$$B(b) = \int_{\underline{s}}^{\bar{s}} x(s,b) f(s) \, ds, \qquad Q(b) = \int_{\underline{s}}^{\bar{s}} \int_{0}^{\infty} e^{-\sigma t} \, d\mathcal{T}(t \mid s,b) \, f(s) \, ds,$$

where $S(s)$ is the discounted expected revenue and $P(s)$ the discounted probability of agreement for seller s, and $B(b)$ is the discounted expected payment and $Q(b)$ the discounted probability of agreement for buyer b. Thus, the seller's and buyer's discounted expected payoffs are given by

$$U(s) = S(s) - sP(s) \qquad \text{and} \qquad V(b) = bQ(b) - B(b),$$

respectively.

Formally, the sequential bargaining mechanism $\langle \mathcal{T}, x \rangle$ is *incentive compatible* if every type of player wants to report truthfully his type; that is, for all s and s' in $[\underline{s}, \bar{s}]$ and for all b and b' in $[\underline{b}, \bar{b}]$,

$$U(s) \geq S(s') - sP(s') \qquad \text{and} \qquad V(b) \geq bQ(b') - B(b').$$

Lemma 1. If the sequential bargaining mechanism $\langle \mathcal{T}, x \rangle$ is incentive compatible, then the seller's expected payoff U is convex and decreasing, with derivative $dU/ds = -P$ almost everywhere on $[\underline{s}, \bar{s}]$; his discounted probability of agreement P is decreasing; and

$$U(s) - U(\bar{s}) = \int_{\underline{s}}^{\bar{s}} P(u) \, du \qquad \text{and} \qquad S(s) - S(\bar{s}) = \int_{\underline{s}}^{\bar{s}} -u \, dP(u). \quad (S)$$

Similarly, the buyer's expected payoff V is convex and increasing, with derivative $dV/db = Q$ almost everywhere on $[\underline{b}, \bar{b}]$; his discounted probability of agreement Q is increasing; and

$$V(b) - V(\underline{b}) = \int_{\underline{b}}^{b} Q(u) \, du \qquad \text{and} \qquad B(b) - B(\underline{b}) = \int_{\underline{b}}^{b} u \, dQ(u). \quad (B)$$

Proof. By definition, seller s achieves the payoff $U(s) = S(s) - sP(s)$. Alternatively, seller s can pretend to be seller s', in which case his payoff is $S(s') - sP(s')$. In the direct revelation game, the seller s must not want to pretend to be seller s', and so we have $U(s) \geq S(s') - sP(s')$ for all $s,s' \in [\underline{s}, \bar{s}]$, or

$$U(s) \geq U(s') - (s - s')P(s'),$$

implying that U has a supporting hyperplane at s' with slope $-P(s') \leq 0$. Thus, U is convex and decreasing with derivative $(dU/ds)(s) = -P(s)$ almost everywhere, and P must be decreasing, which implies the first integral in (S) (I will use the Stieltjes integral throughout, so that any discontinuities in the probability of agreement are accounted for in the integral.) From integration by parts,

$$\int_{s}^{\bar{s}} P(u) \, du = \bar{s}P(\bar{s}) - sP(s) - \int_{s}^{\bar{s}} u \, dP(u),$$

which, together with the definition of U, yields the second integral in (S). The proof for the buyer is identical.

Lemma 1 indicates the stringent requirements that incentive compatibility imposes on the players' utilities. In particular, it suggests how one can construct an incentive-compatible payment schedule x, given a probability of agreement distribution $\mathcal{T}$ for which the seller's discounted probability of agreement $P(s)$ is decreasing in s and the buyer's discounted probability of agreement $Q(b)$ is increasing in b.

Lemma 2.   Given the sequential bargaining mechanism $\langle \mathcal{T}, x \rangle$ such that P is decreasing, Q is increasing, and S and B satisfy (S) and (B) of lemma 1, then $\langle \mathcal{T}, x \rangle$ is incentive compatible.

Proof.   A mechanism is incentive compatible for the seller if for all $s,s' \in [\underline{s}, \bar{s}]$,

$$S(s) - sP(s) \geq S(s') - sP(s').$$

Rearranging terms yields the following condition for incentive compatibility:

$$s(P(s') - P(s)) + S(s) - S(s') \geq 0. \tag{S'}$$

From (S), we have

$$S(s) - S(s') = \int_{s}^{s'} -u \, dP(u),$$

and from the fundamental theorem of integral calculus,

$$s(P(s') - P(s)) = s \int_s^{s'} dP(u).$$

Adding the last two equations results in

$$s(P(s') - P(s)) + S(s) - S(s') = \int_s^{s'} (s - u) \, dP(u) \geq 0,$$

where the inequality follows because the integrand $(s - u) \, dP(u)$ is non-negative for all $s, u \in [s, \bar{s}]$, since P is decreasing. Hence, $\langle \mathcal{T}, x \rangle$ satisfies the incentive-compatibility condition (S'). An identical argument follows for the buyer.

Individual rationality

The sequential bargaining mechanism $\langle \mathcal{T}, x \rangle$ is *individually rational* if every type of player wants to play the game; that is, for all s in $[s, \bar{s}]$ and b in $[\underline{b}, \bar{b}]$,

$$U(s) \geq 0 \quad \text{and} \quad V(b) \geq 0.$$

In light of the monotonicity of U and V proven in lemma 1, any incentive-compatible mechanism $\langle \mathcal{T}, x \rangle$ will satisfy individual rationality if the extreme high-cost seller and low-valuation buyer receive a nonnegative payoff; that is, an incentive-compatible mechanism $\langle \mathcal{T}, x \rangle$ is individually rational if and only if $U(\bar{s}) \geq 0$ and $V(\underline{b}) \geq 0$.

The following lemma describes how one can check whether or not a sequential bargaining mechanism is individually rational. It is convenient to state the lemma in terms of the simplified bargaining mechanism $\langle t, x \rangle$ rather than in terms of $\langle \mathcal{T}, x \rangle$. Recall that for the sequential bargaining mechanism $\langle t, x \rangle$, we have

$$S(s) = \int_{\underline{b}}^{\bar{b}} x(s,b)g(b) \, db, \qquad P(s) = \int_{\underline{b}}^{\bar{b}} e^{-\rho t(s,b)} g(b) \, db,$$

$$B(b) = \int_s^{\bar{s}} x(s,b)f(s) \, ds, \qquad Q(b) = \int_s^{\bar{s}} e^{-\sigma t(s,b)} f(s) \, ds.$$

Lemma 3. If the sequential bargaining mechanism $\langle t,x \rangle$ is incentive compatible and individually rational, then

$$U(\bar{s}) + V(\underline{b}) = \mathscr{E}\left\{\left(b - \frac{1 - G(b)}{g(b)}\right) e^{-\sigma t(s,b)}\right.$$
$$\left. - \left(s + \frac{F(s)}{f(s)}\right) e^{-\rho t(s,b)}\right\} \geq 0, \quad (IR)$$

where the expectation is taken with respect to s and b.

Proof. First note that from lemma 1, for $\langle t,x \rangle$ to be individually rational, it must be that $U(\bar{s}) \geq 0$ and $V(\underline{b}) \geq 0$. For the seller, we have

$$\int_{\underline{s}}^{\bar{s}} U(s)f(s) \, ds = U(\bar{s}) + \int_{\underline{s}}^{\bar{s}} \int_{s}^{\bar{s}} P(u) \, du \, f(s) \, ds$$

$$= U(\bar{s}) + \int_{\underline{s}}^{\bar{s}} F(s)P(s) \, ds$$

$$= U(\bar{s}) + \int_{\underline{b}}^{\bar{b}} \int_{\underline{s}}^{\bar{s}} F(s)e^{-\rho t(s,b)}g(b) \, ds \, db, \qquad (US)$$

where the first equality follows from lemma 1 and the second equality results from changing the order of integration. Similarly, for the buyer we have

$$\int_{\underline{b}}^{\bar{b}} V(b)g(b) \, db = V(\underline{b}) + \int_{\underline{b}}^{\bar{b}} \int_{\underline{s}}^{\bar{s}} (1 - G(b))e^{-\sigma t(s,b)}f(s) \, ds \, db. \qquad (UB)$$

Rearranging terms in (US) and (UB) and substituting the definitions for $U(s)$ and $V(b)$, result in the desired expression (IR) for $U(\bar{s}) + V(\underline{b})$.

Lemma 4. If the function $t(\cdot,\cdot)$ is such that P is decreasing, Q is increasing, and (IR) is satisfied, then there exists a function $x(\cdot,\cdot)$ such that $\langle t,x \rangle$ is incentive compatible and individually rational.

Proof. The proof is by construction. Let

$$x(s,b) = \int_{\underline{b}}^{b} u \, dQ(u) + \int_{\underline{s}}^{s} u \, dP(u) + c,$$

where c is a constant chosen such that $V(\underline{b}) = 0$. To compute c, notice that

$$V(\underline{b}) = \underline{b}Q(\underline{b}) - \int_{\underline{s}}^{\bar{s}} x(s,\underline{b})f(s)\, ds$$

$$= \underline{b}Q(\underline{b}) - c - \int_{\underline{s}}^{\bar{s}} \int_{\underline{s}}^{s} u\, dP(u)\, f(s)\, ds$$

$$= \underline{b}Q(\underline{b}) - c + \int_{\underline{s}}^{\bar{s}} s(1 - F(s))\, dP(s) = 0.$$

Thus,

$$c = \underline{b}Q(\underline{b}) + \int_{\underline{s}}^{\bar{s}} s(1 - F(s))\, dP(s).$$

Incentive compatibility for the seller is verified by showing that the seller s is better off reporting s than $s' \neq s$: For all $s,s' \in [\underline{s},\bar{s}]$,

$$s(P(s') - P(s)) + S(s) - S(s') = s \int_{s}^{s'} dP(u) - \int_{s}^{s'} u\, dP(u)$$

$$= \int_{s}^{s'} (s - u)\, dP(u) \geq 0,$$

since P is decreasing. An identical argument holds for the buyer.

Since $V(\underline{b}) = 0$ and $\langle t,x \rangle$ is incentive compatible and satisfies (IR), it follows from lemma 3 that $U(\bar{s}) \geq 0$. Thus, the bargaining mechanism $\langle t,s \rangle$ is incentive compatible and individually rational.

Sequential rationality

To understand how learning takes place in a sequential bargaining mechanism, it is best to interpret the direct revelation game as follows. At time zero (but after the players know their private information), the players agree to adopt a particular sequential bargaining mechanism $\langle t,x \rangle$ that is interim efficient. (Note that any interim-efficient mechanism can be chosen as a Nash equilibrium in an appropriately defined "choice-of-mechanism" game.) The players then report their private information in sealed envelopes to a mediator, who will then implement the mechanism $\langle t,x \rangle$. (Actually, a third party is not necessary, since the role of the mediator can be carried out by a computer programmed by the bargainers to execute the mechanism.) After opening the envelopes, the mediator does not announce the outcome immediately by saying something like, "Trade shall occur two months from now at the price of one thousand dollars," but instead waits until two months have passed and *then* announces, "Trade shall occur now at the price of one thousand dollars." The mediator must wait until the time of trade in order that the mechanism be sequentially rational, since otherwise the bargainers would have an incentive to ignore the mediator's announcement and trade immediately.

As time passes, the players are able to refine their inferences about the other player's private information based on the information that the mediator has not yet made an announcement about. Initially, it is common knowledge that the players' valuations are distributed according to the probability distributions F and G, but after τ units of time the common-knowledge beliefs become the distributions F and G conditioned on the fact that an announcement has not yet been made; that is,

$$F_\tau(s) = F(s \mid t(s,b) > \tau) \quad \text{and} \quad G_\tau(b) = G(b \mid t(s,b) > \tau).$$

Thus, at any time $\tau > 0$, the mechanism $\langle t,x \rangle$ induces an outcome function $t(s,b) = t(s,b \mid F_\tau, G_\tau)$ for all s and b. A mechanism $\langle t,x \rangle$ is *sequentially rational* if at every time $\tau \geq 0$, the induced outcome function $t(s,b \mid F_\tau, G_\tau)$ is interim efficient, that is, there does not exist a mechanism $\langle t',x' \rangle$ preferable to $\langle t,x \rangle$ at some time $\tau \geq 0$ for all remaining traders and strictly preferred by at least one trader.

The following lemma relates the definition of sequentially rational to common-knowledge dominance.

Lemma 5. A sequential bargaining mechanism $\langle t,x \rangle$ is sequentially rational if and only if it is never common knowledge that the mechanism $t(\,\cdot\,,\,\cdot \mid F_\tau, G_\tau)$ that it induces over time is dominated by an alternative mechanism.

Proof. From theorem 1 of Holmström and Myerson (1983), we know that a mechanism is interim efficient if and only if it is not common knowledge dominated by any other incentive-compatible and individually rational mechanism.

A necessary condition for a mechanism to be sequentially rational is that the bargainers continue negotiations so long as each expects positive gains from continuing. For the model here, since there are no transaction costs (only delay costs), this means that negotiations cannot end if there exists a pair of players that have not yet come to an agreement, but for which agreement is beneficial at some point in the future. Formally, for the bargaining mechanism $\langle t,x \rangle$ to be sequentially rational, it must be that for all potential players, a failure to reach agreement implies that there is some point beyond which agreement is never beneficial; that is, for all s and b,

$$t(s,b) = \infty \Longrightarrow \text{there exists } \hat{t} \geq 0 \text{ such that for every } \tau > \hat{t}, s \geq be^{(\rho - \sigma)\tau}.$$

The condition $s \geq be^{(\rho - \sigma)\tau}$ is simply a statement that trade is not beneficial at time τ, since

$$x - se^{-\rho\tau} + be^{-\sigma\tau} - x \geq 0 \Longleftrightarrow se^{-\rho\tau} \geq be^{-\sigma\tau} \Longleftrightarrow s \geq be^{(\rho - \sigma)\tau}.$$

Notice that the strength of this requirement depends on the relative magnitudes of the players' discount rates. When $\rho > \sigma$, then $e^{(\rho - \sigma)\tau} \to \infty$ as $\tau \to \infty$, and so for all potential pairs of players it is always the case that there exists a time at which trade is beneficial. Thus, when $\rho > \sigma$, the mechanism $\langle t,x \rangle$ is sequentially rational only if trade always occurs; that is, $t(s,b) < \infty$ for all s and b. Likewise, when $\rho < \sigma$, then $e^{(\rho - \sigma)\tau} \to 0$ as $\tau \to \infty$, and so for every pair of players there is always a point at which trade becomes undesirable for all times in the future. Finally, if $\rho = \sigma$, then the necessary condition for sequential rationality becomes $t(s,b) = \infty \Longrightarrow s \geq b$; that is, trade must occur whenever the gains from trade are initially positive.

To state this necessary condition in a lemma, it will be useful to define $\mathscr{B}$ as the set of potential traders for which trade is always beneficial at some time in the future; that is,

$$\mathscr{B} = \{(s,b) \mid \rho > \sigma \text{ or } (\rho = \sigma \text{ and } s \leq b)\}.$$

Lemma 6. Any mechanism $\langle t,x \rangle$ that excludes trade over a nonempty subset of $\mathscr{B}$ violates sequential rationality.

Proof. Let $\mathscr{N} \subset \mathscr{B}$ be the set for which trade never occurs. Then, at some point in time τ, the induced mechanism has $t(s,b \mid F_\tau, G_\tau) = \infty$ for all remaining traders, which includes $\mathscr{N}$. However, this mechanism is not interim efficient, since it is dominated by a mechanism that results in a positive probability of trade for some traders in $\mathscr{N}$ (a partially pooling equilibrium with this property will always exist).

I claim that sequential rationality is a necessary condition for rationality in games with incomplete information in which commitment is not possible. If a mechanism is not sequentially rational, then at some point in time it is common knowledge that *all* potential agents would prefer an alternative mechanism and hence this alternative mechanism will be adopted by the agents at that point in time. Thus, it would be inconsistent for the players to believe that the original mechanism would be carried out faithfully.

Necessary and sufficient conditions for perfection

Lemmas 1 through 5 are summarized in the following theorem, which gives necessary and sufficient conditions for the sequential bargaining mechanism $\langle t,x \rangle$ to be perfect.

Theorem 1. A sequential bargaining mechanism $\langle t,x \rangle$ is incentive compatible if and only if the functions

$$S(s) = \int_{\underline{b}}^{\bar{b}} x(s,b)g(b)\, db, \quad P(s) = \int_{\underline{b}}^{\bar{b}} e^{-\rho t(s,b)}g(b)\, db,$$

$$B(b) = \int_{\underline{s}}^{\bar{s}} x(s,b)f(s)\, ds, \quad Q(b) = \int_{\underline{s}}^{\bar{s}} e^{-\sigma t(s,b)}f(s)\, ds$$

are such that P is decreasing, Q is increasing, and

$$S(s) - S(\bar{s}) = \int_{s}^{\bar{s}} -u\, dP(u) \quad \text{and} \quad B(b) - B(\underline{b}) = \int_{\underline{b}}^{b} u\, dQ(u). \quad (IC)$$

Furthermore, for t such that P is decreasing and Q is increasing, there exists an x such that $\langle t,x \rangle$ is incentive compatible and individually rational if and only if

$$U(\bar{s}) + V(\underline{b}) = \mathscr{E}\left\{ \left(b - \frac{1 - G(b)}{g(b)} \right) e^{-\sigma t(s,b)} - \left(s + \frac{F(s)}{f(s)} \right) e^{-\rho t(s,b)} \right\} \geq 0. \quad (IR)$$

Finally, the mechanism $\langle t,x \rangle$ is sequentially rational if and only if it is never common knowledge that the mechanism it induces over time is dominated by an alternative mechanism.

8.4   Efficiency

The set of perfect bargaining mechanisms is typically quite large, which means that there are many extensive-form games with equilibria satisfying incentive compatibility, individual rationality, and sequential rationality. To narrow down this set, it is natural to assume additional efficiency properties. Three notions of efficiency, described at length by Holmström and Myerson (1983), are ex post, interim, and ex ante efficiency. The difference between these concepts centers on what information is available at the time of evaluation: Ex ante efficiency assumes that comparisons are made before the players know their private information, interim efficiency assumes that the players know only their private information, and ex post efficiency assumes that all information is known.

Ex post efficiency

Ideally, one would like to find perfect bargaining mechanisms that are ex post efficient. The mechanism $\langle t,x \rangle$ is *ex post efficient* if there does not exist an alternative mechanism that can make both players better off in terms of their ex post utilities (after all of the information is revealed). (This is often called *full-information efficiency* in the literature. Holmström and Myerson (1983) term this "ex post classical efficiency" to distinguish it from their concept of ex post incentive-efficiency, in which incentive constraints are recognized.) Equivalently, for a mechanism to be ex post efficient, it must maximize a weighted sum $\alpha_1(s,b)u(s) + \alpha_2(s,b)v(b)$ of the players' ex post utilities for all s and b, where $\alpha_1(\,\cdot\,,\cdot\,)$, $\alpha_2(\,\cdot\,,\cdot\,) \geq 0$ and the ex post utilities of seller s and buyer b are

$$u(s,b) = x(s,b) - se^{-\rho t(s,b)} \quad \text{and} \quad v(s,b) = be^{-\sigma t(s,b)} - x(s,b).$$

Since the payoff functions are additively separable in money and goods, and thus utility is transferable between players, we can assume equal weights (i.e., $\alpha_1(s,b) = \alpha_2(s,b) = 1$ for every s,b) without loss of generality. To simplify notation, define $p(s,b) = e^{-t(s,b)}$, so that $p(s,b)^\rho$ is the discounted probability of agreement for seller s given that the buyer has valuation b, and $p(s,b)^\sigma$ is the discounted probability of agreement for buyer b given that the seller has cost s. With this change, a sequential bargaining mechanism becomes the pair of functions $\langle p,x \rangle$ where p: $[\underline{s},\bar{s}] \times [\underline{b},\bar{b}] \rightarrow [0,1]$. The bargaining mechanism $\langle p,x \rangle$, then, is ex post efficient if for all $s \in [\underline{s},\bar{s}]$ and $b \in [\underline{b},\bar{b}]$, the function $p(s,b)$ is chosen to solve the program

$$\max_{p \in [0,1]} \pi(p) = bp^\sigma - sp^\rho.$$

The first-order condition is

$$\frac{d\pi}{dp} = \sigma b p^{\sigma-1} - \rho s p^{\rho-1} = 0$$

or

$$p = \left(\frac{\sigma b}{\rho s}\right)^{1/(\rho-\sigma)}.$$

Checking the boundary conditions and assuming that $\underline{s}, \underline{b} \geq 0$ yields

$$p^*(s,b) = \begin{cases} 1 & \text{if } s < b, \rho s \leq \sigma b, \\ \left(\dfrac{\sigma b}{\rho s}\right)^{1/(\rho-\sigma)} & \text{if } \rho > \sigma, \rho s > \sigma b, \\ 0 & \text{if } \rho \leq \sigma, s \geq b. \end{cases} \qquad (EP)$$

The following theorem demonstrates that it is impossible to find ex post-efficient mechanisms if the bargainers are uncertain whether or not trade should occur immediately. This result is shown in an example in Cramton (1984).

Theorem 2.   There exists an incentive-compatible, individually rational bargaining mechanism that is ex post efficient if it is common knowledge that trade should occur immediately. However, an ex post-efficient mechanism does not exist if the buyer's delay cost is at least as great as the seller's and it is not common knowledge that gains from trade exist.

Proof.   Suppose that it is common knowledge that trade should occur immediately. Then, three cases are possible: (1) $\rho \leq \sigma$ and $\bar{s} \leq \underline{b}$, (2) $\rho > \sigma$ and $\rho \bar{s} \leq \sigma \underline{b}$, and (3) $\rho = \infty$ and $\sigma < \infty$. What needs to be shown is that $p^*(s,b) = 1$ for all s,b satisfies (IR). For cases (1) and (2),

$$\begin{aligned} U(\bar{s}) + V(\underline{b}) &= \mathscr{E}\left\{\left(b - \frac{1 - G(b)}{g(b)}\right) - \left(s + \frac{F(s)}{f(s)}\right)\right\} \\ &= \mathscr{E}\left\{b - \frac{1 - G(b)}{g(b)}\right\} - \mathscr{E}\left\{s + \frac{F(s)}{f(s)}\right\} \\ &= \int_{\underline{b}}^{\bar{b}} (bg(b) - 1 + G(b))\, db - \int_{\underline{s}}^{\bar{s}} (sf(s) + F(s))\, ds \\ &= bG(b)\,|_{\underline{b}}^{\bar{b}} - \bar{b} + \underline{b} - sF(s)\,|_{\underline{s}}^{\bar{s}} \\ &= \underline{b} - \bar{s} \geq 0, \end{aligned}$$

where the integration is done by parts. In case (3),

$$U(\bar{s}) + V(\underline{b}) = \mathscr{E}\left\{b - \frac{1 - G(b)}{g(b)}\right\} = \underline{b} \geq 0.$$

Then, by lemma 4, there exists an x such that $\langle p, x \rangle$ is incentive compatible and individually rational.

Now, assume that it is not common knowledge that gains from trade exist and the buyer's delay cost is at least as great as the seller's (i.e., $\rho \leq \sigma$). Notice that when $\rho \leq \sigma$, we find that $\langle p, x \rangle$ is ex post efficient if trade occurs without delay whenever there are positive gains from trade:

$$p^*(s, b) = \begin{cases} 1 & \text{if } s < b, \\ 0 & \text{if } s \geq b. \end{cases}$$

Substituting this function for p into (IR) yields

$$U(\bar{s}) + V(\underline{b})$$

$$= \int_{\underline{b}}^{\bar{b}} \int_{\underline{s}}^{\min(b,\bar{s})} (bg(b) + G(b) - 1)f(s) \, ds \, db$$

$$- \int_{\underline{b}}^{\bar{b}} \int_{\underline{s}}^{\min(b,\bar{s})} (sf(s) + F(s)) \, ds \, g(b) \, db$$

$$= \int_{\underline{b}}^{\bar{b}} (bg(b) + G(b) - 1)F(b) \, db - \int_{\underline{b}}^{\bar{b}} \min\{bF(b), \bar{s}\}g(b) \, db$$

$$= -\int_{\underline{b}}^{\bar{b}} (1 - G(b))F(b) \, db + \int_{\bar{s}}^{\bar{b}} (b - \bar{s})g(b) \, db$$

$$= -\int_{\underline{b}}^{\bar{b}} (1 - G(b))F(b) \, db + \int_{\bar{s}}^{\bar{b}} (1 - G(b)) \, db$$

$$= -\int_{\underline{b}}^{\bar{s}} (1 - G(u))F(u) \, du.$$

Thus, any incentive-compatible mechanism that is ex post efficient must have

$$U(\bar{s}) + V(\underline{b}) = - \int\limits_{\underline{b}}^{\bar{s}} (1 - G(u))F(u) \, du < 0,$$

and so it cannot be individually rational.

When the seller's delay cost is greater than the buyer's and it is not common knowledge that trade should occur immediately, a general proof that ex post efficiency is not achievable cannot be given due to the complicated expression for $p^*(s,b)$ in this case. However, analysis of examples (see Section 8.5) suggests that ex post efficiency is typically unobtainable.

Ex ante efficiency

The strongest concept of efficiency, other than ex post efficiency (which is generally unobtainable), that can be applied to games of incomplete information is ex ante efficiency. A player's ex ante utility is his expected utility *before* he knows his type. Thus, given the sequential bargaining mechanism $\langle p,x \rangle$, the seller's and buyer's ex ante utilities are

$$\mathcal{U} = \int\limits_{\underline{s}}^{\bar{s}} U(s)f(s) \, ds = \int\limits_{\underline{s}}^{\bar{s}} \int\limits_{\underline{b}}^{\bar{b}} (x(s,b) - sp(s,b)^\rho)g(b) \, db \, f(s) \, ds,$$

$$\mathcal{V} = \int\limits_{\underline{b}}^{\bar{b}} V(b)g(b) \, db = \int\limits_{\underline{b}}^{\bar{b}} \int\limits_{\underline{s}}^{\bar{s}} (bp(s,b)^\sigma - x(s,b))f(s) \, ds \, g(b) \, db.$$

The mechanism $\langle p,x \rangle$ is *ex ante efficient* if there does not exist an alternative mechanism that can make both players better off in terms of their ex ante utilities. Thus, for a mechanism to be ex ante efficient, it must maximize a weighted sum $\alpha_1 \mathcal{U} + \alpha_2 \mathcal{V}$ of the players' ex ante utilities, where $\alpha_1, \alpha_2 \geq 0$. For tractability and reasons of equity, I will assume equal weights (i.e., $\alpha_1 = \alpha_2 = 1$). (One might think that the assumption of equal weights is made without loss of generality, because the payoff functions here are additively separable in money and goods, and thus utility is transferable between players. Although this intuition is correct in a setting of complete information, it is false when there is incomplete information, because an ex ante transfer of utility will violate individual rationality for some players.) The use of unequal weights would not significantly change the results, but would greatly complicate the analysis.

If the bargainers were to choose a bargaining mechanism *before* they knew their types, it would seem reasonable that they would agree to a scheme that was ex ante efficient. It is generally the case, however, that the players know their private information before they begin negotiations, and therefore would be unable to agree on an ex ante-efficient mechanism, since the players are concerned with their *interim* utilities $U(s)$ and $V(b)$ rather than their ex ante utilities $\mathcal{U}$ and $\mathcal{V}$. Nevertheless, it may be that the sequential bargaining mechanism is chosen by an uninformed social planner or arbitrator, in which case the selection of an ex ante-efficient mechanism would be justified. Alternatively, one might suppose that the choice of a bargaining mechanism is based on established norms of behavior and that these norms have evolved over time in such a way as to produce ex ante-efficient mechanisms. In situations where the choice of a bargaining mechanism does not occur before the players know their types or is not handled by an uninformed third party, ex ante efficiency is too strong a requirement. The weaker requirement of *interim effi-ciency*–that there does not exist a dominating mechanism in terms of the players' interim utilities $U(s)$ and $V(b)$–is more appropriate.

The sum of the players' ex ante utilities for the bargaining mechanism $\langle p,x \rangle$ is given by

$$\mathcal{U} + \mathcal{V} = \int_{\underline{b}}^{\bar{b}} \int_{\underline{s}}^{\bar{s}} (bp(s,b)^{\sigma} - sp(s,b)^{\rho})f(s)g(b)\,ds\,db.$$

A bargaining mechanism, then, is ex ante efficient if it maximizes this sum subject to incentive compatibility and individual rationality:

$$\max_{p(\cdot,\cdot)} \mathcal{E}\{bp(s,b)^{\sigma} - sp(s,b)^{\rho}\}$$

such that $\qquad\qquad\qquad\qquad\qquad\qquad\qquad\qquad\qquad\qquad\qquad$ (P)

$$\mathcal{E}\left\{\left(b - \frac{1 - G(b)}{g(b)}\right)p(s,b)^{\sigma} - \left(s + \frac{F(s)}{f(s)}\right)p(s,b)^{\rho}\right\} \geq 0,$$

where p is chosen such that P is decreasing and Q is increasing. Multiply-ing the constraint by $\lambda \geq 0$ and adding it to the objective function yields the Lagrangian

$$\mathcal{L}(p,\lambda) = \mathcal{E}\left\{\left((1+\lambda)b - \lambda\frac{1-G(b)}{g(b)}\right)p(s,b)^\sigma\right.$$

$$\left. -\left((1+\lambda)s + \lambda\frac{F(s)}{f(s)}\right)p(s,b)^\rho\right\}$$

$$= (1+\lambda)\mathcal{E}\left\{\left[b - \left(\frac{\lambda}{1+\lambda}\right)\left(\frac{1-G(b)}{g(b)}\right)\right]p(s,b)^\sigma\right.$$

$$\left. -\left[s + \left(\frac{\lambda}{1+\lambda}\right)\left(\frac{F(s)}{f(s)}\right)\right]p(s,b)^\rho\right\}.$$

For any $\alpha \geq 0$, define the functions

$$c(s,\alpha) = s + \alpha\frac{F(s)}{f(s)} \quad \text{and} \quad d(b,\alpha) = b - \alpha\frac{1-G(b)}{g(b)}.$$

Then, the Lagrangian (ignoring the constant $(1+\lambda)$) becomes

$$\mathcal{L}(p,\lambda) = \mathcal{E}\{d(b,\alpha)p(s,b)^\sigma - c(s,\alpha)p(s,b)^\rho\},$$

which is easily maximized by pointwise optimization. The first-order condition is

$$\frac{d\mathcal{L}}{dp} = \sigma\,dp^{\sigma-1} - \rho cp^{\rho-1}$$

or

$$p = \left(\frac{\sigma d}{\rho c}\right)^{1/(\rho-\sigma)}.$$

Establishing the boundary conditions and noticing that $c(\cdot,\cdot) \geq 0$ yields the optimal solution

$$p_\alpha(s,b) = \begin{cases} 1 & \text{if } c(s,\alpha) < d(b,\alpha),\ \rho c(s,\alpha) \leq \sigma d(b,\alpha), \\ \left(\dfrac{\sigma d(b,\alpha)}{\rho c(s,\alpha)}\right)^{1/(\rho-\sigma)} & \text{if } \rho > \sigma,\ \rho c(s,\alpha) > \sigma d(b,\alpha) > 0, \\ 0 & \text{if } (\rho \leq \sigma,\ c(s,\alpha) \geq d(b,\alpha)) \text{ or } d(b,\alpha) \leq 0. \end{cases}$$

The following theorem determines how to find an ex ante-efficient mechanism for any sequential bargaining game.

Theorem 3. If there exists an incentive-compatible mechanism $\langle p,x\rangle$ such that $p = p_\alpha$ for some α in $[0,1]$ and $U(\bar{s}) = V(\underline{b}) = 0$, then this mechanism is ex ante efficient. Moreover, if $c(\cdot,1)$ and $d(\cdot,1)$ are increasing functions on $[\underline{s}, \bar{s}]$ and $[\underline{b}, \bar{b}]$, respectively, and ex post efficiency is unobtainable, then such a mechanism must exist.

Proof. The first statement in this theorem follows from the fact that the Lagrangian $\mathcal{L}(p, \lambda)$ is maximized by the function p_α with $\alpha = \lambda/(1 + \lambda)$. Hence, p_α yields an ex ante-efficient mechanism provided that the individual-rationality constraint is binding.

To prove the existence part of the theorem, suppose that $c(\cdot, 1)$ and $d(\cdot, 1)$ are increasing, and that the players are uncertain whether or not trade should occur immediately. Then, for every $\alpha \in [0,1]$, $c(\cdot, \alpha)$ and $d(\cdot, \alpha)$ are increasing, which implies that $p_\alpha(s, b)$ is increasing in s and decreasing in b. Thus, P is decreasing and Q is increasing, as required by incentive compatibility.

It remains to be shown that there is a unique $\alpha \in [0,1]$, for which the individual-rationality constraint is binding. Define

$$R(\alpha) = \mathcal{E}\{d(b,1)(p_\alpha(s,b))^\sigma - c(s,1)(p_\alpha(s,b))^\rho\}$$

so that $R(\alpha)$ is the value of the integral in the individual-rationality constraint as a function of α. First, notice that $R(1) \geq 0$, since the term in the expectation is nonnegative for all s and b. Furthermore, $R(0) < 0$, since there does not exist an ex post-efficient mechanism. Therefore, if $R(\alpha)$ is continuous and strictly increasing in α, then there is a unique $\alpha \in [0,1]$ for which $R(\alpha) = 0$.

The continuity and monotonicity of $R(\cdot)$ are most easily verified by considering two cases.

CASE 1 ($\rho \leq \sigma$). When $\rho \leq \sigma$, then

$$p_\alpha(s,b) = \begin{cases} 1 & \text{if } c(s,\alpha) < d(b,\alpha), \\ 0 & \text{if } c(s,\alpha) \geq d(b,\alpha). \end{cases}$$

Thus, $p_\alpha(s,b)$ is decreasing in α, since

$$d(b,\alpha) - c(s,\alpha) = (b - s) - \alpha \left(\frac{1 - G(b)}{g(b)} + \frac{F(s)}{f(s)} \right)$$

is decreasing in α. Thus, for $\alpha < \beta$, $R(\beta)$ differs from $R(\alpha)$ only because $0 = p_\beta(s,b) < p_\alpha(s,b) = 1$ for some (s,b) where $d(b,\beta) < c(s,\beta)$, and so $d(b,1) < c(s,1)$. Therefore, $R(\cdot)$ is strictly increasing.

To prove that $R(\cdot)$ is continuous, observe that if $c(s,1)$ and $d(b,1)$ are increasing in s and b, then $c(\cdot, \alpha)$ and $d(\cdot, \alpha)$ are strictly increasing for any $\alpha < 1$. So, given b and α, the equation $c(s,\alpha) = d(b,\alpha)$ has at most one solution in s, and this solution varies continuously in b and α. Hence, we may write

$$R(\alpha) = \int\limits_{\underline{b}}^{\overline{b}} \int\limits_{\underline{s}}^{r(b,\alpha)} (d(b,1) - c(s,1))f(s)g(b) \, ds \, db,$$

where $r(b,\alpha)$ is continuous in b and α. Thus, $R(\alpha)$ is continuous in α.

CASE 2 ($\rho > \sigma$). When $\rho > \sigma$, then

$$p_\alpha(s,b) = \begin{cases} 1 & \text{if } \sigma c(s,\alpha) \le \sigma d(b,\alpha), \\ \left(\dfrac{\sigma d(b,\alpha)}{\rho c(s,\alpha)}\right)^{1/(\rho-\sigma)} & \text{if } \rho c(s,\alpha) > \sigma d(b,\alpha) > 0, \\ 0 & \text{if } d(b,\alpha) \le 0. \end{cases}$$

Since

$$\sigma d(b,\alpha) - \rho c(s,\alpha) = \sigma b - \rho s - \alpha\left(\sigma\frac{1 - G(b)}{g(b)} + \rho\frac{F(s)}{f(s)}\right),$$

$$\frac{\sigma d(b,\alpha)}{\rho c(s,\alpha)} = \frac{\sigma}{\rho}\left(\frac{b - \alpha[(1 - G(b))/g(b)]}{S + \alpha[F(s)/f(s)]}\right),$$

and $d(b,\alpha)$ are decreasing in α, $p_\alpha(s,b)$ is decreasing in α. Thus, for $\alpha < \beta$, $R(\beta)$ differs from $R(\alpha)$ only because $p_\beta(s,b) < p_\alpha(s,b)$ for some (s,b) where $\sigma d(b,\alpha) < \rho c(s,\alpha)$. Therefore, $R(\cdot)$ is strictly increasing.

Since $c(\cdot,\alpha)$ and $d(\cdot,\alpha)$ are strictly increasing for any $\alpha < 1$, the equation $d(b,\alpha) = 0$ has at most one solution in b and the equation $\rho c(s,\alpha) = \sigma d(b,\alpha)$ has at most one solution in s, and the solutions vary continuously in b and α. Hence, we may write

$$R(\alpha) = \int\limits_{q(\alpha)}^{\overline{b}} \left(\int\limits_{\underline{s}}^{r(b,\alpha)} (d(b,1) - c(b,1))f(s) \, ds \right.$$

$$\left. + \int\limits_{r(b,\alpha)}^{\overline{s}} [d(b,1)(p_\alpha(s,b))^\sigma - c(s,1)(p_\alpha(s,b))^\rho]f(s) \, ds \right) g(b) \, db,$$

where $q(\alpha)$ and $r(b,\alpha)$ are continuous in b and α. Therefore, $R(\alpha)$ is continuous in α.

Since $R(\cdot)$ is continuous and strictly increasing, with $R(0) < 0$ and $R(1) \ge 0$, there must be a unique $\alpha \in [0,1]$ such that $R(\alpha) = 0$ and $p_\alpha(s,b)$ is ex ante efficient.

It is worthwhile to point out that the requirement in the existence part of theorem 3 that $c(\cdot,1)$ and $d(\cdot,1)$ be increasing functions is satisfied by a large range of distribution functions. A sufficient condition for $c(\cdot,1)$ and $d(\cdot,1)$ to be increasing is for the ratio of the distribution and the density to be increasing. This is a local characterization of the monotone likelihood ratio property and is satisfied by many distributions, such as the uniform, exponential, normal, chi-square, and Poisson distributions.

I now prove that the ex ante-efficient mechanism typically violates sequential rationality, and hence show that bargainers who are unable to make binding commitments are worse off (in an ex ante sense) than bargainers who are able to commit to particular strategies.

Corollary 1. If ex post efficiency is unobtainable, $c(\cdot,1)$ and $d(\cdot,1)$ are increasing functions, and $d(\underline{b},1) < 0$ if $\rho > \sigma$, then the ex ante-efficient mechanism violates sequential rationality.

Proof. By theorem 3, the ex ante-efficient mechanism exists and is given by p_α for some $\alpha > 0$. Consider the set of traders who never trade under p_α, but for whom trade is always beneficial at some point in the future:

$$\mathcal{N} = \{(s,b) \mid p_\alpha(s,b)=0 \text{ and } [\rho>\sigma \text{ or } (\rho=\sigma \text{ and } s\leq b)]\}.$$

By our hypothesis, this set is nonempty. Thus, from lemma 6, the mechanism p_α violates sequential rationality.

8.5 The case of uniform symmetric exchange: An example

To illustrate the theory presented in the earlier sections, it will be useful to look at an example. In particular, consider the case of uniform symmetric exchange in which both the seller's cost and the buyer's valuation are uniformly distributed on $[0,1]$. Then, $c(s,\alpha) = (1 + \alpha)s$ and $d(b,\alpha) = (1 + \alpha)b - \alpha$, which are strictly increasing when $\alpha = 1$, and so by theorem 3 we know that, for some $\alpha \in [0,1]$, the mechanism $p = p_\alpha$ is ex ante efficient. The desired α is found by setting $R(\alpha)$ to zero, so that $U(\bar{s}) = V(\underline{b}) = 0$. Again, it will be useful to consider two cases depending on whether $\rho \leq \sigma$ or $\rho > \sigma$.

CASE 1 ($\rho \leq \sigma$). When $\rho \leq \sigma$, then

$$p_\alpha(s,b) = \begin{cases} 1 & \text{if } s < b - \dfrac{\alpha}{1+\alpha}, \\ 0 & \text{if } s \geq b - \dfrac{\alpha}{1+\alpha}. \end{cases}$$

Define $\mu = \alpha/(1 + \alpha)$. Then, we wish to find $\mu \in [0,\frac{1}{2}]$ such that

$$R(\alpha) = \int_{\mu}^{1} \int_{0}^{b-\mu} (2(b - s) - 1)\, ds\, db = 0.$$

Performing the integration yields

$$\left(\mu - \frac{1}{4}\right)(\mu + 1)^2 = 0,$$

which has a root in $[0,\frac{1}{2}]$ at $\mu = \frac{1}{4}$. Thus, $\alpha = \frac{1}{3}$ and

$$p(s,b) = \begin{cases} 1 & \text{if } s < b - \dfrac{1}{4}, \\[2mm] 0 & \text{if } s \geq b - \dfrac{1}{4}. \end{cases}$$

When $\rho \leq \sigma$, ex ante efficiency is obtained by a mechanism that transfers the object without delay if and only if the buyer's valuation exceeds the seller's by at least $\frac{1}{4}$. Perhaps somewhat surprisingly, the ex ante-efficient mechanism in this case does not depend on ρ or σ. Since the value of the object is declining more rapidly for the buyer than for the seller, it is always better to transfer the item immediately, if at all. Hence, even though the players can reveal information by delaying agreement, in the ex ante-efficient mechanism they choose to trade immediately or not at all, so that a static mechanism ex ante dominates any sequential bargaining mechanism. This static mechanism, however, is not sequentially rational, which illustrates corollary 1.

   An extensive-form game that implements the ex ante-efficient mechanism when $\rho \leq \sigma$ has been studied by Chatterjee and Samuelson (1983). They consider the simultaneous-offers game, in which the players simultaneously announce prices and the object is traded if the buyer's bid exceeds the seller's offer. For this example, the seller's optimal strategy is to offer the price $\frac{2}{3}s + \frac{1}{4}$, and the buyer's best response is to bid $\frac{2}{3}b + \frac{1}{12}$, which implies that trade occurs provided that $\frac{2}{3}s + \frac{1}{4} < \frac{2}{3}b + \frac{1}{12}$ or $s < b - \frac{1}{4}$, as in the ex ante-efficient mechanism. For this equilibrium, the price at which the object is sold is

$$x(s,b) = \begin{cases} \dfrac{1}{3}(b + s) + \dfrac{1}{6} & \text{if } s < b - \dfrac{1}{4}, \\[3mm] 0 & \text{if } s \geq b - \dfrac{1}{4}. \end{cases}$$

The sum of the players' ex ante utilities is

$$\mathcal{U} + \mathcal{V} = \int_{1/4}^{1} \int_{0}^{b-1/4} (b - s) \, ds \, db = \frac{9}{64},$$

whereas the total utility from the ex post-efficient mechanism is

$$\int_{0}^{1} \int_{0}^{b} (b - s) \, ds \, db = \frac{1}{6}.$$

Thus, 15.6 percent of the gains from trade are lost when $\rho \le \sigma$, due to delays in agreement.

CASE 2 $(\rho > \sigma)$. When $\rho > \sigma$, then

$$p_\alpha(s,b) = \begin{cases} 1 & \text{if } s \le \dfrac{\sigma}{\rho}\left(b - \dfrac{\alpha}{1+\alpha}\right), \\[2em] \left(\dfrac{\sigma\left(b - \dfrac{\alpha}{1+\alpha}\right)}{\rho s}\right)^{1/(\rho-\alpha)} & \text{if } s > \dfrac{\sigma}{\rho}\left(b - \dfrac{\alpha}{1+\alpha}\right), \\[2em] 0 & \text{if } b \le \dfrac{\alpha}{1+\alpha}. \end{cases}$$

Making the substitution $\mu = \alpha/(1 + \alpha)$, we wish to find $\mu \in [0, \tfrac{1}{2}]$ such that

$$\int_{\mu}^{1} \left[\int_{0}^{(\sigma/\rho)(b-\mu)} (2b - 1 - 2s) \, ds + \int_{(\sigma/\rho)(b-\mu)}^{1} \left[(2b - 1)\left(\frac{\sigma(b-\mu)}{\rho s}\right)^{\sigma/(\rho-\sigma)} \right. \right.$$
$$\left. \left. - 2s\left(\frac{\sigma(b-\mu)}{\rho s}\right)^{\rho/(\rho-\sigma)} \right] ds \right] db = 0.$$

Let $\delta = \sigma/\rho$ and $\gamma = \sigma/(\rho - \sigma)$, so that $1 + \gamma = \rho/(\rho - \sigma)$. After this substitution, we have

$$\int_{\mu}^{1} \int_{0}^{\delta(b-\mu)} (2b - 1 - 2s) \, ds$$

$$+ \int_{\delta(b-\mu)}^{1} [(2b - 1)[\delta(b - \mu)]^\gamma - 2[\delta(b - \mu)]^{1+\gamma}]s^{-\gamma} \, ds] \, db = 0.$$

Performing the inner integration (assuming $\gamma \neq 1$) yields

$$\int\limits_{\mu}^{1} \Bigg[\delta(b-\mu)[(2-\delta)b + \delta\mu - 1]$$

$$+ \frac{1}{1-\gamma}[2(1-\delta)b + 2\delta\mu - 1][\delta(b-\mu)]^{\gamma}\{1 - [\delta(b-\mu)]^{1-\gamma}\} \Bigg] db$$

$$= \int\limits_{\mu}^{1} \Bigg[\delta\{(2-\delta)b^2 - (2\mu(1-\delta) + 1]b + \mu(1-\delta\mu)\}$$

$$+ \frac{1}{1-\gamma}[2(1-\delta)b + 2\delta\mu - 1]\{[\delta(b-\mu)]^{\gamma} - \delta(b-\mu)\} \Bigg] db$$

$$= \int\limits_{\mu}^{1} \frac{\delta}{1-\gamma} \Bigg[[\delta - \gamma(2-\delta)]b^2 - \{\gamma[1 + 2\mu(1-\delta)] - 2\delta\mu\}b$$

$$+ \delta\mu^2 - \gamma\mu(1-\delta\mu) + [2(1-\delta)b + 2\delta\mu - 1]\delta^{\gamma-1}(b-\mu)^{\gamma} \Bigg] db = 0.$$

Since

$$\int\limits_{\mu}^{1} (b-\mu)^{\gamma}\, db = \frac{(1-\mu)^{1+\gamma}}{1+\gamma} \qquad \text{and}$$

$$\int\limits_{\mu}^{1} b(b-\mu)^{\gamma}\, db = \frac{(1-\mu)^{1+\gamma}}{1+\gamma}\left(1 - \frac{1-\mu}{2+\gamma}\right),$$

after integration we have

$$\frac{\delta}{1-\gamma}\Bigg[\frac{1}{3}(1-\mu^3)[\delta - \gamma(2-\delta)] + \frac{1}{2}(1-\mu^2)\{\gamma[1 + 2\mu(1-\delta)] - 2\delta\mu\}$$

$$+ (1-\mu)[\delta\mu^2 - \gamma\mu(1-\delta\mu)] + \frac{\delta^{\gamma-1}(1-\mu)^{1+\gamma}}{1+\gamma}$$

$$\left[2\delta\mu - 1 + 2(1-\delta)\left(1 - \frac{1-\mu}{2+\gamma}\right)\right]\Bigg] = 0.$$

Dividing by $\delta(1-\mu)/(1-\gamma)$, yields

$$\frac{1}{3}(1 + \mu + \mu^2)[\delta - \gamma(2 - \delta)] + \frac{1}{2}(1 + \mu)\{\gamma[1 + 2\mu(1 - \delta)] - 2\delta\mu\}$$

$$+ \delta\mu^2 - \gamma\mu(1 - \delta\mu) + \frac{\delta^{\gamma-1}(1 - \mu)^{\gamma}}{1 + \gamma} \tag{R}$$

$$\left[2\delta\mu - 1 + 2(1 - \delta)\left(1 - \frac{1 - \mu}{2 + \gamma}\right)\right] = 0.$$

Given $\delta = \sigma/\rho$, a root $\mu \in [0,\tfrac{1}{2}]$ to (R) is easily found numerically.

The sum of the players' ex ante utilities is computed as follows:

$$\mathcal{U} + \mathcal{V} = \int_{\mu}^{1}\left[\int_{0}^{\delta(b-\mu)}(b - s)\,ds + \int_{\delta(b-\mu)}^{1}\right.$$

$$\left.\left[b\left(\frac{\delta(b - \mu)}{s}\right)^{\gamma} - s\left(\frac{\delta(b - \mu)}{s}\right)^{1+\gamma}\right]ds\right]db$$

$$= \int_{\mu}^{1}\left[\delta(b - \mu)\left(\left(1 - \frac{1}{2}\delta\right)b + \frac{1}{2}\delta\mu\right)\right.$$

$$\left. + \frac{1}{1 - \gamma}[(1 - \delta)b + \delta\mu][\delta(b - \mu)]^{\gamma}\{1 - [\delta(b - \mu)]^{1-\gamma}\}\right]db$$

$$= \int_{\mu}^{1}\frac{\delta}{1 - \gamma}\left[\left(\frac{1}{2}\delta(1 + \gamma) - \gamma\right)b^2 + [\mu\gamma - \delta\mu(1 + \gamma)]b\right.$$

$$\left. + \frac{1}{2}\delta\mu^2(1 + \gamma) + \delta^{\gamma-1}[(1 - \delta)b + \delta\mu](b - u)^{\gamma}\right]db$$

$$= \frac{\delta(1 - \mu)}{1 - \gamma}\left[\frac{1}{3}\left(1 + \mu + \mu^2\right)\left(\frac{1}{2}\delta(1 + \gamma) - \gamma\right)\right.$$

$$+ \frac{1}{2}(1 + \mu)[\mu\gamma - \delta\mu(1 + \gamma)]$$

$$\left. + \frac{1}{2}\delta\mu^2(1 + \gamma) + \frac{\delta^{\gamma-1}(1 - \mu)^{\gamma}}{1 + \gamma}\left(\delta\mu + (1 - \delta)\frac{1 + \mu + \gamma}{2 + \gamma}\right)\right].$$

The value of μ and the efficiency of the ex ante-efficient mechanism relative to the first-best (full-information) solution are shown in Figure 8.1 and Figure 8.2, respectively, as the ratio of the players' discount rates is

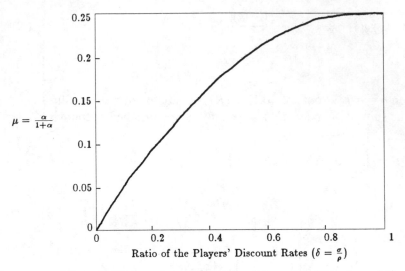

$$\mu = \frac{\alpha}{1+\alpha}$$

Ratio of the Players' Discount Rates $(\delta = \frac{\sigma}{\rho})$

Figure 8.1 Value of μ as a function of the ratio of the players' discount rates.

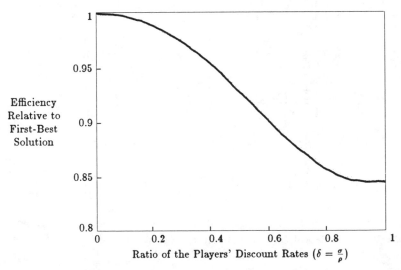

Efficiency Relative to First-Best Solution

Ratio of the Players' Discount Rates $(\delta = \frac{\sigma}{\rho})$

Figure 8.2 Efficiency as a function of the ratio of the players' discount rates.

varied from 0 to 1. Bargaining efficiency improves as the seller's discount rate is increased relative to the buyer's. When the players' discount rates are equal, 15.6 percent of the gains from trade are lost due to delays in agreement. This inefficiency decreases to zero as $\rho \rightarrow \infty$, illustrating theorem 2.

8.6 Conclusion

Two important features of any bargaining setting are information and time. Bargainers typically have incomplete information about each other's preferences, and therefore must communicate some of their private information in order to determine whether or not gains from trade exist. One means of communication is for the agents to signal their private information through their willingness to delay agreement: Bargainers who anticipate large gains from trade will be unwilling to delay agreement and so will propose attractive terms of trade that the other is likely to accept early in the bargaining process, whereas bargainers expecting small gains will prefer to wait for better offers from their opponent. In this chapter, I have described the properties of such a bargaining model, by analyzing a sequential direct revelation game.

Modeling the bargaining process as a sequential game, where the agents communicate their private information over time, has two main advantages. First, from the point of view of realism, one commonly observes bargaining taking place over time. Second, any static bargaining mechanism, because it does not permit the agents to learn about their opponent's preferences, must end with positive probability in a situation where gains from trade are possible and yet no agreement is reached. If both bargainers know that gains from trade exist, what prevents them from continuing negotiations until an agreement is reached? By introducing the time dimension, and hence allowing the bargainers to communicate through their actions over time, one is able to construct perfect bargaining mechanisms, in which the bargainers continue to negotiate so long as they expect positive gains from continuing.

When the bargainers discount future gains according to known and fixed discount rates, it was found that the bargainers may be better off (in terms of their ex ante utilities) using a sequential bargaining mechanism than a static scheme. This is the result of the time dimension introducing an additional asymmetry into the problem, which may be exploited to construct sequential bargaining mechanisms that ex ante dominate the most efficient static mechanisms. Even in situations where a static mechanism is ex ante efficient, it is unlikely that such a mechanism would be adopted by the bargainers, since it necessarily would violate sequential rationality.

The analysis presented here represents an early step toward understanding how agreements are reached in conflict situations under uncertainty. Several simplifying assumptions have been made in order to keep the analysis manageable. First, modeling the agents' time preferences with constant discount rates is an appealing example, but not an accurate description of all bargaining settings. (Fishburn and Rubinstein (1982) derive under which circumstances the discounting assumption is valid. In particular, they prove that any preferences over bargaining outcomes that are monotonic, continuous, and stationary can be represented by discounting provided the bargainers exhibit impatience over all outcomes except that of no agreement.) Second, the agents have been assumed to be risk neutral, but in many bargaining situations the agents' willingness to take risks is an important bargaining factor. Third, I have restricted attention to rational agents who can calculate (at no cost) their optimal strategies. Certainly, few agents are so consistent and calculating. With less-than-rational agents, an agent's capacity to mislead his opponent becomes an important variable in determining how the gains from trade are divided. Finally, I have assumed that the players' valuations are independent. However, in many settings the bargainers' valuations will be correlated, and so, for example, the seller's willingness to trade may be a signal of the valuation of the object to the buyer.

Although it would be useful in future research to weaken the simplifying assumptions made here, perhaps the most fruitful avenue for further study is the analysis of specific extensive-form bargaining games. The advantage of looking at specific extensive-form games is that the bargaining rules are independent of the probabilistic beliefs that the players have about each other's preferences. In a direct revelation game, on the other hand, the bargaining rule depends in a complicated way on these probabilistic beliefs. Because of this dependence, direct revelation games are not played in practice.

Can one find a strategic game that comes close to implementing the ex ante-efficient bargaining mechanism over a wide range of bargaining situations? Initial studies along these lines have been conducted by Cramton (1984), Fudenberg and Tirole (1983), and Sobel and Takahashi (1983). All three papers consider a model in which only one of the bargainers makes offers. When the players' reservation prices are uniformly distributed on [0,1] and their discount rates are equal, it was found that this model results in 32 percent of the gains from trade being lost, as opposed to 16 percent being lost when the ex ante-efficient bargaining mechanism is adopted (Cramton (1984)). Thus, the players' inability to commit to ending negotiations results in a bargaining outcome that is significantly less efficient than if commitment were possible.

Perhaps a better candidate for a strategic bargaining game that is nearly ex ante efficient is the game in which the bargainers alternate offers. This game was analyzed by Rubinstein (1982) in a setting of complete information, but an analysis with incomplete information has yet to be done. Of particular interest is the alternating-offers game as the time between offers goes to zero, because this strategic game represents a very general bargaining rule: At any time, a bargainer may make a new offer or accept the most recent offer of his opponent. It would be a pleasant surprise if such a reasonable bargaining game was nearly ex ante efficient over a variety of circumstances.

A second promising area for research is further study on the implications of sequential rationality to bargaining and to more general games of incomplete information. I intend to address this issue in depth in future research.

REFERENCES

Chatterjee, Kalyan, and William Samuelson (1983): Bargaining under Incomplete Information. *Operations Research,* Vol. 31, pp. 835–51.
Cramton, Peter C. (1984): Bargaining with Incomplete Information: An Infinite-Horizon Model with Continuous Uncertainty. *Review of Economic Studies,* Vol. 51, pp. 579–93.
Fishburn, Peter C., and Ariel Rubinstein (1982): Time Preference. *International Economic Review,* Vol. 23, pp. 719–36.
Fudenberg, Drew, and Jean Tirole (1983): Sequential Bargaining with Incomplete Information. *Review of Economic Studies,* Vol. 50, pp. 221–47.
Gresik, Thomas A., and Mark A. Satterthwaite (1983): *The Number of Traders Required To Make a Market Competitive: The Beginnings of a Theory.* Research Paper No. 551, Graduate School of Management, Northwestern University.
Holmström, Bengt, and Roger B. Myerson (1983): Efficient and Durable Decision Rules with Incomplete Information. *Econometrica,* Vol. 51, 1799–1820.
Kreps, David M., and Robert Wilson (1982): Sequential Equilibria. *Econometrica,* Vol. 50, pp. 863–94.
Myerson, Roger B., and Mark A. Satterthwaite (1983): Efficient Mechanism for Bilateral Trading. *Journal of Economic Theory,* Vol. 28, pp. 265–81.
Selten, R. (1976): Reexamination of the Perfectness Concept for Equilibrium Points in Extensive Games. *International Journal of Game Theory,* Vol. 4, pp. 25–53.
Sobel, Joel, and Ichiro Takahashi (1983): A Multi-Stage Model of Bargaining. *Review of Economic Studies,* Vol. 50, pp. 411–26.
Wilson, Robert (1982): *Double Auctions.* Technical Report No. 391, Stanford Institute for Mathematical Studies in the Social Sciences.

CHAPTER 9

The role of risk aversion in a simple bargaining model

Martin J. Osborne
COLUMBIA UNIVERSITY

The purpose of this paper is to study the effect of a change in an individual's degree of risk aversion on the perfect Bayesian Nash equilibrium in a simple model of bargaining. I find that, contrary to the results in the axiomatic model with riskless outcomes due to Nash, an opponent may be made worse off by such a change. Further, an individual may want to take an action that identifies him as more, rather than less, risk averse than he really is. In the course of the analysis, I fully characterize the equilibria of a class of "wars of attrition" with incomplete information, and single out one as "perfect" in a certain sense; this result may be of independent interest.

9.1 Introduction

The role of risk aversion in bargaining has been widely studied within the axiomatic framework of Nash (1950) (see, for example, Roth (1979), Perles and Maschler (1981)). It has been found that if the negotiation concerns riskless outcomes, then the more risk averse an individual is, the higher the payoff of his opponent. Related results show that in this case it is to the advantage of an individual to "pretend" to be less risk averse than

I am grateful to Vincent Crawford, Vijay Krishna, Carolyn Pitchik, John Riley, Alvin Roth, Ariel Rubinstein, Charles Wilson, Allan Young, and two anonymous referees for very helpful discussions and comments. A number of participants in the Conference on Game-Theoretic Models of Bargaining at the University of Pittsburgh, June 1983, also made valuable comments. I first worked on the issue considered in this paper during a most enjoyable visit to the Institute for Advanced Studies, Hebrew University of Jerusalem, in Spring 1980; I am grateful to the Institute for its hospitality and for partial financial support. This work was also partially supported by grants from the Council for Research in the Social Sciences at Columbia University in the summers of 1981–83, and from the National Science Foundation (SES-8318978).

181

he really is (Kurz (1977, 1980), Thomson (1979), Sobel (1981)). These results have some intuitive appeal: Given any (probabilistic) beliefs about the behavior of his opponent, it seems that an individual should behave more cautiously, the more risk averse he is. However, this fact influences his opponent's behavior, and without a more detailed specification of the information possessed by both parties and of the precise structure of the negotiation, it is not clear how the *equilibrium* behavior changes. (In the case where the potential agreements involve lotteries, the axiomatic model predicts that an increase in an individual's risk aversion may reduce the payoff of his opponent (see Roth and Rothblum (1982)). Here, I restrict attention to the case in which agreements concern riskless outcomes.)

It is natural to investigate these issues by modeling the process of negotiation as a (noncooperative) strategic game, and by studying the effect of changes in the players' risk aversions on the characteristics of the Nash equilibria. For such a comparative static exercise to make sense, the game must have a unique equilibrium. It is clear that if the equilibrium strategies are pure, then a change in a player's risk aversion that preserves his preferences over certain outcomes has no effect on his opponent's payoff. (This is the case, for example, in Rubinstein's (1982) model.[1]) Thus, for the degree of risk aversion to influence the outcome, the equilibrium strategies must involve randomization.

The model that I analyze is designed with these facts in mind. It is a simple version of those formulated by Hicks (1932), Bishop (1964), and Cross (1965). At each time in [0,1], two individuals can produce a flow of one unit of some good desirable to them both. Before production can begin, a contract must be negotiated that specifies how the flow of output will be divided between the two parties. At time 0, each party begins by demanding some fraction of the flow – say individual i demands $d_i(0)$. So long as the demands are incompatible (i.e., sum to more than the output available), no production takes place. In the most general version of the model, at each time, each individual may adjust his demand. If t is the first time at which the demands are compatible, and in fact $d_1(t) + d_2(t) = 1$, then at each time in $[t,1]$ each individual i receives the flow $d_i(t)$. This most general form of the model is unwieldy; in order to get some rather specific results, I assume that the allowable concession patterns are very special.

In the simplest case (considered in Sections 9.2 and 9.3), the demands of both individuals at time 0 are fixed, incompatible, and the same. At each time, each individual may leave his demand the same, or concede to that of his opponent. I model the interaction between the individuals as a strategic game[2] in which a pure strategy of an individual is an element t of

[0,1], with the interpretation that the individual will concede at t if his opponent has not done so by then. (Once his opponent has conceded, there is no cause for further action on his part.) In a slightly richer version of the model (considered in Section 9.4), each individual may choose how much to demand at time zero, but may subsequently only stand firm or concede. Though there are clearly many aspects of negotiation not included in this model, it does capture the tradeoff involved in the intuitive arguments concerning the effects of changes in risk aversion. That is, by delaying concession, an individual sacrifices payoff now in return for the chance that his opponent will concede in the future.

As regards the informational structure of the negotiation, I assume that each individual may be one of many types, which differ in their degrees of risk aversion. The solution is that of Bayesian Nash equilibrium, modified by "perfection" of a certain sort (see Section 9.3). This standard solution captures the idea that each player is uncertain of the type of his opponent. However, it may also be given a more concrete interpretation. Thus, suppose that there are two populations, each consisting of a continuum of individuals of different types. In any play of the game, each member of one population is randomly matched with a member of the other population. A Bayesian Nash equilibrium has the property that if each individual's beliefs about the distribution of concession times in the opponent population is correct, then his equilibrium strategy is optimal. Given this interpretation, it is natural to consider also the case where members of a single population are matched with each other. From the point of view of the Bayesian Nash equilibrium, this is, of course, simply a special case of the two-population model, in which the characteristics of both populations are the same, and attention is restricted to symmetric equilibria (i.e., equilibria in which the strategies used in both populations are the same). However, the comparative static question, which is my main focus, requires separate analysis in the two cases. Viewed as a special case of the two-population model, a change in risk aversion of a potential opponent in the one-population case is a change not only in the characteristics of the opponent population, but also in the characteristics of the player's own population. Given this, I analyze the two cases separately.

First, consider the case in which initial demands are fixed. In the one-population model, there is a unique equilibrium distribution of concession times[3]; in the two-population model, there is a set of equilibria (characterized in theorem 3), but only one is perfect in a certain sense (see proposition 5). In both cases, more risk averse individuals concede earlier in the (perfect) equilibrium. The comparative static results are as follows.

In the one-population case, an individual is made better off by an increase in the risk aversion of his potential opponents, whereas in the two-population case, the opposite is true. Thus, in the two-population model, the prediction of Nash's model is not supported. Unless one argues that the model does not capture some essential aspect of bargaining, or that Nash equilibrium is an inappropriate solution concept, the conclusion is that the effect of a change in an opponent's risk aversion on an individual's negotiated payoff can go in either direction, depending on the precise structure of the negotiation.

To address the issue of "distortion" of preferences in this simple model, I consider how an individual's payoff changes as the fraction of his own population that is less risk averse than him increases. This change causes his opponents to believe with smaller probability that he is risk averse, and so gives him an opportunity to "pretend" that he is not. However, such a change does not affect his equilibrium payoff, although it does reduce the payoff of his less risk averse colleagues.

Although the simple version of the model does not fit into Nash's framework (the set of payoffs to possible agreements may not be convex), it is clear that the solution does not obey appropriately modified versions of his axioms. Most conspicuously, the (perfect) equilibrium is not Pareto-efficient. This lack of efficiency does not derive from uncertainty about opponents' payoffs – even if everyone is identical, the solution is not efficient. Rather, it is the (inevitable) uncertainty about opponents' actions that prevents agreement at time zero. It seems that the continuous nature of the model contributes to this outcome: If disagreement is once-and-for-all (as in Nash's (1953) "demand game"), then it seems less likely that it will be the outcome of negotiation. If, on the other hand, demands may be adjusted continuously (or, in the simple case here, a concession can be made at any time), then it seems quite unlikely that an equilibrium will involve agreement from the very beginning.

My analysis of the case in which initial demands may be chosen is limited. I show that when there are two types in each population and two possible initial demands, there is no separating equilibrium in which all members of a given type choose the same demand and the two types in each population choose different demands. The reason for this is that the less risk averse individuals can benefit from pretending to be more risk averse (see Section 9.4). There is thus another sense in which the model works differently from the axiomatic one of Nash. I also show that there is a continuum of pooling equilibria, in which a positive fraction of each type in each population makes each initial demand. Given this non-uniqueness, it is not possible to perform the comparative static exercises discussed previously; it is an open question whether the model can be modified to produce a unique equilibrium. However, the analysis does show that the basic model does not degenerate when choice of initial demand is allowed.

Recently, a number of authors (e.g., Samuelson (1980), McLennan (1981), Crawford (1982), Rubinstein (1982), Chatterjee and Samuelson (1983), Fudenberg and Tirole (1983a), and Sobel and Takahashi (1983)) have modeled bargaining as a noncooperative strategic game. None of these focuses specifically on the role of risk aversion. In most cases, the bargaining parties are assumed to be risk neutral (although Samuelson (1980) and Chatterjee and Samuelson (1983) do contain some analysis of the effect of changes in the players' risk aversions). The model here, designed specifically to address the role of risk aversion, differs in several respects from these models. Most significantly, time runs continuously, so that the players have great flexibility in choosing their time of action. A player can always wait a short time (thereby losing at most a very small amount of payoff) in case his opponent will concede; if time is discrete, this is not possible. Note, however, that because the possibility for changing demands is so limited, players' actions (or lack thereof) transmit no useful information during the course of play (except for their choice of initial demand, when this is allowed), whereas this information transmission is central to some of the models just cited. Young (1983) analyzes a model that is in some respects similar to the simple model considered here. However, the structure of the payoffs in his model is not quite the same, and time is discrete; he does not consider the effect of changes in risk aversion.

The game associated with the simple version of my model is what is known in the literature as a "war of attrition" (see, for example, Riley (1980)). Nalebuff and Riley (1984) have (independently) found a class of equilibria in a model that is different in some respects from mine (e.g., the time horizon is infinite, and there is a continuum of types), but is similar in general structure. However, they do not show that they have found all of the equilibria; nor do they consider the issue of perfection, or the effect of a change in an individual's risk aversion. Also related is the work of Fudenberg and Tirole (1983b), who have (independently) shown that, in another version of a war of attrition, there is a unique Bayesian Nash equilibrium that is perfect in a certain sense.

9.2   Bargaining within a single population

The model

The population consists of a continuum of individuals. The environment of the negotiation between any two individuals is as follows. Time runs continuously in [0,1]. At each point in time, a flow of one unit of output can be produced, if the individuals can agree how to split it between them. The rules of negotiation are simple. At time 0, each individual demands

$\frac{1}{2} < a < 1$ units of output. At any subsequent time in $[0,1]$, each may concede to the demand of the other. The outcome of negotiation for each individual is an output stream x: $[0,1] \rightarrow [0,1]$ of the form

$$\mathbf{x}(s) = \begin{cases} 0 & \text{if } 0 \le s < t, \\ x & \text{if } t \le s \le 1, \end{cases}$$

where $0 \le t \le 1$ and $0 \le x \le 1$. Such an output stream is characterized by the pair $(x,t) \in [0,1]^2$. If an individual is first to concede, and does so at t, he receives the output stream $(1 - a,t)$; his opponent receives (a,t). If the individuals concede simultaneously at t, the equilibrium of the game that I study is independent of the output stream received by each individual, so long as that stream is of the form (c,t), where $1 - a < c < a$; for notational convenience, I assume that it is $(\frac{1}{2},t)$. There are m *types* of individuals. The fraction $\gamma_i > 0$ of the population is of type $i(= 1, \ldots, m)$. The preferences over lotteries on output streams of individuals of type i are represented by a von Neumann-Morgenstern *utility function* u_i: $[0,1]^2 \rightarrow \mathbb{R}_+$ with the following properties:

(P.1) For each (x,t), $u_i(x,1) = u_i(0,t) = 0$;

(P.2) For each $t < 1$, u_i is increasing in x;

(P.3) For each $x > 0$, u_i is continuous in t, and continuously differentiable and decreasing in t whenever $t < 1$.

In order to isolate the role of risk aversion, I assume that all of the types have the same preferences over sure outcomes; they differ only in their degrees of risk aversion, type i being more risk averse than type $i + 1$. Precisely, a utility function v is *more risk averse* than a utility function u if there is a strictly concave function $f: \mathbb{R}_+ \rightarrow \mathbb{R}_+$ such that $v = f \circ u$. I assume the following:

(P.4) For each $i = 1, \ldots, m - 1$, u_i is more risk averse than u_{i+1}.

It is easy to check that an example of a collection $\{u_i\}$ of utility functions that satisfies (P.1) through (P.4) is that for which $u_i(x,t) = (1 - t)^{\alpha_i} x^{\alpha_i}$, with $0 < \alpha_1 < \alpha_2 < \cdots < \alpha_m < 1$.

The only choice an individual has is the time at which to concede. Thus, a (mixed) *strategy* of an individual is simply a cumulative probability distribution on $[0,1]$. Only the average strategy of individuals of type i is determined in equilibrium, not the strategy of any particular individual. I refer to this average strategy as the *strategy of i*, and denote it E_i. For each $0 \le t \le 1$, let

$$G(t) = \sum_{i=1}^{m} \gamma_i E_i(t), \tag{9.1}$$

so that $G(t)$ is the probability that a randomly selected individual concedes at or before t. I refer to G as the *distribution of concession times in the population*. The distribution of concession times relevant to an individual's choice is the one generated by all of the *other* individuals' strategies. However, since the population is nonatomic, this is the same as G. If an individual of type i uses the pure strategy t, his expected payoff in negotiations with a randomly selected opponent is

$$P_i(t,G) = \int_{[0,t)} u_i(a,s) \, dG(s) + u_i(\tfrac{1}{2},t)J_G(t) + u_i(1-a,t)(1 - G(t)), \quad \textbf{(9.2)}$$

where $J_G(t)$ is the size of the atom in G at t. The payoff to the mixed strategy E_i is $P_i(E_i,G) = \int_{[0,1]} P_i(t,G) \, dE_i(t)$, and $(E_1, \ldots, E_m)$ is a (Bayesian Nash) *equilibrium* if for $i = 1, \ldots, m$ we have

$$P_i(E_i,G) \geq P_i(E,G) \quad \text{for all strategies } E,$$

where G is defined in (9.1).

Equilibrium

There is a unique equilibrium $(E_1, \ldots, E_m)$, defined as follows. There exist numbers $0 = p_0 < \cdots < p_y = \cdots p_m = 1$ such that the support of E_i (denoted supp E_i) is equal to $[p_{i-1},p_i]$ for $i = 1, \ldots, m$. The strategies E_i are nonatomic on $[0,1)$, and such that G causes the payoff $P_i(t,G)$ of an individual of type i to be constant on $[p_{i-1},p_i]$. A distribution G with this property can be found by solving the differential equations obtained by setting equal to zero the derivative with respect to t of each $P_i(t,G)$. We find that, for some $A > 0$, for $p_{i-1} \leq t < p_i$,

$$G(t) = 1 - A \exp\left(\int_0^t U_i(a,a,s) \, ds \right),$$

where, for any $\tfrac{1}{2} < a < 1, \tfrac{1}{2} < b < 1$, and $0 \leq s < 1$, and any utility function $u: [0,1]^2 \to \mathbb{R}_+$, the function U is defined by

$$U(a,b,s) = \frac{-D_2 u(1-a,s)}{u(b,s) - u(1-a,s)}. \tag{9.3}$$

(I have made the definition of U more general than necessary for the present purposes; it will be used also later.) Now, the fact that G is generated by the E_i's means that the equilibrium is as follows. For notational convenience, let $\Gamma(0) = 0$ and $\Gamma(k) = \Sigma_{i=1}^k \gamma_i$ for $k = 1, \ldots, m$. The p_i's are defined iteratively. First, $p_0 = 0$. Now, given $p_{i-1} < 1$, suppose that there exists $\bar{p} < 1$ such that

$$\frac{1 - \Gamma(i)}{1 - \Gamma(i-1)} = \exp\left(-\int\limits_{p_{i-1}}^{\bar{p}} U_i(a,a,s)\, ds\right). \tag{9.4}$$

Then, let $p_i = \bar{p}$, and continue the process. If there is no such $\bar{p}$, set $i = y$ and let $p_y = p_{y+1} = \cdots = p_m = 1$. For $i = 1, \ldots, y$, the equilibrium strategy E_i of type i has support $[p_{i-1}, p_i]$,

$$E_i(t) = [1 - \Gamma(i-1)] \frac{\left[1 - \exp\left(-\int\limits_{p_{i-1}}^{t} U_i(a,a,s)\, ds\right)\right]}{\gamma_i} \quad \text{if } p_{i-1} \le t < p_i, \tag{9.5}$$

and $E_i(t) = 1$ if $p_i \le t$. For $i = y + 1, \ldots, m$, the equilibrium strategy E_i is purely atomic, with mass at $t = 1$ (i.e., $E_i(t) = 0$ if $t < 1$ and $E_i(1) = 1$).

The fact that this defines an equilibrium, and that there is no other, follows from the results of Section 9.3 (see corollary 4). However, it is easy to check that each E_i is a strategy and that $P_i(t,G)$ is constant on $[p_{i-1}, p_i]$ ($= \text{supp } E_i$).

Note that if all individuals are identical, the equilibrium does not degenerate – in fact, all individuals then use mixed strategies with support $[0,1]$. The only efficient outcome is for all to concede at time 0, but this is not an equilibrium. If all individuals in a set S of positive measure concede at time 0, the distribution of concession times in the population contains an atom at 0. Hence, every individual, including those in S, can benefit from waiting a short period, and so it is not optimal for them to concede at time 0.

The effect of a change in risk aversion

Let k be such that $p_k < 1$ (i.e., in the unique equilibrium, individuals of type k concede with probability 1 before time 1). Now, suppose that individuals of type k become more risk averse, but not more so than individuals of type $k - 1$. That is, consider a new game in which the utility function of type k is $\hat{u}_k$, which is more risk averse than u_k, and less risk averse than u_{k-1}. (Throughout, I use a circumflex to denote the new value of an object.) This means that the order in which the types concede in equilibrium is preserved (since the ordering of risk aversions is preserved, and the unique equilibrium has the property that the most risk averse types concede first). In particular, the support of $\hat{E}_k$ lies between those of $\hat{E}_{k-1}$ and $\hat{E}_{k+1}$.

I first argue that this change has no effect on the equilibrium payoffs of types $1, \ldots, k-1$. To see this, note that from the definition of p_i (see (9.4)), we have $\hat{p}_i = p_i$ for $i = 1, \ldots, k-1$, and hence from (9.5) we have $\hat{E}_i = E_i$ for $i = 1, \ldots, k-1$. Thus, $\hat{G}(t) = G(t)$ for all $0 \leq t \leq p_{k-1}$. Now, $P_i(t,G)$ is constant on supp E_i, and so the equilibrium payoff of type i is equal to $P_i(p_{i-1},G)$, which depends on the form of G only on $[0,p_{i-1}]$ (see (9.2)). Hence, the equilibrium payoff of types $1, \ldots, k-1$ is unaffected by the change.

To analyze the changes in the payoffs of the remaining types, I need the following result (see (9.3) for the definition of U). (The result is more general than necessary for the present analysis; it will be used also in the next section.)

Lemma 1.   Suppose that the utility function $\hat{u}$ is more risk averse than the utility function u. Then, for any $\frac{1}{2} < a < 1$ and $\frac{1}{2} < b < 1$, we have $\hat{U}(a,b,s) > U(a,b,s)$ for all $0 \leq s < 1$.

Proof.   Let $\hat{u} = f \circ u$. The result follows from the fact that, since f is strictly concave and $1 - a < \frac{1}{2} < b$, if $0 \leq s < 1$, then

$$f'(u(1-a,s))(u(b,s) - u(1-a,s)) > f(u(b,s)) - f(u(1-a,s)).$$

This result implies that $\hat{U}_k(a,a,s) > U_k(a,a,s)$ for all $0 \leq s < 1$, and thus from (9.4) we have $\hat{p}_k < p_k$, and from (9.5) we have $\hat{E}_k(t) > E_k(t)$ for all $p_{k-1} = \hat{p}_{k-1} < t \leq \hat{p}_k$. Thus, $\hat{G}(t) > G(t)$ on $(p_{k-1},\hat{p}_k]$ (see Figure 9.1). Now, $\hat{u}_i = u_i$ for $i = k+1, \ldots, m$, so that $\hat{U}_i = U_i$; but since $\hat{p}_k < p_k$, we have $\hat{p}_{k+1} \leq p_{k+1}$, with strict inequality if $p_{k+1} < 1$ (see (9.4)), and so from (9.5), we have $\hat{E}_{k+1}(t) > E_{k+1}(t)$ for all $\hat{p}_k < t < \hat{p}_{k+1}$. Thus, $\hat{G}(t) > G(t)$ also on $(\hat{p}_k,\hat{p}_{k+1})$. Continuing this argument, we see that $\hat{G}(t) > G(t)$ on $(p_{k+1},1)$.

Now, as noted previously, the equilibrium payoff of type i is equal to $P_i(p_{i-1},G)$. If we integrate by parts in the expression for $P_i(p_{i-1},G)$ (see (9.2)), using the fact that G is nonatomic on $[0,1)$ and $u_i(x,1) = 0$ for all x (see (P.1)), then, given that each u_i is decreasing in t (see (P.3)) and $\hat{G}(t) > G(t)$ on $(p_{k-1},1)$, we see that $P_i(\hat{p}_{i-1},\hat{G}) > P_i(p_{i-1},G)$ for all $i = k+1, \ldots, m$. That is, the equilibrium payoffs of types $k+1, \ldots, m$ increase. We can summarize these results as follows.

Proposition 2.   Let k be a type that in equilibrium concedes with probability 1 before time 1. Then, if individuals of type k become more risk averse (but not more so than those of type $k-1$), the equilibrium payoffs

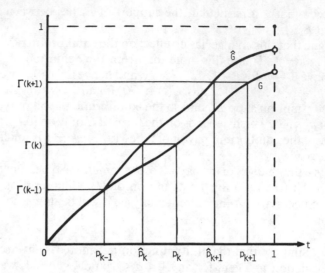

Figure 9.1 Change in the equilibrium distribution of concession times caused by an increase in the risk aversion of individuals of type k in the one-population model

of less risk averse individuals increase, whereas those of more risk averse individuals are unaffected.

9.3   The case of two populations

The model

There are two populations like that described in the previous section. Each individual in population 1 bargains with an individual in population 2. The name of an object in population 2 is the alphabetic successor of the name of the corresponding object in population 1. Thus, in population 2 there are n types. I refer to type i in population ℓ as "type ℓi". The fraction δ_j of population 2 is of type $j (= 1, \ldots, n)$; the sum $\Sigma_{j=1}^{k} \delta_j$ is denoted $\Delta(k)$. At time 0, individuals in population 2 demand $\frac{1}{2} < b < 1$ units of output. Individuals of type $2j$ have a utility function $v_j: [0,1]^2 \rightarrow \mathbb{R}$ satisfying (P.1) through (P.3). The function v_j is more risk averse than v_{j+1}, as in (P.4). A strategy of type $2j$ is denoted F_j, and the distribution of concession times in population 2 is H. If an individual of type $1i$ uses the pure strategy t, then his payoff is

$$P_i(t,H) = \int_{[0,t)} u_i(a,s) \, dH(s) + u_i(\tfrac{1}{2},t)J_H(t) + u_i(1 - b,t)(1 - H(t)); \quad \textbf{(9.6)}$$

if an individual of type $2j$ uses the pure strategy t, then his payoff is

$$Q_j(t,G) = \int\limits_{[0,t)} v_j(b,s)\, dG(s) + v_j(\tfrac{1}{2},t)J_G(t) + v_j(1-a,t)(1-G(t)). \qquad (9.7)$$

(Once again, for convenience I assume that simultaneous concessions give a payoff of $\tfrac{1}{2}$ to each individual.)

Equilibrium

In this model, there are many equilibria; they are fully characterized in theorem 3, to be given later. However, I will argue (in the next subsection) that only one equilibrium is perfect in a certain sense. It is this equilibrium that I describe first. Although the details of its definition are somewhat complex, its structure is easy to outline. Within each population, the pattern of concessions is similar to the equilibrium pattern in the one-population model. That is, there exist numbers $0 = p_0 < \cdots < p_y = \cdots = p_m = 1$ and $0 = q_0 < \cdots < q_z = \cdots = q_n = 1$ such that the support of the equilibrium strategy E_i of type $1i$ is $[p_{i-1}, p_i]$ and that of the equilibrium strategy F_j of type $2j$ is $[q_{j-1}, q_j]$. Informally, the p_i's and q_j's can be defined as follows. First, find the distributions of concession times G_1 and H_1 that make types 11 and 21, respectively, indifferent between conceding at any point in $[0,1]$. Now, the equilibrium distributions G and H have to be generated by the actions of the individuals in the two populations. Since type 11 constitutes the fraction γ_1 of population 1, this means that only that part of G_1 up to the point s_1 where $G_1(s_1) = \gamma_1$ can be generated by the actions of individuals of type 11. After that point, the actions of type-12 individuals have to generate G_1. However, in order for the strategy of type-12 individuals to have support commencing at s_1, from this point H has to be such that these individuals, not those of type 11, are indifferent. Similarly, if we try to generate H_1 by the actions of individuals in population 2, we run out of individuals of type 21 at the point t_1 where $H(t_1) = \delta_1$. After this point, G has to be such that type-22 individuals are indifferent. Thus, the equilibrium distributions G and H can be constructed as follows. Start at $t = 0$ with $G = G_1$ and $H = H_1$. Increase t to the point where either $G_1(t) = \gamma_1$ or $H_1(t) = \delta_1$ (i.e., s_1 or t_1 in the preceding discussion), whichever comes first. Suppose that s_1 comes first. Then, starting from s_1, H has to be modified so that type-12 individuals are indifferent. Then, H no longer reaches δ_1 at t_1, but at some other point, say t_1'. After t_1', G must be modified so that type-22 individuals are indifferent; a new point, s_2, for which $G(s_2) = \gamma_1 + \gamma_2$ $(= \Gamma(2))$, is defined, and the process of building G and H can continue.

Formally, G and H, and hence the equilibrium strategies $E_1, \ldots, E_m$

and $F_1, \ldots, F_n$, can be defined iteratively. The iterative procedure that I describe is slightly more general than necessary to define the present equilibrium, because I will use it later to define other equilibria. For any $0 \le \alpha < 1$ and $0 \le \beta < 1$, the procedure $\Pi(\alpha,\beta)$ is as follows.

Procedure $\Pi(\alpha,\beta)$.   Let w and x be such that $\Gamma(w) \le \alpha < \Gamma(w+1)$ and $\Delta(x) \le \beta < \Delta(x+1)$ (possibly $w=0$ and/or $x=0$), and let $0 = p_0 = \cdots = p_w$ and $0 = q_0 = \cdots = q_x$. Suppose that the numbers $0 < p_{w+1} < \cdots < p_k < 1$ and $0 < q_{x+1} < \cdots < q_\ell < 1$, where $0 \le k \le m-1$, $0 \le \ell \le n-1$, and, say, $q_\ell \le p_k$, satisfy the following properties. First, let $G(0) = \alpha$, and define G on $(q_{j-1},q_j]$ for $j = w+1, \ldots, \ell$ and on $(q_{j-1},p_k]$ for $j = \ell+1$ by

$$G(t) = 1 - (1 - G(q_{j-1}))\exp\left(-\int_{q_{j-1}}^t V_j(a,b,s)\,ds\right); \qquad (9.8)$$

let $H(0) = \beta$, and define H on $(p_{i-1},p_i]$ for $i = x+1, \ldots, k$ by

$$H(t) = 1 - (1 - H(p_{i-1}))\exp\left(-\int_{p_{i-1}}^t U_i(b,a,s)\,ds\right). \qquad (9.9)$$

Now, assume that the p_i's and q_j's are such that $G(p_i) = \Gamma(i)$ for $i = w+1, \ldots, k$, $H(q_j) = \Delta(j)$ for $j = x+1, \ldots, \ell$, and $H(p_k) < \Delta(\ell+1)$. (Refer to Figure 9.2.) Note that G and H are continuous and increasing, and $G(t) < 1$ and $H(t) < 1$ for all $0 \le t \le p_k$. Now, as noted before, for any H the payoff $P_i(t,H)$ of type $1i$ depends on the form of H only on $[0,t]$ (see (9.6)), and similarly for $Q_j(t,G)$. Thus, even though G and H are not yet defined on the whole of $[0,1]$, we can calculate $P_i(t,H)$ on $[p_{i-1},p_i]$ for $i = w+1, \ldots, k$ (i.e., $P_i(t,H)$ is independent of the way in which H is extended to $[0,1]$); it is easy to check that it is constant there. Similarly, G is designed so that $Q_j(t,G)$ (see (9.7)) is constant on $[q_{j-1},q_j]$ for $j = x+1, \ldots, \ell$ and on $[q_{j-1},p_k]$ for $j = \ell+1$.

We now extend G and H to the next p_i or q_j, whichever comes first. To do so, for $p_k \le t \le 1$, let

$$G_{k+1}(t) = 1 - (1 - \Gamma(k))\exp\left(-\int_{p_k}^t V_{\ell+1}(a,b,s)\,ds\right)$$

and let

$$H_{\ell+1}(t) = 1 - (1 - H(p_k))\exp\left(-\int_{q_\ell}^t U_{k+1}(b,a,s)\,ds\right).$$

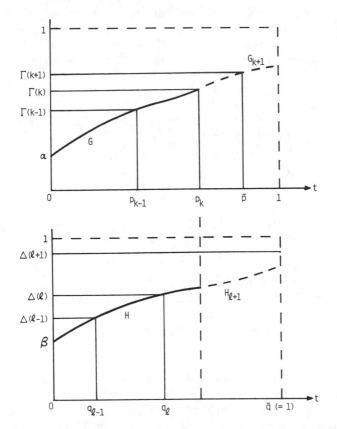

Figure 9.2 Construction of the functions G and H in procedure $\Pi(\alpha,\beta)$

Let $\overline{G}(t) = G(t)$ for $0 \le t \le p_k$ and $\overline{G}(t) = G_{k+1}(t)$ for $p_k < t \le 1$, and define $\overline{H}$ similarly. Then, $P_{k+1}(t,\overline{H})$ and $Q_{\ell+1}(t,\overline{G})$ are constant on $[p_k,1]$. Now, define numbers $\overline{p}$ and $\overline{q}$ as follows. If $\overline{G}(1) \le \Gamma(k+1)$, let $\overline{p} = 1$; otherwise, let $\overline{p}$ be the unique number in $(p_k,1)$ such that $\overline{G}(\overline{p}) = \Gamma(k+1)$. If $\overline{H}(1) \le \Delta(\ell+1)$, let $\overline{q} = 1$; otherwise, let $\overline{q}$ be the unique number in $(p_k,1)$ such that $\overline{H}(\overline{q}) = \Delta(\ell+1)$. (Such numbers exist since $\overline{G}$ and $\overline{H}$ are continuous and increasing.) Now, if $\min(\overline{p},\overline{q}) = 1$, let $p_{k+1} = \cdots = p_m = 1$ and $q_{\ell+1} = \cdots = q_n = 1$; if $\min(\overline{p},\overline{q}) = \overline{p} < 1$, let $p_{k+1} = \overline{p}$; if $\min(\overline{p},\overline{q}) = \overline{q} < 1$, let $q_{\ell+1} = \overline{q}$. In each case, extend G and H to $[0,\min(\overline{p},\overline{q})]$ by letting $G(t) = \overline{G}(t)$ and $H(t) = \overline{H}(t)$ if $0 \le t < 1$, and $G(1) = H(1) = 1$.

If $\min(\overline{p},\overline{q}) = 1$, then the process ends and G and H are defined on the whole of $[0,1]$. If this is not so, then either the collection of p_i's or the collection of q_j's has been augmented and G and H have been extended in a way that satisfies the conditions necessary to repeat the process. Thus, this procedure defines uniquely numbers $0 = p_0 = \cdots = p_w < \cdots < p_y = \cdots = p_m = 1$ and $0 = q_0 = \cdots = q_x < \cdots < q_z = \cdots = q_n = 1$ and continuous and increasing functions G and H on $[0,1)$ with $G(p_i) = \Gamma(i)$ for $i = w + 1, \ldots, y$, $H(q_j) = \Delta(j)$ for $j = x + 1, \ldots, z$, and $G(1) = H(1) = 1$.

Define strategies $E_1, \ldots, E_m$ and $F_1, \ldots, F_n$ as follows:

$$E_i(t) = \begin{cases} 0 & \text{if } 0 \leq t < p_{i-1}, \\ \dfrac{G(t) - \Gamma(i-1)}{\gamma_i} & \text{if } p_{i-1} \leq t < p_i, \\ 1 & \text{if } p_i \leq t \leq 1; \end{cases} \qquad (9.10)$$

$$F_j(t) = \begin{cases} 0 & \text{if } 0 \leq t < q_{j-1}, \\ \dfrac{H(t) - \Delta(j-1)}{\delta_j} & \text{if } q_{j-1} \leq t < q_j, \\ 1 & \text{if } q_j \leq t \leq 1. \end{cases} \qquad (9.11)$$

(Note that this means, for example, that $E_1, \ldots, E_w$ are pure strategies involving concession at $t = 0$, E_{y+1} may have an atom at $t = 1$, and $E_{y+2}, \ldots, E_m$ are pure strategies involving concession at $t = 1$.) This completes the description of the procedure $\Pi(\alpha, \beta)$.

Now, I claim that the strategies defined by $\Pi(0,0)$ constitute an equilibrium of the game. Note that all of the strategies thus defined are non-atomic on $[0,1)$. As noted in the construction, G and H are such that $Q_j(t,G)$ is constant on $[q_{j-1}, q_j]$ for $j = 1, \ldots, n$, and $P_i(t,H)$ is constant on $[p_{i-1}, p_i]$ for $i = 1, \ldots, m$. To show that the E_i's and F_j's constitute an equilibrium, it suffices to show that $Q_j(t,G)$ is increasing on $(0, q_{j-1})$ and decreasing on $(q_j, 1)$, and similarly for $P_i(t,H)$ (since the nonatomicity of G and H on $[0,1)$ implies that P_i and Q_j are continuous in t).

Consider $Q_j(t,G)$ on (q_{h-1}, q_h), with $h \leq j - 1$. Using the definition of G (see (9.8)), the derivative of $Q_j(t,G)$ with respect to t on (q_{h-1}, q_h) is

$$(1 - G(t))(v_j(b,t) - v_j(1 - a,t))(V_h(a,b,t) - V_j(a,b,t)).$$

However, from lemma 1 we have $V_h(a,b,t) > V_j(a,b,t)$ (since h is more risk averse than j), so that the derivative is positive, as required. A similar argument establishes that the derivative on $(q_j, 1)$ is negative, and a like argument can be made for P_i. Hence, the E_i's and F_j's defined by $\Pi(0,0)$ constitute an equilibrium.

The remaining equilibria are of two types. One type is closely related to the equilibrium just defined. In fact, it should be clear (by arguments similar to the preceding) that for any $0 < \alpha < 1$ and any $0 < \beta < 1$, the strategies defined by $\Pi(\alpha,0)$ and those defined by $\Pi(0,\beta)$ are equilibria of the game.

The final type of equilibria involves all individuals in one population conceding with probability 1 at time 0. The members of the other population use any strategies that generate a distribution of concession times that puts enough weight near $t = 1$ to make the members of the first population concede at $t = 0$. (Such strategies clearly exist – for example, all individuals can concede at $t = 1$ with probability 1.) This defines an equilibrium: Since all members of the first population concede at time 0, all members of the second population are indifferent between all concession times in $(0,1]$ (they always receive a payoff stream equal to their demand from time 0).

It is much more difficult to argue that every equilibrium of the game is of one of these types; a proof is given in the Appendix. We can summarize the results as follows.

Theorem 3. $(E_1, \ldots, E_m; F_1, \ldots, F_n)$ is an equilibrium of the two-population model if and only if it is one of the following:

1. $E_i(i = 1, \ldots, m)$ and $F_j(j = 1, \ldots, n)$ are defined by $\Pi(0,0)$.
2. For some $0 < \alpha < 1$ and $0 < \beta < 1$, $E_i(i = 1, \ldots, m)$ and $F_j(j = 1, \ldots, n)$ are defined by either $\Pi(\alpha,0)$ or $\Pi(0,\beta)$.
3. Either (a) $E_i(t) = 1$ for all $0 \le t \le 1$, for all $i = 1, \ldots, m$, and $F_1, \ldots, F_n$ are any strategies that generate a distribution H of concession times for which $P_i(0,H) \ge P_i(t,H)$ for any $0 \le t \le 1$, for $i = 1, \ldots, m$; or (b) the equilibrium is similar to this, with the roles of populations 1 and 2 reversed.

An immediate consequence of this result is the following.

Corollary 4. If the characteristics of populations 1 and 2 are the same, then the only symmetric equilibrium is the one defined by $\Pi(0,0)$. That is, the only equilibrium in the one-population model is the one defined in the previous section.

Perfect equilibrium

Selten (1975) argues that equilibria in games with finite pure strategy sets should possess a certain robustness. Suppose that a game is perturbed by insisting that each player devote at least some small probability to some completely mixed strategy. An equilibrium is *perfect* if it is close to an equilibrium of such a perturbed game. Okada (1981) suggests that one should insist that the equilibrium be close to an equilibrium of *every* such perturbed game; he calls such an equilibrium *strictly perfect*. Kohlberg and Mertens (1982) study a related notion (a strictly perfect equilibrium is a stable component in their sense), and show that the equilibria it generates have a number of attractive properties.

In the game here, each player has a continuum of pure strategies. In such a game, it is not clear how to formulate these notions of perfection. I do not attack this problem. Rather, I consider a small collection of perturbed games, in which the perturbing strategy is concession at time 0 with probability 1. (Note that this is an equilibrium strategy – of type (3)). The following result shows that the only equilibrium that is robust with respect to small perturbations of the strategy sets in the direction of this strategy is the one of type (1). That is, in the game in which each individual thinks that there is a positive probability that his opponent will concede at time 0, the only equilibrium is close to the one of type (1). It seems likely that this equilibrium is the only one that satisfies an appropriately modified version of strict perfection – that is, it is robust with respect to *all* small perturbations of the strategy sets. However, a precise argument to this effect is beyond the scope of this paper.

Proposition 5.   For each $\epsilon > 0$, let Γ^ϵ be the perturbed game in which the strategy space of each player is the set of cumulative probability distributions F on $[0,1]$ such that $F(0) \geq \epsilon$. Then, for each $\epsilon > 0$, the game Γ^ϵ has a unique equilibrium, which converges to the one defined in (1) of theorem 3 as $\epsilon \to 0$.

Proof.   Let $E_i(i = 1, \ldots, m)$ and $F_j(j = 1, \ldots, n)$ be the equilibrium strategies given in (1) of theorem 3, and let G and H be the corresponding distributions of concession times in the two populations. For each $\epsilon > 0$, let $E_i^\epsilon(t) = \epsilon + (1 - \epsilon)E_i(t)$ and $F_j^\epsilon(t) = \epsilon + (1 - \epsilon)F_j(t)$ for all $0 \leq t \leq 1$, $i = 1, \ldots, m$, and $j = 1, \ldots, n$. Now, $(E_1^\epsilon, \ldots, E_m^\epsilon; F_1^\epsilon, \ldots, F_n^\epsilon)$ is an equilibrium of Γ^ϵ, because the derivative with respect to t on $(0,1)$ of the payoff $P_i(t, H^\epsilon)$, where $H^\epsilon(t) = \Sigma_{j=1}^n \delta_j F_j^\epsilon(t) = \epsilon + (1 - \epsilon)H(t)$ for all $0 \leq t \leq 1$, is precisely $(1 - \epsilon)$ times the derivative of $P_i(t, H)$. Hence, $P_i(t, H^\epsilon)$ is increasing on $(0, p_{i-1})$, constant on (p_{i-1}, p_i), and decreasing on $(p_i, 1)$. Also, $P_i(0, H^\epsilon)$ is less than $P_i(\eta, H^\epsilon)$ for some $\eta > 0$, since H^ϵ has an atom at 0 (compare lemma A3 of the Appendix). Similar arguments can obviously be made for the payoffs of individuals in population 2. Further, since there is no other nonatomic equilibrium of the original game (Γ^0), and no equilibrium in which the strategies of players in both populations have atoms at 0, it is clear that this is the only equilibrium of Γ^ϵ. In addition, the E_i^ϵ's and F_j^ϵ's converge (pointwise) to the E_i's and F_j's.

The effect of a change in risk aversion

Here, I investigate the effect of an increase in the risk aversion of individuals of type 2ℓ on the equilibrium singled out as perfect by the preceding arguments. Suppose that the utility function $\hat{v}_\ell$ is more risk averse than v_ℓ, and less risk averse than $v_{\ell-1}$ (so that the ordering of risk aversions in population 2 is preserved).

Suppose that $q_\ell < 1$ and $q_{\ell-1} \in$ supp E_k. Then, as in the one-population case, $\hat{p}_i = p_i$ for $i = 1, \ldots, k-1$, $\hat{q}_j = q_j$ for $j = 1, \ldots, \ell-1$, and $\hat{G}(t) = G(t)$ and $\hat{H}(t) = H(t)$ for $0 \le t \le q_{\ell-1}$, so that the equilibrium payoffs of types $11, \ldots, 1k$ and $21, \ldots, 2(\ell - 1)$ are unaffected.

Now, consider the changes in G and H on $(q_{\ell-1}, 1]$. From lemma 1, we have $\hat{V}_\ell(a,b,s) > V_\ell(a,b,s)$ for all $0 \le s < 1$, so that from (9.8) (with $j = \ell$), we have $\hat{G}(t) > G(t)$ on $(q_{\ell-1}, \min(\hat{q}_\ell, q_\ell)]$ (since on this interval, both G and $\hat{G}$ have to keep type 2ℓ indifferent). (Refer to Figure 9.3.) This means that $q_{\ell-1} < \hat{p}_k < p_k$. On $(q_{\ell-1}, \hat{p}_k)$, H is unchanged (since u_k is unchanged). However, on $[\hat{p}_k, \min(p_k, \hat{p}_{k+1})]$, $\hat{H}$ has to keep type $k + 1$ indifferent, whereas H keeps type k indifferent. Since $H(\hat{p}_k) = \hat{H}(\hat{p}_k)$ and, from lemma 1, $U_{k+1}(b,a,s) < U_k(b,a,s)$ for all $0 \le s < 1$, we have, from (9.9), $\hat{H}(t) < H(t)$ for $\hat{p}_k < t \le \min(p_k, \hat{p}_{k+1})$. Now, there are several cases to consider, but the arguments are very similar. Suppose that $p_k < q_\ell$ and $\hat{G}(q_\ell) < \Gamma(k + 1)$, so that $q_\ell < \hat{p}_{k+1}$. Then, on $[p_k, \min(p_{k+1}, \hat{p}_{k+1})]$, $\hat{H}$ has to keep type $1(k + 1)$ indifferent, as H did. However, since $\hat{H}(p_k) < H(p_k)$, we deduce, from (9.9), that $\hat{H}(t) < H(t)$ on $[p_k, \min(p_{k+1}, \hat{p}_{k+1})]$. Now, suppose that $\hat{H}(\hat{p}_{k+1}) > \Delta(\ell)$. Then, $\hat{q}_\ell > q_\ell$, and we can consider the behavior of $\hat{G}$ on $[q_\ell, \hat{q}_\ell]$. Now, $\hat{G}$ has to keep type 2ℓ indifferent whereas G keeps type $2(\ell + 1)$ indifferent; also, $G(q_\ell) < \hat{G}(q_\ell)$, and so from (9.8), $\hat{G}(t) > G(t)$ on $[q_\ell, \hat{q}_\ell]$. On $[\hat{q}_\ell, q_{\ell+1}]$, both G and $\hat{G}$ keep type $2(\ell + 1)$ indifferent; since $\hat{G}(\hat{q}_\ell) > G(\hat{q}_\ell)$, we have $\hat{G}(t) > G(t)$ on this interval. Continuing in the same way, we see that $\hat{G}(t) > G(t)$ for all $q_{\ell-1} < t < 1$ and $\hat{H}(t) < H(t)$ for all $\hat{p}_k < t < 1$.

Then, arguing exactly as in the one-population case (integrating by parts in the expressions for $P_i(p_{i-1}, H)$ and $Q_j(q_{j-1}, G)$ for $i = k + 1, \ldots, m$ and $j = \ell + 1, \ldots, n$), we find that the equilibrium payoffs of types $1(k + 1), \ldots, 1m$ *decrease* and those of types $2(\ell + 1), \ldots, n$ *increase*. That is, an increase in risk aversion in population 2 causes those individuals in population 1 who in (perfect) equilibrium concede later to be made worse off, whereas the members of population 2 who concede later are better off. Summarizing, we have the following.[4]

Proposition 6. Suppose that individuals of type ℓ in population 2 become more risk averse (but not more so than those of type $\ell - 1$). Suppose

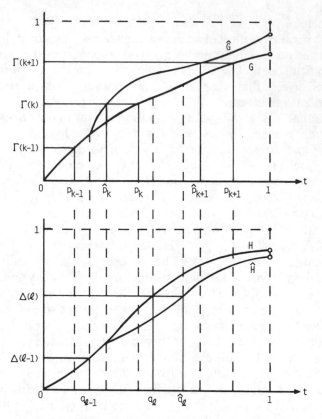

Figure 9.3 Changes in the perfect equilibrium distributions of concession times caused by an increase in the risk aversion of individuals of
type ℓ in population 2 in the two-population model

also that in the old (perfect) equilibrium, type 2ℓ concedes with probability 1 before time 1, and the smallest point in the support of the strategy of
type 2ℓ is a member of the support of the strategy of type $1k$. Then, the
(perfect) equilibrium payoffs of the types at least as risk averse as type k in
population 1 are unaffected, whereas those of the less risk averse types
decrease; the equilibrium payoffs of the types more risk averse than type ℓ
in population 2 are unaffected, whereas those of the less risk averse types
increase.

Thus, in the two-population model the effect of a change in risk aversion is exactly the opposite of that predicted by the axiomatic models. The

reason is that in equilibrium, the concession pattern in population 1 must make the actions of the individuals in population 2 optimal, and vice versa. Thus, if some members of population 2 become more risk averse, the individuals in population 1 have to concede on average earlier in order to keep the members of population 2 indifferent over some interval of concession times. However, if concessions in population 1 are on average earlier, the optimal concessions in population 2 are later; hence, the payoffs of individuals in population 1 decrease. (This type of argument is a standard one concerning mixed-strategy Nash equilibria; it is not made possible by some peculiar feature of the model.)

The effect of a change in the size of a type

Finally, I consider the effect of a change in the fraction of a population that is of a given type. I do so to see if any meaning can be given to the claim that in equilibrium, individuals will pretend to be less risk averse than they really are. Suppose that the fraction of the population taken up by relatively risk neutral individuals increases. Then, one might imagine that since this causes an opponent to ascribe a lower probability to an individual being risk averse, those who are risk averse can do better – they can "hide" among the mass of relatively risk neutral individuals. It turns out that this is not the case, although it *is* true that the ratio of the payoffs of the more risk averse to those of the less risk averse increases; the former are constant, whereas the latter decrease.

To see why this is true, we can use the previous result concerning a change in the degree of risk aversion. Suppose that the fraction of population 2 occupied by individuals of type ℓ increases from δ_ℓ to $\hat{\delta}_\ell = \delta_\ell + \epsilon$, and the fraction of type $\ell - 1$ decreases from $\delta_{\ell-1}$ to $\hat{\delta}_{\ell-1} = \delta_{\ell-1} - \epsilon$ (so that the population becomes on average less risk averse). This change is equivalent to one of the types considered in the previous subsection. Thus, break types $\ell - 1$ and ℓ into three types, which constitute the fractions $\delta_{\ell-1} - \epsilon$, ϵ, and δ_ℓ of the population (the first two types having the same utility function before the change,[5] and the second two having the same utility function after the change). Then, the change defined previously is a decrease in the risk aversion of the middle type. Hence, by proposition 6 the equilibrium payoffs of the types more risk averse than ℓ are unaffected, whereas those of type ℓ and the less risk averse types decrease. That is, we have the following.

Corollary 7. Suppose that the fraction of individuals of type ℓ in some population increases, whereas the fraction of those of type $\ell - 1$ decreases by the same amount, and those of type $\ell - 1$ concede with probability 1 before time 1. Then, the equilibrium payoff of every individual more risk averse than type ℓ in that population is unaffected, whereas the equilibrium payoff of every individual at most as risk averse as type ℓ decreases.

9.4   The case in which there is a choice of initial demand

Here, I elaborate on the previous model by allowing individuals to choose a "demand" at time 0. I assume that there are only two possible demands, a and b ($0 \le a < b < 1$). I study the perfect (Bayesian Nash) equilibria of the two-population model in which each individual simultaneously first chooses a demand, and then negotiates as in the previous model (i.e., subsequently simply chooses a time at which to concede). Throughout, I consider only the perfect equilibrium described in the previous section. To keep the analysis relatively simple, I assume that there are only two types in each population ($m = n = 2$). Note that in this model, the actions of an individual do, in general, convey useful information to his opponent. Unless the same fraction of each type demands a, the demand that an individual makes at time 0 allows his opponent to revise the probability that the individual is of a given type. Note, however, that an individual's subsequent behavior does not convey any additional useful information to his opponent.

I show that if $a > \frac{1}{2}$, there is no separating equilibrium in which the two types in each population choose different demands. I also show that in this case there is a continuum of pooling equilibria, in which a positive fraction of each type in each population chooses each possible demand.

Given the results in the axiomatic models that an individual can benefit from pretending to be less risk averse than he really is, one might imagine that the reason no separating equilibrium exists is that a more risk averse individual can benefit from changing his demand to that of a less risk averse individual. However, given the result of the previous section (proposition 6), it should come as no surprise that the opposite is true. That is, the less risk averse can benefit from pretending to be more risk averse (see the arguments that follow). Thus, there is another sense (in addition to the one considered in the previous subsection) in which the result derived in the axiomatic framework does not hold in my model.

If $a < \frac{1}{2}$, then there is no equilibrium of either type. Later, under the heading "Discussion" I consider briefly what may happen when there are more than two types in each population. However, I do not consider another natural extension, in which there are many, even a continuum, of possible demands. My analysis is not comprehensive, but is simply intended to establish that the basic model considered in the previous sections does not degenerate when at least some choice of initial demand is allowed.

Nonexistence of separating equilibrium

Suppose that $a > \frac{1}{2}$. Consider a situation in which all individuals of type 1 in each population demand a, whereas all those of type 2 demand b. When two individuals meet and reveal their demands, they know immediately each other's type, and the only perfect equilibrium distributions of concession times are given by the two-population model described previously in which each population contains one type. For example, if two type 1's meet, then their perfect equilibrium concession strategies are given by

$$E_{11}(t) = 1 - \exp\left(-\int_0^t V_1(a,a,s)\, ds\right)$$

and

$$F_{11}(t) = 1 - \exp\left(-\int_0^t U_1'(a,a,s)\, ds\right)$$

for $0 \le t < 1$ (see (9.10) and (9.11)). (That is, F_{11} keeps type 11 indifferent over all points in $[0,1]$, and E_{11} keeps type 21 indifferent over all such points.) The payoffs to these strategies are $u_1(1 - a,0)$ and $v_1(1 - a,0)$ (i.e., the payoffs obtained by immediate concession).

Next, consider the consequence of an individual of type 2 in population 1 demanding a rather than b. If he demands b, then his expected payoff is $\delta_1 u_2(1 - a,0) + \delta_2 u_2(1 - b,0)$ (since with probability δ_i, he encounters an individual of type $2i$, who correctly infers that he is of type 2, and uses a strategy that makes such individuals indifferent over $[0,1]$). If he demands a, then any opponent incorrectly identifies him as being of type 11, so that the opponent uses a strategy that makes such individuals indifferent over $[0,1]$. That is, if his opponent is of type 21, his payoff if he concedes at t is

$$P_2(t,F_{11}) \equiv \int_{(0,t]} u_2(a,s)F_{11}(s) + u_2(1 - a,t)(1 - F_{11}(t)); \qquad \textbf{(9.12)}$$

whereas if his opponent is of type 22, it is

$$P_2(t,F_{21}) \equiv \int_{(0,t]} u_2(a,s)F_{21}(s) + u_2(1 - b,t)(1 - F_{21}(t)), \qquad \textbf{(9.13)}$$

where

$$F_{21}(t) = 1 - \exp\left(-\int\limits_0^t U_1(b,a,s)\,ds\right)$$

for all $0 \leq t < 1$. Differentiating with respect to t in (9.12), we obtain

$$(1 - F_{11}(t))(u_2(a,t) - u_2(1 - a,t))(U_1(a,a,t) - U_2(a,a,t)).$$

From lemma 1, this is positive if $t < 1$, so that an optimal action for the individual in this case is to concede at time 1. His payoff is then $P_2(1,F_{11})$, which, since $P_2(t,F_{11})$ is increasing in t, exceeds $P_2(0,F_{11}) = u_2(1 - a,0)$, the payoff he obtains when he demands a in this case. Similarly, differentiating in (9.13), we obtain

$$(1 - F_{21}(t))(u_2(a,t) - u_2(1 - b,t))(U_1(b,a,t) - U_2(b,a,t)).$$

So by the same argument as before, the individual can obtain $P_2(1,F_{21})$, which exceeds $P_2(0,F_{21}) = u_2(1 - b,0)$, the payoff when he demands a in this case. Thus, his expected payoff against a random opponent exceeds $\delta_1 u_2(1 - a,0) + \delta_2 u_2(1 - b,0)$, and therefore he is better off demanding a, pretending to be more risk averse than he really is.

Thus, no separating equilibrium of this type exists. It is easy to see that the same argument also rules out any separating equilibrium in which all individuals of type 1 in one population demand b, whereas all individuals of type 2 in that population demand a, and the members of the other population act either similarly, or as they did before. So there is no separating equilibrium in which within each population the two types choose different demands.

If $a < \frac{1}{2}$, then when two individuals who demand a meet, they can reach agreement immediately; if $a + b < 1$, this is also true if individuals demanding a and b meet. It matters precisely what the payoffs are in these cases. I assume that if individual i demands d_i, $i = 1, 2$, and $d_1 + d_2 < 1$, then individual i receives the output stream $((1 + d_i - d_j)/2,0)$ (i.e., the individuals split equally the amount left over after their demands are satisfied; the precise method of splitting the excess does not matter for my argument, so long as the amount that i receives increases with d_i). First, consider the possibility of a separating equilibrium when $a < \frac{1}{2}$ and $a + b \geq 1$. In such an equilibrium, there are individuals in both populations who demand a. If the opponent of such an individual demands a, then the individual receives the output stream $(\frac{1}{2},0)$, whereas if the opponent demands b, the equilibrium payoff of this individual is the utility of the output stream $(1 - b,0)$. If the individual switches to a demand of b, the output stream he receives if his opponent demands a is $((1 + b - a)/2,0)$, and if his opponent demands b, he again receives the utility of $(1 - b,0)$. Since $(1 + b - a)/2 > \frac{1}{2}$, the individual will switch from a to b. A similar argument can obviously be made if $a + b < 1$. Thus, no separating equilibrium exists for any values of a and b.

Pooling equilibria

Now, consider the possibility of an equilibrium in which the fractions $0 < \pi_i < 1$ of type $1i$ and $0 < \rho_j < 1$ of type $2j$ demand a, whereas all other individuals in both populations demand b. Then, if for example a type-11 individual demands a and bargains with a type-21 individual who demands a, the equilibrium concession times are those given by the two-population model in which the fractions of the types in population 1 are $\pi_1/(\pi_1 + \pi_2)$ and $\pi_2/(\pi_1 + \pi_2)$ and those in population 2 are $\rho_1/(\rho_1 + \rho_2)$ and $\rho_2/(\rho_1 + \rho_2)$. For $(\pi_1,\pi_2,\rho_1,\rho_2)$ to constitute an equilibrium, each individual in each population must be indifferent between demanding a and b.

First, consider the case $a > \frac{1}{2}$. Note than an individual of type 1 in either population is always indifferent between demanding a and b. This is the case because 0 is always an element of the support of the equilibrium strategy of such an individual, whoever is his opponent (since type 1 is the most risk averse). Thus, the equilibrium payoff when the opponent demands a is $u_1(1 - a,0)$ (or $v_1(1 - a,0)$), and when the opponent demands b it is $u_1(1 - b,0)$ (or $v_1(1 - b,0)$), independent of $(\pi_1,\pi_2,\rho_1,\rho_2)$.

Consider the behavior of individuals of type 2 in population 1. Fix $0 < \pi_2 < 1$ and $0 < \rho_2 < 1$, and let $P_i(c;\pi_1,\rho_1)$ be the equilibrium payoff of an individual of type i in population 1 who demands c when the fractions of those who demand a among types 11 and 21 are π_1 and ρ_1; similarly define $Q_j(c;\pi_1,\rho_1)$ for type j in population 2. Suppose that $\pi_1 = 1$ (i.e., that all type-11 individuals demand a). Then, if a type-12 individual demands b, he identifies himself to be of type 2, and the equilibrium reached is the one in a two-population model where there is only one type in population 1. Hence, the support of the individual's strategy is $[0,1]$, and his equilibrium payoff is $u_2(1 - a,0)$ or $u_2(1 - b,0)$, depending on the demand of his opponent. Thus, for each $0 \le \rho_1 \le 1$,

$$P_2(b;1,\rho_1) = (\rho_1 + \rho_2)u_2(1 - a,0) + (1 - \rho_1 - \rho_2)u_2(1 - b,0). \qquad (9.14)$$

Now, fix $0 \le \rho_1 \le 1$ and reduce π_1. As π_1 falls, the fraction of type 2's among those demanding b in population 1 decreases. Hence, by corollary 7, the equilibrium payoff of type 2, whether the opponent demands a or b, increases. That is, for each $0 \le \rho_1 \le 1$,

$$P_2(b;\pi_1,\rho_1) \text{ is decreasing in } \pi_1. \qquad (9.15)$$

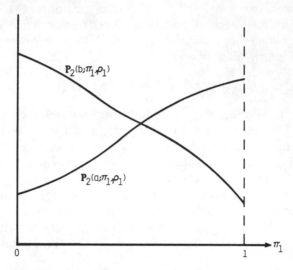

Figure 9.4 Functions $P_2(a; \cdot, \rho_1)$ and $P_2(b; \cdot, \rho_1)$

Next, consider what happens when a type-12 individual demands a. If $\pi_1 = 1$, then the equilibrium distributions of concession times are those for a two-population model in which the fraction $0 < 1/(1 + \pi_2) < 1$ of population 1 is of type 1, and the fraction $0 < \pi_2/(1 + \pi_2) < 1$ is of type 2 (since $\pi_1 = 1$ and $0 < \pi_2 < 1$). Hence, whether the opponent demands a or b, the smallest element in the support of the equilibrium strategy of the type-12 individual exceeds zero, and hence his equilibrium payoff exceeds $u_2(1 - a, 0)$ if his opponent demands a, and exceeds $u_2(1 - b, 0)$ if his opponent demands b. That is, for each $0 \le \rho_1 \le 1$, $P_2(a; 1, \rho_1) > (\rho_1 + \rho_2)u_2(1 - a, 0) + (1 - \rho_1 - \rho_2)u_2(1 - b, 0)$, and so by (9.14) we have, for each $0 \le \rho_1 \le 1$,

$$P_2(a; 1, \rho_1) > P_2(b; 1, \rho_1) \qquad (9.16)$$

(see Figure 9.4). Now, suppose that π_1 decreases. This means that the fraction of type 2's among those demanding a in population 1 increases. Hence, again by corollary 7, for each $0 \le \rho_1 \le 1$,

$$P_2(a; \pi_1, \rho_1) \text{ is increasing in } \pi_1. \qquad (9.17)$$

Finally, suppose that $\pi_1 = 0$. Then, a symmetric argument establishes that for all $0 \le \rho_1 \le 1$,

$$P_2(a; 0, \rho_1) < P_2(b; 0, \rho_1). \qquad (9.18)$$

It is also clear that for each $0 \le \rho_1 \le 1$, the equilibrium payoffs are continuous in π_1. (For example, if π_1 is close to zero, so that almost all type-11 individuals demand b, then the equilibrium payoff of a type-12 individual who demands a is close to $u_2(1 - a,0)$ or $u_2(1 - b,0)$ [depending on the opponent's demand], since the fraction of type 11's in the concession game after the demands are revealed is close to zero, so that the smallest element in the support of the equilibrium strategy of type 12 is close to zero.)

Combining (9.15) through (9.18), we conclude that for each $0 \leq \rho_1 \leq 1$, there exists a unique π_1 such that $P_2(a;\pi_1,\rho_1) = P_2(b;\pi_1,\rho_1)$. Denote this π_1 by $Y(\rho_1)$. Since all of the functions involved are continuous, so is Y. Symmetric arguments can obviously be made for population 2. That is, for each $0 \leq \pi_1 \leq 1$, there exists a unique ρ_1 such that $Q_2(a;\pi_1,\rho_1) = Q_2(b;\pi_1,\rho_1)$. Denote this ρ_1 by $\Phi(\pi_1)$; Φ is continuous.

Now, the function $\Phi \circ Y: [0,1] \to [0,1]$ is continuous and hence has a fixed point, say ρ_1^*. Let $\pi_1^* = Y(\rho_1^*)$. Then, (π_1^*,ρ_1^*) is such that $P_2(a;\pi_1^*,\rho_1^*) = P_2(b;\pi_1^*,\rho_1^*)$ and $Q_2(a;\pi_1^*,\rho_1^*) = Q_2(b;\pi_1^*,\rho_1^*)$. By (9.16) and (9.18), we have $0 < \pi_1^* < 1$ and $0 < \rho_1^* < 1$. That is, given the fixed (π_2,ρ_2), and the fact that type 1 is indifferent between a and b for any $(\pi_1,\pi_2,\rho_1,\rho_2)$, $(\pi_1^*,\pi_2,\rho_1^*,\rho_2)$ is a pooling equilibrium.

Proposition 8. If $a > \frac{1}{2}$, then for each $(\pi_2,\rho_2) \in (0,1)^2$, there exists a pooling equilibrium in which a positive fraction of each type in each population make each demand.

When $a < \frac{1}{2}$, it is easy to show that there is no pooling equilibrium. The reason is that, exactly as in the case of a separating equilibrium, an individual of type 1 in each population can increase his payoff by demanding b.

Discussion

Given the continuum of pooling equilibria in proposition 8, we cannot perform the comparative static exercises of Section 9.3. It is not clear whether there are assumptions under which a unique equilibrium is selected. One possibility is to increase the number of types in each population. The arguments presented establish that the most risk averse individuals in both populations are always indifferent between demanding a and b. All other types are indifferent only in particular cases. This suggests that however many types there are, there is always a one-dimensional continuum of equilibria; as the size of the most risk averse type shrinks, the range of the equilibria may contract. Thus, in the limit, when there is a continuum of types, there is a possibility that an essentially determinate equilibrium is defined.

APPENDIX
The Characterization of All Equilibria in the Two-Population Model

I repeatedly use the following expression for the difference between the payoffs of conceding at r and at t. If $r \leq t$, then

$$P_i(t,H) - P_i(r,H) = J_H(r)(u_i(a,r) - u_i(\tfrac{1}{2},r))$$

$$+ \int\limits_{(r,t)} (u_i(a,s) - u_i(1-b,r))\, dH(s) + J_H(t)(u_i(\tfrac{1}{2},t) - u_i(1-b,r)) \qquad \text{(A.1)}$$

$$+ (1 - H(t))(u_i(1-b,t) - u_i(1-b,r)).$$

Throughout, E_i $(i = 1, \ldots, m)$ is an equilibrium strategy of $1i$, and F_j $(j = 1, \ldots, n)$ is an equilibrium strategy of $2j$; G and H are the equilibrium distributions of concession times in populations 1 and 2, respectively. Let $J(G)$ and $J(H)$ be the set of atoms (jumps) of G and H, respectively. Note that

$$\text{If } t \notin J(H) \text{ and } t \in \text{supp } E_i, \text{ then } P_i(t,H) = P_i(E_i,H). \qquad \text{(A.2)}$$

The following gives conditions on a distribution of concession times under which more risk averse individuals concede earlier.

Lemma A1. If $[0,s_0] \subset \text{supp } H$, H is atomless on $(0,s_0] \cap (0,1)$, $r \in [0,s_0]$, $t \in [0,s_0]$, $r \in \text{supp } E_i$, and $t \in \text{supp } E_{i-1}$, then $t \leq r$.

Proof. If $r = s_0 = 1$, the result is immediate. So suppose that $r < 1$. Let $r \in \text{supp } E_i$ and suppose that $0 \leq r < t \leq s_0$. Then, $P_i(t,H) - P_i(r,H) \leq 0$. Now, $u_{i-1} = f \circ u_i$, where f is strictly concave, so that $f(w) - f(z) \leq f'(z)(w - z)$, with strict inequality if $w \neq z$. Hence,

$$u_{i-1}(a,s) - u_{i-1}(1-b,r) < f'(u_i(1-b,r))(u_i(a,s) - u_i(1-b,r))$$

unless s is such that $u_i(a,s) = u_i(1-b,r)$; by (P.2) and (P.3), there is only one such s. Hence, given that $[0,s_0] \subset \text{supp } H$,

$$\int\limits_{(r,t)} (u_{i-1}(a,s) - u_{i-1}(1-b,r))\, dH(s) <$$

$$f'(u_i(1-b,r)) \int\limits_{(r,t)} (u_i(a,s) - u_i(1-b,r))\, dH(s).$$

Also,

$$u_{i-1}(1-b,t) - u_{i-1}(1-b,r) < f'(u_i(1-b,r))(u_i(1-b,t) - u_i(1-b,r)).$$

However, since $t \in \operatorname{supp} H$, then either $H(t) - H(r) > 0$ or $H(t) < 1$. Hence, given that r is not an atom of H, and either t is not an atom of H, or $t = s_0 = 1$ and hence $u_i(\frac{1}{2},t) = 0 = u_i(1 - b,t)$, the preceding inequalities imply, using (A.1), that

$$P_{i-1}(t,H) - P_{i-1}(r,H) < f'(u_i(1 - b,r))(P_i(t,H) - P_i(r,H)) \le 0.$$

Hence, $t \notin \operatorname{supp} E_{i-1}$. So if $t \in \operatorname{supp} E_{i-1}$, then $t \le r$.

Corollary A2. If $[0,s_0] \subset \operatorname{supp} G$, $[0,s_0] \subset \operatorname{supp} H$, G is atomless on $(0,s_0] \cap (0,1)$, and H is atomless on $[0,s_0] \cap (0,1)$, then there exist $0 = p_0 = p_1 = \cdots = p_\ell < p_{\ell+1} < \cdots < p_{k-1} < s_0$ and $0 = q_0 < q_1 < \cdots < q_{h-1} < s_0$ such that

$[0,s_0] \cap \operatorname{supp} E_i = \{0\}$ for $i = 1, \ldots, \ell$;

$[0,s_0] \cap \operatorname{supp} E_i = [p_{i-1},p_i]$ for $i = \ell + 1, \ldots, k - 1$,

$$\text{and } [0,s_0] \cap \operatorname{supp} E_k = [p_{k-1},s_0];$$

$[0,s_0] \cap \operatorname{supp} F_j = [q_{j-1},q_j]$ for $j = 1, \ldots, h - 1$,

$$\text{and } [0,s_0] \cap \operatorname{supp} F_h = [p_{h-1},s_0].$$

Proof. Immediate from lemma A1 (using (9.1), and the analogous relation between H and the F_j's).

Now, I show that G and H cannot have atoms at the same point, except possibly at 1. The reason is simple: If, for example, G has an atom at t_0, then all members of population 2 obtain a higher payoff by conceding just after t_0, rather than at t_0.

Lemma A3. If $t_0 \in J(G)$ and $t_0 < 1$, then $t_0 \notin J(H)$.

Proof. Let $t_0 \in J(H)$, $t_0 < 1$. Then, for each $\delta > 0$ there exists $0 < \epsilon < \delta$ such that $t_0 + \epsilon \notin J(H)$. Next, consider $P_i(t_0 + \epsilon, H) - P_i(t_0,H)$ (see (A.1)). The first term is positive, independent of ϵ; the second term is nonnegative for small ϵ; the third is zero; and the fourth can be made as small as necessary for choosing ϵ small enough. Hence, for ϵ small enough, we have $P_i(t_0 + \epsilon,H) > P_i(t_0,H)$.

The following is a very useful result, which says that if G has an atom at $t_0 \in (0,1)$, then no member of population 2 concedes in some open interval before t_0 (when t_0 is imminent, it is better to wait until afterward, since there is a positive probability of a concession occurring at t_0).

Lemma A4.   If $t_0 \in J(G)$ and $0 < t_0 < 1$, then there exists $\epsilon > 0$ such that $(t_0 - \epsilon, t_0) \cap \operatorname{supp} H = \emptyset$.

Proof.   Let $\delta > 0$. For any $j = 1, \ldots, n$, we have

$$Q_j(t_0, G) - Q_j(t_0 - \delta, G) = J_G(t_0 - \delta)(v_j(b, t_0 - \delta) - v_j(\tfrac{1}{2}, t_0 - \delta))$$

$$+ \int\limits_{(t_0 - \delta, t_0)} (v_j(b, s) - v_j(1 - a, t_0 - \delta)) \, dG(s)$$

$$+ J_G(t_0)(v_j(\tfrac{1}{2}, t_0) - v_j(1 - a, t_0 - \delta)) +$$
$$(1 - G(t_0))(v_j(1 - a, t_0) - v_j(1 - a, t_0 - \delta))$$

(see (A.1)). However, $v_j(b, t_0 - \delta) - v_j(\tfrac{1}{2}, t_0 - \delta) \geq 0$ and, since $t_0 < 1$, we can find $\epsilon_1 > 0$ and $\alpha > 0$ such that for all $0 < \delta < \epsilon_1$, we have

$$v_j(\tfrac{1}{2}, t_0) > v_j(1 - a, t_0 - \delta) + \alpha,$$

and for all $t_0 - \delta < s < t_0$, we have

$$v_j(b, s) > v_j(b, t_0) > v_j(\tfrac{1}{2}, t_0) > v_j(1 - a, t_0 - \delta).$$

Hence, for all $0 < \delta < \epsilon_1$,

$$Q_j(t_0, G) - Q_j(t_0 - \delta, G) \geq \alpha J_G(t_0)$$
$$+ (1 - G(t_0))(v_j(1 - a, t_0) - v_j(1 - a, t_0 - \delta)).$$

However, there also exists $\epsilon_2 > 0$ such that for all $\delta < \epsilon_2$, we have $v_j(1 - a, t_0) - v_j(1 - a, t_0 - \delta) > -\alpha J_G(t_0)/2$. But then for all $0 < \delta < \epsilon = \min(\epsilon_1, \epsilon_2)$, we have

$$Q_j(t_0, G) - Q_j(t_0 - \delta, G) > \frac{\alpha J_G(t_0)}{2} > 0,$$

and so $Q_j(t, G) < Q_j(t_0, G)$ for all $t \in (t_0 - \epsilon, t_0)$. Hence, $(t_0 - \epsilon, t_0) \cap \operatorname{supp} H = \emptyset$.

The following states that if there is an interval not in the support of H, at the endpoints of which G does not have atoms, then the largest point in the interval can be in the support of G only if H is already 1 at that point. The reason is that the payoff to any member of population 1 is decreasing in the interval whenever there is a positive probability of a future concession by an opponent.

Lemma A5.   If $H(r) = H(t)$, $0 \leq r < t \leq 1$, $r \notin J(H)$, $t \notin J(H)$, and $t \in \operatorname{supp} G$, then $H(t) = 1$.

Proof. For all $i = 1, \ldots, m,$

$$P_i(t,H) - P_i(r,H) = (1 - H(t))(u_i(1 - b,t) - u_i(1 - b,r))$$

(using (A.1)). Hence, $P_i(t,H) < P_i(r,H)$ unless $H(t) = 1$. Since $t \notin J(H)$, this means (from (A.2)) that $t \notin$ supp G.

We can now restrict quite substantially the nature of the supports of the equilibrium distributions of concession times.

Lemma A6. If $t_0 \in J(G)$ and $0 < t_0 < 1$, then there exists $s_0 \in [0,t_0)$ such that supp $H = [0,s_0]$, $[0,s_0] \subset$ supp G, and G and H are atomless on $(0,s_0]$.

Proof. From lemma A4, there exists $\epsilon > 0$ such that $(t_0 - \epsilon,t_0) \cap$ supp $H = \emptyset$. Now, let $r = t_0 - \epsilon/2$ and $t = t_0$ in lemma A5. Since $t_0 \in J(G)$, $t_0 \notin J(H)$ by lemma A3, and so $H(r) = H(t)$. Hence, by lemma A5, $H(t_0) = 1$. Let $s_0 = $ max supp H. Then, $s_0 < t_0$. Now, if there is an atom of G in $(0,s_0]$, say at t_1, the same argument establishes that $H(t_2) = 1$ for some $t_2 < t_1$, contradicting the fact that $s_0 \in$ supp H. Similarly, H can have no atom in $(0,s_0]$.

Now, suppose that there exists $y \in$ supp H, and $0 < x < y$ such that $H(x) = H(y)$. Then, $y < s_0$, and so $H(y) < 1$, and $x \notin J(H)$, $y \notin J(H)$ by the preceding argument, and thus by lemma A5 we know that $y \notin$ supp G. But then we know that there exists $w < y$ such that $G(w) = G(y) < 1$; reversing the roles of G and H in lemma A5, and letting $r = w$ and $t = y$, we conclude that $y \notin$ supp H, a contradiction. Hence, supp $H = [0,s_0]$ and, similarly, supp $G \supset [0,s_0]$.

Now, we can conclude that if one distribution of concession times has an atom in the interior of its support, then all individuals in the opponent population must concede at time 0 with probability 1.

Lemma A7. If $t_0 \in J(G)$ and $0 < t_0 < 1$, then supp $H = \{0\}$.

Proof. By lemma A3, G and H cannot both have atoms at 0. Let s_0 come from lemma A6, and assume that $s_0 > 0$. Then, from corollary A2 and lemma A6, we know that there exist k and $0 \le p_{k-1} < s_0$ such that $[0,s_0] \cap$ supp $E_k = [p_{k-1},s_0]$. Hence, H is such that $P_k(t,H)$ is constant, equal to $P_k(E_k,H)$, for all $t \in (p_{k-1},s_0]$. That is,

$$\int_{[0,t]} u_k(a,s) \, dH(s) + (1 - H(t))u_k(1 - b,t) = P_k(E_k,H)$$

(since H is atomless on $(p_{k-1}, s_0]$) for all $p_{k-1} < t \le s_0$. Because the integral is (as a function of t) absolutely continuous, H is absolutely continuous. But then we can integrate by parts to obtain

$$u_k(a,t)H(t) - u_k(a,0)H(0) - \int_{[0,t]} H(s)\, D_2 u_k(a,s)\, ds$$

$$+ (1 - H(t))u_k(1 - b,t) = P_k(E_k H).$$

Since $D_2 u_k$ is continuous in s, and H is atomless on $(0, s_0]$, this shows that H is differentiable. Differentiating, we find that every solution of the resulting differential equation is of the form

$$H(t) = 1 - A \exp\left(-\int_0^t U_k(b,a,s)\, ds\right) \tag{A.3}$$

for some $A > 0$. Now, we need $H(s_0) = 1$. Since $s_0 < t_0 < 1$, the integral with $t = s_0$ is always finite, and so we must have $A = 0$. But then $H(u_{k-1}) = 1$, and thus $s_0 \notin \operatorname{supp} H$. So the only possibility is $s_0 = 0$.

As noted in the text, there exists an equilibrium of this type. For example, if supp $E_i = \{1\}$ for $i = 1, \ldots, m$, and supp $F_j = \{0\}$ for $j = 1, \ldots, n$, then $(E_1, \ldots, E_m; F_1, \ldots, F_n)$ is an equilibrium.

We can now use lemma A5 to restrict the nature of the supports of G and H when G and H are atomless on $(0,1)$.

Lemma A8. If G and H are atomless on $(0,1)$ and there exists $0 < t < 1$ such that $G(t) < 1$ and $H(t) < 1$, then $[0,t] \subset \operatorname{supp} H$.

Proof. Suppose, to the contrary, that $0 < x < t$ and $x \notin \operatorname{supp} H$. Let $y_G = \min\{z \ge x : z \in \operatorname{supp} G\}$ and define y_H similarly. Since $x \notin \operatorname{supp} H$, we have $y_H > x$. Also, $y_G > x$ (since if $y_G = x$, then there exists $y > x$, $y \in \operatorname{supp} G$ such that $H(x) = H(y)$ and $H(y) < 1$, contradicting lemma A5). Let $y = \min\{y_G, y_H\} > x$. First, suppose that $y < 1$. If $y = y_G$, then $G(x) = G(y) < 1$, $x \notin J(G)$ and $y \notin J(G)$, and so by lemma A5, $y \notin \operatorname{supp} H$. Hence, there exists $w < y$ such that $H(w) = H(y)$, $w \notin J(H)$, $y \notin J(H)$, and $H(y) < 1$, and so by lemma A5 again, $y \notin \operatorname{supp} G$, contradicting the definition of y ($= y_G$). If $y = y_H$, a similar argument can be made. Hence, the only possibility is $y = 1$. But then

$$P_i(y,H) - P_i(x,H) = J_H(y)(u_i(\tfrac{1}{2},y) - u_i(1 - b,x)).$$

However, $u_i(\tfrac{1}{2},y) = 0$ if $y = 1$, and so this is negative unless $J_H(y) = 0$. But this is impossible, since we assumed that $G(t) = G(y) - J_H(y) = 1 -$

$J_H(y) < 1$. Hence, $[0,t] \subset$ supp H. A symmetric argument implies that $[0,t] \subset$ supp G.

Lemma A9. If neither supp $G = \{0\}$ nor supp $H = \{0\}$, then neither supp $G = \{1\}$ nor supp $H = \{1\}$.

Proof. If, for example, supp $G = \{1\}$, then clearly $Q_j(0,G) > Q_j(t,G)$ for all $t > 0$, so that supp $H = \{0\}$.

Corollary A10. If neither supp $G = \{0\}$ nor supp $H = \{0\}$, then there exists $0 < t < 1$ such that $G(t) < 1$ and $H(t) < 1$.

Lemma A11. If G and H are atomless on $(0,1)$ and neither supp $G = \{0\}$ nor supp $H = \{0\}$, then there exists $s_0 > 0$ such that either supp $G = [0,s_0]$ and supp $H \supset [0,s_0]$, or supp $H = [0,s_0]$ and supp $G \supset [0,s_0]$.

Proof. Let $z_G = \max$ supp $G > 0$ and $z_H = \max$ supp $H > 0$, and let $s_0 = \min\{z_G,z_H\} > 0$. The result then follows by letting $t = s_0 - \epsilon$ for any $\epsilon > 0$ in lemma A8, and using corollary A10.

Lemma A12. If G and H are atomless on $(0,1)$ and neither supp $G = \{0\}$ nor supp $H = \{0\}$, then there exist $0 \leq \alpha < 1$ and $0 \leq \beta < 1$ such that G and H are as specified either by the procedure $\Pi(\alpha,0)$ or by the procedure $\Pi(0,\beta)$.

Proof. Suppose that supp $H = [0,s_0]$ (see lemma A11). Then, from corollary A2, there exist k and $p_{k-1} < s_0$ such that $[0,s_0] \cap$ supp $E_k = [p_{k-1},s_0]$. But then we can argue, as in the proof of lemma A7, that H has the form given in (A.3) on $[p_{k-1},s_0)$. Now, if $s_0 < 1$, then by assumption, s_0 is not an atom of H, and so we need $H(s_0) = 1$; but this is possible only if $A = 0$, in which case $s_0 = 0$, contradicting the assumption that supp $H \neq \{0\}$. Hence, $s_0 = 1$, and so supp $G =$ supp $H = [0,1]$. By lemma A3, at most one of G and H have an atom at 0. But then using corollary A2, and solving the differential equation on each $[p_{i-1},p_i]$ and $[q_{j-1},q_j]$, as before, we find that the only solutions are those defined in the procedure $\Pi(\alpha,0)$ or $\Pi(0,\beta)$ by (9.8) and (9.9).

We have now proved that the only equilibria are those characterized in theorem 3. Lemma A12 states that the only equilibria in which G and H are atomless on $(0,1)$ and neither supp $G = \{0\}$ nor supp $H = \{0\}$ are those described in (1) and (2) of theorem 3; lemma A7 states that whenever G or H has an atom in $(0,1)$, then either supp $G = \{0\}$ or supp $H = \{0\}$, when the equilibrium is of the type specified in (3) of theorem 3.

NOTES

1. The change in risk aversion considered in Roth (1985) does not preserve a player's preferences over certain outcomes.
2. A continuous extensive game fits more directly with the preceding description. By analogy with discrete extensive games, a pure strategy in such a game specifies, for each time t, whether or not to concede. That is, it is a function from $[0,1]$ to $\{C(\text{oncede}),S(\text{tand firm})\}$. However, for each such strategy of an opponent, every strategy of an individual that has the same time of first concession yields the same outcome. Thus, there is a reduced strategic form for the game in which the pure strategies of each individual are those functions f from $[0,1]$ to $\{C,S\}$ such that $f(t) = S$ if $0 \le t < t_0$ and $f(t) = C$ if $t_0 \le t \le 1$, for some t_0. This reduced strategic form is isomorphic to the strategic form specified in the text, and its Nash equilibria are of course outcome equivalent to the Nash equilibria of the extensive form.
3. Given the discussion of the previous paragraph, this is the same as saying that there is a unique *symmetric* equilibrium in the two-population model when the characteristics of the two populations are identical.
4. If a type that, in equilibrium, concedes with probability 1 at time 1 becomes more risk averse, then no individual's equilibrium payoff is affected.
5. This violates (P.4) (the function relating the utility functions of the two identical types is not *strictly* concave), but it should be clear that this assumption affects only some of the finer details of the results.

REFERENCES

Bishop, R. L. (1964): A Zeuthen-Hicks Theory of Bargaining. *Econometrica, 32,* 410-17.
Chatterjee, K., and W. Samuelson (1983): Bargaining under Incomplete Information. *Operations Research,* 31, 835-51.
Crawford, V. P. (1982): A Theory of Disagreement in Bargaining. *Econometrica,* 50, 607-37.
Cross, J. G. (1965): A Theory of the Bargaining Process. *American Economic Review,* 55, 66-94.
Fudenberg, D., and J. Tirole (1983a): Sequential Bargaining with Incomplete Information. *Review of Economic Studies,* 50, 221-47.
     (1983b): A Theory of Exit in Oligopoly. Draft.
Hicks, J. (1932): *The Theory of Wages.* Macmillan, London.
Kohlberg, E., and J.-F. Mertens (1982): *On the Strategic Stability of Equilibrium.* Discussion Paper 8248, C.O.R.E., November.
Kurz, M. (1977): Distortion of Preferences, Income Distribution, and the Case for a Linear Income Tax. *Journal of Economic Theory,* 14, 291-8.
     (1980): Income Distribution and the Distortion of Preferences: The ℓ-Commodity Case. *Journal of Economic Theory,* 22, 99-106.
McLennan, A. (1981): A General Noncooperative Theory of Bargaining. Draft, Department of Political Economy, University of Toronto.
Nalebuff, B., and J. Riley (1984): *Asymmetric Equilibrium in the War of Attrition.* Working Paper 317, University of California at Los Angeles, January.
Nash, J. F. (1950): The Bargaining Problem. *Econometrica,* 28, 155-62.
     (1953): Two-Person Cooperative Games. *Econometrica,* 21, 128-40.

Okada, A. (1981): On Stability of Perfect Equilibrium Points. *International Journal of Game Theory,* 10, 67–73.

Perles, M. A., and M. Maschler (1981): The Super-Additive Solution for the Nash Bargaining Game. *International Journal of Game Theory,* 10, 163–93.

Riley, J. G. (1980): Strong Evolutionary Equilibrium and the War of Attrition. *Journal of Theoretical Biology,* 82, 383–400.

Roth, A. E. (1979): *Axiomatic Models of Bargaining.* Springer-Verlag, New York.

Roth, A. E. (1985): A Note on Risk Aversion in a Perfect Equilibrium Model of Bargaining. *Econometrica,* 53, 207–11.

Roth, A. E., and U. G. Rothblum (1982): Risk Aversion and Nash's Solution for Bargaining Games with Risky Outcomes. *Econometrica,* 50, 639–47.

Rubinstein, A. (1982): Perfect Equilibrium in a Bargaining Model. *Econometrica,* 50, 97–109.

Samuelson, W. (1980): First Offer Bargains. *Management Science,* 26, 155–64.

Selten, R. (1975): Reexamination of the Perfectness Concept for Equilibrium Points in Extensive Games. *International Journal of Game Theory,* 4, 25–55.

Sobel, J. (1981): Distortion of Utilities and the Bargaining Problem. *Econometrica,* 49, 597–619.

Sobel, J., and I. Takahashi (1983): A Multistage Model of Bargaining. *Review of Economic Studies,* 50, 411–26.

Thomson, W. (1979): *The Manipulability of the Shapley-Value.* Discussion Paper 79–115, Center for Economic Research, Department of Economics, University of Minnesota.

Young, A. R. (1983): Iterated Demand Game. Draft, August.

CHAPTER 10

Risk sensitivity and related properties for bargaining solutions

Stef Tijs
UNIVERSITY OF NIJMEGEN, THE NETHERLANDS

Hans Peters
UNIVERSITY OF NIJMEGEN, THE NETHERLANDS

10.1 Introduction

In this chapter, we consider *n-person bargaining games* ($n \geq 2$), that is, pairs (S,d) where

(G.1) The *space S of feasible utility payoffs* is a compact and convex subset of $\mathbb{R}^n$,

(G.2) The *disagreement outcome d* is an element of S.

Furthermore, for mathematical convenience, we will also assume that

(G.3) $x \geq d$ for all $x \in S$,
(G.4) There is an $\hat{x} \in S$ with $\hat{x}_i > d_i$ for each $i \in N = \{1,2,\ldots,n\}$,
(G.5) For all $y \in \mathbb{R}^n$ with $d \leq y \leq x$ for some $x \in S$, we have $y \in S$.

Such a game (S,d) corresponds to a situation involving n bargainers (players) $1, 2, \ldots, n$, who may cooperate and agree upon choosing a point $s \in S$, which has utility s_i for player i, or who may not cooperate. In the latter case, the outcome is the point d, which has utility d_i for player $i \in N$. The family of all such bargaining games, satisfying (G.1) through (G.5), is denoted by G^n.

For a bargaining game $(S,d) \in G^n$, the *Pareto-set P(S)* is defined by

$$P(S) := \{x \in S; \forall_{y \in S}[y \geq x \Longrightarrow y = x]\}$$

The authors are indebted to Ehud Kalai for drawing their attention to the twist property of bargaining solutions and for some helpful discussions, and to Al Roth for numerous valuable comments. The paper has benefitted also from the comments of two anonymous referees.

215

and the *utopia point* $h(S) = (h_1(S), \ldots, h_n(S)) \in \mathbb{R}^n$ by

$$h_i(S) := \max\{x_i; (x_1, \ldots, x_i, \ldots, x_n) \in S\} \quad \text{for all } i \in N.$$

(The letter h is the first letter of *heaven*.)

We call a map $\phi\colon G^n \to \mathbb{R}^n$ an *n-person bargaining solution*. If, additionally, the following two properties hold, we call ϕ a *classical bargaining solution*:

PO: For each $(S,d) \in G^n$, we have $\phi(S,d) \in P(S)$ (*Pareto-optimality*).

IEUR: For each $(S,d) \in G^n$ and each transformation $A\colon \mathbb{R}^n \to \mathbb{R}^n$ of the form

$A(x_1, x_2, \ldots, x_n) = (a_1 x_1 + b_1, a_2 x_2 + b_2, \ldots, a_n x_n + b_n)$ for all $x \in \mathbb{R}^n$,

where $b_1, b_2, \ldots, b_n$ are real numbers and $a_1, a_2, \ldots, a_n$ are positive real numbers, we have $\phi(A(S), A(d)) = A(\phi(S,d))$ (*independence of equivalent utility representations*).

The PO property can be considered a basic property (see also our remark with regard to this point in Section 10.6). One of the arguments for taking the IEUR property as basic is a theorem in Kihlstrom, Roth, and Schmeidler (1981), which states that every (2-person) bargaining solution that is Pareto-optimal and risk sensitive satisfies also IEUR; so this latter property is, under the assumption of PO, a necessary condition for risk sensitivity.

Since, in this chapter, we will consider only classical solutions, we may without loss of generality restrict our attention here to n-person bargaining games with disagreement outcome 0. From now on, we assume that every $(S,d) \in G^n$, besides (G.1) through (G.5), satisfies

(G.6) $d = 0$,

and we will write S instead of (S,d).

The purpose of this chapter is to establish relations between some well-known and some new properties of bargaining solutions, where a central position is given to the risk-sensitivity property. Special attention will be paid to the risk aspects of solutions satisfying the following property, which was introduced by J. F. Nash (1950) in his fundamental paper.

IIA: A solution $\phi\colon G^n \to \mathbb{R}^n$ is called *independent of irrelevant alternatives* if for all S and T in G^n, we have $\phi(S) = \phi(T)$ if $S \subset T$ and $\phi(T) \in S$.

In addition, risk aspects of individually monotonic solutions (see Kalai and Smorodinsky (1975), Roth (1979b)) will be discussed.

IM: A bargaining solution $\phi\colon G^n \to \mathbb{R}^n$ is called *individually monotonic* if, for every $i \in N$, the following condition holds:

IM_i: For all $S, T \in G^n$ with $S \subset T$ and $h_j(S) = h_j(T)$ for each $j \in N - \{i\}$ we have $\phi_i(S) \le \phi_i(T)$.

The organization of the chapter is as follows. Section 10.2 is devoted to the risk-sensitivity property of bargaining solutions and contains an overview of known results. In Section 10.3, the relation between risk sensitivity and twist sensitivity of two-person classical solutions is studied. We prove in Section 10.4 that all two-person classical IIA solutions and also all individually monotonic classical solutions are risk sensitive, using the result of Section 10.3, which states that all 2-person twist-sensitive classical solutions are risk sensitive. Section 10.5 discusses the risk profit opportunity and its relation to risk sensitivity and twist sensitivity for n-person classical solutions. Section 10.6 summarizes the results, and some concluding remarks are made.

10.2   Risk sensitivity of bargaining solutions

Pioneering work on the problem of how to compare the aversion to risk of decision makers was done by Pratt (1964), Yaari (1969), Arrow (1971), and Kihlstrom and Mirman (1974). Let A be the set of riskless alternatives for decision makers and $L(A)$ the set of finite lotteries over A. Let u and v be von Neumann–Morgenstern utility functions on $L(A)$ for two decision makers. Closely following Yaari (1969) and Kihlstrom and Mirman (1974), the following result was derived.

Theorem 1.   (Peters and Tijs (1981)): The following two assertions are equivalent:

1. For all $a \in A$: $\{\ell \in L(A); v(\ell) > v(a)\} \subset \{\ell \in L(A); u(\ell) > u(a)\}$.
2. There exists a nondecreasing concave function $k: u(A) \to \mathbb{R}$ such that $v(a) = k \circ u(a)$ for all $a \in A$.

In view of this result, we have the following.

Definition 2.   If u and v satisfy one of the equivalent conditions in theorem 1, then we say that the decision maker with utility function v is *more risk averse* than the decision maker with utility function u.

In the recent literature, the effects of increasing or decreasing risk aversion in bargaining situations have been studied in two directions. In the first direction, attempts have been made to answer the question of whether it is advantageous or disadvantageous for bargainers to have more risk averse opponents. This question was raised for the first time by Kihlstrom, Roth, and Schmeidler (1981). It also represents the approach followed in this chapter. In the second direction, investigators have tried to determine whether it is advantageous for a bargainer to *pretend* to be more (or less) risk averse in a bargaining situation. Interesting, in this context, is a remark by Kannai (1977, p. 54) – that in a resource-allocation problem of two agents, where the Nash bargaining solution is used, and where each bargainer knows only the preferences of the other bargainer and not the utility function, it is advantageous to announce that one's utility function is a minimally concave utility function, corresponding to the preferences. Other contributions in this second direction can be found in Kurz (1977, 1980), Crawford and Varian (1979), and Sobel (1981).

Let us first introduce some notation and then give the definition of risk sensitivity that we will use here. In this definition, it is implicitly assumed that all Pareto-optimal elements in a game S correspond to riskless alternatives (i.e., elements of A).

For $S \in G^n$ and $i \in N$, let $C_i(S)$ be the *family of nonconstant, nondecreasing continuous concave functions* on the closed interval $[0, h_i(S)]$ that have value 0 on 0; and for each $k_i \in C_i(S)$, let

$$K_i(x) = (x_1, \ldots, x_{i-1}, k_i(x_i), x_{i+1}, \ldots, x_n) \text{ for each } x \in S,$$
$$K_i(S) = \{K_i(x); x \in S\}.$$

Lemma 3.   Let $S \in G^n$, $i \in N$, and $k_i \in C_i(S)$. Then, $K_i(S) \in G_n$.

Proof.   We have to prove (G.1) through (G.6) for $K_i(S)$.

1. $0 = K_i(0) \in K_i(S)$, and so (G.2) and (G.6) hold.
2. Let $y \in \mathbb{R}^n$ and $x \in S$ such that $0 \le y \le K_i(x)$. Then, $0 \le y_i \le k_i(x_i)$, and so since k_i is continuous, there exists $z_i \in [0, x_i]$ such that $k_i(z_i) = y_i$. Hence, $y = (y_1, \ldots, y_{i-1}, k_i(z_i), y_{i+1}, \ldots, y_n) \in K_i(S)$ since $0 \le (y_1, \ldots, z_i, y_{i-1}, y_{i+1}, \ldots, y_n) \le x$. Thus, (G.5) holds.
3. $K_i(x) \ge K_i(0) = 0$ for all $x \in S$ since k_i is nondecreasing. Therefore, (G.3) holds.
4. Since S is compact and K_i is continuous, $K_i(S)$ is compact. Let $x, y \in S$ and $\lambda \in (0,1)$. Then, $\lambda K_i(x) + (1 - \lambda) K_i(y) \le K_i[\lambda x + (1 - \lambda)y] \in K_i(S)$ since k_i is concave and S is convex. So $K_i(S)$ is convex, in view of (2) and (3). Hence, (G.1) holds
5. Let $\hat{x} \in S$, with $\hat{x} > 0$. Then, $k_i(\hat{x}_i) > 0$ since k_i is nondecreasing, nonconstant, and concave. So $K_i(\hat{x}) > 0$, and (G.4) holds.

The bargaining game $K_i(S)$ can be seen as the game that arises from the bargaining game S, if the ith player there (with utility function u) is replaced by a more risk averse player (with utility function $k_i \circ u$).

Definition 4.   A bargaining solution is called *risk sensitive* (RS) if for all $S \in G^n$, $i \in N$, and $k_i \in C_i(S)$, we have for all $j \in N\setminus\{i\}$,

$$RS_i; \phi_j(K_i(S)) \ge \phi_j(S).$$

We can interpret risk sensitivity of a bargaining solution as follows: The solution assigns higher utilities to all bargainers in $N - \{i\}$, if bargainer i is replaced by a more risk averse opponent.

Our risk-sensitivity property is fairly strong. It is even stronger than, for example, the risk-sensitivity property in Roth (1979a), since we allow k_i to be nondecreasing in view of theorem 1. The difference, however, is only a minor one and it allows us the advantage of simplifying the proof of theorem 9, to follow. For more information on risk sensitivity for $n > 2$, see the end of this section, and Section 10.5.

In their fundamental paper, Kihlstrom, Roth, and Schmeidler (1981) prove that the symmetric 2-person bargaining solutions proposed by Nash (1950), Kalai and Smorodinsky (1975), and Perles and Maschler (1981) are all risk sensitive. Peters and Tijs (1981) prove that every nonsymmetric two-person classical IIA solution, as proposed in Harsanyi and Selten (1972), is also risk sensitive. In de Koster, Peters, Tijs, and Wakker (1983), it is shown that all two-person classical IIA solutions are risk sensitive; moreover, this class is described there. The class consists of the Harsanyi–Selten solutions and two other dictatorial bargaining solutions, D^1 and D^2. Here, $D^i(S)$ is the point of the Pareto-set $P(S)$ with maximal ith coordinate ($i = 1, 2$). As is well known, the Harsanyi–Selten solutions are the solutions F^t: $G^2 \rightarrow \mathbb{R}^2$ ($t \in (0,1)$) where, for every $S \in G^2$ and $t \in (0,1)$, $F^t(S)$ maximizes the product $x_1^t x_2^{1-t}$ on S. In Peters and Tijs (1982a), it is proved that every individually monotonic two-person classical solution is risk sensitive. Moreover, all of these solutions are described in that paper, as follows. In view of IEUR, it is sufficient to look at games S in G^2 with $h(S) = (1,1)$. A *monotonic curve* is a map λ: $[1,2] \rightarrow$ conv$\{(1,0),(0,1),(1,1)\}$ with $\lambda_1(s) \le \lambda(t)$ and $\lambda_1(s) + \lambda_2(s) = s$ for all $s,t \in$ $[1,2]$ with $s \le t$. For every monotonic curve λ, the classical solution π^λ: $G^2 \rightarrow \mathbb{R}^2$ is defined as follows: $\pi^\lambda(S)$ is the unique point in $P(S) \cap \{\lambda(t);$ $t \in [1,2]\}$, for every $S \in G^2$ with $h(S) = (1,1)$. Then, $\{\pi^\lambda;\ \lambda$ is a monotonic curve$\}$ is the family of all individually monotonic 2-person classical solutions. In particular, the Kalai–Smorodinsky solution is the solution $\pi^{\lambda*}$ with $\lambda_*(T): = (\tfrac{1}{2}t, \tfrac{1}{2}t)$ for every $t \in [1,2]$, and $D^1 = \pi^{\underline{\lambda}}$, $D^2 = \pi^{\bar{\lambda}}$ where $\underline{\lambda}(t): = (1, t - 1)$ and $\bar{\lambda}(t): = (t - 1, 1)$ for every $t \in [1,2]$. So D^1 and D^2 also satisfy IM.

For all results with regard to risk sensitivity mentioned thus far, it is assumed implicitly that all points of the Pareto-set correspond to riskless alternatives. For results in the case of risky Pareto-points, we refer to Peters and Tijs (1981, 1983) and Roth and Rothblum (1982). In Peters and Tijs (1984), for a subclass of G^n, all individually monotonic n-person classical solutions are described, and it is proved that all of these bargaining solutions are risk sensitive. (It is well known (Roth (1979b)) that there does not exist a symmetric n-person classical solution on the whole class G^n that is individually monotonic.) In Section 10.5, we will see that the n-person Nash solution is not risk sensitive. This is one of the indications that for $n > 2$, risk sensitivity is a rather strong property. Two suitable weaker properties, risk profit opportunity and the worse-alternative property, will be introduced in that section. All of the n-person classical IIA solutions possess these properties (see Peters and Tijs (1983)). In the next section, we compare for two-person classical solutions the risk-sensitivity property and the twist-sensitivity property, and in Section 10.4 we present new short proofs of the fact that all two-person classical IIA solutions and all classical IM solutions are risk sensitive.

10.3   Risk sensitivity and twist sensitivity

Let $S, T \in G^n$, $i \in N$, and $\alpha_i \in [0, h_i(S)]$. Then, we say that T is a *favorable twisting of S for player i at level α_i* if

$$x_i > \alpha_i \text{ for all } x \in T \backslash S, \tag{10.1}$$

$$x_i < \alpha_i \text{ for all } x \in S \backslash T, \tag{10.2}$$

and an *unfavorable twisting of S for player i at level α_i* if

$$x_i < \alpha_i \text{ for all } x \in T \backslash S, \tag{10.3}$$

$$x_i > \alpha_i \text{ for all } x \in S \backslash T. \tag{10.4}$$

Definition 5.   A bargaining solution $\phi: G^n \to \mathbb{R}^n$ is called *twist sensitive* (TW) if for each S and $T \in G^n$, with $\phi(S) \in P(T)$, we have for each $i \in N$,

TW$_1$: $\phi_i(T) \geq \phi_i(S)$, if T is a favorable twisting of S for player i at level $\phi_i(S)$.
TW$_2$: $\phi_i(T) \leq \phi_i(S)$, if T is an unfavorable twisting of S for player i at level $\phi_i(S)$.

Twist-sensitive bargaining solutions respond with a better payoff for a player in case a favorable twisting for that player is made at his payoff level in the solution point. Note that if $n = 2$, for Pareto-optimal solutions this notion TW is equal to the twisting property Tw, introduced by Thomson and Myerson (1980, p. 39). In general, Tw $\Rightarrow$ TW for $n = 2$.

The following theorem is one of the main results of the present discussion.

Theorem 6.   Each twist-sensitive two-person classical solution is risk sensitive.

Proof. Let $\phi: G^2 \to \mathbb{R}^2$ be a twist-sensitive classical solution. We have to prove RS$_1$ and RS$_2$. We show only RS$_2$. Let $S \in G^2$ and $k_2 \in C_2(S)$. We have to prove that

$$\phi_1(K_2(S)) \geq \phi_1(S). \tag{10.5}$$

If $\phi_2(K_2(S)) = 0$, then by PO,

$$\phi_1(K_2(S)) = h_1(K_2(S)) = h_1(S) \geq \phi_1(S),$$

and thus (10.5) holds. Suppose now that $\phi_2(K_2(S)) > d_2$. Since ϕ satisfies the IEUR property, it is no loss of generality to suppose that

$$k_2(q_2) = q_2, \tag{10.6}$$

where $q = (q_1, q_2)$ is the point of $P(S)$ with first coordinate $\phi_1(K_2(S))$. By the concavity of k_2, we then have

$$k_2(x) \geq x \text{ for all } x \in [0, q_2] \qquad k_2(x) \leq x \text{ for all } x \geq q_2. \tag{10.7}$$

From (10.6) and (10.7) it follows that S is an unfavorable twisting of $K_2(S)$ for player 1 at level $\phi_1(K_2(S))$. From TW$_2$, we may conclude that (10.5) holds.

The converse of theorem 6 does not hold, as example 10 at the end of this section shows. We introduce now another property for two-person bargaining solutions, which, for classical solutions, is also implied by twist sensitivity.

Definition 7. A bargaining solution $\phi: G^2 \to \mathbb{R}^2$ is said to have the *slice property* (SL), if for all $S, T \in G^2$, with $h(S) = h(T)$ and $T \subset S$, we have

SL$_1$: $\phi_1(T) \geq \phi_1(S)$ if $x_2 > \phi_2(S)$ for all $x \in S \backslash T$,
SL$_2$: $\phi_2(T) \geq \phi_2(S)$ if $x_1 > \phi_1(S)$ for all $x \in S \backslash T$.

Thus, a bargaining solution $\phi: G^2 \to \mathbb{R}^2$ is said to have the slice property if it favors the opponent of a player i when a piece of the set of utility payoffs, preferred by i over $\phi(S)$, is sliced off, the utopia point remaining the same. For $n = 2$, the slice property resembles the cutting axiom of Thomson and Myerson (1980). The difference (for Pareto-optimal solutions) is that in the cutting axiom, there is no condition on the utopia point. Therefore, SL is considerably weaker than cutting. Theorem 9, to follow, shows that risk-sensitive classical solutions are twist sensitive if they additionally satisfy SL.

Theorem 8. Each twist-sensitive two-person classical solution has the slice property.

Proof.   Let $\phi: G^2 \rightarrow \mathbb{R}^2$ be twist sensitive. We prove only that SL_1 holds. Therefore, let $S, T \in G^2$, with $h(S) = h(T)$, $T \subset S$, and $x_2 > \phi_2(S)$ for all $x \in S \backslash T$. We must show that

$$\phi_1(T) \geq \phi_1(S). \tag{10.8}$$

Note that $\phi(S) \in P(T)$ and $x_1 < \phi_1(S)$ for all $x \in S \backslash T$ because $\phi(S) \in P(S)$. Since $T \backslash S = \phi$, we may conclude that T is a favorable twisting of S for player 1 at level $\phi_1(S)$. Thus, (10.8) follows from TW_1.

Example 11 will show that the converse of theorem 8 does not hold.

The following theorem gives a characterization of twist sensitivity of two-person classical solutions.

Theorem 9.   A 2-person classical solution is twist sensitive if and only if it has the slice property and is risk sensitive.

Proof.   (See Figure 10.1.) In view of theorems 6 and 7, we have only to show the "if" part of the theorem. Hence, let $\phi: G^2 \rightarrow \mathbb{R}^2$ be a risk-sensitive classical solution having the slice property. We demonstrate only that TW_2 for $i = 1$ holds. Suppose that TW_2 does not hold for $i = 1$. Then, there are S and $T \in G^2$ with $\phi(S) \in P(T)$ and

$$\phi_1(T) > \phi_1(S) \qquad \phi_2(T) < \phi_2(S), \tag{10.9}$$

whereas

$$x_1 < \phi_1(S) \text{ for all } x \in T \backslash S, \tag{10.10}$$

$$x_1 > \phi_1(S) \text{ for all } x \in S \backslash T. \tag{10.11}$$

Let $k_1: [0, h_1(S)] \rightarrow \mathbb{R}$ be the function defined by $k_1(\lambda) = \lambda$ if $0 \leq \lambda \leq h_1(T)$ and $k_1(\lambda) = h_1(T)$ if $h_1(T) \leq \lambda \leq h_1(S)$. Then, $k_1 \in C_1(S)$, and

$$K_1(S) = \{x \in S; x_1 \leq h_1(T)\}. \tag{10.12}$$

Since ϕ is risk sensitive, we have

$$\phi_2(K_1(S)) \geq \phi_2(S). \tag{10.13}$$

Formula (10.13) and $P(K_1(S)) \subset P(S)$ imply that

$$\phi_1(K_1(S)) \leq \phi_1(S). \tag{10.14}$$

Let $D = S \cap T$. Then,

$$h(D) = h(K_1(S)) = (h_1(T), h_2(S)). \tag{10.15}$$

By (10.11), (10.12), and (10.14), we have

$$x_1 > \phi_1(S) \geq \phi_1(K_1(S)) \text{ for all } x \in K_1(S) \backslash D. \tag{10.16}$$

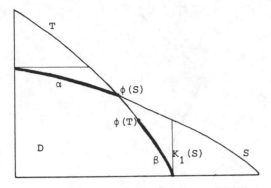

Figure 10.1 $\phi(D) \in \alpha$ as well as $\phi(D) \in \beta$, a contradiction

Since $D \subset K_1(S)$, we have, by (10.15), (10.16), and the slice property of ϕ,

$$\phi_2(D) \geq \phi_2(K_1(S)). \tag{10.17}$$

From (10.14), (10.11), and PO, it follows that $\phi(K_1(S)) \in P(D)$. Then, (10.17) implies that

$$\phi_1(K_1(S)) \geq \phi_1(D). \tag{10.18}$$

By (10.18) and (10.14), we obtain

$$\phi_1(D) \leq \phi_1(S). \tag{10.19}$$

Since, by (10.9), $\phi_1(T) > \phi_1(S)$, we can apply the same line of reasoning for T instead of S, interchanging the roles of players 1 and 2, to finally obtain

$$\phi_1(D) \geq \phi_1(T). \tag{10.20}$$

Now, (10.9), (10.19), and (10.20) yield a contradiction. Hence, TW_2 holds for $i = 1$.

We now discuss some examples of bargaining solutions with respect to the three properties that play a role in this section.

Example 10. The superadditive solution of Perles and Maschler (1981) is risk sensitive but not twist sensitive and does not have the slice property. See counter-example 7.1, p. 189, in Perles and Maschler (1981).

Example 11. Let the classical solution $\phi\colon G^2 \to \mathbb{R}^2$ be defined by the following: For all $S \in G^2$ with $h(S) = (1,1)$, $\phi(S)$ is the point of intersection of $P(S)$ with γ with maximal second coordinate, where γ is the curve depicted in Figure 10.2. Let $\alpha\colon = \frac{3}{2} - \frac{1}{2}\sqrt{3}$, then between $(1,1)$ and (α,α),

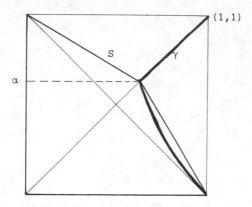

Figure 10.2 Curve γ, and game S

$\gamma = \text{conv}\{(1,1),(\alpha,\alpha)\}$, and between (α,α) and $(1,0)$, γ is an arc of the circle $(x_1 - 2)^2 + (x_2 - 1)^2 = 2$. By IEUR, ϕ is determined for all $S \in G^2$. It is easy to see that ϕ has the slice property. However, ϕ is not twist sensitive. Let $S: = \text{conv}\{(0,0),(1,0),(\alpha,\alpha),(0,1)\}$ and $T: = \text{conv}\{(0,0),(1,0), (0,\alpha(1 - \alpha)^{-1})\}$. Then, T is an unfavorable twisting of S for player 1 at level $\alpha = \phi_1(S)$, but $\phi_1(T) = 1 > \alpha = \phi_1(S)$, and so ϕ is not twist sensitive.

Example 12. Let $\alpha: G^2 \to \mathbb{R}^2$ be the *equal area split solution;* that is, for every $S \in G^2$, $\alpha(S)$ is that point of $P(S)$ such that the area in S lying above the line through 0 and $\alpha(S)$ equals half the area of S. Then, α is a classical solution, which is twist sensitive, and consequently is also risk sensitive and has the slice property.

In the next section, we investigate the classical IIA and IM solutions with respect to the three properties in this section.

10.4   Two-person classical IIA solutions and IM solutions

We start with considering the family $\{D^1,D^2,F^t;t \in (0,1)\}$ of two-person classical IIA solutions (compare with Section 10.2). In de Koster, Peters, Tijs, and Wakker (1983), it was proved that all elements in this family are risk sensitive. A new proof of this fact is given now, using theorem 9. See also Thomson and Myerson (1980, lemma 5).

Theorem 13. All two-person classical IIA solutions are risk sensitive, twist sensitive, and have the slice property.

Proof. Let $\phi: G^2 \to \mathbb{R}^2$ be a classical IIA solution. In view of theorem 9, it is sufficient to show that ϕ is twist sensitive. We prove only TW_1 for player 1. Let S and T be elements of G^2 and suppose that T is a favorable twisting of S for player 1 at level $\phi_1(S)$, that is, $\phi(S) \in T$ and

$$x_1 > \phi_1(S) \text{ for all } x \in T\backslash S, \tag{10.21}$$

$$x_1 < \phi_1(S) \text{ for all } x \in S\backslash T. \tag{10.22}$$

We have to prove that

$$\phi_1(T) \ge \phi_1(S). \tag{10.23}$$

Let $D = S \cap T$. Since $D \subset S$ and $\phi(S) \in T$, the IIA property implies that

$$\phi(D) = \phi(S). \tag{10.24}$$

Since $D \subset T$, the IIA property implies

$$\phi(D) = \phi(T) \quad \text{or} \quad \phi(T) \notin D.$$

In the case where $\phi(D) = \phi(T)$, we have $\phi(T) = \phi(S)$ in view of (10.24), and so (10.23) holds. If $\phi(T) \notin D$, then $\phi(T) \in T\backslash S$, and then (10.23) follows from (10.21).

Now, we want to look at the family of two-person individually monotonic classical solutions, that is, the family $\{\pi^\lambda; \lambda \text{ is a monotonic curve}\}$ as described in Section 10.2. In Peters and Tijs (1985), it was proved that all classical two-person IM solutions are risk sensitive. A new proof is presented now, using theorem 6.

Theorem 14. All classical two-person IM solutions are risk sensitive, twist sensitive, and have the slice property.

Proof. Let $\phi: G^2 \to \mathbb{R}^2$ be a classical IM solution. In view of theorems 6 and 8, we only have to show that ϕ is twist sensitive. We prove only that TW_1 holds for player 1. Let $S,T \in G^2$ and suppose that $\phi(S) \in T$ and that (10.21) and (10.22) hold. We have to show that

$$\phi_1(T) \ge \phi_1(S). \tag{10.25}$$

Let $D = S \cap T$. Since $D \subset S$ and $h_1(D) = h_1(S)$ by (10.22), the IM_2 property implies that $\phi_2(S) \ge \phi_2(D)$. Then, since $\phi(S) \in D$ and $\phi(D) \in P(D)$, $\phi_2(S) \ge \phi_2(D)$ implies that

$$\phi_1(S) \le \phi_1(D). \tag{10.26}$$

From $D \subset T$, $h_2(D) = h_2(T)$, and IM_1, we may conclude that

$$\phi_1(D) \leq \phi_1(T). \tag{10.27}$$

Now, (10.26) and (10.27) imply (10.25).

Thomson and Myerson (1980) show (lemma 9, for $n = 2$) that their property WM (which is somewhat stronger than IM) together with WPO (for all $S \in G^2$ and $x \in \mathbb{R}^2$, if $x > \phi(S)$, then $x \notin S$) implies Tw.

In this section, we have proved that the family of two-person twist-sensitive classical solutions T contains the families of classical IIA solutions and IM solutions. The family T also contains solutions that are neither IIA or IM, as example 12 shows.

10.5   New risk properties for n-person bargaining solutions

In this section, we want to extend some of the results of Sections 10.3 and 10.4 to n-person bargaining solutions. Not all results can be extended, as the following example illustrates.

Example 15.   Let S be the three-person bargaining game with S the convex hull of the points $(0,0,0)$, $(1,0,0)$, $(0,1,0)$, $(0,0,1)$, and $(1,0,1)$. Let N be the three-person IIA Nash solution, assigning to S the unique point at which the function $(x_1,x_2,x_3) \rightarrow x_1 x_2 x_3$ takes its maximum. Let $k_3 \in C_3(S)$ be the function with $k_3(x) = \sqrt{x}$. Then, $P(S) = \{(\alpha,1 - \alpha,\alpha) \in \mathbb{R}^3; 0 \leq \alpha \leq 1\}$,

$$P(K_3(S)) = \{(\alpha,1 - \alpha,\sqrt{\alpha}) \in \mathbb{R}^3; 0 \leq \alpha \leq 1\},$$
$$N(S) = (\tfrac{2}{3},\tfrac{1}{3},\tfrac{2}{3}), \quad N(K_3(S)) = (\tfrac{3}{5},\tfrac{2}{5},\tfrac{1}{5}\sqrt{15}).$$

Note that $N_2(K_3(S)) > N_2(S)$ but $N_1(K_3(S)) < N_1(S)$. Hence, N is not risk sensitive. However, $O_{-3}(S,N) \subset O_{-3}(K_3(S),N)$, where

$$O_{-3}(S,N) := \{(x_1,x_2) \in \mathbb{R}^2; (x_1,x_2,N_3(S)) \in S\},$$
$$O_{-3}(K_3(S),N) := \{(x_1,x_2) \in \mathbb{R}^2; (x_1,x_2,N_3(K_3(S))) \in S\}.$$

Nielsen (1984) also shows, using the same example, that the three-person IIA Nash solution is not risk sensitive. In addition, he proves that the n-person IM Kalai–Smorodinsky solution is risk sensitive (see Peters and Tijs (1984)), and that both the n-person IIA Nash and IM Kalai-Smorodinsky solutions satisfy a weaker property, the worse-alternative property, which can also be found in Peters and Tijs (1983), in definition 17, to follow. In Peters and Tijs (1983), it is shown that none of the nonsymmetric strongly individually rational n-person classical IIA solutions (see Roth (1979a, p. 16)), for $n > 2$, satisfy the risk-sensitivity property. Of all n-person classical IIA solutions (described in Peters (1983)), only a small subclass is risk sensitive, and all of these solutions are dictatorial (see Peters and Tijs (1983)). This motivated us to look for weaker risk properties. Before introducing two such weaker properties, we provide some notation.

For $i \in N$, the map $\pi_{-i} : \mathbb{R}^n \to \mathbb{R}^{n-1}$ assigns to a vector $x \in \mathbb{R}^n$ the vector $\pi_{-i}(x) = (x_1, \ldots, x_{i-1} x_{i+1}, \ldots, x_n)$, which is obtained from x by deleting the ith coordinate. Let ϕ be an n-person bargaining solution, $S \in G^n$ and $i \in N$. Then, the *opportunity set* $O_{-i}(S,\phi)$ for the bargainers in $N - \{i\}$ with respect to S and ϕ, is defined by

$$O_{-i}(S,\phi) := \pi_{-i}\{x \in S; x_i = \phi_i(S)\}.$$

The opportunity set $O_{-i}(S,\phi)$ consists of those payoff $(n-1)$-tuples, available for the collective $N - \{i\}$, if bargainer i obtains $\phi_i(S)$. We are interested in bargaining solutions where, if one of the players is replaced by a more risk averse player, the opportunity set of the other players increases. Formally, we have the following.

Definition 16. We say that a bargaining solution $\phi : G^n \to \mathbb{R}^n$ has the *risk profit opportunity* (RPO) *property* if for all $S \in G^n$, $i \in N$, and $k_i \in C_i(S)$, we have

$$O_{-i}(S,\phi) \subset O_{-i}(K_i(S),\phi).$$

Peters and Tijs (1983) show that, for classical solutions, risk profit opportunity is equivalent to another property, which here we call the worse-alternative property. We first state this property informally. Let $S \in G^n$ and $i \in N$, and suppose that player i is replaced by a more risk averse player, $\hat{\imath}$. If, in such a situation, both player i and player $\hat{\imath}$ prefer the alternative (in the underlying set of alternatives A; see Section 10.2) assigned by an n-person classical solution ϕ in the game with player i to the alternative assigned by ϕ in the game with player $\hat{\imath}$, then we say that ϕ has the worse-alternative property (WA). Peters and Tijs (1983) show that, for games with risky outcomes, the equivalence between RPO and WA breaks down, and argue there that WA is the most elementary property. We think, however, that the RPO property is attractive because it says something about the possible benefits for the other players, if one player is replaced by a more risk averse one. We will now give the formal definition of the worse-alternative property. To avoid having to introduce many additional notations, we will state it in terms of utilities rather than alternatives.

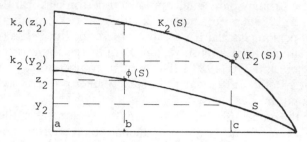

Figure 10.3 $z = \phi(S)$, $y_1 = \phi_1(K_2(S))$, $ab = O_{-2}(S,\phi)$, $ac = O_{-2}(K_2(S),\phi)$

Definition 17. We say that a bargaining solution $\phi: G^n \to \mathbb{R}^n$ has the *worse-alternative* (WA) *property* if all $S \in G^n$, $i \in N$, and $k_i \in C_i(S)$, we have

$$z_i \geq y_i,$$

where $z = \phi(S)$, and $y \in S$ such that $K_i(y) = \phi(K_i(S))$.

Of course, we also have $k_i(z_i) \geq k_i(y_i)$ in definition 17, since k_i is nondecreasing. For a two-person classical solution $\phi: G^2 \to \mathbb{R}^2$ and $S \in G$, we have

$$O_{-1}(S,\phi) = [0,\phi_2(S)] \qquad O_{-2}(S,\phi) = [0,\phi_1(S)].$$

From this and (essentially only the) Pareto-optimality (of a classical solution) follows immediately.

Theorem 18. For two-person classical solutions, the properties RS, RPO, and WA are equivalent.

Example 15 shows that there are RPO solutions that are not risk sensitive. In general, the RPO property is weaker than the RS property, as the following theorem demonstrates.

Theorem 19. Each risk-sensitive classical solution has the RPO property.

Proof. Let $\phi: G^n \to \mathbb{R}^n$ be a risk-sensitive classical solution. Take $S \in G^n$, $k_i \in C_i(S)$. Let y be the point in $P(S)$ for which

$$K_i(y) = (y, \ldots, y_{i-1}, k_i(y_i), y_{i+1}, y_n) = \phi(K_i(S)). \tag{10.28}$$

By risk sensitivity, we have

$$y_j \geq \phi_j(S) \text{ for all } j \in N - \{i\}. \tag{10.29}$$

Since $y \in P(S)$ and $\phi(S) \in P(S)$, the PO property and (10.29) imply

$$y_i \leq \phi_i(S). \tag{10.30}$$

But then by (10.30), G.5, and (10.28),

$$\begin{aligned}
O_{-i}(S,\phi) &= \pi_{-i}\{x \in S; x_i = \phi_i(S)\} \subset \pi_{-i}\{x \in S; x_i = y_i\} \\
&= \pi_{-i}\{u \in K_i(S); u_i = k_i(y_i)\} \\
&= \pi_{-i}\{u \in K_i(S); u_i = \phi_i(K_i(S))\} = O_{-i}(K_i(S),\phi).
\end{aligned}$$

Hence, ϕ has the RPO property.

In Peters and Tijs (1983), it is proved that all n-person classical IIA solutions have the RPO property. Another proof of this result can be given by looking at twist sensitivity. Then, by modifying in a trivial way the proofs of theorems 13 and 6, we obtain the following.

Theorem 20.

    1. Each n-person classical IIA solution is twist sensitive;
    2. Each n-person twist-sensitive classical solution has the RPO property.

10.6   Summary and remarks

In the foregoing, we have shown that for two-person classical solutions, the following logical implications between the discussed properties hold:

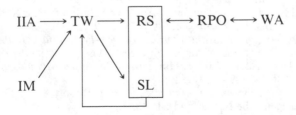

For n-person classical solutions, we have the following implications:

$$\text{IIA} \longrightarrow \text{TW} \longrightarrow \text{RPO}, \qquad \text{RS} \longrightarrow \text{RPO} \longleftrightarrow \text{WA}.$$

In an obvious way, many results in this chapter can be extended to WPO (weak Pareto-optimal; see text immediately following theorem 14) solutions. Similar results can be derived for bargaining multisolutions

(i.e., correspondences μ: $G^n \to \mathbb{R}^n$ such that $\mu(S) \subset S$ for every $S \in G^n$).
See Peters, Tijs, and de Koster (1983) for a description of (two-person)
weak (multi-)solutions with the IIA or the IM property.

REFERENCES

Arrow, K. J.: *Essays in the Theory of Risk Bearing.* Markham, Chicago, 1971.
Crawford, V. P., and H. R. Varian: Distortion of Preferences and the Nash Theory
     of Bargaining. *Economics Letters* 3, 203–6, 1979.
Harsanyi, J. C., and R. Selten: A Generalized Nash Solution for Two-Person
     Bargaining Games with Incomplete Information. *Management Science* 18,
     80–106, 1972.
Kalai, E., and M. Smorodinsky: Other Solutions to Nash's Bargaining Problem.
     Econometrica 43, 513–18, 1975.
Kannai, Y.: Concavifiability and Constructions of Concave Utility Functions.
     J. of Math. Econ. 4, 1–56, 1977.
Kihlstrom, R. E., and L. J. Mirman: Risk Aversion with Many Commodities. *J. of
     Econ. Theory* 8, 361–88, 1974.
Kihlstrom, R. E.; A. E. Roth; and D. Schmeidler: Risk Aversion and Solutions to
     Nash's Bargaining Problem, pp. 65–71 in *Game Theory and Mathematical
     Economics* (O. Moeschlin, D. Pallaschke, eds.). North Holland, Amster-
     dam, 1981.
de Koster, R.; H. J. M. Peters; S. H. Tijs; and P. Wakker: Risk Sensitivity, Inde-
     pendence of Irrelevant Alternatives and Continuity of Bargaining Solu-
     tions. *Mathematical Social Sciences* 4, 295–300, 1983.
Kurz, M.: Distortion of Preferences, Income Distribution, and the Case for a
     Linear Income Tax. *J. of Econ. Theory* 14, 291–8, 1977.
Income Distribution and the Distortion of Preferences: The ℓ-Commodity Case.
     J. of Econ. Theory 22, 99–106, 1980.
Nash, J. F.: The Bargaining Problem. *Econometrica* 18, 155–62, 1950.
Nielsen, L. T.: Risk Sensitivity in Bargaining with More Than Two Participants.
     Journal of Economic Theory 32, 371–76, 1984.
Perles, M. A., and M. Maschler: The Super-Additive Solution for the Nash Bar-
     gaining Game. *Int. J. of Game Theory* 10, 163–93, 1981.
Peters, H.: *Independence of Irrelevant Alternatives for n-Person Bargaining Solu-
     tions.* Report 8318, Dept. of Math., Nijmegen, The Netherlands, 1983.
Peters, H., and S. Tijs: Risk Sensitivity of Bargaining Solutions. *Methods of Oper-
     ations Research* 44, 409–20, 1981.
     Risk Properties of n-Person Bargaining Solutions. Report 8323, Dept. of
     Math., Nijmegen, The Netherlands, 1983.
     Individually Monotonic Bargaining Solutions for *n*-Person Bargaining
     Games. *Methods of Operations Research* 51, 377–84, 1984.
     Characterization of All Individually Monotonic Bargaining Solutions. *Int. J.
     of Game Theory* (forthcoming).
Peters, H.; S. Tijs; and R. de Koster: Solutions and Multisolutions for Bargaining
     Games. *Methods of Operations Research* 46, 465–76, 1983.
Pratt, J. W.: Risk Aversion in the Small and in the Large. *Econometrica* 32,
     122–36, 1964.
Roth, A. E.: *Axiomatic Models of Bargaining.* Springer-Verlag, Berlin, 1979*a*.

An Impossibility Result concerning n-Person Bargaining Games. *Int. J. of Game Theory* 8, 129–32, 1979*b*.

Roth, A. E., and U. G. Rothblum: Risk Aversion and Nash's Solution for Bargaining Games with Risky Outcomes. *Econometrica* 50, 639–47, 1982.

Sobel, J.: Distortion of Utilities and the Bargaining Problem. *Econometrica* 49, 597–619, 1981.

Thomson, W., and R. B. Myerson: Monotonicity and Independence Axioms. *Int. J. of Game Theory* 9, 37–49, 1980.

Yaari, M. E.: Some Remarks on Measures of Risk Aversion and on Their Uses. *J. of Econ. Theory* 1, 315–29, 1969.

CHAPTER 11

Axiomatic theory of bargaining with a variable population: A survey of recent results

William Thomson
UNIVERSITY OF ROCHESTER

11.1 Introduction

In the traditional formulation of the bargaining problem, it is typically assumed that a fixed number of agents are involved. The possibility that their number varies has recently been the object of a number of studies, which it is the purpose of the present chapter to review in a unified way, with emphasis on the main results and on the main lines of their proofs.

I propose to evaluate solutions by focusing on their behavior in circumstances where new agents come in without their entry being accompanied by an expansion of opportunities. The standard economic problem that motivated much of the work presented here is that of dividing fairly a bundle of goods among a group of agents. The number of agents involved in the division is allowed to vary while the resources at their disposal remain fixed. (Technically, this implies that the intersection in utility space of the set of alternatives available to the enlarged group with the coordinate subspace corresponding to the original group coincides with the set of alternatives initially available to that group.) Of course, this does not mean that new agents are required never to bring in additional resources nor that their presence itself may not affect the alternatives available to the original group. I simply want to *allow* for the case of fixed resources, and I claim that a study of this special situation yields important insights into the relative merits of solutions.

This review is organized around three themes. The first one deals with the possibility that when new agents come in, one of the agents originally present gains despite the fact that the claims of more agents on a pie that

The author thanks NSF for its support under grant 8311249, and the referee and the editor for their helpful comments.

has remained fixed have to be accommodated. I see this possibility as a negative feature of a solution, and investigate the existence of solutions that would not permit it. I show that such solutions exist and offer axiomatic characterizations of two of them involving this requirement of *monotonicity*.

If a solution does not satisfy monotonicity, it is natural to be concerned with the extent to which it permits violations of the property. A measure of the *opportunity* for gain offered by solutions to agents initially present when new agents come in is proposed, and it is used to rank solutions. Conversely, one may be concerned with the losses that a solution may inflict on an agent initially present upon the arrival of new agents and prefer solutions for which these losses are small. A measure of the *guarantees* offered by solutions is defined and also is used to rank solutions. The two rankings essentially agree. However, if solutions are ranked on the basis of either the opportunities for gains or the guarantees offered to initial *groups* seen as a whole, different answers are obtained. These considerations of opportunities and guarantees constitute the second theme.

The third theme is that of *stability*. This is the property that a solution recommends for each group and for each problem faced by this group, an outcome that is consistent with what the solution recommends for any subgroup when facing the problem derived from the original one by giving all agents not in the subgroup what had been decided they should receive in the original problem. Although not all solutions satisfy this property, some do, and I conclude by presenting characterizations involving the requirement of stability.

In the course of this review, we will encounter all of the best known solutions – the Nash, Kalai–Smorodinsky, egalitarian, and utilitarian solutions. Each of the three themes will highlight different solutions, and the reader should not expect a definite recommendation in favor of a particular one. However, it is hoped that the results presented here will elucidate their relative merits.

The chapter is organized as follows. Section 11.2 introduces definitions and notation. The following three sections are successively devoted to questions of monotonicity, opportunity and guarantees, and stability. Section 11.6 offers some conclusions.

11.2   Bargaining problems and solutions

A bargaining problem, or simply a *problem*, is given by specifying a list of "alternatives" available to a group of agents through some joint action. Agents are equipped with von Neumann–Morgenstern utility functions, and the problem is given directly as a subset of the utility space. Because the agents' preferences over the alternatives usually conflict, the question arises how to establish a compromise, that is, how to select an alternative that achieves an acceptable balance between the agents' respective aspirations and sacrifices. When such problems are repeatedly encountered, it becomes natural to look for a general rule that could be used to solve all of them. This requires that the class of the possible problems be identified; then, the desired rule can be described as a function defined on that class, which associates to each problem in the class a feasible alternative for that problem, interpreted as the recommended compromise. Such a function is called a *solution,* and the value it takes when applied to a particular problem is termed the *solution outcome* for that problem.

The axiomatic study of solutions consists of formulating properties that one would expect, or desire, solutions to satisfy, and in checking whether there are solutions satisfying these properties. A theorem giving a list of axioms that are satisfied by, and only by, a particular solution is said to be an *axiomatic characterization* of the solution. This is the methodology that Nash (1950) adopted in his pioneering paper on the bargaining problem, and that will be followed here. However, whereas Nash considered only the two-person case, the focus of the present study is on situations in which the number of agents may vary. This more general situation is formally described as follows.

There is an infinite population I of agents, indexed by the positive integers. Arbitrary finite subsets of I may be confronted by a problem. The family of these subsets is denoted $\mathcal{P}$. Given $P \in \mathcal{P}$, Σ^P is the class of problems that the group P may conceivably face. Each $S \in \Sigma^P$ is a subset of $\mathbb{R}_+^P$, the nonnegative portion of the $|P|$-dimensional euclidean space with coordinates indexed by the members of P, with each point of S representing the von Neumann–Morgenstern utilities achievable by the members of P through some joint action. It is assumed that

1. S is a compact subset of $\mathbb{R}_+^P$ containing at least one strictly positive vector;
2. S is convex;
3. S is comprehensive (i.e., if $x, y \in \mathbb{R}_+^P$, $x \in S$, and $x \geq y$, then $y \in S$).[1]

Compactness of S is a technical assumption, made for convenience. Requiring that $S \subseteq \mathbb{R}_+^P$ implies that an appropriate choice of a zero of the utilities has been made. We could have dispensed with that assumption, but at a significant notational cost. Assuming that S contains a strictly positive vector ensures that all agents are nontrivially involved in the bargaining. Convexity of S holds in particular if agents can randomize jointly, since utilities are von Neumann–Morgenstern utilities, but this property of S may hold even in situations where randomization is not permitted. Similarly, comprehensiveness holds in particular if, but not only if, utilities are freely disposable.

We will also consider the domain $\tilde{\Sigma}^P$ of problems satisfying the additional condition

4. If $x,y \in S$ and $x \geq y$, then there exists $z \in S$ with $z > y$.

Then, the undominated boundary of S contains no segment parallel to a coordinate subspace. Note that any element of Σ^P can be approximated in the Hausdorff topology by a sequence of elements of $\tilde{\Sigma}^P$.

Finally, we set

$$\Sigma \equiv \underset{P \in \mathscr{P}}{U} \Sigma^P \quad \text{and} \quad \tilde{\Sigma} \equiv \underset{P \in \mathscr{P}}{U} \tilde{\Sigma}^P.$$

Because an important motivation for the work reviewed here is the "economic" problem of dividing among a group of agents P a fixed bundle of freely disposable and infinitely divisible commodities, it is of interest that the image in the utility space of the set of such possible divisions is an element of Σ^P if the utilities are continuous, nonconstant and nondecreasing, concave, and normalized by assigning zero utility to the zero bundle. (An element of $\tilde{\Sigma}^P$ results if utilities are, in fact, strictly increasing.) The converse question, whether any subset of Σ^P satisfying (1) through (3) represents some economic problem satisfying the preceding regularity assumptions, is studied by Billera and Bixby (1973).

A *solution* is a function defined on Σ and associating for each $P \in \mathscr{P}$ and to each $S \in \Sigma^P$, a unique point of S called the *solution outcome* of S.

Finally, we turn to a formal presentation of the main solutions discussed in the literature on bargaining. All of these solutions will continue to be central to the analysis of bargaining with a variable population.

Letting P be an arbitrary element of $\mathscr{P}$ and S an arbitrary element of Σ^P, for the *Nash solution*,[2] $N(S)$ is the unique maximizer of $\Pi_P\, x_i$ for x in S; for the *Kalai–Smorodinsky solution*,[3] $K(S)$ is the maximal feasible point on the segment connecting the origin to the "ideal point" $a(S)$ where for each i in P, $a_i(S) \equiv \max\{x_i \,|\, x \in S\}$; and for the *egalitarian solution*,[4] $E(S)$ is the maximal feasible point with equal coordinates. Mention will also be made of *utilitarian solutions;* in this case, for each member of the family, $U(S)$ is chosen among the maximizers of $\Sigma_P\, x_i$ for x in S. Note that the Kalai–Smorodinsky solution is a normalized version of the egalitarian solution. Even on the somewhat restricted domain considered here, these two solutions may fail to yield Pareto-optimal outcomes, but their lexicographic extensions do. For the *lexicographic maximin solution*,[5] $L(S)$ is obtained as follows: Given $x \in \mathbb{R}^P$, let $\bar{x} \in \mathbb{R}^P$ be defined by

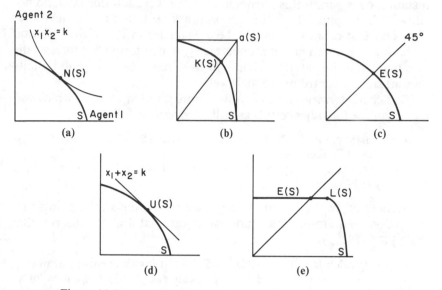

Figure 11.1

rewriting the coordinates of x in decreasing order; given $x, y \in \mathbb{R}^P$, x is said to be lexicographically greater than y if for some k $\bar{x}_k > \bar{y}_k$ while $\bar{x}_i = \bar{y}_i$ for all $i > k$; finally, $L(S)$ is the unique point of S that is lexicographically greater than all other points of S. A similar extension of the Kalai–Smorodinsky solution can be defined. Several natural variants of these solutions, some new, will also be discussed. The definitions just given are illustrated in Figure 11.1 for $P = \{1,2\}$.

We conclude this section by introducing some additional notation. Given P in $\mathscr{P}$ and $x_1, \ldots, x_k$ in $\mathbb{R}^P$, $cch\{x_1, \ldots, x_k\}$ is the *convex and comprehensive hull* of these k points, that is, the smallest convex and comprehensive subset of $\mathbb{R}^P$ containing them. Also, e_P is the vector in $\mathbb{R}^P$ whose coordinates are all equal to one. Given i in P, e_i is the ith unit vector. Given P, Q in $\mathscr{P}$ with $P \subset Q, y$, a point of $\mathbb{R}^Q$, and T, a subset of $\mathbb{R}^Q$, y_P and T_P designate the projections on $\mathbb{R}^P$ of y and T, respectively.

11.3 Monotonicity

We will begin the discussion here by asking whether it is possible for a solution to assign greater utility to an agent initially present, after the arrival of some newcomers with equally valid claims on the fixed resources, than the utility he had been assigned originally. The answer is yes, and it is easy to construct examples showing that the Nash solution, for instance, does permit this phenomenon. Are there solutions that do not allow it? Yes again. The Kalai–Smorodinsky solution is one such solution. Our first result will, in fact, be a characterization of that solution involving a requirement of monotonicity, which formally expresses the idea that if more agents have claims on given resources, all agents initially present should contribute to their welfare.

This characterization also involves more familiar axioms, which will play a role in the other results as well. They are as follows.

> *Weak Pareto-optimality* (WPO): For all $P \in \mathcal{P}$, for all $S \in \Sigma^P$, for all $y \in \mathbb{R}^P_+$, if $y > F(S)$, then $y \notin S$.
> *Pareto-optimality* (PO): for all $P \in \mathcal{P}$, for all $S \in \Sigma^P$, for all $y \in \mathbb{R}^P_+$, if $y \geq F(S)$, then $y \notin S$.

We denote by WPO(S) and PO(S), respectively, the sets of points that are weakly Pareto-optimal and Pareto-optimal for S (observe that PO(S) $\subset$ WPO(S)).

> *Symmetry* (SY): for all $P \in \mathcal{P}$, for all $S \in \Sigma^P$, if for all one-one functions γ: $P \to P, S = \{x' \in \mathbb{R}^P_+ \mid \exists x \in S \text{ such that } \forall i \in P, x'_{\gamma(i)} = x_i\}$, then for all $i,j \in P$, $F_i(S) = F_j(S)$. A related condition is
> *Anonymity* (AN): For all $P,P' \in \mathcal{P}$ with $|P| = |P'|$, for all one-one functions γ: $P \to P'$, for all $S \in \Sigma^P$, $S' \in \Sigma^{P'}$, if $S' = \{x' \in \mathbb{R}^P_+ \mid \exists x \in S \text{ such that } \forall i \in P, x'_{\gamma(i)} = x_i\}$, then for all $i \in P$, $F_{\gamma(i)}(S') = F_i(S)$.
> *Scale invariance* (S.INV): For all $P \in \mathcal{P}$, for all $S, S' \in \Sigma^P$, for all $a \in \mathbb{R}^P_{++}$, if $S' = \{x' \in \mathbb{R}^P \mid \forall i \in P, x'_i = a_i x_i\}$, then for all $i \in P$, $F_i(S') = a_i F_i(S)$.
> *Continuity* (CONT)[6]: For all $P \in \mathcal{P}$, for all sequences $\{S^\nu\}$ of elements of Σ^P, if $S^\nu \to S \in \Sigma^P$, then $F(S^\nu) \to F(S)$. (In this definition, convergence of S^ν to S is evaluated in the Hausdorff topology.)

These axioms are standard. WPO states that it is infeasible to make all agents simultaneously better off, and PO that it is infeasible to make one agent better off without hurting some other agent. SY states that if a problem is invariant under all permutations, then all agents should get the same amount. AN states that the names of the agents do not matter; only the geometrical structure of the problem at hand is relevant. S.INV states that the solution is independent of the choice of particular members of the equivalence classes of utility functions representing the agents' von Neumann–Morgenstern preferences. CONT states that small changes in the data defining the problem cause only small changes in solution outcomes.

The following axiom is the first one to relate solution outcomes across cardinalities.

> *Monotonicity with respect to changes in the number of agents* (MON): For all $P, Q \in \mathcal{P}$ with $P \subset Q$, for all $S \in \Sigma^P$, $T \in \Sigma^Q$, if $S = T_P$, then $F(S) \geq F_P(T)$.

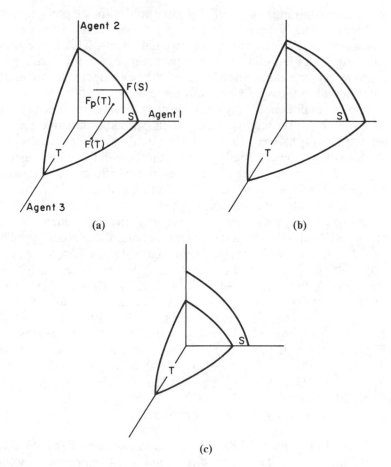

Figure 11.2

This axiom is illustrated in Figure 11.2a, where $P = \{1,2\}$ and $Q = \{1,2,3\}$. (Unless indicated otherwise, the indexing of the axes by agents of all forthcoming figures will be as in Figure 11.2a.) S is a two-person problem in the 1-2 plane. It is obtained from the three-person problem T by setting the utility of agent 3 equal to 0. The axiom states that the projection of $F(T)$ on the 1-2 plane is weakly dominated by $F(S)$.

An example of a situation that gives rise to this particular relationship between S and T is the economic problem of fair division mentioned earlier. In the usual specification of the problem, there is a fixed amount of privately appropriable commodities to which the agents are collectively entitled. If one more agent were to be added to the list of claimants, the intersection of the problem faced by the large group with the coordinate subspace pertaining to the initial group would coincide precisely with the problem originally faced by that group, provided that the presence of the new agents itself does not create external effects. This is the situation represented in Figure 11.2a. The requirement of monotonicity is that in order to accommodate the claims of the newcomers, sacrifices are required of all of the agents orginally present.

The axiom does not apply when the newcomers come in with their own resources (e.g., commodity endowments, special productive abilities) or when their very existence has positive external effects (e.g., if they are the children of the agents initially present); these possibilities are illustrated in Figure 11.2b, and the case of negative external effects (e.g., crowding) in Figure 11.2c. Note that we are not excluding such cases. We simply want our solution to behave well (also) when they do not occur.

In Figure 11.3, we present examples showing that none of N, L, or U satisfy MON and illustrating the fact that both K and E do. In the examples, $P = \{1,2\}$ and $Q = \{1,2,3\}$. In Figure 11.3a, $T \equiv cch\{e_1,e_2,e_3,x\}$ with $x \equiv (\frac{2}{12},\frac{10}{12},\frac{2}{12})$, $S \equiv T_P = cch\{e_1,e_2\}$, $N(T) = x$, and $N(S) = \frac{1}{2}e_P$; therefore, N does not satisfy MON since $N_2(T) > N_2(T_P)$. In Figure 11.3b, $T \equiv cch\{e_1,e_2,e_3,(\epsilon + \frac{1}{2})e_P,x\}$ for $\epsilon > 0$ small, $S \equiv T_P = cch\{e_1,e_2,(\epsilon + \frac{1}{2})e_P\}$, $U(T) = x$, and $U(S) = (\epsilon + \frac{1}{2})e_P$; therefore, U does not satisfy MON since $U_2(T) > U_2(T_P)$. It should be clear intuitively from Figure 11.3c that E, and consequently K, which is a normalized version of E, satisfy MON. In Figure 11.3d, $T \equiv cch\{y,e_2,e_3\}$ with $y \equiv (1,\frac{1}{2},\frac{1}{2})$, $S \equiv T_P = cch\{(1,\frac{1}{2}),e_2\}$, $L(T) = y$, and $L(S) = (\frac{2}{3},\frac{2}{3})$; therefore, L does not satisfy MON since $L_1(T) > L_1(T_P)$.

We are now ready for our first main result.

Theorem 1 (Thomson (1983c)). A solution satisfies WPO, AN, S.INV, MON, and CONT if and only if it is the Kalai–Smorodinsky solution.

Proof.   The proof that the Kalai–Smorodinsky solution satisfies the five axioms is omitted. Conversely, let F be a solution satisfying the five axioms. Also, let $P \in \mathscr{P}$ and $S \in \Sigma^P$ be given. We will only show that $F(S) = K(S)$ if $|P| = 2$. Without loss of generality, we suppose that $P = \{1,2\}$ and, appealing to S.INV, that S is normalized so that $a(S) = e_P$ (see Figure 11.4). We introduce agent 3, and we define $Q \equiv \{1,2,3\}$ and $T \in \Sigma^Q$ by $T \equiv cch\{S,S^1,S^2,\alpha e_Q\}$, where S^1 and S^2 are replicas of S in $\mathbb{R}^{(2,3)}$ and $\mathbb{R}^{(1,3)}$, respectively, and α is the common value of the coordinates of $K(S)$. More precisely, $S^1 \equiv \{(x_2,x_3) | \exists\ (x_1',x_2') \in S$ with $x_2 = x_1'$ and $x_3 = x_2'\}$ and $S^2 \equiv \{(x_1,x_3) | \exists\ (x_1',x_2') \in S$ with $x_3 = x_1'$ and $x_1 = x_2'\}$. We note that T is invariant under rotations of the agents, so that by AN, $F(T)$ has equal coordinates. This in conjunction

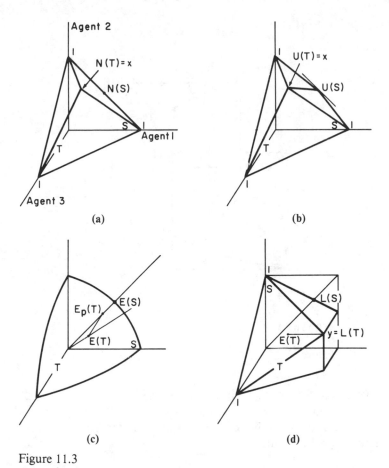

Figure 11.3

with WPO and the fact that $\alpha e_Q \in \text{WPO}(T)$ implies that $F(T) = \alpha e_Q$.
Also, $T_P = S$. By MON, $F(S) \geqq F_P(T) = \alpha e_P = K(S)$. Since $\alpha e_P \in$
$\text{PO}(S)$, $F(S) = K(S)$.

Several remarks concerning the case in which $|P| > 2$ are in order. First,
it may not be sufficient to add only one agent in order to reach the desired
conclusion. Second, CONT, which was not used in the preceding proof,
becomes necessary; we did not need it there because for $|P| = 2$, K satisfies
PO (and not just WPO). To adapt the proof to the case $|P| > 2$, we first
show that $F(S) = K(S)$ for all S in Σ^P such that $K(S) \in \text{PO}(S)$. Then, we
extend the argument to the case where $K(S) \in \text{WPO}(S) \backslash \text{PO}(S)$ by applying CONT. Third, there is no solution satisfying PO (instead of just

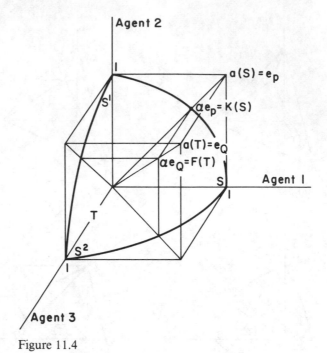

Figure 11.4

WPO), AN, S.INV, and MON (i.e., even if CONT is sacrificed). Finally, on the subdomain $\tilde{\Sigma}$, K satisfies PO (and not just WPO) and can be characterized by the list PO, AN, S.INV, and MON (i.e., CONT is not needed for this result).

The Kalai–Smorodinsky solution is not the only one to satisfy MON. The egalitarian solution also does. In fact, E satisfies all but one, (S.INV) of the axioms used to characterize K, and a characterization of E can be obtained by replacing S.INV by the axiom of independence of irrelevant alternatives. This is our second result.

Independence of Irrelevant Alternatives (IIA): For all $P \in \mathcal{P}$, for all $S,S' \in \Sigma^P$, if $S' \subset S$ and $F(S) \in S'$, then $F(S) = F(S')$.

Theorem 2 (Thomson (1983*d*)).   A solution satisfies WPO, SY, CONT, IIA, and MON if and only if it is the egalitarian solution.

Proof.   The proof that the egalitarian solution satisfies the five axioms is omitted. Conversely, let F be a solution satisfying the five axioms. Also, let $P \in \mathscr{P}$ with $|P| = 2$ and $S \in \Sigma^P$ be given. We will show that $F(S) = E(S)$. Without loss of generality, we suppose that $P = \{1,2\}$ and that $E(S) = e_P$ (see Figure 11.5a). Let n be an integer such that $n \geqq \max\{x_1 + x_2 \mid x \in S\} + 1$. Note that $n \geqq 3$. Let $Q \equiv \{1, \ldots, n\}$ and $T \in \Sigma^Q$ be defined by $T \equiv \{x \in \mathbb{R}_+^Q \mid \Sigma_Q x_i \leqq n\}$ (in Figure 11.5a, $Q \equiv \{1,2,3\}$). By WPO and SY, we have that $F(T) = e_Q$. Let $T' \in \Sigma^Q$ be defined by $T' \equiv cch\{S, e_Q\}$. We note that $T' \subset T$ and $F(T) \in T'$. By IIA, $F(T') = F(T)$. Also, $T'_P = S$. By MON, $F(S) \geqq F_P(T) = e_P$. If $S \in \tilde{\Sigma}^P$, this is possible only if $F(S) = e_P$. Otherwise, we approximate S by a sequence $\{S^k\}$ of elements of $\tilde{\Sigma}^P$ with $E(S^k) = e_P$ for all k. Then, $F(S^k) = e_P$ for all k and, $F(S) = e_P$ by CONT.

Next, let $Q \in \mathscr{P}$ with $|Q| > 2$ and $T \in \Sigma^Q$ be given. We will show that $F(T) = E(T)$. Without loss of generality, we suppose that $Q = \{1, \ldots, n\}$ for $n > 2$ (in Figure 11.5b, $Q \equiv \{1,2,3\}$) and, in a first step, that $T \in \tilde{\Sigma}^Q$. Supposing, by way of contradiction, that $F(T) \neq E(T)$, we conclude from WPO and the fact that $T \in \tilde{\Sigma}^Q$, that there exist $i, j \in Q$ such that $F_i(T) > E_i(T) = E_j(T) > F_j(T)$. Then, let $T' \in \Sigma^Q$ be defined by $T' \equiv cch\{E(T), F(T)\}$. Clearly, $T' \subset T$ and $F(T) \in T'$, so that $F(T) = F(T')$ by IIA. Now, let $P \equiv \{i, j\}$ and $S \equiv T'_P$. We have that $E(S) = E_P(T)$. Since $F(S) = E(S)$ by the first step of the proof, we conclude that $F_i(T') > F_i(T'_P) = F_i(S) = E_i(S)$, in contradiction to MON. The conclusion for $T \in \Sigma^Q \setminus \tilde{\Sigma}^Q$ follows from an application of CONT.

When WPO is dropped from the list of axioms of theorem 2, the new family of *truncated egalitarian* (TE) solutions is obtained. To define such a solution, let $\alpha = \{\alpha^P \mid P \in \mathscr{P}\}$ be a list of nonnegative numbers such that $\alpha^P \geqq \alpha^Q$ if and only if $P \subset Q$. Then, the TE solution relative to α, E_α, is defined by setting $E_\alpha(S) = E(S)$ if $\alpha^P e_P$ does not belong to S and $E_\alpha(S) = \alpha^P e_P$ otherwise. For each P, E_α behaves like E for "small problems," that is, if not too much is at stake, but selects some maximal feasible point $\alpha^P e_P$ otherwise. However, weak Pareto-optimality is less and less likely to be achieved as a group enlarges. This result, due to the monotonicity condition imposed on the α^P, reflects the fact that negotiations are more difficult in large groups than in small groups.

It can be shown (Thomson (1983a)) that any solution satisfying SY, IIA, MON, and CONT differs from a TE solution only for two-person problems, in which case some limited utility substitution becomes feasible. This is of course of interest because of the central role played by two-person problems, both in practice and in theoretical developments. As an example, define α by $\alpha^P = 1$ for all P and choose F to coincide with E_α on all Σ^P except when $|P| = 2$. If $|P| = 2$, given $S \in \Sigma^P$, select $F(S) = E(S)$ if $e_P \notin S$ and $\operatorname{argmax}\{x_1 x_2 \mid x \in S, x_1 + \epsilon x_2 \geqq 1 + \epsilon, \epsilon x_1 + x_2 \geqq 1 + \epsilon\}$ otherwise, where ϵ is some small positive number.

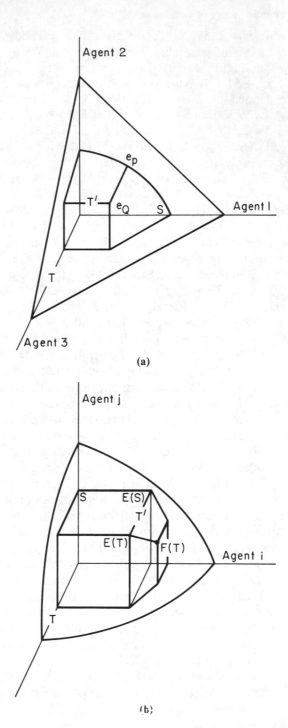

Figure 11.5

11.4   Guarantees and opportunities

Note that the axiom of monotonicity specifies that agents should not gain when new agents come in. If a solution satisfies WPO, (at least) one of the agents originally present will (usually) lose upon the arrival of the new agents. It is natural to worry about the magnitude of these losses and be more interested in solutions for which they are smaller. However, in attempting to formulate this notion precisely, we come up against two difficulties. The first difficulty is that the loss incurred by an agent will typically depend on the specific initial and the final problems. If some probabilistic structure were given on the class of admissible problems, one could measure "expected" losses and evaluate a solution on that basis, but the conclusions so obtained would only be relative to that structure. Instead, our approach here will be to focus on the maximal loss that the solution may inflict on an agent when new claimants come in. Seen positively, we will look for the minimum that an agent will always retain upon the arrival of the newcomers. This minimum can be viewed as the *guarantee* offered by the solution to the individual. In general, of course, agents will do better than their minima.

The second difficulty involves the way losses themselves are measured. Whatever measure we adopt should be consistent with the invariance properties the solutions are assumed to satisfy. We will require here solutions to be invariant under positive scale changes (i.e., to satisfy S.INV); and to ensure that our measures of guarantees are also invariant under the same transformations, we will base them on proportional losses. Given some original problem S involving the members of some group P, we consider the problem T obtained after the expansion of P to some larger group Q. As before, we assume that the new agents do not bring in additional resources, so that $S = T_P$, and we consider the ratio $F_i(T)/F_i(S)$ of final utility to initial utility of some member i of P. The guarantee offered by F to i is then given by the infimum taken by this ratio subject to the preceding conditions on S and T. Of course, the guarantee so measured pertains to the triple (i,P,Q), but if a solution satisfies AN, it is, in fact, only the cardinalities of P and Q that matter; then, we can speak of the guarantee α_F^{mn} offered by F to *any* agent originally part of *any* group of cardinality m upon the arrival of *any* group of cardinality n. Formally, $\alpha_F^{mn} \equiv \inf\{F_i(T)/F_i(S) \mid i \in P, \ P \subset Q, \ |P| = m, \ |Q| = m + n, \ S \in \Sigma^P, \ T \in \Sigma^Q, S = T_P\}$. The *collective guarantee structure* of F is finally defined as the list $\alpha_F \equiv \{\alpha_F^{mn} \mid m,n \in I\}$.

We are now ready to compare solutions on the basis of their guarantee structures. Among the solutions discussed thus far, only two satisfy S.INV – the Nash solution and the Kalai–Smorodinsky solution. First, we compute the guarantee structure of the Nash solution. Figure 11.6a depicts an example of a pair S,T for which $\alpha_N^{2,1}$ is attained: $P = \{1,2\}$, $Q = \{1,2,3\}$, $T \in \Sigma^Q$ is defined by $Q \equiv cch\{e_Q,(a,b,0)\}$, where $a = 6/(6 - \sqrt{12})$ and $b = 3 - a$. Let $S \equiv T_P = cch\{e_P,(a,b)\}$. We note that $N(T) = e_Q$ and that $N(S) = (a,b)$. Also, $N_1(T)/N_1(S) = 1/a$. This pair (S,T) is an example of a worst configuration for agent 1 as the number of agents increases from 2 to 3. More generally, we have

Theorem 3 (Thomson and Lensberg (1983)).   The guarantee structure of the Nash solution is given by

$$\alpha_N^{mn} = \frac{m(n+2) - \sqrt{mn(mn + 4m - 4)}}{2(m+n)}$$

for all $m,n \in I$.

Proof.   The proof is outlined here and can be followed on Figure 11.6a. In searching for a worst configuration (S,T) for some agent, we can assume by S.INV that $T \in \Sigma^Q$ is normalized so that $N(T) = e_Q$. This implies that T is below the hyperplane in $\mathbb{R}^Q$ of equation $\Sigma_Q x_i = |Q|$ and that (1) $S \equiv T_P$ is below the hyperplane in $\mathbb{R}^P$ of equation $\Sigma_P x_i = |Q|$; because T is comprehensive, and e_P is the projection of $e_Q \in T$ on $\mathbb{R}^P$, we also need (2) $e_P \in S$. Our task reduces to finding $S \in \Sigma^P$ satisfying (1) and (2) and being such that (3) $x \equiv N(S)$ has the greatest jth coordinate, agent j being an arbitrary member of P (in Figure 11.6a, $j = 1$). It is enough to find $x \in \mathbb{R}_+^P$ with the greatest jth coordinate such that $\Sigma_P x_i \leqq |Q|$ (because of (1)) and since N satisfies IIA, such that $x = N(cch\{e_P,x\})$ (because of (2) and (3)). The proof involves showing that the inequality $\Sigma_P x_i \leqq |Q|$ should be satisfied as an equality (in Figure 11.6a, this means that x must be on the line segment $[3e_1,3e_2]$), that all of the coordinates of x different from the one that is being maximized must be equal, and that the segment $[x,e_P]$ must be tangent at x to the level curve of the function $\Pi_P x_i' = k$ that goes through x. The proof concludes with some elementary but laborious algebra, which is omitted here. (In Figure 11.6a, $x = (a,b)$.)

Several observations are in order. First, we note that $\alpha_N^{mn} \leqq \frac{1}{2}$ for all $m,n \in I$. Moreover, and somewhat paradoxically, for each fixed n, the maximal proportional loss inflicted by the Nash solution on one of the original agents increases with the size of the original group. One would hope that the burden of supporting one additional person be light on each of the original agents if there are many of them, and perhaps even go to 0 as their number increases to infinity. But this is not the case for the Nash solution.

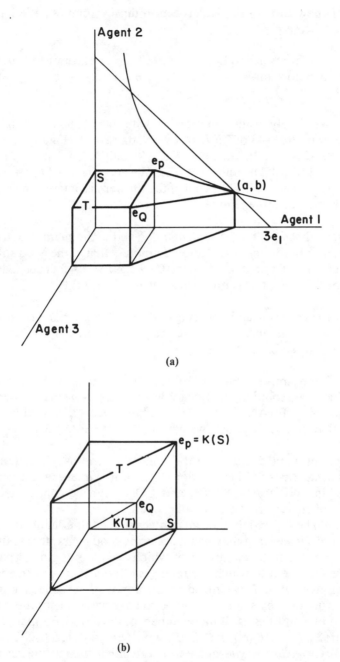

(a)

(b)

Figure 11.6

Let us now turn to the Kalai–Smorodinsky solution. We have the following theorem.

Theorem 4 (Thomson and Lensberg (1983)).   The guarantee structure of the Kalai–Smorodinsky solution is given by $\alpha_K^{mn} = 1/(n+1)$ for all $m,n \in I$.

Proof. We simply exhibit an example with $m = 2$ and $n = 1$ for which the minimum $\alpha_K^{2,1} = \frac{1}{2}$ of $K_i(T)/K_i(S)$ is attained (see Figure 11.6b). Let $P \equiv \{1,2\}$, $Q \equiv \{1,2,3\}$, and let $T \in \Sigma^Q$ and $S \in \Sigma^P$ be defined by $T \equiv cch\{(1,1,0)(0,1,1)\}$ and $S \equiv T_P$. We note that $K(S) = e_P$ and $K(T) = \frac{1}{2}e_Q$, as desired. The proof of the theorem is obtained by a simple generalization of this example.

We note that $\alpha_K^{mn} \geqq \alpha_N^{mn}$ for all $m,n \in I$, and so the guarantee structure of the Kalai–Smorodinsky solution *dominates* that of the Nash solution. However, it is still not the case that $\alpha_K^{mn} \to 1$ as $m \to \infty$ for each fixed n, as was hoped. In fact, this is impossible, as is shown next.

Theorem 5 (Thomson and Lensberg (1983)).   If a solution satisfies WPO and AN, then its guarantee structure is dominated by $\bar{\alpha}$ defined by $\bar{\alpha}^{mn} = 1/(n+1)$ for all $m,n \in I$.

Proof.   The example of Figure 11.6b can be used to prove this for $m = 2$, $n = 1$. Let F be a solution satisfying WPO and AN. Note that by WPO and AN, $F(S) = e_P$. By AN, $F_1(T) = F_3(T)$, but any $x \in T$ satisfying $x_1 = x_3$ is such that $x_1 \leqq \frac{1}{2}$. Together, we have that $F_1(T)/F_1(S) \leqq \frac{1}{2}$.

Theorems 4 and 5 show that the Kalai–Smorodinsky solution offers *maximal guarantees*. Other solutions offering maximal guarantees as well as satisfying WPO, AN, S.INV, and CONT can be constructed. The problem of characterizing them all is open.

It should be stressed that the guarantees studied thus far are *individual* guarantees. However, it may be that offering good guarantees to individuals is very costly to the group of which they are originally part. To measure the extent to which the interests of *groups* are protected by an anonymous solution F, we introduce the notion of the collective guarantee structure of F by setting β_F^{mn} to be the average value of the ratios of initial to final utilities of all the members of the group. Formally, $\beta_F^{mn} \equiv (1/m)\inf\{\Sigma_P F_i(T)/F_i(S) \mid P \subset Q, |P| = m, |Q| = m+n, S \in \Sigma^P, T \in \Sigma^Q, S = T_P\}$. The *collective guarantee structure* of F is then defined as the list $\beta_F \equiv \{\beta_F^{mn} \mid m,n \in I\}$.

If we compare solutions on the basis of their collective guarantee structures, we find that the ordering previously obtained on the basis of individual-guarantee structures is reversed.

Theorem 6 (Thomson (1983b)).   The Nash solution offers better collective guarantees than the Kalai–Smorodinsky solution, and in fact than any other solution satisfying WPO and AN. However, it is not the only solution to have that property, even among solutions satisfying S.INV and CONT as well.

Proof.   Computations analogous to those in the proofs of theorems 3 and 4 show that $\beta_N^{mn} = n/(n + 1)$ for all $m,n \in I$, and that $\beta_K = \alpha_K$.

The results described above concern the losses to the original agents inflicted by a solution, but it is just as natural to study the gains that the solution permits the original agents to achieve. Earlier, a preference was expressed for solutions that do not allow such gains; however, since many solutions do allow them, it seems desirable to be able to rank them on the basis of the extent to which they do. Such a ranking would constitute a useful complement to the ranking obtained by examining guarantees. Proceeding as we did for guarantees, we measure the opportunity for gain offered by an anonymous solution F to some agent originally part of some group of cardinality m when the group enlarges to some group of cardinality $m + n$, by $\gamma_F^{mn} \equiv \sup\{F_i(T)/F_i(S) \mid i \in P, \ P \subset Q, \ |P| = m, \ |Q| = m + n, \ S \in \Sigma^P, \ T \in \Sigma^Q, \ S = T_P\}$. The *opportunity structure* of F is then defined as the list $\gamma_F \equiv \{\gamma_F^{mn} \mid m,n \in I\}$.

The following results are established in Thomson (1983e).

Theorem 7.   The opportunity structure of the Nash solution is given by $\gamma_N^{mn} = m/(m + n)\alpha_N^{mn}$ for all $m,n \in I$.

Theorem 8.   The opportunity structure of the Kalai–Smorodinsky solution is given by $\gamma_K^{mn} \equiv 1$ for all $m,n \in I$.

Theorem 9.   If a solution satisfies WPO and AN, then its opportunity structure dominates $\bar{\gamma}$ defined by $\bar{\gamma}^{mn} = 1$ for all $m,n \in I$.

These results confirm the ordering of N and K obtained earlier on the basis of individual-guarantee structures, since they imply that the Kalai–Smorodinsky solution is better than any solution satisfying WPO and AN, and, in fact, strictly better than the Nash solution.

If we focused on the opportunities for gains offered to *groups* instead of those offered to *individuals,* we would compute $\delta_F^{mn} \equiv (1/m)\sup\{\Sigma_P F_i(T)/F_i(S) \mid P \subset Q, |P| = m, |Q| = m + n, S \in \Sigma^P, T \in \Sigma^Q, S = T_P\}$ and define the *collective opportunity structure* of F as $\delta_F \equiv \{\delta_F^{mn} \mid m,n \in I\}$. However, this concept permits a less fine discrimination among solutions than the previous one.

Theorem 10. The collective opportunity structures of the Kalai–Smorodinsky and Nash solutions are given by $\delta_K^{mn} = \delta_N^{mn} = 1$ for all $m,n \in I$, and for any F satisfying WPO and AN, $\delta_F^{mn} \geqq 1$ for all $m,n \in I$.

11.5   Stability

We turn now to considerations of stability. The idea here is that what solutions recommend for any group should be consistent with what they recommend for subgroups.

Given $P,Q \in \mathscr{P}$ with $P \subset Q$, $T \in \Sigma^Q$, and $x \in \mathbb{R}_+^Q$, $t_P^x(T)$ denotes the intersection of T with a hyperplane through x parallel to $\mathbb{R}_+^P$. We are now ready to formally introduce the axiom of stability.

Stability (STAB): For all $P,Q \in \mathscr{P}$ with $P \subset Q$, for all $S \in \Sigma^P$, $T \in \Sigma^Q$, if $S = t_P^x(T)$, where $x = F(T)$, then $x_P = F(S)$.

This axiom is illustrated in Figure 11.7, where $P = \{1,2\}$ and $Q = \{1,2,3\}$. The large problem $T \in \Sigma^Q$ is solved at x. The small problem $S \in \Sigma^P$ is obtained by taking a "slice" of T through x parallel to $\mathbb{R}^P$. The requirement is that the solution outcome of S coincide with the restriction of x to P.

Several motivations can be offered for the axiom. First of all, it can be interpreted as stating that an overall compromise is acceptable only if it is compatible with what negotiations among small groups would yield. Checking this involves, for each group of agents, setting the utilities of its members at the values specified by the proposed compromise and considering the resulting subset of the original problem as a problem involving the complementary group; then requiring that this problem be solved at a point that also assigns to each of the members of that group the utility of the proposed compromise. This motivation was offered by Harsanyi (1959), who first introduced the condition.

The axiom also has an interesting interpretation when agents receive their payoffs at different times. After a compromise x has been agreed upon, some of the agents may receive their payoffs first. The alternatives that are left open to the remaining agents constitute a problem S', which in general will be a subset of the intersection S of the original problem with a plane through x parallel to the coordinate subspace pertaining to that

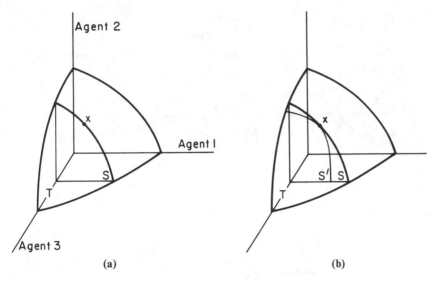

Figure 11.7

group. For the stability of the agreement to be guaranteed, the solution outcome of S' should coincide with the restriction of x to the group P. The axiom applies only if $S' = S$, which will happen in particular if the feasible set is derived from an economic problem of fair division in the one-commodity case. Since, in general, it is known only that S' is a subset of S containing x, as illustrated in Figure 11.7b the requirement is a weak one. This motivation of stability under temporal implementation of the solution was offered by Lensberg (1981).

Figure 11.8 presents examples illustrating that U, N, and L satisfy STAB and proving that neither K nor E do. In these examples, $P = \{1,2\}$, $Q = \{1,2,3\}$, $S \in \Sigma^P$, $T \in \Sigma^Q$, and $S = t_P^x(T)$, where $x = F(T)$ for the solution F under consideration.

To illustrate that N and U satisfy STAB, note that if the product $x_1 x_2 x_3$ is maximized over T at $x^* > 0$, then the product $x_1 x_2 x_3^*$ (and therefore the product $x_1 x_2$) is maximized over $S = t_P^{x^*}(T) = T \cap \{x \in \mathbb{R}^Q \mid x_3 = x_3^*\}$ at (x_1^*, x_2^*) (see Figure 11.8a). Similarly, if the sum $x_1 + x_2 + x_3$ is maximized over T at x^*, then the sum $x_1 + x_2 + x_3^*$ (and therefore the sum $x_1 + x_2$) is maximized over S at (x_1^*, x_2^*) (see Figure 11.8b). (In the case of U, we ignore the difficulties that occur when a tie-breaking rule has to be used to yield a well-defined [that is, single-valued] solution.) To show that E does not satisfy STAB, note that in Figure 11.8c, where $T \equiv cch\{(2,2,1)\}$, $E(T) = e_Q \equiv x$, and $E(S) = E(cch\{2e_P\}) = 2e_P \neq x_P$.

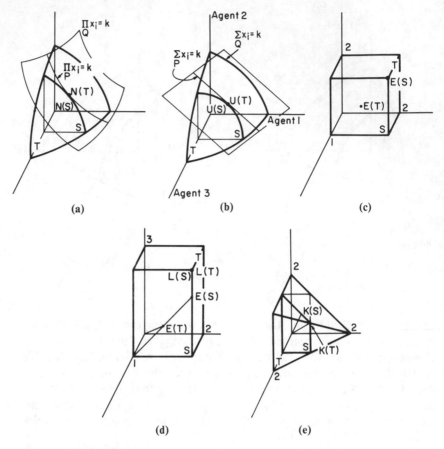

Figure 11.8

The example represented in Figure 11.8*d* illustrates that L satisfies STAB. There, $T \equiv cch\{(2,3,1)\}$, $L(T) = (2,3,1) = x$, $L(S) \equiv L(cch\{(2,3)\}) = (2,3) = x_p$. In Figure 11.8*e*, $T \equiv cch\{2e_1,(0,2,2)\}$, $K(T) = e_Q \equiv x$, $K(S) = K(cch\{e_P,2e_2\}) = (\frac{4}{3},\frac{4}{3}) \neq x_P$. Therefore, K does not satisfy STAB.

Harsanyi (1959) proved that if F satisfies STAB and coincides with the Nash solution for groups of cardinality 2, then it coincides with the Nash solution for all cardinalities. Of course, this is not a complete characterization of the Nash solution. Lensberg gave the following full characterization.

Theorem 11 (Lensberg (1981)).   If a solution satisfies PO, AN, S.INV, and STAB, then it is the Nash solution.

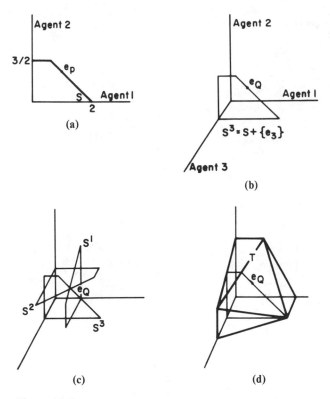

Figure 11.9

Proof. It is clear that N satisfies the four axioms. Conversely, we first establish that if F satisfies the four axioms, then $F = N$ for two-person problems. Without loss of generality, we take $P = \{1,2\}$ and, appealing to S.INV, we take $S \in \Sigma^P$ with $N(S) = e_P$. The idea of the proof is to add a third agent, agent 3, yielding $Q \equiv \{1,2,3,\}$ and to construct a three-person problem whose solution outcome x is easy to determine – by appealing only to PO and AN – and such that its slice parallel to $\mathbb{R}^P$ through x is precisely S. This approach is illustrated with the example of Figure 11.9. Let $S \equiv cch\{2e_1,(\frac{1}{2},\frac{3}{2})\}$ (Figure 11.9a). First, S is translated parallel to $\mathbb{R}^{(3)}$ by the vector e_3, yielding $S^3 \equiv S + \{e_3\}$ (Figure 11.9b). Then, S^1 and S^2 are obtained from S^3 by replications analogous to the ones performed in the proof of theorem 1 (Figure 11.9c). Formally, $S^1 \equiv \{x \in \mathbb{R}^Q_+ | \exists x' \in S^3$ such that, $x'_1 = x_2, x'_2 = x_3,$ and $x'_3 = x_1\}$, and $S^2 \equiv \{x \in \mathbb{R}^Q_+ | \exists x' \in S^3$ such that $x'_1 = x_3, x'_2 = x_1,$ and $x'_3 = x_2\}$. Finally, $T \equiv cch\{S^1,S^2,S^3\}$ is constructed (Figure 11.9d). We note that $e_Q \in PO(T)$ and that T is invari-

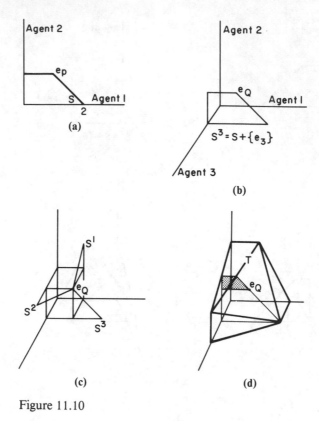

Figure 11.10

ant under rotations of the agents, and so by PO and AN, $F(T) = e_Q \equiv x$. Also, $t_P^x(T) = S^3$, and thus by STAB, $F(S^3) = x_P$, implying that $F(S) = N(S)$, the desired conclusion.

This argument is unfortunately not applicable to all S, as illustrated in Figure 11.10, where $S \equiv cch\{2e_1, e_P\}$. If we follow the same sequence of steps for that example, we still obtain that $F(T) = e_Q \equiv x$ (note, in fact, that T is the same here as it was in the previous example), but now $t_P^x(T) \supsetneq S^3$. Thus, an application of STAB tells us nothing about S^3, and therefore nothing about S.

To obtain an argument applicable to all S, S^3 may have to be replicated more than twice, that is, more than one agent may have to be added; how many additional agents are necessary depends on how "flat" S is around $N(S)$. The piece $t_P^x(T) \backslash S^3$ that is added on to S^3 by the convexification yielding T gets smaller and smaller as the number of additional agents increases. For a number sufficiently large, nothing is added if the Pareto-

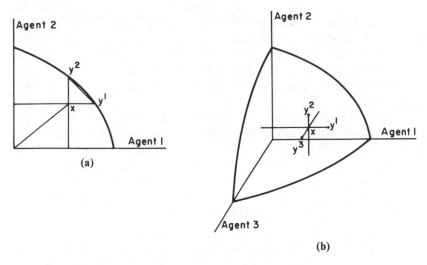

Figure 11.11

optimal boundary of S contains a nondegenerate segment around $N(S)$ (the conclusion can be extended to all S by a continuity argument) and the proof concludes as for the first example. The laborious algebra necessary to make the argument rigorous is omitted.

Having proved that $F = N$ for $|P| = 2$, we then appeal to Harsanyi's result to conclude for an arbitrary number of agents.

It is of particular interest here to see what happens when PO is deleted from the list of axioms of theorem 11, a question that is investigated in Thomson (1982a). If a solution F is required to satisfy only AN, S.INV, and STAB, it can be shown that either it satisfies PO as well, and therefore it is the Nash solution by theorem 11, or there exists $\lambda < 1$ such that given any $P \in \mathcal{P}$ and any $S \in \Sigma^P$, $F(S)$ is a point x such that for all $i \in P$, $x_i / \max\{x'_i \mid (x'_i, x_{-i}) \in S\} = \lambda$, where (x'_i, x_{-i}) designates the vector x after replacement of its ith coordinate by x'_i. This definition is illustrated in Figure 11.11 for $|P| = 2$ and $|P| = 3$. In the illustrations, $(x_i / \lambda, x_{-i})$ is denoted y_i.

Note that as $\lambda \to 1$, any point x so defined converges to $N(S)$. This can be seen most easily in the two-person example since the slope of the segment $[0, x]$ is the negative of the slope of the segment $[y_1, y_2]$. As $\lambda \to 1$, x approaches the boundary of S, the latter slope approaches the slope of a line of support of S at x, and the equality of slopes at the limit is the one that characterizes the Nash solution.

There is no difficulty in showing, for any $0 \leqq \lambda < 1$, the existence of a point x satisfying the equalities $x_i/\max\{x_i' \mid (x_i', x_{-i}) \in S\} = \lambda$ for all i. However, uniqueness is not guaranteed (Lensberg (1938b), Moulin (1983)). Therefore, the list of axioms SY, S.INV, and STAB does not seem to characterize a unique one-parameter family N_λ of solutions, although there may be some ways of performing selections that would have appealing properties.

We will conclude this section by stating two additional results based on the stability axiom. In addition to stability, the first result involves the natural generalization to an arbitrary number of agents of the axiom of individual monotonicity formulated by Kalai and Smorodinsky (1975) for the two-person case and used by them to characterize their solution. This axiom states that if a problem is expanded "in a direction favorable to an agent," the agent should not lose. Formally, we have

Individual monotonicity (I.MON): For all $P \in \mathcal{P}$, for all $S, S' \in \Sigma^P$, for all $i \in P$, if $S_{P \setminus i} = S'_{P \setminus i}$ and $S' \supset S$, then $F_i(S') \geqq F_i(S)$.

I.MON is satisfied by K as well as by E and L. However, L also satisfies STAB, which neither K nor E do. Again, L satisfies PO almost by definition. In fact, we have

Theorem 12 (Lensberg (1982)).   A solution satisfies PO, AN, I.MON, and STAB if and only if it is the lexicographic maximin solution.

The last theorem is interesting in that it involves considerations of both monotonicity and stability. Recall that E satisfies WPO, AN, MON, and CONT, but that it fails to satisfy STAB. However, on the domain $\tilde{\Sigma}$ of problems whose set of weakly Pareto-optimal points coincides with the set of Pareto-optimal points, STAB is in fact also satisfied. Obviously, on this restricted domain, E satisfies PO and not just WPO. Our final result is

Theorem 13 (Thomson (1982b)).   A solution defined on the restricted domain $\tilde{\Sigma}$ satisfies PO, AN, MON, CONT, and STAB if and only if it is the egalitarian solution.

11.6   Concluding comments

This review was intended to show that much of the theory of bargaining can be rewritten in the context of a variable population and that useful insights into the behavior of solutions can be gained by studying them in this more general framework. This work is far from complete. Of particularly interest are the recent results of Lensberg (1983a), in which PO,

CONT, and STAB are shown to characterize the general class of solutions defined by the maximization of a sum (one for each agent) of increasing and strictly concave functions. The axiom of stability is shown there to be closely related to the axioms of revealed preference in demand theory, and certain formal similarities between that theory and axiomatic bargaining are brought out in an illuminating way.

NOTES

1. Given $x,y \in \mathbb{R}^P$, $x \geqq y$ means that $x_i \geqq y_i$ for all $i \in P$; $x \geq y$ means that $x \geqq y$ and $x \neq y$; $x > y$ means that $x_i > y_i$ for all $i \in P$.
2. The Nash solution was introduced by Nash (1950) and further discussed by him (1953), as well as by many other writers.
3. This solution was introduced and characterized by Kalai and Smorodinsky (1975) for the two-person case. A closely related solution had been defined previously, but not axiomatized, by Raiffa (1953). Rosenthal (1976) proposed and axiomatized another related solution. Although the definition of the Kalai–Smorodinksy solution can be generalized easily to the n-person case, the property it has in the two-person case of yielding Pareto-optimal outcomes does not extend unless comprehensiveness of the problems is required, as is the case here (to be precise, this assumption guarantees only weak Pareto-optimality). It is not straightforward to extend the characterization of the solution given in the two-person case to the n-person case, as discussed by Roth (1980), although such extensions are possible, as shown by Segal (1980) and Imai (1983), who is concerned with the lexicographic extension of the solution.
4. This solution and variants of it have been characterized by Kalai (1977), Myerson (1977), Roth (1979a, 1979b), Thomson and Myerson (1980), and Myerson (1981).
5. This solution has been characterized by Imai (1983).
6. For a thorough study of the continuity properties of various solutions, see Jansen and Tijs (1983).

REFERENCES

Billera, L. F., and R. E. Bixby (1973): A Characterization of Pareto Surfaces. *Proceedings of the American Mathematical Society* 41: 261–7.
Harsanyi, J. C. (1959): A Bargaining Model for the Cooperative n-Person Game. In Tucker, A. W., and R. D. Luce (eds.). *Contributions to the Theory of Games,* Vol. 4. Princeton University Press, 324–56.
   (1977): *Rational Behaviour and Bargaining Equilibrium in Games and Social Situations.* Cambridge University Press.
Imai, H. (1983): Individual Monotonicity and Lexicographic *Maxmin* Solution. *Econometrica* 51: 389–401.
Jansen, M., and S. Tijs (1983): Continuity of Bargaining Solutions. *International Journal of Game Theory* 12: 91–105.
Kalai, E. (1977): Proportional Solutions to Bargaining Situations: Interpersonal Utility Comparisons. *Econometrica* 45: 1623–30.

Kalai, E., and M. Smorodinsky (1975): Other Solutions to Nash's Bargaining Problem. *Econometrica* 43: 513–18.

Lensberg, T. (1981): *The Stability of the Nash Solution.* Norwegian School of Management and Economics, Discussion Paper No. 05.

(1982): The Lexicographic Maximin Solution. Mimeograph.

(1983*a*): A Family of Pareto–Bergson–Samuelson Solutions. Mimeograph.

(1983*b*): Private communication.

Moulin, H. (1983): Private communication.

Myerson, R. B. (1977): Two-Person Bargaining Problems and Comparable Utility. *Econometrica* 45: 1631–7.

(1981): Utilitarianism, Egalitarianism, and the Timing Effect in Social Choice Problems. *Econometrica* 49: 883–97.

Nash, J. F. (1950): The Bargaining Problem. *Econometrica* 18: 155–62.

(1953): Two-Person Cooperative Games. *Econometrica* 21: 129–40.

Raiffa, H. (1953): Arbitration Schemes for Generalized Two-Person Games. In Kuhn, H. W., and A. W. Tucker (eds.). *Contribution to the Theory of Games,* Vol. 2. Princeton University Press.

Rosenthal, R. W. (1976): An Arbitration Model for Normal Form Games. *Mathematics of Operations Research* 2: 82–8.

Roth, A. E. (1977): Individual Rationality and Nash's Solution to the Bargaining Problem. *Mathematics of Operations Research* 2: 64–5.

(1979*a*): Proportional Solutions to the Bargaining Problem. *Econometrica* 47: 775–8.

(1979*b*): *Axiomatic Models of Bargaining.* Springer-Verlag.

(1980): An Impossibility Result for *N*-Person Games. *International Journal of Game Theory* 8: 129–32.

Segal, U. (1980): The Monotonic Solution for the Bargaining Problem: A Note. Hebrew University. Mimeograph.

Thomson, W. (1982*a*): Notes on Solving Choice Problems without Pareto-Optimality. Mimeograph.

(1982*b*): *Monotonicity, Stability, and Egalitarianism.* Harvard University, Discussion Paper No. 895. Forthcoming in *Mathematical Social Sciences.*

(1983*a*): *Truncated Egalitarian and Monotone Path Solutions.* University of Minnesota Discussion paper (January).

(1983*b*): Collective Guarantee Structures. *Economics Letters* 11: 63–8.

(1983*c*): The Fair Division of a Fixed Supply among a Growing Population. *Mathematics of Operations Research* 8: 319–26.

(1983*d*): Problems of Fair Division and the Egalitarian Solution. *Journal of Economic Theory* 31: 211–226.

(1983*e*): Individual and Collective Opportunities. University of Rochester Discussion paper (October).

Thomson, W., and T. Lensberg (1983): Guarantee Structures for Problems of Fair Division. *Mathematical Social Sciences* 4: 205–18.

Thomson, W., and R. B. Myerson (1980): Monotonicity and Independence Axioms. *International Journal of Game Theory* 9: 37–49.

CHAPTER 12

Toward a focal-point theory of bargaining

Alvin E. Roth
UNIVERSITY OF PITTSBURGH

12.1 Introduction

The purpose of this chapter is to consider some recent experimental evidence that existing models of bargaining, both axiomatic and strategic, are incomplete in ways that make them unlikely candidates from which to build powerful descriptive models of bargaining. After reviewing some of this evidence, a direction will be proposed that seems to offer some promising possibilities, and this will be briefly explored with the aid of an extremely simple preliminary model.

The plan of the chapter is as follows. Section 12.2 reviews some experiments in which certain kinds of information that are assumed by existing game-theoretic models not to influence the outcome of bargaining were nevertheless observed to have a dramatic effect. The data from these experiments make it plausible to suggest that bargainers sought to identify initial bargaining positions that had some special reason for being credible, and that these credible bargaining positions then served as *focal points* that influenced the subsequent conduct of negotiations, and their outcome. Section 12.3 explores this idea by investigating a simple model of coordination between two well-defined focal points. This model exhibits some of the same qualitative features observed in the bargaining data, concerning the frequency of disagreements as a function of the focal points. The section concludes with a brief discussion.

12.2 Review of four experiments

To test theories that depend on the expected utilities of the players, it is desirable to design experiments that allow the participants' utility functions to be determined. A class of games allowing this was introduced in

This work has been supported by grants from the National Science Foundation and the Office of Naval Research, and by Fellowships from the John Simon Guggenheim Memorial Foundation and the Alfred P. Sloan Foundation.

Roth and Malouf (1979). In that experiment, players bargained over the probability that they would receive some monetary prize, possibly a different prize for each player. Specifically, they bargained over how to distribute "lottery tickets" to determine the probability that each player would win his personal lottery (i.e., a player who received 40 percent of the lottery tickets would have a 40-percent chance of winning his monetary prize and a 60-percent chance of winning nothing). The rules of the game specified which distributions of lottery tickets were allowable. If no agreement was reached in the allotted time, each player received nothing. We call such games, in which each player has only two possible monetary payoffs, *binary lottery games.*

To interpret the outcomes of a binary lottery game in terms of each player's utility for money, recall that if each player's utility function is normalized so that the utility for receiving his prize is 1, and the utility for receiving nothing is 0, then the player's utility for any lottery between these two alternatives is the probability of winning the lottery. The set of feasible utility payoffs in such a game equals the set of allowable divisions of lottery tickets. Thus, binary lottery games can be used to test experimentally theories of bargaining that depend on the set of feasible utility payoffs. Note that the set of feasible utility payoffs does not depend on the prizes, and so a binary lottery game in which the players know the allowable divisions of lottery tickets is a game of complete information, regardless of whether each player also knows the other's prize. The classical models of bargaining that follow the work of John Nash (1950) and depend on only the set of feasible utility payoffs to the players (see Roth (1979)) thus predict that the outcome of a binary lottery game will not depend on whether the players know their opponent's prize.

The experiment of Roth and Malouf (1979) was designed to test this hypothesis, among others. Participants played binary lottery games under either full or partial information. In the full-information condition, each player knew his own potential prize and his opponent's potential prize. Under partial information, each player knew only his own prize. Contrary to the predictions of the classical models in the tradition of Nash (1950), the outcomes observed in the two information conditions exhibited dramatic differences: Under partial information, outcomes tended to be very close to an equal division of the lottery tickets, whereas under full information, outcomes showed a pronounced shift toward equal expected payoffs.

Of course, other classical models describe games in greater detail. The strategic form of a game describes not only the feasible utility payoffs, but also the strategies available to the players. In the games described previously, strategy choices concern the formulation of messages and proposals during negotiations. Since the strategies available to the players depend on the information those players possess, we must consider whether the observed results can be accounted for by the different strategies available to the players in the two information conditions.

The experiment of Roth, Malouf, and Murnighan (1981) was designed to address this question and involved binary lottery games with prizes stated in terms of an intermediate commodity. Prizes were expressed in chips having monetary value, and each player played four games under either *high, intermediate,* or *low* information. (See Table 12.1.) In each condition, each player knew the number of chips in his own potential prize and their value, but a player's information about his opponent's prize varied with the information condition. In the high-information condition, each player knew the number of chips in his opponent's prize, and their value. Under intermediate information, each player knew the number of chips in his opponent's prize, but not their value. Under low information, each player knew neither the number of chips in his opponent's prize, nor their value. In the latter two conditions, players were prevented from communicating the missing information about the prizes.

The experiment took advantage of two kinds of strategic equivalence relations.[1] Binary lottery games with prizes expressed in both chips and money, played in the low-information condition of this experiment, are strategically equivalent to binary lottery games with the same monetary prizes expressed in money alone, played in the partial-information condition of the previous experiment, because under the rules of the two information conditions, any legal message in one kind of game would be legal in the other. So the strategy sets are the same for both kinds of games, as are the utility functions and the underlying set of alternatives. Also, games expressed in both chips and money, played in the intermediate-information condition of this experiment, are strategically equivalent to games

Table 12.1.

	Player 1			Player 2		
	Number of chips	Value per chip	Value of prize	Number of chips	Value per chip	Value of prize
Game 1	60	$0.05	$ 3.00	20	$0.45	$9.00
Game 2	80	0.03	2.40	240	0.04	9.60
Game 3	100	0.09	9.00	300	0.01	3.00
Game 4	150	0.08	12.00	50	0.06	3.00

expressed in money alone, played in the full-information condition of the previous experiment. This is the result of the fact that any legal message in one kind of game can be transformed into a legal message in the other kind of game by substituting references to chips for references to money (or vice versa) in any message concerning the value of the prizes.

If the observed difference between the partial- and full-information conditions of the previous experiment was due to the players' different strategy sets in the two conditions (the *strategic hypothesis*), then a similar difference should be observed between the low- and intermediate-information conditions of the present experiment. The observed results did not support the strategic hypothesis. The low- and high-information conditions replicated the partial- and full-information conditions of the previous experiment, but the outcomes observed in the intermediate-information condition did not differ significantly from those in the low-information condition: The observed agreements tended to give both players equal probabilities, regardless of the size of their prize in chips. Thus, information about the artificial commodity, chips, did not affect the outcomes in the same way as did strategically equivalent information about money.

Both of the experiments discussed here revealed an effect of information that cannot be explained by existing models. The experiment of Roth and Murnighan (1982) was conducted to separate this effect into components resulting from the possession of specific information by specific individuals, and to assess the extent to which the observed behavior can be characterized as equilibrium behavior.[2]

In the two earlier experiments, either both bargainers knew their opponents's prize, or neither bargainer knew his opponent's prize. Also, it was always common knowledge whether the bargainers knew one another's prizes. Information is common knowledge in a game if it is known to all of the players, and if every player knows that all the players know, and that every player knows the others know that he knows, and so forth. Two bargainers can be thought of as having common knowledge about an event if the event occurs when both of them are present to see it, so that they also see each other seeing it, and so on. In these experiments, a set of instructions provides common knowledge to the bargainers if it contains the information that both of them are receiving exactly the same instructions.

Each game of the third experiment was a binary lottery game in which one player had a $20 prize and the other a $5 prize. In each of the eight conditions of the experiment, each player knew at least his own prize. The experiment used a 4 (information) $\times$ 2 (common knowledge) factorial design. The information conditions were: (1) *neither knows* his opponent's prize; (2) the *$20 player knows* both prizes, but the $5 player knows only his own prize; (3) the *$5 player knows* both prizes, but the $20 player knows only his own prize; and (4) *both players know* both prizes. The second factor made this information common knowledge for half of the bargaining pairs, but not common knowledge for the other half.

The results of this experiment permitted three principal conclusions. First, the effect of information on the agreements reached is primarily a function of whether the player with the smaller prize knows both prizes. Second, whether this information is common knowledge influences the frequency of disagreement, with more disagreements occurring in the noncommon-knowledge conditions. Third, in the noncommon-knowledge conditions, the relationship among the outcomes showed virtually no departure from equilibrium.

Together, these three experiments allowed fairly specific speculation as to the cause of the observed information effects. The first experiment demonstrated an effect of information about the prizes that could not be accounted for in terms of players' preferences over consequences (lotteries). The second experiment showed that this effect could not be accounted for by the set of available actions (strategies). The third experiment showed that the effect is consistent with rational (equilibrium) behavior. Thus, if we continue to hypothesize that the players are (approximately) Bayesian utility maximizers, it must be that the effect of information is due to a change in the players' subjective beliefs.

The experiment of Roth and Schoumaker (1983) was conducted to investigate this hypothesis. The design of the experiment took advantage of the fact that agreements in the previous experiments tended to cluster around two divisions of the lottery tickets: One kind of agreement split the lottery tickets equally between the bargainers, and the other gave the bargainers equal expected monetary payoffs. The experiment of Roth and Schoumaker investigated whether, by manipulating the bargainers' expectations, one or the other of these two kinds of agreements could be obtained as a stable equilibrium.

Each player played 25 identical binary lottery games. Although players were told that they bargained with another individual in each game, each individual in fact played against a programmed opponent in the first 15 games. Half the participants had a prize of $40 and half a prize of $10; both players knew both prizes, and players whose prize was $40 always bargained against players whose prize was $10 (each player had the same prize in all 25 games). Subjects were divided into three experimental conditions. The first was a 20–80 condition in which the programmed opponent promoted a 20–80 division of the lottery tickets, which yields equal expected payoffs. The second was a 50–50 condition in which subjects bargained with a programmed opponent designed to promote the equal division of lottery tickets. The third condition was the control: Subjects never bargained with a programmed opponent, but always with other members of the control group.

The experiment was designed to distinguish between two competing hypotheses. The classical game-theoretic hypothesis, which states that the outcome of a game can be predicted from the set of feasible utility payoffs and strategic possibilities, implies that, in this experiment, the different experimental conditions should have no continuing effect. Specifically, if this is correct, we would expect to observe that, starting with trial 16, any differences between the two experimental conditions and the control condition would begin to disappear and the outcomes in the three conditions should converge over time, as continued play removes any transient effects due to the initial experience of players in the 20–80 and 50–50 conditions.

However, if the expectations have a critical role in determining the outcome, as suggested by the earlier experiments, then we should expect to see divergent outcomes, established in the first 15 trials, persist in a stable fashion in each of the three conditions. We would expect the first condition's mean agreement to be near 20–80 and the second condition's to be near 50–50. The control condition's mean agreement should be somewhere between these two. This would be consistent with the hypothesis that the players' expectations were the uncontrolled factor accounting for the results of the previous experiments. The observed results clearly supported this latter hypothesis, since the observed agreements in the three conditions diverged just as the hypothesis predicts.

12.3   Focal points

The agreements observed in the experiment of Roth and Murnighan (1982) were distributed bimodally. One mode was at the 50,50 agreement, which gave the bargainers an equal chance of winning their prize; the other was at the 80,20 agreement, which gave the bargainers an equal expected (monetary) value by giving the bargainer with a $5 prize four times the probability of winning his prize as the bargainer with a $20 prize. This suggests that these *equal-probability* (EP) and *equal-value* (EV) agreements served as some sort of focal points for the bargaining. Examination of the transcripts from all the experiments supports this suggestion, since the EP and EV agreements also figure in the discussions between bargainers.

Recall, however, that in the experiment of Roth, Malouf, and Murnighan (1981), the "equal-chips" agreement failed to function as a focal

Table 12.2.

50,50	$(50 + h)/2, (150 - h)/2$
d_1,d_2	$h,100 - h$

$h \geq 50 \geq d_1$
$50 \geq 100 - h \geq d_2$

point in the intermediate-information condition, even though it was strategically equivalent to the EV agreement in the high-information condition. Thus, focal points are not determined by the usual (strategic) data with which existing theories describe a game. Nevertheless, focal points appear to play a significant role in determining the outcome of bargaining. For this reason, it seems sensible to attempt to construct theories of bargaining that treat focal points as an (empirically determined) part of the data used to model a game, and to test the ability of such theories to predict and explain other observable regularities of bargaining behavior.

Let us therefore take the focal points in a bargaining situation as given. In the binary lottery games that we have been considering, the EP agreement has always been a focal point, whereas the EV agreement appears as a focal point only when there is sufficient information about the prizes to allow the bargainer who would prefer it to identify it.

Perhaps the simplest model of bargaining with focal points is the *coordination game* in which each player has only two strategies: to demand the focal point that is more favorable to himself, or to acquiesce to the less favorable focal point. If both players demand the focal point that favors them, a disagreement results. If only one player demands the focal point that favors him, then that focal point is the resulting agreement. If both players acquiesce to their less favored focal point, some sort of compromise between the two focal points is the final agreement. Table 12.2 represents the simple coordination game in which the outcomes are binary lotteries of the kind discussed here, and the second focal point (aside from $(50,50)$) is $(h,100 - h)$ for some $h \geq 50$. For simplicity, compromise agreements are here taken to have an expected value halfway between the two focal points. (In all of the experiments discussed here, the disagreement payoffs d_1 and d_2 have been equal to zero.)

For $h > 50$, this coordination game has two pure-strategy equilibria (corresponding to the focal points), and one mixed-strategy equilibrium. When $h = 50$ (so that there is only one focal point), there is a unique, pure-strategy, equilibrium.

The data from the bargaining experiments conducted to date are suggestive of the hypothesis that, when there is only one focal point, we are observing the unique equilibrium in such a coordination game, and when there are two, we are observing the mixed-strategy equilibrium. This

Table 12.3. *Frequency of disagreement*

Experiment	(h,100 − h)		
	(50,50)	(75,25)	(80,20)
Roth and Malouf (1979)	2% (1/54)[a]	14% (3/21)[b]	
Roth, Malouf, and Murnighan (1981)	6% (2/32)[c]	20% (6/30)[d]	24% (7/29)[e]
Roth and Murnighan (1982)	11% (7/63)[f]		25% (37/146)[g]
All experiments combined	7% (10/149)	18% (9/51)	25% (44/175)
Prediction of the coordination model (mixed-strategy equilibrium)	0%	7%	10%

[a] Games with only a (50,50) focal point in this experiment are all those in the partial-information condition, and games with equal prizes for both bargainers in the full-information condition.
[b] Games with a (75,25) focal point in this experiment are games 3 and 4 in the full-information condition.
[c] Games with only a (50,50) focal point in this experiment are all games in the low-information condition.
[d] Games with a (75,25) focal point in this experiment are games 1 and 3 in the high-information condition.
[e] Games with an (80,20) focal point in this experiment are games 2 and 4 in the high-information condition.
[f] Games with only a (50,50) focal point in this experiment are those in which neither player knows both prizes, in the common- and noncommon-knowledge conditions.
[g] Games with an (80,20) focal point in this experiment are all those in conditions in which the $5 player knows both prizes.

hypothesis allows predictions to be made about observable bargaining phenomena, such as the frequency of disagreement, as a function of the focal points.[3] Table 12.3 compares this predicted frequency with the observed frequency of disagreements as a function of the second focal point $(h,100 - h)$ for each of the experiments discussed previously (except that of Roth and Schoumaker, in which the degree of coordination was subjected to experimental manipulation).

Note that a prediction of the coordination model is that the frequency of disagreement should increase as h increases, and that this is, in fact, observed within each experiment and across experiments. Comparing the disagreement frequency predicted by the coordination model with the frequency observed across all experiments, it appears plausible that there is a *coordination component* to the observed disagreements. Of course, such connections between disagreement in bargaining and disagreements arising from coordinating between two focal points must remain speculation until they can be subjected to a test by means of experiments specifically designed for the purpose.

It should be noted in passing that the coordination model makes other testable predictions that appear plausible as well. For example, it predicts that the frequency of disagreement should increase as the disagreement payoff to either player increases. Of course, the model is also incomplete in a number of important ways. For example, it gives no guidance as to when we should expect to observe a mixed-strategy equilibrium as opposed to a pure-strategy equilibrium as the parameters of the model vary. This kind of incompleteness in the coordination model can perhaps be seen as complementary to the different sorts of incompleteness in the axiomatic models, which, for example, make no predictions about the frequency of disagreement.

In closing, it should be emphasized that the disagreements discussed here are quite different in origin from the disagreements predicted by the chapters in this volume that study strategic models of bargaining under incomplete information. In those papers, the positive probability of disagreement at equilibrium is entirely due to the presence of incomplete information. Here, both the disagreements observed in the experiments discussed, and those predicted by the coordination model, occur in games having complete information. The purpose of this chapter, therefore, is to suggest that some of the disagreement observed in bargaining has nothing to do with incomplete information, and might better be understood as resulting from the questions of coordination inherent in bargaining.

NOTES

1. Two games are strategically equivalent if they both can be represented by the same game in strategic form. Thus, any theory of games that depends only on the strategic form of a game yields the same prediction for strategically equivalent games.
2. Reference here is to the familiar noncooperative equilibrium of Nash (1951).
3. The frequency of disagreement at the mixed-strategy equilibrium of the coordination game is equal to the product of two probabilities: the probability x that player 1 demands the EV focal point, and the probability y that player 2 demands the EP focal point. These quantities are given by $x = (h/2 - 25)/(75 - h/2 - d_2)$, and $y = (h/2 - 25)/(h/2 + 25 - d_1)$. At the mixed-strategy equilibrium, the probability chosen by each player is the one that makes his opponent indifferent between playing either of his two pure strategies. This has the (perverse) effect of having each player's probability of choosing either of his pure strategies at equilibrium depend only on his opponent's payoffs.

REFERENCES

Nash, John: The Bargaining Problem. *Econometrica,* 1950, 18, 155–62.
  Non-Cooperative Games. *Annals of Mathematics,* 1951, 54, 286–95.
Roth, Alvin E.: *Axiomatic Models of Bargaining.* Berlin: Springer, 1979.
Roth, Alvin E., and Malouf, Michael: Game-Theoretic Models and the Role of
  Information in Bargaining. *Psychological Review,* 1979, 86, 574–94.
Roth, Alvin E., and Murnighan, J. Keith: The Role of Information in Bargaining:
  An Experimental Study. *Econometrica,* 1982, 50, 1123–42.
Roth, Alvin E., and Schoumaker, Francoise: Expectations and Reputations in
  Bargaining: An Experimental Study. *American Economic Review,* 1983,
  73, 362–72.
Roth, Alvin E.; Malouf, Michael; and Murnighan, J. Keith: Sociological versus
  Strategic Factors in Bargaining. *Journal of Economic Behavior and Organization,* 1981, 2, 153–77.

CHAPTER 13

Bargaining and coalitions

K. G. Binmore
LONDON SCHOOL OF ECONOMICS

13.1 Introduction

This chapter represents the first of several putative papers on bargaining among a small number of players. The problem treated in the current paper may be thought of as the "three-player/three-cake" problem. Each pair of players exercises control over the division of a different cake, but only one of the cakes can be divided. Which of the cakes is divided and how much does each player receive? This problem is, of course, a paradigm for a much wider class of problems concerning the conditions under which coalitions will or will not form.

The general viewpoint is the same as that adopted in our previous papers on bargaining (e.g., [3], [4], and [5]). Briefly, we follow Nash ([15], [16], and [17]) in regarding "noncooperative games" as more fundamental than "cooperative games."[1] Operationally, this means that cooperative solution concepts need to be firmly rooted in noncooperative theory in the sense that the concept should be realizable as the solution of at least one interesting and relevant noncooperative bargaining game[2] (and preferably of many such bargaining games).

The cooperative concept that we wish to defend in the context of the three-person/three-cake problem is a version of the "Nash bargaining solution." A precise statement of the version required is given in Section 13.3. For the moment, we observe only that the notion can be thought of as synthesizing to some extent the different approaches of Nash and von Neumann and Morgenstern.[3] The *n*-player version of the Nash bargaining solution that is usually quoted (see, for example, Roth [19]) is, of course, not relevant to the three-player/three-cake problem but to the three-player/one-cake problem.

Our defense of what we feel to be the appropriate version of the Nash bargaining solution is based on the construction of noncooperative bargaining models in which the bargaining process is described explicitly. Our purpose in studying these models is not to attempt to show that the cooperative concept on which we focus is the only one worthy of attention. Indeed, it is well known that a considerable variety of cooperative concepts can be implemented noncooperatively by using sufficiently ingenious bargaining models (see, for example, Moulin [14]). Our purpose is rather to provide some reasonably solid grounding for judgments about the circumstances under which our cooperative solution concept is likely to be applicable instead of another.

In particular, it seems often to be the imperfections in the negotiation process that resolve the indeterminacy of the basic bargaining problem. But it is seldom obvious a priori precisely how the final outcome and the imperfections of the negotiation process are related. The use of a specific bargaining model (in which imperfections are modeled by constraining a player to remain within his strategy set) allows one to get some feel for this issue. Of course, if a particular bargaining model imposes constraints on a player's behavior that he would prefer to violate and no mechanism exists in the situation one is trying to model that would prevent such violations, then little insight can be expected from the model. The question of whether a model is vulnerable to such criticism is a matter for the judgment of the modeler. This approach therefore does not avoid the necessity of exercising one's judgment but at least one does succeed in transferring the judgment from the rather diffuse question of what is a "reasonable outcome" to the more down to earth question of the nature of the "imperfections" in the negotiation process.

The noncooperative bargaining models to be considered here are based on the very natural two-person model described by Rubinstein[4] in [21]. In this model, the imperfections of the negotiation process lie in the fact that a player cannot respond immediately with a counter offer to an offer made by his opponent but must wait for a given time period.[5] We follow Rubinstein in studying the perfect equilibria of such games where "perfect" is used in Selten's original sense (i.e. subgame perfect[6]). It is worth noting that Rubinstein's arguments can be simplified even when the model is generalized (see Binmore [5] and Fudenberg and Levine [7]). For models with some element of stationarity over time, an especially simple technique is described in Shaked and Sutton [25]. My indebtedness to Shaked and Sutton however is much wider, and I would like to take this opportunity to acknowledge the numerous useful discussions I have had with them, both separately and together, on this topic and others.

We conclude this introduction by noting that Sections 13.5 and 13.6 contain some implications of our results for the Raiffa/Kalai–Smorodinsky bargaining solution and for the nontransferable utility Shapley value. As far as the former is concerned, we hope that our remarks will be seen as evidence that the notion is complementary to the Nash bargaining solution rather than contradictory. As far as the latter is concerned, we contend that this is perhaps best not thought of as a bargaining concept except possibly in a modified form and then only under restrictive conditions.

13.2   The two-player/one-cake problem

Our version of the Nash bargaining solution for the three-player/three-cake problem requires some preliminary discussion of the two-player/one-cake problem. The "cake" is identified with a set $\mathscr{X}$ in $\mathbb{R}_+^2$. (We use $\mathbb{R}_+$ for the nonnegative reals and $\mathbb{R}_{++}$ for the positive reals.) Each point $\underline{x}$ represents a pair of utilities corresponding to a possible division of the cake. We assume that $\mathscr{X}$ is compact, strictly convex,[7] and satisfies

$$\underline{x} \in \mathscr{X} \iff \forall \underline{y} \in \mathbb{R}^2(\underline{0} \le \underline{y} \le \underline{x} \implies \underline{y} \in \mathscr{X}).$$

The "status-quo" point is normalized at $\underline{0}$. We use quotation marks here because we will not always wish to identify the "status-quo" point with a utility pair that results from disagreement. As far as the mathematical derivation of the Nash bargaining solution from Nash's axioms is concerned, the interpretation of the "status-quo" point is irrelevant. All that is necessary is that a reference point $\underline{\xi}$ be given with the property that the solution $f(\mathscr{X}, \underline{\xi})$ depends only on the feasible set $\mathscr{X}$ and the given reference point $\underline{\xi}$.

A basic assumption in this paper is that the two-person/one-cake problem as just described should be "solved" with an (asymmetric) Nash bargaining solution as presented, for example, by Roth in [19]. Various noncooperative justifications can be advanced (see, for example, [3] or [5]). One of these justifications is mentioned below in a somewhat more elaborate context. The word "asymmetric" is used in association with the Nash bargaining solution to indicate that we intend to use the version in which each player is assigned a positive[8] "bargaining power[9]". The asymmetric Nash bargaining solution corresponding to the bargaining powers τ_1 and τ_2 is the point $\underline{\sigma} \in \mathscr{X}$ at which $x_1^{\tau_1} x_2^{\tau_2}$ is maximized subject to the constraints $\underline{x} \in \mathscr{X}$ and $\underline{x} \ge \underline{0}$.

In this section, we will be concerned with the stability of this resolution of the two-player/one-cake problem given that one or both of the players may have the opportunity to go and bargain elsewhere if displeased with the course of the negotiations thus far. Any bargaining solution must presumably be stable in the presence of small enough perturbations from outside of this type, if it is to have any hope of realistic application.

Suppose that, if the first player breaks off negotiations and goes elsewhere to bargain, then the first player will obtain a utility m_1 and the

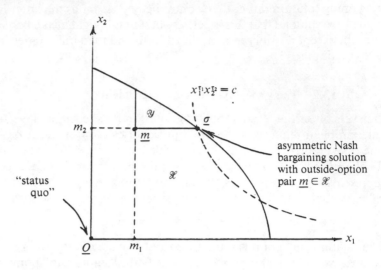

Figure 13.1

second player will be left with utility 0; similarly for the second player, with m_2 replacing m_1. It seems not unreasonable under these circumstances to propose that the fact that m_1 and m_2 might be positive should be irrelevant provided that the asymmetric Nash bargaining solution $\underline{\sigma}$ satisfies $\underline{\sigma} \geq \underline{m}$. We will go somewhat farther than this and resolve the two-player/one-cake problem with an "outside-option" pair $\underline{m} \in \mathscr{X}$ by maximizing $x_1^{\tau_1}x_2^{\tau_2}$ subject to the constraints $\underline{x} \in \mathscr{X}$ and $\underline{x} \geq \underline{m}$ (see Figure 13.1). Note that we do not use $\underline{m}$ as a new "status quo". The "status quo" remains[10] at $\underline{0}$. The outside-option pair $\underline{m}$ is accommodated by replacing $\mathscr{X}$ with

$$\mathscr{Y} = \{\underline{x}: \underline{x} \in \mathscr{X} \text{ and } \underline{x} \geq \underline{m}\}$$

and then applying the (asymmetric) Nash bargaining solution as usual.[11]

We now briefly describe a version of the Rubinstein bargaining model that supports the preceding resolution of the two-person/one-cake problem with outside-option pair $\underline{m}$. A feature of this model is that, if the bargaining question is still open at time T, then matters look much the same to the players at time T as they did at time 0 (except that all payoffs are appropriately discounted). In so far as traditional thinking about a status-quo point is concerned it follows that, if the bargaining is not over by time T, then the status-quo point $\underline{\xi}(T)$ used by the players at time T and the solution $\underline{\sigma}(T)$ of their bargaining problem at time T should be related by an equation of the form

$$\underline{\xi}(T) = \underline{\sigma}(T + \delta T).$$

Such considerations would seem relevant whenever forward commitment in the bargaining process is not possible. But the case of forward commitment would seem by far the less interesting. Thus, although $\underline{0}$ will continue to be called the "status-quo" point, and although it is true that if the players never agree to anything (including their outside options), then the result will be $\underline{0}$, it is nevertheless misleading to think of $\underline{0}$ in terms of a "disagreement point."

Returning to the appropriate version of the Rubinstein model, we first assign each player a discount factor from the interval $(0,1)$. These factors are labeled δ_1 and δ_2. Next, we fix $t > 0$ as the time interval between successive "negotiation rounds." At time $2nt$ ($n = 0,1, \ldots$), player 2 makes an offer (d_1, d_2) to player 1. If player 1 agrees, then the offer is implemented provided $(\delta_1^{-2nt}d_1, \delta_2^{-2nt}d_2) \in \mathscr{X}$. If player 1 disagrees, he may either take up his outside option,[12] thereby implementing $(\delta_1^{2nt}m_1, 0)$, or else wait until time $(2n + 1)t$ and make a counteroffer (e_1, e_2) to player 2. If player 2 agrees, then the offer is implemented provided $(\delta_1^{-(2n+1)t}e_1, \delta_2^{-(2n+1)t}e_2) \in \mathscr{X}$. Alternatively, player 2 may take up his outside option. Otherwise, we pass to time $(2n + 2)t$ and proceed as before, with $n + 1$ replacing n.

As far as the analysis of the game is concerned, there is nothing worth adding to what is stated in [3] and [5]. The unique (subgame) perfect equilibrium converges to what we have called the (asymmetric) Nash bargaining solution for the two-person/one-cake problem with outside-option pair $\underline{m} \in \mathscr{X}$ as the time interval between successive proposals becomes vanishingly small (i.e., $t \rightarrow 0+$). The appropriate bargaining powers are given by $\tau_i = (-\log \delta_i)^{-1}$ ($i = 1, 2, \ldots$).

Note that, in the limit as $t \rightarrow 0+$, it does not matter to the outcome whether we begin with player 1 or with player 2 making an offer at time 0. The result will be the same in either case.

We have two motives for reviewing the Rubinstein model in this context. The first is to clarify the "status-quo" issue, on which we now undertake to remain silent in the remainder of this chapter. The other is to provide a rationale for the assumptions we wish to make about what happens when $\underline{m} \notin \mathscr{X}$, that is, when the outside-option pair is *not* feasible.

We are interested in the situation in which one player or the other can be regarded as having the "initiative" in the sense that, if disagreement arises, then it will be the player with the "initiative" who secures his outside option[13] if there is competition among the players.[14] We regard the "initiative" as an ephemeral phenomenon in that, if not taken up, it

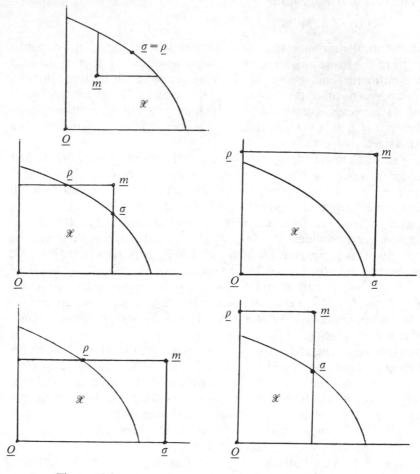

Figure 13.2

passes to the other player. Thus, in the preceding bargaining model, the "initiative" at time 0 is with player 1, although this makes no difference to the outcome if $\underline{m} \in \mathscr{X}$ and $t \to 0+$. However, if $\underline{m} \notin \mathscr{X}$, a perfect equilibrium will clearly have to assign player 1 a payoff of m_1, whereas if the roles of 1 and 2 were reversed, player 2 would be assigned a payoff of m_2.

In the diagrams of Figure 13.2, we suppose that player 1 has the "initiative". The point $\underline{\sigma}$ represents the actual outcome of the bargaining process, and $\underline{\rho}$ represents the "standby" outcome. By this we mean the outcome that *would* result if player 2 had the "initiative". In particular, $\underline{\rho}$ is the outcome of the game that will result if player 1 fails, or is unable for some reason, to exercise his "initiative". We suggest that the plausibility of the proposed "solutions" be studied with the help of the bargaining model introduced earlier in the case when $\underline{m} \notin \mathscr{X}$ and $t \to 0+$.

Although the nomenclature is clumsy, we will refer to $\underline{\sigma}$ in the diagrams of Figure 13.2 as the (asymmetric) Nash bargaining solution with outside-option pair $\underline{m}$ when player 1 has the initiative.

13.3   The three-player/three-cake problem

We label the three players with the numerals 1, 2, and 3. The coalitions $\{2,3\}$, $\{3,1\}$, and $\{1,2\}$ are labeled I, J, and K, respectively. Associated with each coalition C is a cake $\mathscr{X}^C$ in $\mathbb{R}^3_+$ with the property that if $\underline{x} \in \mathscr{X}^C$ and p is the player excluded from C, then $x_p = 0$. In so far as the players other than p are concerned, we assume that $\mathscr{X}^C$ satisfies properties analogous to those assumed in Section 13.2 for $\mathscr{X}$. The situation is illustrated in Figure 13.3.

We are interested in a bargaining game in which at most one of the coalitions I, J, or K can form. The formation of a coalition consists of an agreement by its members on a point $\underline{x} \in \mathscr{X}^C$. If no coalition forms, each player receives $\underline{0}$; that is, the "status-quo" point is normalized at $\underline{0}$.

The question we address is: *If* coalition C forms, on what point $\underline{x} \in \mathscr{X}^C$ will its members agree? Insufficient structure has been provided to resolve the question of *which* coalition will form in the general case.[15] Of course, in taking this view we simply follow von Neumann and Morgenstern. We refer to our proposed resolution of this question as the three-player/three-cake (asymmetric) Nash bargaining solution.

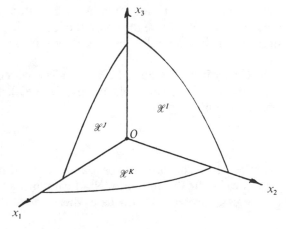

Figure 13.3

Before describing this proposed solution, we wish to make some comments on the possible "stickiness" of the two-person/one-cake solution. That the two-person/one-cake solution should remain unaffected by the introduction of a third player and two further cakes is not surprising if all divisions of the new cakes yield a utility to the original players of less than what they will enjoy at their original agreement point. This observation was incorporated in the discussion of Section 13.2. It might be thought however that, if the third player were able to offer one or both of the original players more than they enjoy at the original agreement point, then the original agreement point would automatically be abandoned. Indeed, perfect-competition arguments in this context take the proposition for granted. Thus, for example, the introduction of a second buyer to a one-buyer/one-seller problem is usually assumed to result in an outcome in the core[16], and the bargaining solution described shortly will also yield this result. However, the three-player noncooperative model considered in Section 13.4 shows that the two-player/one-cake solution can be surprisingly resistant to the introduction of a third player even when this player is able to offer both original players more than they obtain at the original agreement point. In this model, although the original players are free to open a channel of communication to the third player, it is optimal for them not to do so and the third player has no means of forcing his attentions on them. The result is that the two-player/one-cake solution survives the introduction of the third player. It follows that, when an "outsider" is not able to guarantee the attention of the "insiders," it may be rational for the insiders to ignore the outsider even though they are aware of his existence and of the cakes that can be divided with his cooperation. The bargaining solution we now describe is not intended to apply in these circumstances but to the "mainstream" situation[17] in which potential outsiders do not require the consent of potential insiders in order to gain an ear for their proposals. The idea is very simple and not particularly original.[18]

We begin with three positive[8] parameters, τ_1, τ_2, and τ_3, which represent the bargaining powers of the three players. If $C = \{p,q\}$ and the excluded player is r, we define[19] a point

$$\underline{\sigma}^{C,p}$$

in $\mathbb{R}^3_+$ as follows. We take the rth coordinate to be 0, and the remaining pair of coordinates is taken to be the (asymmetric) Nash bargaining solution for the two-player/one-cake problem for the case when

1. The players are p and q
2. The cake is $\mathscr{X}^C$ (with the rth coordinate suppressed)

3. The status quo is $\underline{0}$
4. The outside-option vector is $\underline{m}^C$ as defined shortly (but with the rth coordinate suppressed)
5. Player p has the initiative.

The outside-option vectors $\underline{m}^C$ are defined[19] by

6. $\underline{m}^I = (0, \sigma_2^{K,1}, \sigma_3^{J,1})$,
7. $\underline{m}^J = (\sigma_1^{K,2}, 0, \sigma_3^{I,2})$,
8. $\underline{m}^K = (\sigma_1^{I,3}, \sigma_2^{J,3}, 0)$.

We will interpret $\underline{\sigma}^{C,p}$ as the outcome that will result *if* the negotiations conclude with the formation of coalition C and the division of the cake that C controls. This interpretation requires that, when $\underline{\sigma}^{C,p} \notin \mathcal{X}^C$, coalition C will *never* form.

Some comment is also necessary on the interpretation of the outside-option vectors. Observe that, if p exercises his initiative and defects from $C = \{p,q\}$, it is assumed[20] that it will be r who holds the initiative in the subsequent negotiations between p and r. One may imagine that the bargaining model of Section 13.2 is employed, with p playing the role of player 2 and r that of player 1.

We now define an (asymmetric) Nash bargaining solution for the three-player/three-cake problem to be a function

$$f: \{I,J,K\} \longrightarrow \mathbb{R}^3_+$$

such that

1. For each $C \in \{I,J,K\}$, there exists a $p \in C$ for which

$$\underline{\sigma}^C = f(C) = \underline{\sigma}^{C,p};$$

2. The outside-option vectors defined by (6), (7) and (8) also satisfy

$$\underline{m}^I = (0, \sigma_2^K, \sigma_3^J),$$
$$\underline{m}^J = (\sigma_1^K, 0, \sigma_3^I),$$
$$\underline{m}^K = (\sigma_1^J, \sigma_2^I, 0).$$

The rationale for condition (1) will be clear from the discussion accompanying the definition of $\underline{\sigma}^{C,p}$. Condition (2) simply requires that, where f assigns the initiative to a player, then this assignment be consistent with the assumptions players are making about the values of their outside options.

To characterize the function f, it is necessary to distinguish two cases (Figure 13.4). Observe that the coordinates of the point P illustrated for case I are strictly decreasing functions of x, and hence the locus of P cuts the Pareto-boundary of $\mathcal{X}^I$ in at most one point. If there is a point of

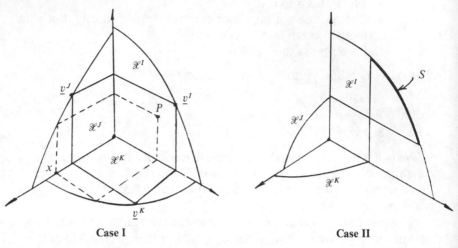

Case I   Case II

Figure 13.4

intersection, it follows that there exists a unique triple $(\underline{v}^I,\underline{v}^J,\underline{v}^K)$ as illustrated for case I. For obvious reasons, we call $(\underline{v}^I,\underline{v}^J,\underline{v}^K)$ a "von Neumann–Morgenstern triple." If there is no point of intersection, then the game has a nonempty "core" S, as illustrated for case II (although S might equally well be a subset of $\mathscr{X}^J$ or $\mathscr{X}^K$ in the general case).

Proposition 1. An (asymmetric) Nash bargaining solution for the three-player/three-cake problem always exists and is unique (for fixed values of τ_1, τ_2, and τ_3).

I. If a von Neumann–Morgenstern triple $(\underline{v}^I,\underline{v}^J,\underline{v}^K)$ exists, then

$$f(C) = \underline{v}^C$$

for each $C \in \{I,J,K\}$ (Figure 13.5)

II. If a von Neumann–Morgenstern triple does not exist, then the game has a nonempty core S, which is a subset of either $\mathscr{X}^I$, $\mathscr{X}^J$, or $\mathscr{X}^K$. If $S \subseteq \mathscr{X}^C$, then $f(C)$ is the (asymmetric) Nash bargaining solution for the two-player/one-cake problem in which the players are the members of C, the status quo is $\underline{0}$ and the cake has Pareto-boundary S. If D is a coalition other than C, then $f(D)$ is the point on the Pareto-boundary of $\mathscr{X}^D$ that assigns 0 to the player excluded from C (Figure 13.5).

Note 1. Given proposition 1, one may ask which coalition would be expected to form. This question clearly is unanswerable as far as case I is concerned[15] without further structure being supplied. In case II, however,

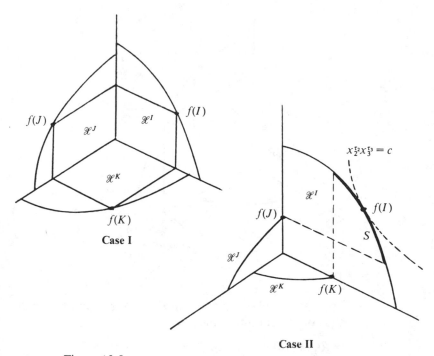

Case I

Case II

Figure 13.5

one might reasonably focus attention on the coalition C with $S \subseteq \mathscr{X}^C$. But some care is necessary here. The situation in case II is rather similar to an example given by Roth [20], in which he argues that coalition C will necessarily form. Roth then advances the example as a criticism of the nontransferable utility Shapley value. Aumann [2] has challenged Roth's conclusion, and his arguments certainly cast doubt on the proposition that coalition C will *necessarily* form. On the other hand, Aumann's arguments do not seem adequate to demolish the somewhat more temperate claim that the formation of C should be seen as the "mainstream" result.[21]

Proof of proposition 1. There is no difficulty in verifying that the functions f described in proposition 1 satisfy the conditions for an (asymmetric) Nash bargaining solution for the three-player/three-cake problem. We therefore concentrate on the uniqueness question. Suppose therefore that there exists an appropriate $f: \{I, J, K\} \to \mathbb{R}_+^3$.

    I. Suppose that each outside-option vector $\underline{m}^C$ is either exterior to $\mathscr{X}^C$ or else is Pareto-efficient in $\mathscr{X}^C$. Under these conditions,

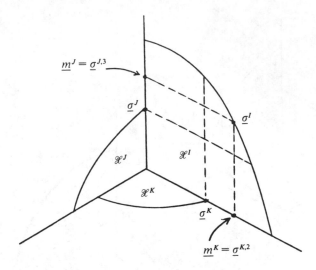

Figure 13.6

$m^C \geq \underline{\sigma}^C$ with equality if and only if $m^C \in \mathscr{X}^C$. But, by condition (2) of the definition of f,

$$\underline{m}^I = (0,\sigma_2^K,\sigma_3^J) \leq (0,m_2^K,m_3^J) = (0,\sigma_2^I,\sigma_3^I) = \underline{\sigma}^I,$$

and thus $\underline{m}^I = \underline{\sigma}^I$. Similarly, $\underline{m}^J = \underline{\sigma}^J$ and $\underline{m}^K = \underline{\sigma}^K$. We conclude that $(\underline{\sigma}^I,\underline{\sigma}^J,\underline{\sigma}^K)$ is a von Neumann–Morgenstern triple.

II. If the hypothesis of case I just considered does not hold, then at least one $\underline{m}^C \in \mathscr{X}^C$ but is not Pareto-efficient in $\mathscr{X}^C$. Suppose that this is true in the case $C = I$. Either $m_2^I < \sigma_2^I$ or $m_3^I < \sigma_3^I$. Suppose the former. Because $m_2^K = \sigma_2^I$ and $\sigma_2^K = m_2^I$, it follows that $m_2^K > \sigma_2^K$ and hence that $m_1^K = \sigma_1^K = \sigma_1^{K,1}$. But $m_1^J = \sigma_1^K$, and also $m_1^J = \sigma_1^{K,2}$. We deduce that $\sigma_1^{K,1} = \sigma_1^{K,2}$. But, since $m_2^K > \sigma_2^K$, $\underline{m}^K \notin \mathscr{X}^K$, and it must therefore be the case that $m_1^K = \sigma_1^{K,1} = \sigma_1^{K,2} = 0$. Since $m_1^J = \sigma_1^K$ and $m_1^J = \sigma_1^{J,1}$, we also conclude that $m_1^J = \sigma_1^{J,1} = \sigma_1^{J,2} = 0$. We are therefore left with the configuration shown in Figure 13.6.

Note 2.   The considerations of this section are closely related to Albers' notion of "stable demand vectors" described by Selten in [24]. In fact, in case I, a stable demand vector is a member of the von Neumann–Morgenstern triple, whereas in case II, the stable demand vectors are the elements of the core S (assuming the obvious adaptation of Albers' definition necessary in the absence of a characteristic function description of the game). If this were not the case, there would be grounds for concern in view of the noncooperative implementation results that Selten obtains in [24]. In this paper, Selten characterizes stable demand vectors as certain equilibrium outcomes of noncooperative bargaining games related to those studied here.

Note 3. It is natural to ask what happens if there are more players and/or more cakes. We do not have adequate bargaining models to defend the obvious generalizations. However, for the three-player/four-cake problem (i.e. one "large" cake under the control of all three players and three "small" cakes, each under the control of a different pair of players), it seems clear that one should first calculate the subset S of the big cake that assigns each player at least as much as he would obtain at his most favored solution outcome for the corresponding three-player/three-cake problem. If S is empty, then one would expect the result of the bargaining to be a solution outcome of the three-player/three-cake problem. If S is nonempty, then one would expect the result of the bargaining to be the (asymmetric) Nash bargaining solution for the three-player/one-cake problem with cake S and "status quo" $\underline{0}$.

The four-player/six-cake problem is less easily dealt with. But assuming that only *one* cake can be divided, presumably the solution outcomes can be described in terms of one of the four three-player/three-cake problems obtained by omitting one of the four players. Where *two* cakes can be divided simultaneously, a two-stage analysis would seem necessary. This approach clearly involves combinatorial difficulties but such difficulties are presumably intrinsic to the problem.

13.4 Noncooperative bargaining models

The origin of the models discussed in this section is the Rubinstein [21] model for the two-player/one-cake problem. For alternative methodologies and related models, see Binmore [5], Fudenberg and Levine [7] and Shaked and Sutton [25]. As a first step in the direction of an incomplete-information analysis, see Rubinstein [22]. It is perhaps worth noting that, although Rubinstein-type models accord better with our intuitive feelings about the nature of negotiation processes, nevertheless the results one obtains often turn out to be the same as those obtained by studying simpler models based on Nash's original demand game [15] and the fact that we do not employ the latter in this paper does not mean that we now regard it as redundant.

To recapitulate some of what was said in Section 13.2, the version of the two-player/one-cake model of Rubinstein that we wish to generalize has the following properties. Two players, labeled 1 and 2, alternate in making offers in the presence of a shrinking cake. The shrinkage is to be interpreted as representing disutilities derived from delays in agreement. At time 0, the cake is assumed to be a set $\mathscr{X}$ satisfying the conditions of Section 13.2, and at time tn, the cake is

$$\mathscr{X}_n = \{(\delta_1^{tn} x_1, \delta_2^{tn} x_2): (x_1, x_2) \in \mathscr{X}\},$$

where δ_1 and δ_2 are real numbers in the interval $(0,1)$ representing the players' respective discount rates.[22] At time $2nt$ $(n = 0, 1, 2, \ldots)$, player 1 makes an offer $\underline{x} \in \mathscr{X}_{2n}$, which player 2 may accept or reject. If the offer is accepted, the game terminates with the implementation of $\underline{x}$. If the offer is rejected, then player 2 makes an offer $\underline{y} \in \mathscr{X}_{2n+1}$; and so on. This game has a unique perfect-equilibrium outcome. The interesting case occurs when $t \rightarrow 0+$, since without constraint on their behavior, players would wish to get their offers in as early as possible (see [5], p. 29). As $t \rightarrow 0+$, the unique perfect-equilibrium outcome approaches an (asymmetric) Nash bargaining solution in which the "bargaining powers" satisfy $\tau_i = (-\log \delta_i)^{-1}$ $(i = 1, 2)$. For the latter result, see Binmore [3], MacLennan [13] or Moulin [14].

There are problems in generalizing this model to more complicated bargaining solutions and it would be misleading simply to present a model that implements the results of Section 13.3 without drawing attention to them. We therefore propose to discuss a number of possible generalizations in the three-player context. (Readers who prefer to ignore these considerations should skip forward to the subsection entitled "A market bargaining model.")

The problems with these generalizations fall into two distinct classes, which it seems important to separate carefully. The first class of problem is that of multiple equilibria. In the absence of an adequate theory of equilibrium selection, we do not know how to proceed in general when there is more than one equilibrium.[23] Personally, I feel that progress can be made on this front via refinements of the perfect-equilibrium concept, but this is too large a subject for the current paper. Here, we simply set aside models with multiple equilibria.

The second class of problem concerns the range of application of the model. This is the more difficult type of problem since it calls for the exercise of good judgment rather than technical expertise. The traditional view is that if there are no "imperfections" in the bargaining procedure, then the result of the bargaining will be indeterminate. If this not-unreasonable proposition is accepted, then we must look for the force that drives bargainers to a determinate outcome among the imperfections (i.e. costs, delays etc.) of the bargaining procedure. But what is it reasonable to assume about such imperfections? The difficulty is compounded by the fact that, if one were to observe rational bargainers using, for example, the Rubinstein two-player/one-cake model, one would never directly observe the imperfections resulting from the necessary delays in making counter-offers because all plays of the game would end with the acceptance of the opening offer. The existence of potential imperfections would therefore have to be deduced indirectly from the value of the opening offer and the fact of its acceptance. All I feel able to do is point out that any bargainers *will* be subject to constraints on their behavior (if only physical con-straints), and although one may be tempted to neglect these constraints for the same reason that a physicist might neglect a very low coefficient of friction or for the reason that the constraints seldom seem "active," *never-theless* it is to be expected that such constraints will, in fact, determine the bargaining outcome. In the future, it is to be hoped that we will obtain a better understanding of which constraints really matter. The only firm principle would seem to be that one cannot expect players to submit to constraints that limit their payoffs unless there is some mechanism that forces the constraints on them. Although these remarks may not be very constructive, they may serve to indicate that we do not subscribe to the school that maintains that a bargaining model (or a cooperative solution concept) is "successful" *because* it has a unique equilibrium or *because* it implements a favored economic notion. Such considerations may well be necessary for "success" in some circumstances but are most certainly not sufficient.

Returning to the specifics of the Rubinstein model, the most natural generalization is to the three-player/one-cake problem. The three players, labeled 1, 2, and 3, rotate in making offers. The player making an offer at time nt ($n = 0, 1, 2, \ldots$) will be denoted by p_n, where $p_0 = 1$, $p_1 = 2$, $p_2 = 3$, $p_3 = 1$, $p_4 = 2, \ldots$, that is, $p_n = n(\mod 3) + 1$. At time nt, player p_n makes an offer $\underline{x} \in \mathscr{X}_{nt}$, and the game terminates if the offer is accepted by both of the players.[24] This game has a unique "stationary"[25] perfect-equilibrium outcome, and the perfect-equilibrium outcomes of the corre-sponding finite-horizon games converge to this outcome as the horizon recedes to infinity. Moreover, this outcome is the unique "strong"[26] per-fect equilibrium (this is a result of Maria Herrero). None of this evidence, however, seems adequate in the context of this paper to counterbalance the fact that *any* efficient point of $\mathscr{X}$ is an ordinary perfect-equilibrium point provided t is sufficiently small. We propose to consider the three-player/one-cake problem in a later paper since we are anxious to avoid multiple-equilibrium problems in what is already a lengthy discussion.

This paper is concerned with the three-player/three-cake problem, and here the simplest Rubinstein-type model would again seem to be the one in which the players rotate in having the opportunity to make offers. As

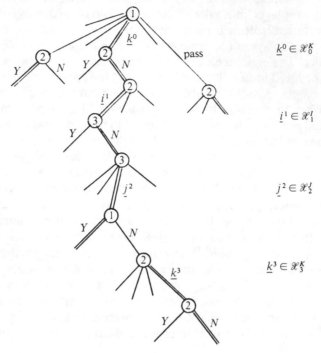

Figure 13.7

before, we denote the player with the opportunity to offer at time nt ($n = 0, 1, 2, \ldots$) by $p_n = n(\text{mod } 3) + 1$. At time nt, we suppose that the cake available is that controlled by coalition $C_n = \{p_n, p_{n+1}\}$. Thus, $C_0 = K$, $C_1 = I$, $C_2 = J$, $C_3 = K$, $C_4 = I, \ldots$ An offer by player p_n at time nt therefore consists of a vector $\underline{x} \in \mathscr{X}_n^{C_n}$. If an offer is made by player p_n and accepted by player p_{n+1}, the game terminates at time nt with the implementation of $\underline{x}$. The game tree is illustrated in Figure 13.7. The double lines in this figure indicate strategy choices leading to the acceptance of an offer of $\underline{j}^2$ by player 3 *to* player 1 being accepted at time $2t$.

Not only is this game the most direct generalization of the two-player/ one-cake problem. In addition, the two-player analysis of, for example, [5] can be applied directly to this model. As is pointed out in Shaked and Sutton [25], a perfect-equilibrium analysis of the game will be unaffected if we replace our three players by only two players who alternate in making offers, provided we make a suitable assumption about the cake available at time nt in the new situation. The assumption is that, if q_n is the player making an offer at time nt in the new situation whereas it was p_n in the old situation, then the utility pairs available to q_n and q_{n+1} respectively, at time nt will be the same as the utility pairs available at time nt to p_n and p_{n+1} respectively.

We illustrate the technique in the most primitive case when $\delta_1 = \delta_2 = \delta_3 = \delta$ and

$$\mathcal{X}^I = \{(0,x_2,x_3): x_2 \geq 0,\ x_3 \geq 0,\ x_2 + x_3 \leq 1\},$$

with symmetric definitions for $\mathcal{X}^J$ and $\mathcal{X}^K$.

Observe that, in Figure 13.8, the cake available to coalition $I = \{2,3\}$ at time t has been drawn with player 3's utility plotted on the x_1-axis. Similarly, the cake available to coalition $J = \{3,1\}$ at time $2t$ has been drawn with player 3's utility still plotted on the x_1-axis but with player 1's utility now plotted on the x_2-axis. The argument of [5] for the two-player case survives and shows that the set of perfect-equilibrium outcomes is the intersection of the sets $E_n(n = 0, 1, 2, \ldots)$. In the current case, this is a single point that converges to $(\tfrac{1}{2},\tfrac{1}{2},0)$ as $t \to 0+$.

To link this result with Section 13.3, it is necessary only to observe that for this version of the three-player/three-cake problem, there is a unique von Neumann–Morgenstern triple,[27] namely, $\{(0,\tfrac{1}{2},\tfrac{1}{2}),\ (\tfrac{1}{2},0,\tfrac{1}{2}),\ (\tfrac{1}{2},\tfrac{1}{2},0)\}$. The bargaining model considered implements the third point of the triple,

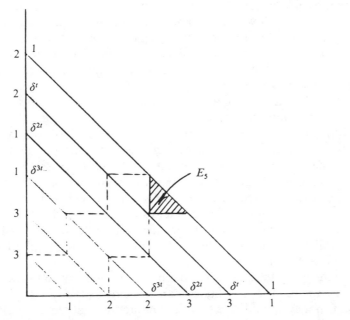

Figure 13.8

because the coalition $K = \{1,2\}$ has the first opportunity to form. The other points in the triple may be obtained either by permuting the players in the bargaining model or by examining the perfect-equilibrium outcomes of subgames in the original model.

In Figure 13.8, the cakes shrink steadily, allowing an easy calculation of the set E_n. However, the analysis of [5] works even when the cakes do not shrink steadily. But, in the latter case, a unique perfect-equilibrium outcome is not guaranteed, and sometimes there will be multiple perfect-equilibrium outcomes (see [5], p. 42). This is not the only difficulty. If case II of Section 13.3 arises (see Figure 13.4), then the model imposes an unnatural constraint on player 3, who would typically wish to address an offer to player 2 given the opportunity whereas the model insists that any offers made by player 3 be to player 1. The model therefore suffers from both types of difficulty mentioned earlier and we therefore set it aside. It is worth noting, however, that in those special cases when these difficulties are absent (i.e. case I with a unique perfect-equilibrium outcome), the model does implement the appropriate result of Section 13.3 (i.e., the von Neumann – Morgenstern triple).

To avoid the second difficulty mentioned in the previous paragraph, one can relabel the decision nodes of Figure 13.7 in such a way that the players are treated more symmetrically. Alternatively, one can introduce chance moves to determine who makes an offer to whom at each time nt ($n = 0, 1, 2, \ldots$). However, both of these alternatives seem too contrived for it to be possible to bestow much significance on the result of their analysis. Instead, we prefer to look at models in which a player with the initiative is not subject to an exogenous constraint that determines to whom he can make an offer.

Two models suggest themselves. The first is based on the practicalities of telephone conversations and so we refer to this as the "telephone bargaining model". One player phones another and they exchange offers until there is agreement or one of them hangs up and phones the third player, whereupon the situation repeats itself. This story is very similar to that of Section 13.2, and it is perhaps surprising that an analysis does *not* yield the results presented there. The second model is based on what transpires at gatherings of brokers and so we call this the "market bargaining model". Players shout their offers and settle with the first player who is willing to meet their terms. It is this model that implements the results of Section 13.3.

It seems likely that there is some practical significance to the dichotomy just mentioned. To the layman it seems extraordinary that large sums of money should be risked in commodity markets by individuals who shout and wave their arms in the air, and the temptation is to dismiss

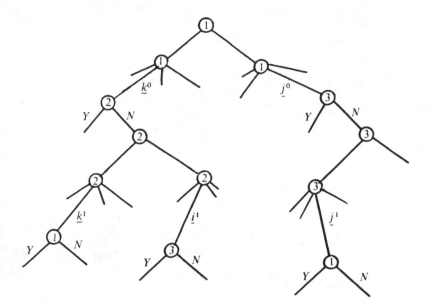

Figure 13.9

this exchange mechanism as an archaic survival. However, even recently established markets operate in this way,[28] and our analysis suggests that there may be good reasons for this. In particular, if it were the custom to deal exclusively by telephone (or bilaterally through private conversations), then there would be players who would wish to disturb the custom by advertising or shouting or whatever else was necessary to gain attention for their offers.

A telephone bargaining model

The game tree is illustrated in Figure 13.9. It differs from that illustrated in Figure 13.7 in that a player with the initiative is free to choose to whom to make an offer, whereupon the initiative is transferred to the object of that choice.

We consider the special case in which

$$\mathscr{X}^I = \{0, x_2, x_3): x_2 \geq 0, \; x_3 \geq 0, \; x_2 + x_3 \leq 1\},$$

with symmetric definitions for $\mathscr{X}^J$ and $\mathscr{X}^K$. The case $\delta_1 = \delta_2 = \delta_3 = \delta$ is not very instructive here, and instead we assume that $\delta_1 < \delta_2 < \delta_3$. We will exhibit a perfect equilibrium in which the outcome is the same as it would be if player 3 were absent.[29]

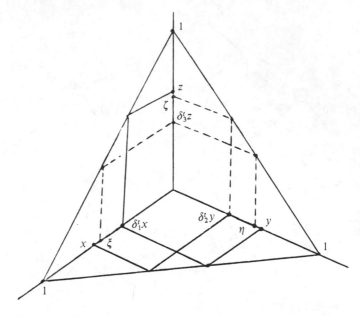

Figure 13.10

The perfect equilibrium is a stationary equilibrium in which player 1 plans on always making an offer to player 2 when the opportunity arises, player 2 plans on always making an offer to player 1 when the opportunity arises and player 3 plans on always making an offer to player 1 when the opportunity arises. The offers that the players will make if they have the opportunity to make an offer at time nt are as follows:

$$\text{Player 1: } (x\delta_1^{nt}, (1-x)\delta_2^{nt}, 0) \in \mathscr{X}_n^K,$$
$$\text{Player 2: } ((1-y)\delta_1^{nt}, y\delta_2^{nt}, 0) \in \mathscr{X}_n^K,$$
$$\text{Player 3: } ((1-z)\delta_1^{nt}, 0, z\delta_3^{nt}) \in \mathscr{X}_n^J,$$

where the values of x, y, and z are as indicated in the Figure 13.10.

As far as responses are concerned, the players plan to accept at time nt any offer that assigns them a utility at least as great as that listed below and to refuse any offer that assigns them less:

$$\text{Player 1: } x\delta_1^{(n+1)t},$$
$$\text{Player 2: } y\delta_2^{(n+1)t},$$
$$\text{Player 3: } z\delta_3^{(n+1)t}.$$

To obtain this equilibrium, we require that $x \geq \xi$, $y \geq \eta$, and $z \geq \zeta$. Otherwise, the players would wish to switch the player to whom they plan to make offers. Checking these inequalities involves some elementary algebra. Equilibrium requires that

$$\left.\begin{array}{l} x + \delta_2^t y = 1 \\ y + \delta_1^t y = 1 \end{array}\right\}$$

$$\left.\begin{array}{l} z + \delta_1^t x = 1 \\ \xi + \delta_3^t z = 1 \end{array}\right\} \Longrightarrow z = y$$

$$\left.\begin{array}{l} \eta + \delta_3^t z = 1 \\ \zeta + \delta_2^t y = 1 \end{array}\right\} \Longrightarrow \xi = \eta$$

From the first pair of equations, we obtain

$$x = \frac{1 - \delta_2^t}{1 - \delta_1^t \delta_2^t} \quad \text{and} \quad y = \frac{1 - \delta_1^t}{1 - \delta_1^t \delta_2^t},$$

which are the values one would obtain if player 3 were absent and players 1 and 2 were involved in a two-player Rubinstein bargaining model. Since $\delta_1 < \delta_2$, we have that $y > x$. Also,

$$\begin{aligned} x \geq \xi &\Longleftrightarrow x \geq 1 - \delta_3^t z = 1 - \delta_3^t y \\ &\Longleftrightarrow x + \delta_3^t y \geq 1 \\ &\Longleftrightarrow \delta_3^t y - \delta_2^t y \geq 0 \quad \text{(Because } x + \delta_2^t y = 1\text{)} \\ &\Longleftrightarrow \delta_3 \geq \delta_2. \end{aligned}$$

Similarly,

$$\begin{aligned} z \geq \xi &\Longleftrightarrow y \geq 1 - \delta_2^t y \\ &\Longleftrightarrow y \geq (1 + \delta_2^t)^{-1} \\ &\Longleftrightarrow (1 - \delta_1^t)(1 + \delta_2^t) \geq 1 - \delta_1^t \delta_2^t \\ &\Longleftrightarrow \delta_2 \geq \delta_1. \end{aligned}$$

As always, the most interesting situation is when $t \to 0+$. Then, players 1 and 2 split the cake $\mathscr{X}^K$ according to the (asymmetric) Nash bargaining solution with "bargaining powers" $\tau_1 = (-\log \delta_1)^{-1}$, $\tau_2 = (-\log \delta_2)^{-1}$. This remains true if we allow player 2 to open the bidding. If player 3 opens the bidding, then players 1 and 3 will split the cake $\mathscr{X}^J$, but *not* according to the (asymmetric) Nash bargaining solution with $\tau_1 = (-\log \delta_1)^{-1}$ and $\tau_3 = (-\log \delta_3)^{-1}$. Instead, player 1 will receive the *same* as he would if he were bargaining with player 2 and player 3 has to be content with what remains of the cake.

Note that this conclusion means that the stronger a player would be in a two-player problem, the weaker he will be in a three-player problem. In particular, player 3 is either excluded altogether or else, if he happens to begin with the initiative, can secure only what player 2 would secure in

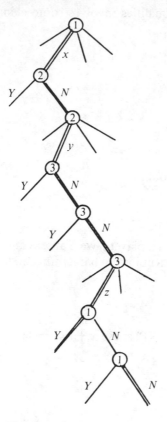

Figure 13.11

this position. But player 3 is the least impatient and hence has the largest value of τ. Clearly, an instability is built into this model.

The same phenomenon occurs with the one-seller/two-buyer case in which $\mathscr{X}^J$ and $\mathscr{X}^K$ are as in the previous discussion but $\mathscr{X}^I = \{(0,0,0)\}$. The considerations remain exactly the same and the object is sold by player 1 to player 2 as if the second buyer, player 3, did not exist.

A market bargaining model

In this model, player 1 begins by announcing a real number x, which represents the utility he requires if agreement is to be reached. This requirement is conveyed to both player 2 *and* player 3 but player 2 has the first opportunity to accept. If player 2 refuses, then player 2 announces a real number y, which represents the utility he requires if agreement is to be reached. If the game reaches this stage, player 3 then has two offers to consider and we suppose that he first considers player 1's offer and then player 2's offer. If he refuses both, then player 3 announces a real number z and it is now player 1 who has two offers to consider. If player 1 refuses both, then the entire situation is repeated from the beginning. The game tree of this model is illustrated in Figure 13.11. The strategy choices indicated by double lines result in the acceptance of player 2's demand of y by player 1.

This bargaining model implements the (asymmetric) Nash bargaining solution for the three-player/three-cake problem as described in Section 13.3 provided suitable assumptions are made about discounting and the timing of offers. As explained in proposition 1, the solution has different descriptions depending on whether case I or case II applies and it will simplify the discussion to consider the two cases separately.

Case I. Here we have a von Neumann–Morgernstern triple $\{\underline{v}^I, \underline{v}^J, \underline{v}^K\}$ (see Figure 13.12). The problem is to show that a perfect-equilibrium outcome of the game is one of the points in this triple. (It will, in fact, be $\underline{v}^K$ because player 1 opens the bidding and player 2 has first refusal.) To obtain the required result in case I, we do not even need to assume that the players suffer disutilities from delays in agreement and we will present the argument for the case $\delta_1 = \delta_2 = \delta_3 = 1$.

The argument is based on Figure 13.12. We will show that a perfect equilibrium in pure strategies requires player 1 to open with the demand α and that this offer will be accepted by player 2, thereby implementing $\underline{v}^K$. That a perfect equilibrium exists with this property is trivial.

The first observation is that a perfect equilibrium in pure strategies for the subgame that follows an initial offer of $a < \alpha$ by player 1 cannot have

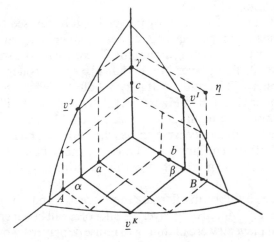

Figure 13.12

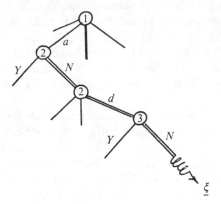

Figure 13.13

the property that a is refused by both players 2 and 3. To prove this, we suppose, on the contrary, that the equilibrium strategies are as in Fig. 13.13. Here, d is player 2's counteroffer and $\underline{\xi}$ (depending on a and d) is the payoff vector that results from the use of the putative equilibrium strategies in the subgame.

There are three possibilities for $\underline{\xi}$: $\underline{\xi} \in \mathscr{X}^I$, $\underline{\xi} \in \mathscr{X}^J$ or $\underline{\xi} \in \mathscr{X}^K$. If $\underline{\xi} \in \mathscr{X}^I$, then at least one of players 2 and 3 will prefer his coordinate of η to that of $\underline{\xi}$ (see Figure 13.12) and hence would wish to amend his refusal of a. If $\underline{\xi} \in \mathscr{X}^J$ or $\underline{\xi} \in \mathscr{X}^K$, one of players 2 and 3 will receive 0 and hence again will wish to amend his refusal of a. It follows that, in equilibrium, any offer $a < \alpha$ by player 1 will be accepted by either player 2 or player 3 and hence no $a < \alpha$ can be an equilibrium offer because player 1 would receive more by offering $\frac{1}{2}(a + \alpha)$.

Next, observe that an offer $A > \alpha$ by player 1 will be refused by both players 2 and 3. The reason that player 2 refuses is that he can guarantee b (see Figure 13.12), by the preceding argument. There are two possibilities for player 3. If player 2 offers player 3 more than player 1 has offered, then clearly player 1's offer will be refused. If player 2 offers player 3 no more than player 1 has offered (e.g. B in Figure 13.12), then player 3 will refuse both A and B because he can guarantee c (see Figure 13.12).

It remains to observe that once a player has the initiative, he is guaranteed a positive payoff (in equilibrium). Thus, it cannot be optimal for player 1 to offer A and have it refused since his resulting payoff will then be 0.

The only possible equilibrium offers are therefore α, β and γ by players 1, 2, and 3, respectively. Moreover, player 1's offer of α will be accepted by player 2 (because, if player 2 were planning to refuse α, player 1 would bid $\alpha - \epsilon$).

If disutilities arise from delays in agreement (i.e. $0 < \delta_1 < 1, 0 < \delta_2 < 1, 0 < \delta_3 < 1$), then the argument needs to be modified. However, it will be clear that, if the time interval t between successive offers is sufficiently small, then equilibrium offers will have to be correspondingly close to $a, b,$ and c respectively and hence the same result will be obtained as $t \to 0+$.

Case II. We consider only the version of case II when the core S is a subset of $\mathscr{X}^I$. The position is illustrated in Figure 13.14. If t is sufficiently small, player 2 can guarantee a payoff of $b < \beta - \epsilon$ (by refusing any offer by player 1 that yields a lesser payoff and then offering b, which will be accepted by player 3 or by player 1 in consequence of the argument given for case I). Similarly, player 3 can guarantee a payoff of $c < \gamma - \epsilon$ provided player 2 refuses player 1's opening offer.

Having made these observations, we can now apply the usual two-player/one-cake arguments to players 2 and 3. As $t \to 0+$, a perfect-equilibrium outcome approaches the (asymmetric) Nash bargaining solution calculated for a cake with Pareto-boundary S, status quo $\underline{0}$, and bargaining powers $\tau_2 = (-\log \delta_2)^-, \tau_3 = (-\log \delta_3)^{-1}$, unless this is equal to $\underline{u}$ or $\underline{v}$ (see Figure 13.14), in which case the points $(0, \beta, 0)$ and $(0, 0, \gamma)$ are also possible.

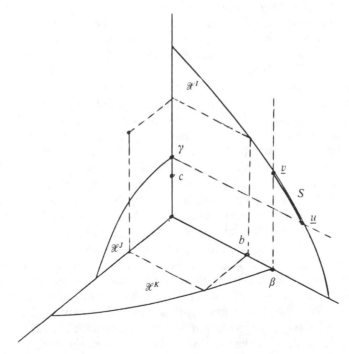

Figure 13.14

13.5   The nontransferable utility Shapley value

For a general discussion of this concept together with an axiomatic derivation, we refer to a recent paper by Aumann [1]. In this paper, Aumann suggests that the notion is best seen as a "group decision" or an "arbitrated outcome" or a "reasonable compromise." This viewpoint implies that the nontransferable utility (NTU) Shapley value is best studied under the heading of social-choice theory rather than of game theory proper. However, it remains the case that the Shapley value is often cited in the latter context (as the Aumann/Roth debate mentioned in note 1 of Section 13.3 confirms). It is therefore necessary to explain how the material of this paper relates to the NTU Shapley value.

In particular, one might ask whether the results of this paper are consistent with the use of the NTU Shapley value when one imposes the symmetry requirements that $\tau_1 = \tau_2 = \tau_3$ and that equal probabilities are assigned to the formation of each of the coalitions I, J, and K. Since there appears to be much confusion on this issue (not least in the mind of the author) it does not seem adequate simply to remark that the answer is that our results are *not* consistent with the NTU Shapley value. For some readers, it may be enough to comment that neither Pareto-efficiency (in the context of an averaging process) nor Additivity makes much sense for a game-theoretic interpretation (although this certainly does not apply in the social choice context). However, we propose to examine more closely the question of why our considerations diverge from those implicit in the use of a Shapley value.

The first point to be made is that our whole approach is founded on the notion that forward commitments are not possible. Any threats that the players make must therefore be "credible threats" if they are to influence the outcome: hence the use of a perfect-equilibrium analysis. We made this point about single players in Section 13.2. But, obviously, it would make little sense to forbid forward commitment for single players but to allow forward commitment for coalitions. Consistency therefore requires that we forbid binding agreements between players concerning the conduct of the future negotiations between themselves and other players. Indeed, the only binding agreements admissible are cake-division agreements (and note that our utilities are very definitely nontransferable). None of this is meant to imply that games with forward commitment are never relevant, only that we prefer to study what seems to be the logically prior and more natural case in which forward commitment is not possible. A consequence of this assumption is that, if a coalition C forms, *all* that it can do is agree to an *unconditional* division of the cake $\mathscr{X}^C$. It *cannot* agree to a *conditional* division of the cake contingent on some event being observed during the future negotiations. This means that Harsanyi's idea of all coalitions simultaneously guaranteeing their members a minimum payoff with which he defends the transferable utility (TU) Shapley-value notion is not applicable. Or, to put the same point more crudely, one cannot think in terms of coalitions forming by accretion, with each extra player contributing a little more, as is the essence of the TU Shapley-value idea. The claim that our assumptions are logically prior to these necessary for dealing with conditional agreements or other forward commitments is based on the proposition that a formal analysis of forward commitment should incorporate the appropriate commitments within the game structure itself, which should then be analyzed without commitment assumptions. This view derives from Nash and has been emphasized by Harsanyi and Selten. The claim that our assumptions are more natural refers to the practical difficulties in making commitments stick. This view has been stressed by Schelling, among others. To me, it seems that the role of the legal profession in this context has been much overrated. A consideration of greater relevance is the fact that games are often in reality stages in a supergame but then, of course, a formal analysis would be directed toward the supergame to which the consideration would not apply.

An example may assist. Consider a "transferable utility" game with characteristic function V that assigns single players 0 and otherwise has

$$V(J) = V(K) = 2,$$
$$V(I) = V(G) = 3,$$

where G is the grand coalition $\{1,2,3\}$. One may compute the TU Shapley value from the following table:

Order of Players	1 2 3 (1)	1 3 2 (2)	2 1 3 (3)	2 3 1 (4)	3 1 2 (5)	3 2 1 (6)	Sum of rows	Shapley value
Player 1	0	0	2	0	2	0	4	2/3
Player 2	2	1	0	0	1	3	7	7/6
Player 3	1	2	1	3	0	0	7	7/6

Note that all but columns 4 and 6 implicitly assume a "two-stage" agreement. It is therefore not surprising that the Shapley value $(\frac{2}{3},\frac{7}{6},\frac{7}{6})$ differs from $(\frac{1}{3},1,1)$, which is the average of the von Neumann–Morgenstern triple $\{(0,\frac{3}{2},\frac{3}{2}),(\frac{1}{2},0,\frac{3}{2}),(\frac{1}{2},\frac{3}{2},0)\}$, since the latter is computed on the assumption that we are dealing with a "one-stage" process. But suppose that we compute a "one-stage" Shapley value as in the following table.

Order of players	1 2 3 (1)	1 3 2 (2)	2 1 3 (3)	2 3 1 (4)	3 1 2 (5)	3 2 1 (6)	Sum of rows	One-stage Shapley value
Player 1	0	0	2	0	2	0	4	2/3
Player 2	2	0	0	0	0	3	5	5/6
Player 3	0	2	0	3	0	0	5	5/6

Note that $(\frac{2}{3},\frac{5}{6},\frac{5}{6})$ still differs from the average $(\frac{1}{3},1,1)$ of the von Neumann–Morgenstern triple. There is a good reason for this difference, which we now discuss.

In the presentation of Section 13.13, the order in which potential coalitions formed was essentially "endogenous" in that it was the player who broke off negotiations with another player who gained the ear of the third player in the subsequent negotiations. However, Shapley-value considerations implicitly require that the order of coalition formation be "exogenously" determined by a random mechanism. It is therefore of interest to reexamine Section 13.3 with this alternative (and considerably simpler) assumption in mind. An appropriate modification would seem to be to redefine the outside-option vectors $\underline{m}^I$, $\underline{m}^K$, and $\underline{m}^K$ appearing in the definition of the function f so that

$$\underline{m}^I = (0,\tfrac{1}{2}\sigma_2^K,\tfrac{1}{2}\sigma_3^I),$$
$$\underline{m}^J = (\tfrac{1}{2}\sigma_1^K,0,\tfrac{1}{2}\sigma_3^I),$$
$$\underline{m}^K = (\tfrac{1}{2}\sigma_1^J,\tfrac{1}{2}\sigma_2^I,0).$$

Figure 13.15 illustrates the impact that this redefinition will have on the nature of the function f in a typical situation (which includes the preceding example provided that $\tau_1 = \tau_2 = \tau_3$). Observe that, for this typical case, each $f(C)$ is simply the (asymmetric) Nash bargaining solution for $\mathcal{X}^C$. When $\tau_1 = \tau_2 = \tau_3$, it happens that $f(C)$ also coincides with the NTU Shapley value for the two-person problem with cake $\mathcal{X}^C$.

For our example, $f(I)$, $f(J)$, and $f(K)$ are easily calculated. When $\tau_1 = \tau_2 = \tau_3$, they are equal to $(0,\frac{3}{2},\frac{3}{2})$, $(1,0,1)$, and $(1,1,0)$, respectively, for which the average is $(\frac{2}{3},\frac{5}{6},\frac{5}{6})$. This is what we called the one-stage Shapley value.

It probably is obvious that this result is a special case of a more general proposition. However, we do not feel the general result is worth formulat-

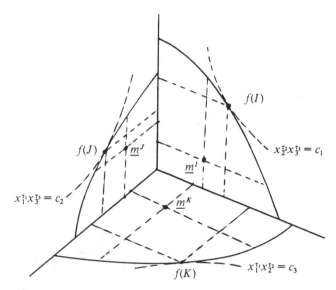

Figure 13.15

ing for two reasons. The first is that the general result will apply only in the typical case illustrated in Figure 13.15 (and which corresponds to case I of Section 13.13). For situations corresponding to that of case II, the result will not hold (and, in any event, one would be very suspicious about attaching equal probabilities to the coalitions). Second, the considerations necessary to try to force some relevance for the NTU Shapley value for problems more complex than the three-player/three-cake problem seem excessively Machiavellian.

Where does this leave the NTU Shapley value? Certainly nothing that has been said affects the notion in so far as it is a construct of social choice (or social valuation) theory. Likewise, nothing has been said that denies the validity of Harsanyi's [9] analysis *given* the basic assumptions on which the analysis is based. However, it is to be hoped that the discussion offered does raise doubts about the use of the NTU Shapley value as a general principle in bargaining theory except in the case of the two-player/one-cake problem. Even here, the observation that the (symmetric) Nash bargaining solution and the NTU Shapley value happen to coincide would seem more reasonably attributable to the fact that only a limited number of invariances are available in such a simple situation than to any intrinsic merit of the NTU Shapley value. (Of course, independent arguments are available in favor of the Nash bargaining solution.)

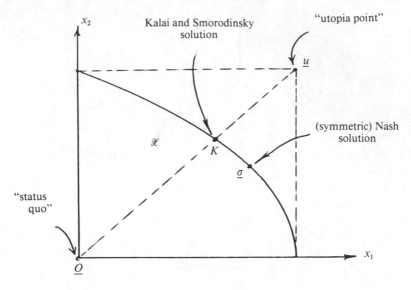

Figure 13.16

13.6   The Raiffa/Kalai–Smorodinsky solution

Various alternatives have been offered to the Nash bargaining solution for the two-player/one-cake problem (see Roth [19]). Some of these are clearly not genuine competitors because they relate to informational assumptions that differ from those appropriate to the Nash bargaining solution. However, the Kalai–Smorodinsky [11] solution certainly does share the same informational base as the Nash solution (Figure 13.16).

In this section, we hope to offer a reason for regarding the Nash bargaining solution and a variant of the Kalai–Smorodinsky solution as complementary rather than rival notions. Perhaps this variant is better described as the Raiffa solution. The difficulty with Kalai and Smorodinsky's monotonicity axiom is its implicit assumption that the replacement of one cake, $\mathscr{X}$, by another cake $\mathscr{Y}$, may put one player in a "stronger bargaining position" than previously, and hence he ought to receive at least the payoff he would have received with the original cake, $\mathscr{X}$. However, it is difficult to understand what mechanism could generate this stronger bargaining position given that we are supposed to assume that the only threat available to either player is the threat to disagree and that disagreement by either player leads simply to the status quo. We propose to avoid this difficulty by arguing as in Section 13.2 that the status quo should be seen as a reference point rather than a unique disagreement point. We are then free to admit the possibility discussed in Section 13.2 of the players having open the opportunity to bargain elsewhere if the negotiations are unsatisfactory. The simplest such situation is precisely that discussed in Section 13.3 with a single third player in the background, and we will work with this situation although it will be evident that similar considerations may apply with a more complex scenario.

We adapt the notation of Section 13.3 by taking $\mathscr{X}$ to be $\mathscr{X}^K$ but with the third coordinate of its elements suppressed. Similarly, we suppress the first and second coordinates, respectively, of the sets $\mathscr{X}^I$ and $\mathscr{X}^J$, and assume that the resulting sets are both $\mathscr{Y}$. Since the Kalai–Smorodinsky solution requires a symmetry axiom, we cannot dispense with this assumption. We regard $\mathscr{Y}$ as fixed and $\mathscr{X}$ as a variable. Where does the Nash bargaining solution for the three-person/three-cake problem place the agreement point $\underline{\sigma}^K$ for the coalition $\{1,2\}$ as a function of the set $\mathscr{X}$? The question is answered in Figure 13.17 provided that the point $\underline{v}$ illustrated does not lie in $\mathscr{X}$.

For circumstances under which the best possible result for the players will be the same no matter with whom this result is negotiated (i.e.,

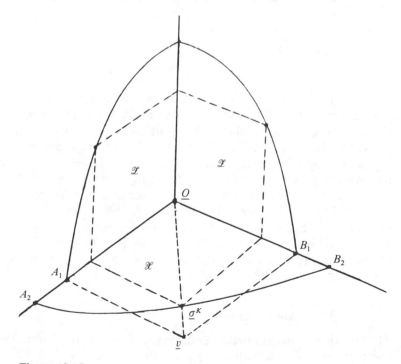

Figure 13.17

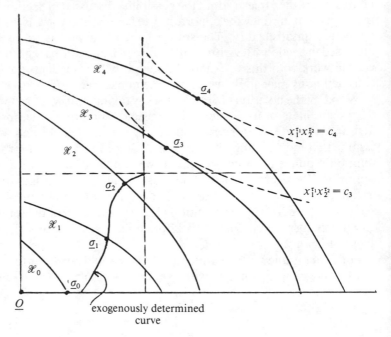

Figure 13.18

$A_1 = A_2$ and $B_1 = B_2$), the "utopia point" $\underline{u}$ of Figure 13.16 and the point $\underline{v}$ of Figure 13.17 will be the same, and hence $\underline{\sigma}^K$ will be precisely the Kalai–Smorodinsky solution $\underline{\kappa}$. Without a symmetry assumption, the straight line joining $\underline{0}$ and $\underline{v}$ in Figure 13.17 will be replaced by a curve.

Finally, it may be worth noting what an outside observer would record after watching a sequence of independent bargaining games with different cakes $\mathscr{X}$ and a fixed status quo $\underline{0}$ in ignorance of the existence of a third player and two further fixed cakes $\mathscr{X}^I$ and $\mathscr{X}^J$. This situation is illustrated in Figure 13.18. The "solution" for $\mathscr{X}_i$ on the basis of the analysis of Section 13.3 is denoted by $\underline{\sigma}_i$. (Of course, $\underline{\sigma}_0$ is to be interpreted as the result *if* agreement were reached, which would seem unlikely in general.) Note the mixture of different ideas.

13.7 Axiomatization

The question of an axiomatic characterization has been left until last for two reasons. The first reason is that it seems inappropriate to say more than a few words unless the general m-player/n-cake problem is to be examined. The second reason is that undue weight seems to be attached to concepts that admit simple axiomatic characterizations.

Briefly, however, we note that [3] provided an axiomatic characterization of the Nash bargaining solution in the two-player/one-cake case in which the "independence of irrelevant alternatives" axiom was replaced by a "multiplicative axiom." The latter bears a family resemblance to the Shapley "additivity axiom" but requires invariance when two games are "multiplied" rather than "added". Refer to [3] for an explanation of why it may be reasonable to wish to multiply two games. In the current context of the three-player/three-cake example, such a multiplicative axiom would reduce the problem to the consideration of games that admit a characteristic function description; that is, the use of the multiplicative axiom would correspond to the reduction in the Shapley context of non-transferable utility games to transferable utility games. How one deals with a game in characteristic function form remains a matter for debate but at least this is familiar ground.

NOTES

1. This view has been championed perhaps most effectively by Harsanyi and Selten.
2. This observation is not of course intended to apply to cooperative solution concepts that are justified as "fair arbitration schemes" or the like. My own view is that "fair arbitration schemes" are best studied under the heading of social-choice theory rather than game theory (although admittedly some blurring of the distinction is inevitable once the question of implementation arises).
3. It is important to note that various n-person cooperative concepts have a tendency to coalesce in the three-person/three-cake case and that, in choosing to couch the required cooperative idea in terms of Nash bargaining solutions, I am vulnerable to accusations of prejudice. It would be possible, for example, to make do with the two-person Nash solution and graft this onto the notion of the core of a game together with Vickrey's strengthening of the von Neumann–Morgenstern idea of a stable set to that of a strongly stable set (see, for example, [12], p. 213). Alternatively, one could use a stability notion of Albers as a substitute for the core and strongly stable sets. This path is followed by Selten [24] in a paper with similar aims to the current paper. Yet, again, one could adopt the Aumann–Maschler notion of a bargaining set (see [18]). What is certain is that, if there is a "correct" description of the appropriate cooperative bargaining concept, the three-person/three-cake problem has too simple a structure to reveal this.
4. Rubinstein worked independently, but his work is of course closely related to that of Ståhl [26], and of Harsanyi and Selten and others. Rubinstein has recently made an important advance in extending his work to a case where information is not complete (see [22]).
5. Such a constraint must exist if only for physical reasons. Naturally, however,

players would prefer to respond at the earliest possible moment and so interest centers on what happens when the response times are small compared with the other parameters of the problem.

6. This means that strategy n-tuples are Nash equilibria not only in the game as a whole but also in every subgame (see Selten [23]).

7. The assumption that $\mathscr{X}$ is compact and convex is standard. The other assumptions on $\mathscr{X}$ are not essential and are introduced to avoid the discussion of technicalities.

8. For simplicity, we exclude the degenerate case of zero bargaining powers.

9. This usage of the term "bargaining power" is quite different from that of Harsanyi. Incidentally, it is important that the parameters τ_1 and τ_2 be determined entirely by the *players* and are independent of $\mathscr{X}$. In Section 13.4, τ_1 and τ_2 measure the players' impatience at delays in agreement but other interpretations are possible.

10. To ignore the location of the original "status quo" point would certainly not be correct with the interpretation of $\underline{m}$ given in this section, although this is disguised to some extent by the fact that the original "status quo" is normalized at $\underline{0}$. However, even if one assumed that *both* player 1 and player 2 receive their respective coordinates of $\underline{m}$ if negotiations break down (i.e. $\underline{m}$ is the disagreement point), it does *not* necessarily follow that one should simply use the Nash bargaining solution with "status quo" transferred to $\underline{m}$. It still may be appropriate, as in the entirely natural bargaining model described later in this section, to use a point other than $\underline{m}$ (in our case $\underline{0}$) as a reference point.

11. As far as an axiomatic characterization is concerned, one simply needs to classify those $\underline{x} \in \mathscr{X}$ that do not satisfy $\underline{x} \geq \underline{m}$ as "irrelevant alternatives".

12. For the purposes of interpretation, one may imagine that player 1 threatens to use his outside option *before* the preceding offer by player 2. Player 2 will then have to consider whether this threat is credible. This consideration is taken care of by using a perfect-equilibrium analysis.

13. The player with the initiative, for example, might be the first to notice the opportunity for outside activity.

14. We do not consider the situation in which *both* players can *simultaneously* secure their outside options, although this is an easier case to analyze. This case is not relevant to the application required in Section 13.3.

15. As Selten observes in [24], in practice one would expect this question to be resolved by issues such as who first notices that a bargaining situation exists and whom it is convenient for him to contact first. Since the factors governing such items are likely to be ephemeral, there seems little point in trying to model them explicitly other than by attaching equal probabilities to the three coalitions where necessary.

16. Sometimes this is assumed, as in [27], even when the possibility of the buyers being able to form an unbreakable coalition has not been excluded.

17. The fact that we reject the survival of the two-person/one-cake solution in the presence of the three-person/three-cake problem as "mainstream", does not mean that we deny the existence of important situations in which such "stickiness" is the overriding factor.

18. It is similar to an idea of Harsanyi ([9], p. 248) embodied in what has been called the Harsanyi/Nash/Shapley value. An important difference between the situation considered here and that considered by Harsanyi is that, in his case, a coalition is able to *guarantee* its members certain utility levels *inde-*

pendently of the guarantees made by other coalitions, whereas for the three-person/three-cake problem considered in this paper, this is impossible. Among other things, this means that there is a difference in the interpretation of the solution payoffs. For Harsanyi, these are actual payoffs, whereas in this paper they are potential payoffs contingent on an appropriate coalition being formed.

19. The word "define" is premature since it remains to be established that the property offered is consistent and categorical.

20. Of course, there may be situations in which if player p breaks off negotiations, then he will not necessarily gain the ear of player r; that is, the idea of the "initiative" is inappropriate. If, for example, the breaking off of negotiations between players 2 and 3 led to a random move with probability $\frac{1}{2}$ that player 2 would be involved in the subsequent negotiations with player 1 and probability $\frac{1}{2}$ that player 3 would be involved, then it would make sense to take $m_3^I = \frac{1}{2}\sigma_3^I + \frac{1}{2}0$ and $m_2^I = \frac{1}{2}0 + \frac{1}{2}\sigma_2^K$.

21. In the sense that, if one were assigning probabilities to the three possible outcomes in the spirit of the Shapley value, one would attach a high probability to $f(C)$.

22. As explained in [5], the argument goes through under very much more general conditions on $\mathcal{X}_n$, but there seems little point in describing a very general model for our purposes.

23. Indeed, we sometimes do not know how to proceed when there is a unique equilibrium. However, at least the bargaining games considered here are free of this type of problem. As far as the general problem of equilibrium selection is concerned, attention should be drawn to the theory of Harsanyi and Selten [10]. I cannot claim to appreciate fully the guiding philosophy behind this theory but the relevance of much of what is said cannot be denied. My problem lies in fitting all the many considerations into a coherent whole. In any case, I am not competent to attempt to apply the theory in the current context.

24. One may model them as voting in sequence or simultaneously. In the latter case, it would seem sensible to introduce a Selten "trembling hand" to avoid the trivial equilibrium in which all players always vote in the negative. For a study of a finite-horizon version, see Dutta and Gevers [6].

25. One in which actions chosen at time t are independent of history, that is, of what happened at times $s < t$.

26. Strong in the sense of Aumann (i.e. the strategies are optimal not only for single players but also for coalitions, given no deviations by outsiders).

27. The "discriminating" von Neumann–Morgenstern solution sets do not appear in any of the bargaining models considered here.

28. We have the London financial futures market in mind here.

29. One can use the method of Shaked and Sutton [25] to show that this is the only perfect-equilibrium outcome in this particular case but I do not know of a technique adequate to handle the general case.

REFERENCES

[1] Aumann, R.: *An Axiomatization of the Non-Transferable Utility Value.* Working paper (1983*a*).

[2] *On the Non-Transferable Utility Value.* Working paper (1983*b*).

[3] Binmore, K. G.: *Nash Bargaining Theory I, II, and III.* ICERD Discussion Papers 9, 14, and 15, LSE (1980–81).

[4] *Nash Bargaining and Incomplete Information.* Economic Theory Discussion Paper No. 45, Dept. of Applied Economics, Cambridge University (1981).

[5] *Perfect Equilibria in Bargaining Models.* ICERD Discussion Paper 58, LSE (1982).

[6] Dutta, G., and L. Gevers: *On Majority Rules and Perfect Equilibrium Allocation of a Shrinking Cake.* Working paper, Namur University (1981).

[7] Fudenberg, D., and J. Levine: *Perfect Equilibria of Finite and Infinite Horizon games.* Working Paper 216, Dept. of Economics, UCLA (1981).

[8] Harsanyi, J.: An Equilibrium-Point Interpretation of Stable Sets and a Proposed Alternative Definition. *Management Science* 20 (1974), 1422–95.

[9] *Rational Behaviour and Bargaining Equilibrium in Games and Social Situations.* Cambridge University Press, Cambridge (1977).

[10] Harsanyi, J., and R. Selten: *A Non-Cooperative Solution Theory with Cooperative Applications.* Working Papers, Institute of Economics, Bielefeld, Nos. 91, 92, 105, and 114 (1980–82).

[11] Kalai, E., and M. Smorodinsky: Other Solutions to Nash's Bargaining Problem". *Econometrica* 43 (1975), 513–18.

[12] Luce, R., and H. Raiffa: *Games and Decisions.* Wiley, New York (1957).

[13] MacLennan, A.: *A General Non-Cooperative Theory of Bargaining.* Working paper, Dept. of Political Economy, University of Toronto (1980).

[14] Moulin, H.: *Bargaining and Non-Cooperative Implementation.* Ecole Polytechnique (Laboratoire d'Econometrie) Discussion Paper A239 0282 (1982).

[15] Nash, J. F.: The Bargaining Problem. *Econometrica* 18 (1950), 155–62.

[16] Non-Cooperative Games. *Annals of Mathematics* 54 (1951), 286–95.

[17] Two-Person Cooperative Games. *Econometrica* 21 (1953), 128–40.

[18] Owen, G.: *Game Theory* (2nd Ed.). Academic Press, New York (1982).

[19] Roth, A. E.: *Axiomatic Models of Bargaining.* Lecture Notes in Economics and Mathematical Systems No. 170, Springer-Verlag, Berlin (1979).

[20] Values for Games without Side Payments: Some Difficulties with Current Concepts. *Econometrica* 48 (1980), 457–65.

[21] Rubinstein, A.: Perfect Equilibrium in a Bargaining Model. *Econometrica* 50 (1981), 97–110.

[22] *A Bargaining Model with Incomplete Information.* Working paper, Dept. of Economics, Hebrew University (1983).

[23] Selten, R.: Re-Examination of the Perfectness Concept for Equilibrium Points in Extensive Games. *International Journal of Game Theory* 4 (1975), 25–55.

[24] *A Non-Cooperative Model of Characteristic Function Bargaining.* Working paper, Institute of Mathematical Economics, Bielefeld, No. 90 (1980).

[25] Shaked, A., and J. Sutton: Involuntary Unemployment as a Perfect Equilibrium in a Bargaining Model. ICERD Discussion Paper 63 (1983).

[26] Ståhl, I.: *Bargaining Theory.* Economic Research Institute, Stockholm (1972).

[27] Weintraub, R.: *Conflict and Cooperation in Economics.* Macmillan, London (1975).

CHAPTER 14

Axiomatic approaches to coalitional bargaining

Sergiu Hart
TEL-AVIV UNIVERSITY

14.1 Introduction

The simplest bargaining situation is that of two persons who have to agree on the choice of an outcome from a given set of feasible outcomes; in case no agreement is reached, a specified disagreement outcome results. This *two-person pure bargaining problem* has been extensively analyzed, starting with Nash (1950).

When there are more than two participants, the *n*-person straightforward generalization considers either unanimous agreement or complete disagreement (see Roth (1979)). However, intermediate subsets of the players (i.e., more than one but not all) may also play an essential role in the bargaining. One is thus led to an *n-person coalitional bargaining problem,* where a set of feasible outcomes is specified for each coalition (i.e., subset of the players). This type of problem is known as a *game in coalitional form without side payments* (or, *with nontransferable utility*). It frequently arises in the analysis of various economic and other models; for references, see Aumann (1967, 1983*a*).

Solutions to such problems have been proposed by Harsanyi (1959, 1963, 1977), Shapley (1969), Owen (1972), and others. All of these were constructed to coincide with the Nash solution in the two-person case. Unlike the Nash solution, however, they were not defined (and determined) by a set of axioms.

Recently, Aumann (1983*b*) has provided an axiomatization for the Shapley solution. Following this work, further axiomatizations were obtained: for the Harsanyi solution by Hart (1983), and for a new class of monotonic solutions by Kalai and Samet (1983). The purpose of this chapter is to review and compare these three approaches.

The discussion is organized as follows. The mathematical model is described in Section 14.2, and is followed by the definitions of the solutions in Section 14.3. The axioms that determine these solutions are presented in Section 14.4, and Section 14.5 includes some general remarks together with a comparison of the solutions in terms of the axioms of Section 14.4.

It should be emphasized that this chapter includes only a minimal discussion of the various concepts; it is intended as a summary and a directory to the existing literature on the subject. In particular, the reader should consult the papers of Aumann (1983b), Hart (1983), and Kalai and Samet (1983) for extensive presentations and comments.

14.2   The mathematical model

We start by introducing the notations. The real line is denoted $\mathbb{R}$. For a finite set I, let $|I|$ be the number of elements of I, and let $\mathbb{R}^I$ be the $|I|$-dimensional euclidean space with coordinates indexed by the elements of I (when I is the empty set ϕ, $\mathbb{R}^\phi$ contains just one element, namely, ϕ). We will thus write $x = (x^i)_{i \in I} \in \mathbb{R}^I$ and, for $J \subset I$, $x^J = (x^i)_{i \in J} \in \mathbb{R}^J$ (hence, $x = x^I$; note that we use the symbol $\subset$ for weak inclusion). Some distinguished vectors in $\mathbb{R}^I$ are: the origin $0 = (0, \ldots, 0)$; and for every $J \subset I$, its indicator 1_J, with $1_J^i = 1$ if $i \in J$ and $1_J^i = 0$ if $i \notin J$.

For x and y in $\mathbb{R}^I$, the inequalities $x \geq y$ and $x > y$ are to be understood coordinatewise: $x^i \geq y^i$ and $x^i > y^i$, respectively, for all $i \in I$. The nonnegative, the positive, and the nonpositive orthants of $\mathbb{R}^I$ (defined by the inequalities $x \geq 0$, $x > 0$, and $x \leq 0$, respectively) are denoted $\mathbb{R}^I_+$, $\mathbb{R}^I_{++}$, and $\mathbb{R}^I_-$. For λ and x in $\mathbb{R}^I$, we write $\lambda \cdot x$ for the real number $\sum_{i \in I} \lambda^i x^i$ (their scalar product), and λx for that element of $\mathbb{R}^I$ given by $(\lambda x)^i = \lambda^i x^i$ for all $i \in I$.

Let A be a closed subset of $\mathbb{R}^I$; its boundary is denoted ∂A. For λ in $\mathbb{R}^I$, the set λA is $\{\lambda a \mid a \in A\}$; for another closed subset B of $\mathbb{R}^I$, $A + B$ is the *closure* of $\{a + b \mid a \in A, b \in B\}$. Note that $A - B$ will denote the set difference $\{x \in A \mid x \notin B\}$.

A *coalitional bargaining problem* – c.b.p., for short – is an ordered pair (N, V), where N is a finite set and V is a set-valued function that assigns to every $S \subset N$ a subset $V(S)$ of $\mathbb{R}^S$. The set N is the set of *players*; a subset S of N is a *coalition*; and V is the *characteristic function*.

The interpretation is as follows. Let A be the set of all possible outcomes. For each player $i \in N$, let $u^i : A \to \mathbb{R}$ be his utility function. Finally, for every coalition $S \subset N$, let $A(S) \subset A$ be the set of outcomes that can be reached by S. Then, $V(S)$ is the set of utility payoff vectors that are feasible for S, namely,

$$V(S) = \{(u^i(a))_{i \in S} \in \mathbb{R}^S \mid a \in A(S)\}.$$

In game theory, such a pair (N, V) is called a *game in coalitional* (or, *characteristic function*) *form with nontransferable utility* (or, *without side payments*).

The set N of players will be fixed throughout this chapter; a c.b.p. will thus be given by its characteristic function V. The space $\Gamma \equiv \Gamma(N)$ of all c.b.p.'s that we will consider consists of all members of V that satisfy the following conditions:

(1) For every $S \subset N$, the set $V(S)$ is
  a. A non-empty subset of $\mathbb{R}^I$,
  b. Closed,
  c. Convex,
  d. Comprehensive (i.e., $x \in V(S)$ and $x \geq y$ imply $y \in V(S)$).

We will also consider the following additional regularity conditions:

(2) The set $V(N)$ is
  a. Smooth (i.e., $V(N)$ has a unique supporting hyperplane at each point of its boundary $\partial V(N)$),
  b. Nonlevel (i.e., $x, y \in \partial V(N)$ and $x \geq y$ imply $x = y$).
(3) For every $S \subset N$, there exists $x \in \mathbb{R}^N$ such that

$$V(S) \times \mathbb{R}_{-}^{N-S} \subset V(N) + \{x\}.$$

(4) For every $S \subset N$ and every sequence $\{x_m\}_{m=1}^{\infty} \subset V(S)$ that is non-decreasing (i.e., $x_{m+1} \geq x_m$ for all $m \geq 1$), there exists $y \in \mathbb{R}^S$ such that $x_m \leq y$ for all $m \geq 1$.

Denote the set of all V in Γ that satisfy (2) by Γ_1, those that satisfy (4) by Γ_2, and those that satisfy (2) and (3) by Γ_3.

Conditions (1) are standard. Condition (2b) is a commonly used regularity condition, meaning that weak and strong Pareto-optimality coincide for $V(N)$. The smoothness of $V(N)$ is an essential condition; (2a) implies that, for every $x \in \partial V(N)$, there exists a unique normalized vector λ in $\mathbb{R}^N$ such that $\lambda \cdot x \geq \lambda \cdot y$ for all y in $V(N)$. Note that λ must be positive (i.e., $\lambda \in \mathbb{R}_{++}^N$) by (1d) and (2b). Condition (3) may be viewed as an extremely weak kind of monotonicity: There exists some translate of $V(N)$ that includes all of the payoff vectors that are feasible for S and assign zero to the players outside S. Finally, (4) is a boundedness-from-above condition. A thorough discussion on assumptions and their impact can be found in Sections 9 and 10 in Aumann (1983b).

For a coalition $S \subset N$, an *S-payoff vector* is simply an element of $\mathbb{R}^S$; when $S = N$, it is a *payoff vector*. A collection $\mathbf{x} = (x_S)_{S \subset N}$ of S-payoff vectors for all coalitions S is called a *payoff configuration* (thus, $x_S = (x_S^i)_{i \in S} \in \mathbb{R}^S$ for all $S \subset N$). The space of payoff configurations

$\Pi_{S \subset N} \mathbb{R}^S$ will be denoted X. In particular, the payoff configuration **x** with $x_S = 0$ for all S will be denoted **0**.

Note that every c.b.p. V may be regarded as a (rectangular) subset of X, namely, $\Pi_{S \subset N} V(S)$. Operations are thus always understood coalitionwise. Hence, $V + W$ is given by $(V + W)(S) = V(S) + W(S)$ for all $S \subset N$; $V \subset W$ means $V(S) \subset W(S)$ for all S; and ∂V is $\Pi_{S \subset N} \partial V(S) \subset X$. If λ is a vector in $\mathbb{R}^N_{++}$, then λV is defined by

$$(\lambda V)(S) = \lambda^S V(S) = \{(\lambda^i x^i)_{i \in S} \mid x = (x^i)_{i \in S} \in V(S)\}$$

(recall that $\lambda^S = (\lambda^i)_{i \in S}$ is the restriction of λ to $\mathbb{R}^S_{++}$). Moreover, for a subset Y of X, we write λY for $\{(\lambda^S y_S)_{S \subset N} \mid \mathbf{y} = (y_S)_{S \subset N} \in Y\}$.

14.3 Solutions

In this section, we will define the three solutions of Harsanyi, Shapley, and Kalai and Samet. The following conditions will be considered, where V is a coalitional bargaining problem; λ is a vector in $\mathbb{R}^N_{++}$; and for each $S \subset N$, $x_S \in \mathbb{R}^S$ is an S-payoff vector and $\xi_S \in \mathbb{R}$ a real number:

(5) $x_S \in \partial V(S)$,
(6) $\lambda^S \cdot x_S \geq \lambda^S \cdot y$ for all $y \in V(S)$,
(7) $\lambda^i x_S^i = \Sigma_{T \subset S, i \in T} \xi_T$ for all $i \in S$.

The solutions are then defined as follows:

Definition 1.   A payoff vector $x \in \mathbb{R}^N$ is a *Harsanyi (NTU) solution* of a c.b.p. V if there exist $\lambda \in \mathbb{R}^N_{++}$, $\mathbf{x} = (x_S)_{S \subset N} \in X$ with $x_N = x$, and $\xi_S \in \mathbb{R}$ for all $S \subset N$ such that the following are satisfied:

  Condition (5) for all $S \subset N$,
  Condition (6) for $S = N$,
  Condition (7) for all $S \subset N$.

Definition 2.   A payoff vector $x \in \mathbb{R}^N$ is a *Shapley (NTU) solution* of a c.b.p. V if there exist $\lambda \in \mathbb{R}^N_{++}$, $\mathbf{x} = (x_S)_{S \subset N} \in X$ with $x_N = x$, and $\xi_S \in \mathbb{R}$ for all $S \subset N$ such that the following are satisfied:

  Condition (5) for all $S \subset N$,
  Condition (6) for all $S \subset N$,
  Condition (7) for $S = N$.

Definition 3.   Let λ be a vector in $\mathbb{R}^N_{++}$. A payoff vector $x \in \mathbb{R}^N$ is the *Kalai and Samet λ-egalitarian solution* of a c.b.p. V if there exist

$\mathbf{x} = (x_S)_{S \subset N} \in X$ with $x_N = x$ and $\xi_S \in \mathbb{R}$ for all $S \subset N$ such that the following are satisfied:

Condition (5) for all $S \subset N$,
Condition (7) for all $S \subset N$.

Note that Kalai and Samet define a *class* of solutions, parameterized by λ (which is thus *exogenously* given, besides V); moreover, each c.b.p. can have at most one λ-egalitarian solution (for every λ; see the end of this section). In both the Harsanyi and Shapley solutions, λ is *endogenously* determined, and there may be no solution or more than one. When the λ^i are all equal (i.e., $\lambda = c1_N$ for some $c \in \mathbb{R}_+$), the corresponding Kalai and Samet solution is called the *symmetric egalitarian solution*. The vector λ yields an interpersonal comparison of the utility scales of the players; whether it is obtained from the bargaining problem itself, or it is an additional datum of the problem, is thus an essential distinction (see also Section 14.5).

The associated payoff configuration $\mathbf{x} = (x_S)_{S \subset N}$ specifies for *every* coalition S a feasible (and even efficient, by condition (1)) outcome x_S. One may view x_S as the payoff vector that the members of S agree upon from their feasible set $V(S)$; if coalition S "forms," then x_S^i is the amount that player i (in S) will receive (note that these are contingent payoffs – *if S forms*). Following Harsanyi, one may furthermore regard x_S as an optimal *threat* of coalition S (against its complement $N - S$), in the bargaining problem. More discussion on these interpretations can be found at the end of section 5 in Hart (1983).

The three conditions (5), (6), and (7) may be interpreted as *efficiency, λ-utilitarity,* and *λ-equity* (or *fairness*), respectively. Indeed, condition (5) means that the S-payoff vector x_S is Pareto-efficient for the coalition S: There is no vector $y \in \mathbb{R}^S$ that is feasible for S (i.e., $y \in V(S)$) such that all members of S prefer y to x_S (i.e., $y > x_S$). Condition (6) means that x_S is λ-utilitarian for S, since it maximizes the sum of the payoffs for members of S, weighted according to λ, over their feasible set $V(S)$. And, finally, the weighted payoff $\lambda^i x_S^i$ of each member of the coalition S is the sum of the *dividends* ξ_T that player i has accumulated from all subcoalitions T of S to which he belongs; because the dividend ξ_T is exactly the same for all members of T (for each T), x_S is thus λ-equitable or λ-fair.

In the two-person simple bargaining problem, the Nash solution is efficient, and for an appropriate vector $\lambda > 0$, it is both λ-utilitarian and λ-equitable. Both the Harsanyi and the Shapley solutions to the general coalitional bargaining problem require efficiency (5) for all coalitions together with utilitarity (6) and equity (7) for the grand coalition N. They differ in the condition imposed on subcoalitions (other than N and the singletons): The Harsanyi solution requires equity, and the Shapley solution utilitarity. The Kalai and Samet solutions do not consider utilitarity at all, but only equity (for all coalitions). Thus, the weights λ have to be given exogenously, whereas in the other two solutions they are determined by the conjunction of (6) and (7). Note further that, in the two-person case, all of the egalitarian solutions (including the symmetric one) differ from the Nash solution (they are the *proportional solutions* of Kalai (1977)).

In general, some of the coordinates of λ may be zero (and thus $\lambda \in \mathbb{R}_+^N - \{0\}$ instead of $\lambda \in \mathbb{R}_{++}^N$); the simplifying assumption (2b) rules out this for the Harsanyi and the Shapley solutions (by (6) for $S = N$); for the egalitarian solutions, the positivity of λ is part of the definition.

The three definitions have been stated in order to facilitate comparison among the solutions. For alternative (and more constructive) definitions, we need the following.

A *transferable utility game* (*TU game,* for short) consists of a finite set of players N and a real function v that assigns to each coalition $S \subset N$ its *worth* $v(S)$, with $v(\phi) = 0$. The *Shapley* (1953) *value* of such a TU game (N,v) is a payoff vector $x \in \mathbb{R}^N$, which will be denoted $Sh(N,v) = (Sh^i(N,v))_{i \in N}$. It is defined by a set of axioms, and it equals the vector of average marginal contributions of each player to those preceding him in a random order of all the players.

Using this concept, one can rewrite the condition "there exist real numbers $\xi_T \in \mathbb{R}$ for all $T \subset S$ such that (7) is satisfied for all $T \subset S$" as:

(8) $\lambda^i x_S^i = Sh^i(S,v)$, where $v(T) = \lambda^T \cdot x_T = \Sigma_{i \in T} \lambda^i x_T^i$ for all $T \subset S$.

We then obtain the following.

Definition 1'.   A payoff vector $x \in \mathbb{R}^N$ is a *Harsanyi solution* of a c.b.p. V if there exist $\lambda \in \mathbb{R}_{++}^N$ and $\mathbf{x} = (x_S)_{S \subset N} \in X$ with $x_N = x$ such that conditions (5) and (8) are satisfied for all $S \subset N$ and condition (6) is satisfied for $S = N$.

Definition 2'.   A payoff vector $x \in \mathbb{R}^N$ is a *Shapley solution* of a c.b.p. V if $x \in V(N)$ and there exists $\lambda \in \mathbb{R}_{++}^N$ such that

$$\lambda^i x^i = Sh^i(N,v),$$

where $v(S) = \max\{\lambda^S \cdot y \mid y \in V(S)\}$ for all $S \subset N$.

(Note that (6) implies (5) and that the TU game v in (8) coincides with v defined previously.)

Definition 3'. Let $\lambda \in \mathbb{R}^N_{++}$. A payoff vector $x \in \mathbb{R}^N$ is the *Kalai and Samet λ-egalitarian solution* of a c.b.p. V if there exists $\mathbf{x} = (x_S)_{S \subset N} \in X$ with $x_N = x$ such that conditions (5) and (8) are satisfied for all $S \subset N$.

How are the solutions of a given c.b.p. V constructed? In the case of the Shapley solution, for each $\lambda \in \mathbb{R}^N_{++}$, one computes the TU game v_λ by

$$v_\lambda(S) = \max\{\lambda^S \cdot y \mid y \in V(S)\}$$

for all $S \subset N$, and then obtains its Shapley TU value $Sh(N,v_\lambda)$. If the payoff vector $x = (x^i)_{i \in N}$ given by $x^i = Sh^i(N,v_\lambda)/\lambda^i$ for all $i \in N$ belongs to $V(N)$, then x is a Shapley solution of V.

The Kalai and Samet λ-egalitarian solution (for a given $\lambda \in \mathbb{R}^N_{++}$) is obtained as follows. Inductively on the lattice of all subsets S of N, we define

$$\xi_S = \max\{t \in \mathbb{R} \mid z_S(t) \in V(S)\},$$

where $z_S(t) = (z^i_S(t))_{i \in S} \in \mathbb{R}^S$ is given by

$$z^i_S(t) = \frac{1}{\lambda^i}\left(t + \sum_{\substack{T \subset S \\ T \neq S \\ i \in T}} \xi_T\right)$$

If we put

$$x_S = z_S(\xi_S),$$

then x_N is the λ-egalitarian solution of V.

Finally, to obtain the Harsanyi solution, we compute the λ-egalitarian solution $x(\lambda)$ for each $\lambda \in \mathbb{R}^N_{++}$; then, $x = x(\lambda)$ is a Harsanyi solution of V whenever $\lambda \cdot x(\lambda) = \max\{\lambda \cdot y \mid y \in V(N)\}$.

Thus, both the Harsanyi and the Shapley approaches require essentially a fixed-point construction, whereas the Kalai and Samet approach does not (again, λ is exogenously given there). It is now clear that each V in Γ has at most one λ-egalitarian solution, and precisely one (for each λ) if V belongs to Γ_2.

14.4 Axiomatizations

In this section, we will present an axiomatization for each one of the three solutions defined previously. By *axiomatization* is meant a set of axioms that uniquely characterize the corresponding solution.

As is usually the case, there are various ways of choosing an appropriate set of axioms. We will follow here the choices made by each author in the papers we review. This will enable us to exhibit a large number of axioms emphasizing a variety of reasonable principles for solving coalitional bargaining problems.

The first solution studied will be the Shapley solution, according to Aumann's (1983*b*) pioneering paper. For every c.b.p. V in Γ, let $\Lambda(V)$ denote the set of Shapley solutions of V; $\Lambda(V)$ is thus a (possibly empty) subset of $\mathbb{R}^N$.

Let Γ_4 denote the set of all c.b.p.'s in Γ_3 that possess at least one Shapley solution (i.e., $\Gamma_4 = \{V \in \Gamma \mid V$ satisfies (2), (3), and $\Lambda(V) \neq \phi\}$). The set-valued function Λ from Γ_4 to $\mathbb{R}^N$ will be called the *Shapley function*. The following axioms will characterize it.

A0. Φ is a non-empty-set-valued function from Γ_4 to $\mathbb{R}^N$.

(For each $V \in \Gamma_4$, $\Phi(V)$ is a nonempty subset of $\mathbb{R}^N$.)

A1. $\Phi(V) \subset \partial V(N)$ for all $V \in \Gamma_4$.

(*Efficiency:* Every solution must be Pareto-efficient [for the grand coalition].)

A2. $\Phi(\lambda V) = \lambda \Phi(V)$ for all $\lambda \in \mathbb{R}^N_{++}$ and $V \in \Gamma_4$.

(*Scale covariance:* If the payoffs of the players are rescaled independently, all solutions will be rescaled accordingly.)

A3.   If $U = V + W$, then $\Phi(U) \supset (\Phi(V) + \Phi(W)) \cap \partial U(N)$ for all $U, V, W \in \Gamma_4$.

(*Conditional additivity:* If $x \in \Phi(V)$ is a solution of V, $y \in \Phi(W)$ is a solution of W, and $z = x + y$ is efficient for $U = V + W$, then z is a solution of U[i.e., $z \in \Phi(U)$].)

A4.   If $V(N) \subset W(N)$ and $V(S) = W(S)$ for all $S \neq N$, then $\Phi(V) \supset \Phi(W) \cap V(N)$ for all $V, W \in \Gamma_4$.

(*Independence of irrelevant alternatives:* If V is obtained from W by restricting the feasible set of the grand coalition, then any solution of W that remains feasible in V will be a solution of V as well.)

For the next axiom, we define a class of c.b.p.'s usually referred to as *unanimity games.* For every nonempty $T \subset N$ and every real number c, let $u_{T,c}$ be the TU game given by $u_{T,c}(S) = c$ if $S \supset T$ and $u_{T,c}(S) = 0$ otherwise; then, $U_{T,c}(S) = \{x \in \mathbb{R}^S \mid \Sigma_{i \in S} x^i \leq u_{T,c}(S)\}$ for all $S \subset N$.

A5. $\Phi(U_{T,1}) = \{1_T/|T|\}$ for all $T \subset N$, $T \neq \phi$.

(*Unanimity games:* $U_{T,1}$ models the situation where each coalition S can arbitrarily divide among its members the amount 1, if it contains *all* the players of T – or nothing, otherwise. This c.b.p. has a unique solution, where the members of T receive equal shares $(1/|T|)$, and the other players zero.)

Theorem A (Aumann (1983*b*)).　There exists a unique function Φ satisfying A0 through A5; it is the Shapley function Λ.

We continue next with the Harsanyi solution, according to Hart (1983). We will consider here not only the payoff vector $x = x_N$ of the grand coalition, but rather the full payoff configuration $\mathbf{x} = (x_S)_{S \subset N}$. Let $H(V)$ stand for the set of all $\mathbf{x} = (x_S)_{S \subset N} \in X$ associated with a Harsanyi solution of a c.b.p. V; that is, $\mathbf{x} = (x_S)_{S \subset N} \in H(V)$ if there exists $\lambda \in \mathbb{R}^N_{++}$ such that conditions (5) and (8) are satisfied for all $S \subset N$ and condition (6) is satisfied for $S = N$; see definition 2′). The set-valued function H from Γ_1 to X will be called the *Harsanyi function;* we will refer to $\mathbf{x} = (x_S)_{S \subset N} \in H(V)$ as a Harsanyi solution of V (rather than just to x_N). Note that $H(V)$ may well be an empty set for some $V \in \Gamma_1$. Consider now the following axioms.

B0. Ψ is a set-valued function from Γ_1 to X.

(For each $V \in \Gamma_1$, $\Psi(V)$ is a subset of X.)

B1. $\Psi(V) \subset \partial V$ for all $V \in \Gamma_1$.

(*Efficiency:* Every solution $\mathbf{x} = (x_S)_{S \subset N} \in H(V)$ must be Pareto-efficient for all coalitions: $x_S \in \partial V(S)$ for all $S \subset N$.)

B2. $\Psi(\lambda V) = \lambda \Psi(V)$ for all $\lambda \in \mathbb{R}^N_{++}$ and $V \in \Gamma_1$.

(*Scale covariance:* If the payoffs of the players are rescaled independently, all solutions will be rescaled accordingly.)

B3. If $U = V + W$, then $\Psi(U) \supset (\Psi(V) + \Psi(W)) \cap \partial U$ for all $U, V, W \in \Gamma_1$.

(Conditional additivity: If $\mathbf{x} = (x_S)_{S \subset N} \in \Psi(V)$ is a solution of V, $\mathbf{y} = (y_S)_{S \subset N} \in \Phi(W)$ is a solution of W, and $\mathbf{z} = \mathbf{x} + \mathbf{y}$ is efficient for $U = V + W$ [i.e., $z_S \in \partial V(S)$ for all $S \subset N$], then z is a solution of U [i.e., $\mathbf{z} \in \Psi(U)$].)

B4. If $V \subset W$, then $\Psi(V) \supset \Psi(W) \cap V$ for all $V, W \in \Gamma_1$.

(Independence of irrelevant alternatives: If V is obtained from W by restricting the feasible set of some coalition(s), then any solution of W that remains feasible in V will be a solution of V as well: $\mathbf{x} = (x_S)_{S \subset N} \in \Psi(W)$ and $x_S \in V(S) \subset W(S)$ for all $S \subset N$ imply $\mathbf{x} \in \Psi(V)$.)

B5. $\Psi(U_{T,c}) = \{\mathbf{z}(T,c)\} = \{z_S(T,c))_{S \subset N}\}$ for all $T \subset N$, $T \neq \phi$, and all $c \in \mathbb{R}$, where $z_S(T,c) = c1_T/|T|$ if $S \supset T$ and $z_S(T,c) = 0$ otherwise.

(Unanimity games: $U_{T,c}$ models the situation where each coalition S can arbitrarily divide among its members the amount c if it contains *all* the players of T – or nothing, otherwise. This c.b.p. has a unique solution $\mathbf{z} \equiv \mathbf{z}(T,c)$; the S-payoff vector z_S of a coalition S that contains T assigns equal shares $(c/|T|)$ to all members of T and zero to the rest; if S does not contain T, everyone gets zero.)

B6. If $\mathbf{0} \in \partial V$, then $\mathbf{0} \in \Psi(V)$.

(Inessential games: A c.b.p. is called *zero inessential* if $\mathbf{0} \in \partial V(S)$ for all $S \subset N$, that is, if the zero payoff vector is efficient for all coalitions. This means that for all coalitions, $\mathbf{0}$ is feasible, whereas no positive vector is feasible. In particular, $V(\{i\}) = \{x^i \in \mathbb{R}^{(i)} \mid x^i \leq 0\}$. For such a game, where there is nothing to bargain on, the payoff configuration zero is a solution.)

Theorem B (Hart (1983)).   There exists a unique function Ψ satisfying B0 through B6; it is the Harsanyi function H.

It is remarkable that the two solutions of Shapley and Harsanyi are determined by very similar sets of axioms. The main difference lies in the range: payoff vectors for the former versus payoff configurations for the latter (see Section 5 in Hart (1983) for further discussion of this subject).

We come now to the class of Kalai and Samet solutions. For every $\lambda \in \mathbb{R}^N_{++}$, let E^λ be the function from Γ_2 into $\mathbb{R}^N$ that assigns to each $V \in \Gamma_2$ its λ-egalitarian solution $E^\lambda(V)$. We will refer to E^λ as the *λ-egalitarian function*. Consider now the following axioms, according to Kalai and Samet (1983).

C0. F is a function from Γ_2 into $\mathbb{R}^N$.

As usual, we will write $F(V) = (F^i(V))_{i \in N} \in \mathbb{R}^N$ and $F^T(V) = (F^i(V))_{i \in T} \in \mathbb{R}^T$ for all $T \subset N$. Given a c.b.p. V, a coalition $T \subset N$ is a *carrier* of V if $V(S) = V(S \cap T) \times \mathbb{R}^{S-T}$ for all $S \subset N$.

C1. If T is a carrier of V, then $F^T(V) \in \partial V(T)$ for all $V \in \Gamma_2$ and $T \subset N$.

(*Carrier:* The solution is Pareto-efficient for any carrier of V.) This axiom implies both an *efficiency* axiom and a *dummy* axiom (where any player outside a carrier is a dummy). Note that if T is a carrier of V, then any $T' \supset T$ (in particular $T' = N$, for all V) is also a carrier, and thus $F^{T'}(V) \in \partial V(T')$.

Given a c.b.p. V, let V_+ denote its *individually rational restriction*, defined as follows:

$$v^i = \max\{x \mid x \in V(\{i\})\} \text{ for all } i \in N,$$

$$V_+(S) = \{x \in V(S) \mid x^i \geq v^i \text{ for all } i \in S\},$$

for $S \subset N$. Note that V_+ does not belong to Γ (it does not satisfy comprehensiveness nor possibly nonemptiness [see (1) in Section 14.2]). A c.b.p. V is *individually rational monotonic* (*monotonic* in Kalai and Samet (1983)) if for all $S \subset N$ and $i \notin S$.

$$V_+(S \cup \{i\}) \supset V_+(S) \times V_+(\{i\}).$$

In such a c.b.p., the contribution of a player is never detrimental, so long as only individually rational outcomes are considered. Note that $V_+(\{i\}) = \{v^i\}$, and repeated applications of the preceding inclusion imply $v^S \in V_+(S) \subset V(S)$ for all $S \subset N$.

C2. If V is individually rational monotonic, then $F(V) \geq v$ for all $V \in \Gamma_2$.

(*Individual rationality:* The solution is individually rational (i.e., $F^i(V) \geq v^i$ for all $i \in N$), provided that every player always contributes nonnegatively to all coalitions he may join.)

Given a nonempty coalition $T \subset N$ and a payoff vector $a \in \mathbb{R}^N$ with $a^i = 0$ for all $i \notin T$, let A_T be the c.b.p. defined by

$$A_T = \begin{cases} \{a^S\} + \mathbb{R}^S_- & \text{if } S \supset T, \\ \mathbb{R}^S_- & \text{otherwise.} \end{cases}$$

C3. If $F(A_T) = a$, then $F(V + A_T) = F(V) + a$ for all $V \in \Gamma_2$.

(*Translation invariance:* If the payoffs of each member i of T in each coalition that contains T are translated by a^i, and moreover the vector a is acceptable (meaning that the solution of the c.b.p. A_T is precisely a), then the solution of the new c.b.p. will be translated by a; note that the c.b.p. $W = V + A_T$ is given by $W(S) = V(S) + \{a^S\}$ for $S \supset T$ and $W(S) = V(S)$ otherwise.)

C4.   If $T \subset N$ is such that $V(S) = W(S)$ for all $S \neq T$ and $V(T) \subset W(T)$, then $F^T(V) \leq F^T(W)$ for all $V, W \in \Gamma_2$.

(*Monotonicity:* If the feasible set of some coalition T is enlarged (and all the other feasible sets remain unchanged), then the payoff of each member of T does not decrease.)

On the space of c.b.p.'s, consider the product of the Hausdorff topologies for all $S \subset N$: A sequence $\{V_m\}_{m=1}^{\infty}$ converges to V if, for each $S \subset N$, the sequence $\{V_m(S)\}_{m=1}^{\infty}$ of subsets of $\mathbb{R}^S$ converges in the Hausdorff topology to $V(S)$.

C5.   The function F is continuous on Γ_2.

(*Continuity:* If a sequence $\{V_m\}_{m=1}^{\infty}$ in Γ_2 converges to $V \in \Gamma_2$, then $F^i(V_m)$ converges to $F^i(V)$ for all $i \in N$.)

Theorem C (Kalai and Samet (1983)).   A function F satisfies axioms C0 through C5 if and only if there exists $\lambda \in \mathbb{R}_{++}^N$ such that $F = E^\lambda$ is the λ-egalitarian function.

Thus, each E^λ (for $\lambda \in \mathbb{R}_{++}^N$) satisfies C0 through C5; moreover, those are the only functions to do so.

This completes the presentation of the three axiomatic systems. We note again that we have considered here only one of the various ways of characterizing the three solutions; there are other combinations of the postulates given (and others) that could do as well.

14.5   Discussion

This last section will include some remarks on the solutions presented earlier, together with a comparison of their properties in terms of the axioms presented in Section 14.4.

The basic assumption underlying all the approaches is that the only information available is the characteristic function of the coalitional bargaining problem. Thus, nothing is given on the extensive form of the bargaining process: how the players are discussing, who talks to whom, whether there are procedures for making proposals – or threats – and for rejecting them, for making coalitions, and so on. The solutions thus cannot depend on such data; moreover, any particular assumptions of this kind must necessarily be ad hoc. This implies that the solutions proposed must be based on rather general principles, which should hold in all situations described by the same characteristic function. The Nash solution in the two-person case is an example of such an axiomatic approach applied to the characteristic-function form. (See Sections 5 through 7 in Aumann (1983a) for further discussion on this point; and see Binmore (1983) for an "extensive-form" approach to three-person coalitional bargaining.)

The solutions discussed in this chapter are of two types. The Harsanyi and Shapley solutions depend only on the cardinal representation of the utility of each player separately. Thus, if a positive linear transformation is applied to some player's payoffs, the same transformation applies to the solutions as well (for rescaling, see axioms A2 and B2). The Kalai and Samet solutions are different. If only one player's utility is rescaled, the solution may change completely. Only *joint rescaling* of the utilities of *all* players leads to the same change in the solution as well. In the former two solutions, *independent* rescaling is allowed; here, only *common* rescaling. Formally, for every $i \in N$, let $l_i: \mathbb{R} \to \mathbb{R}$ be a positive linear transformation given by $l_i(x) = a^i x + b^i$, where $a^i > 0$ and b^i are real constants. For each c.b.p. V, let $W = l(V)$ be the transformed c.b.p., namely,

$$W(S) = \{l(x) = (l^i(x^i))_{i \in S} \in \mathbb{R}^S \mid x = (x^i)_{i \in S} \in V(S)\}$$

for all $S \subset N$. If a payoff vector $x \in \mathbb{R}^N$ is a Harsanyi or a Shapley solution of V, then the payoff vector $l(x) \in \mathbb{R}^N$ is a Harsanyi or a Shapley solution, respectively, of $W = l(V)$. Let $\lambda \in \mathbb{R}^N_{++}$; if a payoff vector $x \in \mathbb{R}^N$ is the Kalai and Samet λ-egalitarian solution of V, and *moreover* all the a^i are identical (i.e., $a^i = a$ for all $i \in N$), then the payoff vector $l(x)$ is the λ-egalitarian solution of $W = l(V)$.

According to Shapley's (1983) classification, the Harsanyi and Shapley solutions are both of category $CARD^N$, whereas the egalitarian solutions are of category $CARD_N$. The interpersonal comparison of utility is obtained endogenously in the former, and it is exogenously given in the latter.

We conclude this paper with a comparison of the three solutions via the axioms presented in Section 14.4. Table 14.1 points out for each solution function which axioms it satisfies and which it does not. The domain is Γ_1 for the Shapley and the Harsanyi functions, and Γ_2 for the Kalai and Samet functions. Note that axioms A1 through A5 regard the solution as a set-valued function that assigns a subset of $\mathbb{R}^N$ to each c.b.p. (possibly empty, since we consider Γ_1 and not Γ_4); similarly for axioms B1 through

Table 14.1.

	Solution function		
Axiom	Shapley	Harsanyi	Kalai and Samet
A1 (efficiency)	Yes	Yes	Yes
A2 (scale)	Yes	Yes	No[a]
A3 (additivity)	Yes	No[b]	No[b]
A4 (irrelevant alternatives)	Yes	Yes	Yes
A5 (unanimity games)	Yes	Yes	No[c]
B1 (efficiency)	Yes	Yes	Yes
B2 (scale)	Yes	Yes	No[a]
B3 (additivity)	Yes	Yes	Yes
B4 (irrelevant alternatives)	Yes	Yes	Yes
B5 (unanimity games)	No[d]	Yes	No[c]
B6 (inessential games)	No[e]	Yes	Yes
C1 (carrier)	Yes	Yes	Yes
C2 (individual rationality)	Yes	Yes	Yes
C3 (translation)	No[f]	No[f]	Yes
C4 (monotonicity)	No[g]	No[g]	Yes
C5 (continuity)	No[h]	No[h]	Yes

The instances where axioms are satisfied ("yes" in the table) follow easily from theorems A, B, and C, and straightforward arguments (see also Section 5 in Hart (1983) and Section 8 in Kalai and Samet (1983)).

[a] If $\lambda = c1_N$ for some $c \in \mathbb{R}_+$, then "yes."

[b] Let $N = \{1,2,3\}$, $U = U_{N,0}$, and $W = U_{\{1,2\},1}$; let $V(S) = U_{N,1}(S)$ for $S \neq \{1,2\}$ and $V(\{1,2\}) = \{x \in \mathbb{R}^{(1,2)} \mid x^1 + 2x^2 \leq 0 \text{ and } 2x^1 + x^2 \leq 3\}$. Then, $W = V + U$; each of the three games W, V, and U has a unique Harsanyi solution, namely, $z = (\frac{1}{2},\frac{1}{2},0)$, $x = (\frac{1}{3},\frac{1}{3},\frac{1}{3})$, and $y = (0,0,0)$, respectively; and $z \neq x + y$. Furthermore, the symmetric egalitarian solution coincides with the Harsanyi solution for each of the three games.

[c] "Yes" for the symmetric egalitarian solution.

[d] See proposition 5.4 and axiom B5 in Hart (1983).

[e] See example 5.6 in Hart (1983).

[f] "No" already in the two-person case (the Nash solution): Let $N = \{1,2\}$, $a = (2,1)$, $T = N$, $V(\{i\}) = \mathbb{R}^{(i)}$, and $V(N) = \{x \in \mathbb{R}^N \mid x^1 + x^2 \leq 2\}$; the Nash (=Shapley = Harsanyi) solutions of A_N, V, and $V + A_N$ are, respectively, (2,1), (1,1), and (2.5,2.5).

[g] See Sections 1 and 2 in Kalai and Samet (1983).

[h] Upper-semi-continuity only: If x_m is a solution of V_m for every $m \geq 1$, $x_m \rightarrow x$, and $V_m \rightarrow V$, then x is a solution of V (recall condition (2b) in Section 14.2).

B6, with the range being the subsets of X (the set of payoff configurations). Axioms C1 through C5 refer to a (point-valued) function into $\mathbb{R}^N$, although they can be extended in a straightforward manner to apply to a set-valued function.

REFERENCES

Aumann, R. J. (1967): A Survey of Cooperative Games without Side Payments. In *Essays in Mathematical Economics in Honor of Oskar Morgenstern*, ed. by M. Shubik. Princeton University Press, Princeton, New Jersey, 3–27.

(1983a): *On the Non-Transferable Utility Value*. RM-55, Center for Research in Mathematical Economics and Game Theory, The Hebrew University, Jerusalem, forthcoming in *Econometrica*.

(1983b): *An Axiomatization of the Non-Transferable Utility Value*. RM-57, Center for Research in Mathematical Economics and Game Theory, The Hebrew University, Jerusalem, forthcoming in *Econometrica*.

Binmore, K. (1983): *Bargaining and Coalitions I*. Theoretical Economics DP-83/71, ICERD, London School of Economics.

Harsanyi, J. C. (1959): A Bargaining Model for the Cooperative *n*-Person Game. In *Contributions to the Theory of Games IV* (Annals of Mathematics Studies 40), ed. by A. W. Tucker and R. D. Luce. Princeton University Press, Princeton, New Jersey, 325–55.

(1963): A Simplified Bargaining Model for the *n*-Person Cooperative Game. *International Economic Review*, 4, 194–220.

(1977): *Rational Behavior and Bargaining Equilibrium in Games and Social Situations*. Cambridge University Press, Cambridge.

Hart, S. (1983): *An Axiomatization of Harsanyi's Non-Transferable Utility Solution*. DP-573, The Center for Mathematical Studies in Economics and Management Science, Northwestern University, Evanston, Illinois, forthcoming in *Econometrica*.

Kalai, E. (1977): Proportional Solutions to Bargaining Situations: Interpersonal Utility Comparisons. *Econometrica*, 45, 1623–30.

Kalai, E., and D. Samet (1983): *A Monotonic Solution to General Cooperative Games*. DP-567, The Center for Mathematical Studies in Economics and Management Science, Northwestern University, Evanston, Illinois, forthcoming in *Econometrica*.

Nash, J. F. (1950): The Bargaining Problem. *Econometrica*, 18, 155–62.

Owen, G. (1972): Values of Games without Side Payments. *International Journal of Game Theory*, 1, 94–109.

Roth, A. E. (1979): *Axiomatic Models of Bargaining*. Springer-Verlag, Berlin, Heidelberg, New York.

Shapley, L. S. (1953): A Value for *n*-Person Games. In *Contributions to the Theory of Games II* (Annals of Mathematics Studies 28), ed. by H. W. Kuhn and A. W. Tucker. Princeton University Press, Princeton, New Jersey, 307–17.

(1969): Utility Comparison and the Theory of Games. In *La Décision: Aggrégation et Dynamique des Ordres de Préférence*, Editions du Centre National de la Recherche Scientifique, Paris, 251–63.

(1983): Bargaining without Cardinal Utility. Paper presented at the Conference on Game-Theoretic Models of Bargaining, University of Pittsburgh.

CHAPTER 15

A comment on the Coase theorem

William Samuelson
BOSTON UNIVERSITY SCHOOL OF MANAGEMENT

15.1 Introduction

Beginning with the observation of Ronald Coase, it has long been held
that private bargaining can provide an antidote to the inefficiencies
caused by externalities. Coase (1960) argued that

1. A pair of agents, by striking a mutually advantageous agreement, would
   obtain an efficient economic solution to the externality, and
2. A change in the assignment of property rights or in the liability rule
   would not affect the attainment of efficient agreements.

The Coase "theorem" relies on a number of assumptions, some explicit,
some implicit, among which are that: agents have perfect knowledge of
the economic setting including each other's utility function; in the absence of transaction costs, the agents will strike mutually beneficial agreements; and there exists a costless mechanism (a court system) for enforcing such agreements.

As many observers have pointed out, the presumptions that the bargainers have perfect knowledge of, and pursue, mutually beneficial agreements – assumptions borrowed from the theory of cooperative games –
are crucial for the Coase results.[1] The usual argument is that rational
bargainers would (should) never settle on a given set of agreement terms if
instead they could agree on alternative terms that were preferred by both
sides. The conclusion, according to this argument, is that any final agreement must be Pareto-optimal.

Although this argument seems compelling, it leaves a number of questions unanswered. By what bargaining procedure do the individuals actually arrive at a Pareto-efficient agreement? Will alternative procedures
attain such agreements? The usual presentation of the Coase theorem

This research was supported by National Science Foundation Grant
SES-8309345.

321

omits the specifics of the bargaining process. The presumption is simply that such agreements can and will be reached since it is in the joint interest of the parties to do so. Although this conclusion is appealing, it is considerably stronger than the economist's customary hypothesis of *individual* rationality. Even under perfect information, this presumption is far from obvious. Each individual seeks only to maximize his individual utility and does not seek a point on the utility-possibility frontier per se. Moreover, in any interesting problem, there will be a multiplicity (in fact, an infinity) of efficient agreements – such that an improvement in one agent's welfare necessitates a sacrifice in the other's. Thus, one would expect the agents to negotiate (or haggle) over these candidates – a process that may in turn expend resources and delay agreement. Other types of strategic behavior are also possible. In pursuit of a preferred agreement, one party may threaten the other and, for credibility's sake, bind himself to carry out the threat some portion of the time. When he does, efficiency fails.[2] Alternatively, the parties may adopt the standard negotiation bluff, insisting on ultrafavorable (and incompatible) terms of agreement. If agents persist in these demands, a mutually beneficial agreement may be lost. Although proponents of the Coase presumption may regard these actions as irrational, it is no less true that such behavior (e.g., strikes, the carrying out of costly threats) frequently occurs.

Moreover, it is unrealistic to suppose that the bargaining setting is one of perfect information. To a greater or lesser degree, each party will be uncertain about key aspects of the bargaining situation – possibly about his own payoffs for alternative agreements and almost certainly about the other side's potential payoffs. As an example, consider a simple setting of bilateral monopoly in which a single seller and buyer are negotiating the sale price of a good. Although each may have relatively precise information about his own monetary value for the good, each will have only a probabilistic assessment of the other's walk-away price. In the case of an externality, two firms (e.g., one a polluter and one a victim of the pollution) would be engaged in negotiations aimed at a mutually beneficial agreement. Each firm would be knowledgeable about its own cost (cleanup cost or pollution cost) but would have limited information about the cost of the other side.

The presence of limited or imperfect information is an impediment to the attainment of efficient agreements. Before the fact, neither side will know whether, or what, mutually beneficial agreements are available. Such agreements, when they exist, must be uncovered by the bargaining process itself. Thus, the key question is whether there exists a suitable bargaining method, conducted by self-interested individuals, that can always achieve Pareto-efficient agreements.

This chapter addresses this question by exploring the Coase theorem in a setting of *incomplete* information. In contrast to the traditional version of the Coase theorem, the propositions under incomplete information are as follows:

1. The parties affected by an externality will, in general, be unable to negotiate efficient agreements all of the time, or if an efficient agreement is reached it may come only after costly delay;
2. The degree of efficiency of a negotiated agreement depends on
   a. which party is assigned the specific property right, and
   b. the bargaining process used by the parties;
3. Efficiency can be increased by allocating the property right via competitive bid, rather than relying on some preassignment.

Proposition 1 indicates that the presence of incomplete information imposes a second-best negotiation solution – one in which agent welfare falls short of that attainable under perfect information. Once an initial rights assignment is made, bargaining cannot ensure the costless transfer of the right to the party that values it most highly.[3] In this sense, the condition of incomplete information creates a kind of trading friction or a barrier to trade. Proposition 2 follows as an immediate consequence. Given the informational barriers to trade, the ultimate solution to the externality depends directly on the initial assignment of the right and on the bargaining method adopted by the parties. Proposition 3 indicates a potential remedy: Efficiency can be increased by foregoing the rights assignment in the first place. Instead, the right is allocated via competitive bid (so that the agent willing to pay the most for the right obtains it) without recontracting.

The main propositions in this chapter are applications or extensions of recent results in the area of resource allocation under uncertainty. Important contributions are provided by Myerson (1979) and Harris and Townsend (1981). Despite their importance, many of these results are not well known (or if known, not assimilated into mainstream economic thinking). Proposition 1 has been noted by several authors – by Arrow (1979) and Samuelson (1980) for specific bargaining procedures and in an important paper by Myerson and Satterthwaite (1983) for the class of all bargaining procedures (under independent information). Nonetheless, the importance of this amendment to the Coase theorem has gone largely unrecognized. Thus, the conventional wisdom holds that in the absense of transaction costs (caused, for instance, by numerous interested parties), bargaining can solve in principle the externality problem. However, whether bargaining is an appropriate remedy depends on the kind of market failure present. If external effects are the sole cause of the failure, a bargaining solution that, in effect, internalizes the externality will be appropriate. But in the common case when external effects are accompanied by the presence of imperfect information, a property-rights assignment followed by private bargaining will not be a fully efficient remedy. The present study emphasizes this basic point and attempts to explore its logical consequences, for example, the importance, so far as efficiency is concerned, of the bargaining method used by the agents and of the initial rights assignment.

The chapter is organized as follows. Section 15.2 outlines the basic model and presents propositions 1 and 2. Section 15.3 suggests a remedy in the form of rights bidding, and Section 15.4 examines a specific application – the siting of hazardous-waste-processing facilities. A final section offers a summary and concluding remarks.

15.2   Bargaining and externalities

The Coase theorem is a proposition not only about externalities and their remedies, but also about the efficiency of bargaining in general. Coase viewed the externality problem (its specific features notwithstanding) as a member of the general class of bargaining problems. Examples in this class range from negotiated purchase-and-sale agreements to the signing of international treaties to management – labor contract bargaining. Why should parties to the externality not negotiate mutually beneficial agreements as in these other cases? In the spirit of cooperative game theory, Coase concluded that they could, provided that a definite property-right assignment was made. This assignment would specify the outcome in the event that the interested parties failed to reach an agreement. For instance, in the purchase-and-sale example, the seller retains the good in the event of a disagreement. In the externality example, the property right would reside with one of the parties in the event of a disagreement. Clearly, then, one can think of the right holder as a kind of seller and the other party as a buyer who must compensate the holder if he is to obtain a better outcome (than the disagreement alternative) for himself.

To begin, it will be convenient to focus on the general bargaining problem, of which the externality problem is a special case. The simplest such problem can be described as follows. Suppose that two individuals are negotiating over two possible outcomes. Agent preferences are in conflict. The first agent prefers one outcome, the second prefers the other. To keep things simple, let us suppose that each individual is risk neutral and assigns a monetary value to his preferred outcome—a value that is independent of income effects. If negotiations end in a disagreement, one agent (labeled the right holder) will obtain his preferred alternative. Thus, the would-be acquirer, if he is to secure his favored outcome, must provide monetary compensation to the right holder.

When individual values are common knowledge, ex post efficiency requires that the agent with the greater value obtain his preferred outcome (or, equivalently, the right to this outcome). Short of this full-information case, ex post-efficient outcomes *cannot* always be secured, a result contained in an initial proposition.

Proposition 1. The parties affected by an externality will, in general, be unable to negotiate efficient agreements all of the time, or if an efficient agreement is reached it may come only after costly delay.

The following is a simple but graphic example of this basic result.

Example 1. A buyer and a seller are negotiating the price at which a single, indivisible good might be sold. Both parties know that the buyer has a comparative advantage for the good. In fact, the buyer's monetary value for the good is 50 percent greater than the seller's value, that is, $v_b = 1.5 v_s$. The complication is that only the seller knows these underlying values v_s and v_b. The buyer knows only that v_s is uniformly distributed on the interval [0,1].

To examine bargaining possibilities, we model the negotiation process as a two-person game of incomplete information following Harsanyi (1967). The information structure of this game is as specified previously. Because both parties know of the buyer's 50 percent advantage, it is natural to expect a sale always to occur, and, of course, ex post efficiency requires this. Nevertheless, it is straightforward to confirm that self-interested and rational bargainers can *never* conclude a mutually beneficial agreement in these circumstances. For instance, suppose that under the rules of the bargaining game, the buyer has the opportunity to make a first-and-final price offer, which the seller can then accept or reject. What offer should he make? An offer of (let us say) .6 will be accepted 60 percent of the time by a seller holding an average value $\bar{v}_s = .6/2 = .3$. Thus, the buyer's average acquisition value is $\bar{v}_b = (1.5)(.3) = .45$, and his expected profit is $(.6)(.45 - .6) = -0.9$. More generally, any buyer offer b results in a negative profit of $-.25b^2$. Clearly, no offer that the buyer can make is profitable.

What if the informed seller makes the first-and-final offer? For instance, consider a seller who demands a price that is 30 percent greater than his value, that is, $s = 1.3v_s$. Anticipating this strategy, a buyer can profitably accept all seller offers (even a price of 1.3). Against such an accepting buyer, however, a profit-maximizing seller would choose to price at 1.3 for *all* v_s, in which case the buyer would suffer an average loss of .75 − 1.3, or −.55, in accepting this offer. The same result holds if the buyer commits himself to accept any seller offer no greater than s, for any s. The seller's best response is to quote s for all $v_s \leq s$, leaving the buyer with an average loss. Thus, in equilibrium, no offer made by a rational seller could ever be profitably accepted by the buyer. Although these two procedures do not exhaust the bargaining possibilities (e.g., offer, counteroffer, and so on), more general methods can be used to show that the buyer's *most* preferred bargaining procedure is to make a first- and final offer.[4] Since even this is unprofitable, mutually beneficial agreements under any bargaining procedure are impossible.

This example points up the conflict between the collective and individual interests of the parties. Even though the bargainers share the desire to conclude a mutually beneficial agreement, each individual pursues a negotiation strategy that maximizes his own expected profit. In the presence of asymmetric information, bargaining self-interest precludes the attainment of any agreements. Thus, despite his comparative advantage for the good, it is impossible for the uninformed buyer to conclude a profitable agreement. It is not only the buyer who suffers. The information asymmetry robs the *informed* seller of trading profit as well. Clearly, this barrier to trade would not exist if both players knew v_b and v_s, in which case they could conclude an agreement at some $P \in [v_s, v_b]$. In short, although a mutually beneficial agreement is always economically feasible, such an agreement is impossible given the self-interest of the parties.

This finding of bargaining inefficiency is not limited to the case of asymmetric information. As a second example, consider a bargaining setting in which each side holds a personal monetary value concerning the issue at stake—a value that is known only to himself. For instance, suppose that an upstream paper mill is negotiating a pollution agreement with a downstream fishery that has the right to clean water. The mill seeks to obtain the right to discharge moderate amounts of pollution and is willing to pay the fishery for the privilege. Denote the mill's value for this right by v_m (embodying the clean-up cost it avoids) and the fishery's pollution cost by v_f. Then, if $v_f < v_m$, both sides can profit from a pollution agreement whereby the mill obtains the right to pollute and makes a payment P to the fishery, where $P \in [v_f, v_m]$. The difficulty is that each value is known only to the player himself. The fishery's probabilistic belief about the mill's value is summarized by the cumulative distribution function $G_f(v_m)$, the mill's probability assessment is denoted by $G_m(v_f)$, and these distributions are common knowledge.

The usual description of bargaining involves unrestricted offers and counteroffers until an agreement is concluded or an impasse is reached. To bring out the main points, however, it is convenient to begin by presenting a highly stylized bargaining procedure such as the following.

> a. *Ascending offers.* The agents place oral ascending bids for the right, where the last and highest bidder obtains it. If this last and highest bidder is the right holder, he retains the right. If this bidder is the other agent, he purchases the right and pays the holder his bid price.

Though unconventional, this bargaining procedure has the virtue of being "competitive." The would-be acquirer can secure the right by making an unmatched competitive bid and paying this amount to the holder. Alternatively, the right holder retains the right by "outbidding" the other agent. How will profit-maximizing individuals bargain under these ground rules? The answer to this question requires a complete description of each agent's bargaining strategy, that is, a specification of the offers he will make contingent on his value and the offer history to date. In general, this may be a formidable task. Under ascending offers, however, the strategy description is quite simple. The mill, seeking to acquire the right, has a dominant strategy: If necessary, it should bid up to a price not exceeding its true value, that is, make a maximum bid $b_m = v_m$. Anticipating this behavior, the fishery determines its own "ceiling bid" to maximize its expected profit:

$$(b_f - v_f)\text{Prob}(b_m < b_f) = (b_f - v_f)(1 - G_f(b_f)).$$

Here, it is presumed that the mill obtains the right by matching the fishery's offer b_f (or, in an alternative interpretation, by bidding $b_f + \epsilon$). Thus, if the right is transferred, the fishery's profit is $b_f - v_f$, and this event occurs with probability $1 - G_f(b_f)$. The fishery's optimal strategy determines b_f by trading off the probability and profitability of an agreement (where the latter is increasing in and the former decreasing in b_f). It is evident that the fishery's ceiling bid is in excess of its value ($b_f > v_f$). Consequently, the bargaining procedure fails to attain an ex post-efficient outcome when $b_f > v_m > v_f$. Here, the fishery retains the right although it is more valuable to the mill.

A similar finding of bargaining inefficiency occurs under more conventional bargaining methods. In the usual description of negotiations, the bargainers begin with incompatible demands, and over time the sides converge to an agreement (if one is possible) by making staged concessions. In keeping with the postulate of individual rationality, it is natural to insist that each side use a Nash-equilibrium bargaining strategy; that is, each should make offers (contingent upon its personal value) that maximize its expected profit given the bargaining strategy of the other side.

Then, given the actual values v_m and v_f, the agents will engage in bargaining (according to their specified strategies), with the result that an agreement is reached or bargaining terminates with no settlement.

The attainment of efficient outcomes requires that both bargainers be willing to concede up to their true values if necessary, thereby securing a mutually beneficial agreement, whenever trading gains (no matter how small) are present. It can be shown, however, that such concession making cannot constitute an equilibrium. More specifically, against a concession-making opponent, a profit-maximizing bargainer should stop conceding short of his true value. (The right holder makes a final demand $b_f > v_f$, and the other bargainer a final offer $b_m < v_m$.) Although this sacrifices some probability of agreement, the bargainer more than compensates by improving the terms of those agreements that are reached. As a result, bargaining fails to attain certain ex post-efficient agreements.

Proposition 1's finding of bargaining inefficiency is the foundation for a second basic result.

Proposition 2.   The degree of efficiency of a negotiated agreement depends on (a) which party is assigned the property right, and (b) the bargaining process used by the parties.

To demonstrate proposition 2, it is convenient to compare the negotiation outcomes under the ascending-offer procedure with outcomes under the following pair of stylized bargaining procedures.

  b. *Sealed offers.* The agents submit written sealed bids, and the high bidder obtains the right. If the high bidder is the right holder, no payment is made. If this bidder is the other agent, he purchases the right and pays the holder his bid price.
  c. *Split-the-difference offers.* The parties submit written sealed bids, and the high bidder obtains the right. If the other agent's bid exceeds the holder's bid, the right is transferred at a price that "splits the difference" between the bids. Otherwise, the holder retains the right and no payment is made.

Consider agent bargaining behavior under each of these procedures. Suppose, as before, that the fishery holds the water right. Then, under sealed offers, it is easy to check that the fishery has a dominant strategy whereby it submits a sealed bid equal to its true value, that is, $b_f = v_f$. Clearly, it should not bid any less, since this would risk transferring the right at a price less than its value. Nor should it bid any more. Such a deviation from truthful bidding is of no benefit if $v_f < b_f < b_m$ but results in a loss of a profitable sale if $v_f < b_m < b_f$. Thus, truthful bidding is optimal.

The mill, on the other hand, submits an optimal bid to maximize its expected profit:

$$(v_m - b_m)\text{Prob}(b_m \geq b_f) = (v_m - b_m)G_m(b_m),$$

where the equality stems from the fact that the right holder bids truthfully. It is evident from this expression that the mill uses a "shading" strategy, submitting a bid below its true value.

Under split-the-difference offers, if $b_m \geq b_f$, then the mill purchases the right and pays the fishery a price $P = (b_m + b_f)/2$. Otherwise, the fishery retains the right. Here, the sale price depends on both offers, not on one side's offer as in the ascending-offer and sealed-offer procedures. It can be shown (see Chatterjee and Samuelson (1983)) that in equilibrium the fishery uses a "mark-up" strategy and the mill a "shading" strategy; that is, $b_f = b_f(v_f) \geq v_f$ for all v_f and $b_m = b_m(v_m) \leq v_m$ for all v_m.

Example 2. Suppose that it is common knowledge that the agents' values are uniformly and independently distributed on the interval [0,1]. When the fishery holds the property right, the bargaining methods yield the following results.

   a. *Ascending offers.* The fishery's optimal strategy is $b_f = .5 + .5v_f$. Thus, the mill obtains the right if and only if $v_m \geq b_f = .5 + .5v_f$.
   b. *Sealed offers.* The mill's optimal bargaining strategy is $b_m = .5v_m$, and so it obtains the right if and only if $b_m = .5v_m \geq v_f$ or, equivalently, when $v_m \geq 2v_f$.
   c. *Split-the-difference offers.* The agents' optimal bargaining strategies are $b_f = \frac{1}{4} + \frac{2}{3}v_f$ and $b_m = \frac{1}{12} + \frac{2}{3}v_m$. Thus, the mill obtains the right if and only if $b_m \geq b_f$ or, equivalently, if and only if $v_m \geq v_f + \frac{1}{4}$.

These outcomes are depicted in Figures 15.1a – c, which indicate the agent who obtains the right via bargaining for all possible combinations of player values. Efficiency in the ex post sense requires that the fishery retain the right if and only if $v_f \geq v_m$ (i.e., in the domain to the southeast of the 45° line in each figure). But under incomplete information, the original right holder retains the right over a larger domain of values (extending to the northwest of the line), regardless of the specific bargaining procedure – that is, the fishery may retain the right even though $v_f < v_m$. As the figures indicate, the domains of inefficient outcomes vary according to the bargaining procedure. (Of course, if the mill were originally assigned the right, the domain of the mill's retention would extend to the southeast of the 45° line under each procedure.)

Under *perfect* information, the mill would obtain the right with probability $\frac{1}{2}$. By comparison, under either the ascending-offer or sealed-offer

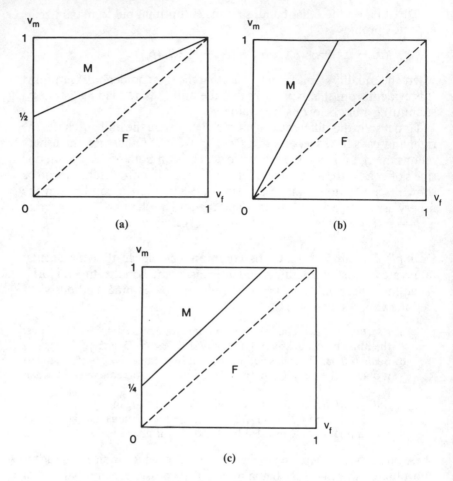

Figure 15.1 (a) Ascending offers. (b) Sealed offers. (c) Split-the-difference offers.

procedures, the probability that the mill obtains the right is $\frac{1}{4}$, whereas under split-the-difference offers, this probability is slightly higher, $\frac{9}{32}$. A natural measure of bargaining performance is the expected collective benefit that is generated. If ex post-efficient outcomes were always achieved, the expected benefit sum would be $E[\Sigma\ B] = E[\max(v_f,v_m)] = \frac{2}{3}$, where the expectation is taken over all possible values v_f and v_m. By comparison, the expected group benefit is $\frac{5}{8}$ under either the ascending-offer or sealed-offer procedures and is slightly higher, $\frac{41}{64}$, under split-the-difference offers.[5]

Example 3.   Now, suppose that the values are independently and uniformly distributed with $v_f \in [0,2]$ and $v_m \in [0,1]$, reflecting the fact that the right is worth more on average to the fishery.

It is straightforward to derive equilibrium strategies and outcomes under each of the bargaining procedures and for each initial assignment of the right. Figure 15.2 displays the bargaining outcomes for different value combinations, as well as the expected benefits generated. It is evident that these benefits vary systematically according to the original rights assignment. In this example, if a rights assignment is made, it should be to the fishery, the firm that values the right more highly on average. However, although this assignment rule seems to be appealing, it is easy to construct other examples in which the attainment of maximum benefits calls for exactly the reverse assignment.

15.3   Rights bidding

There is a simple remedy to the failure of bargaining based on a rights preassignment. In the absense of a preassignment, let the parties bid for the right. For historical, political, or legal reasons, an initial right assignment may be a foregone conclusion in many settings. In other circumstances, however, bidding for the right is natural and feasible.

The bidding method envisioned is akin to a standard auction with one exception. There is no seller to collect the proceeds; instead, the proceeds are returned to the parties themselves. Thus, failing to acquire the right, an agent will obtain compensation. Consider the following bidding procedure.

> *Split-the-difference bidding.* Agents submit sealed bids, and the high bidder acquires the right and pays the sum $(b_f + b_m)/4$ to the other agent, where b_m and b_f are the respective bids of the parties.

Although the assignment of the right is straightforward, the amount of compensation deserves comment. The payment is most easily understood by noting that the agents are, at the same time, bidders for and joint owners of the right. In this light, the bidding procedure described here parallels split-the-difference offers. First, the purchase price is determined by the average of the bids, $(b_f + b_m)/2$. This revenue is collected and shared equally by the joint owners of the right, so that the acquirer's *net* payment is simply $(b_f + b_m)/4$.

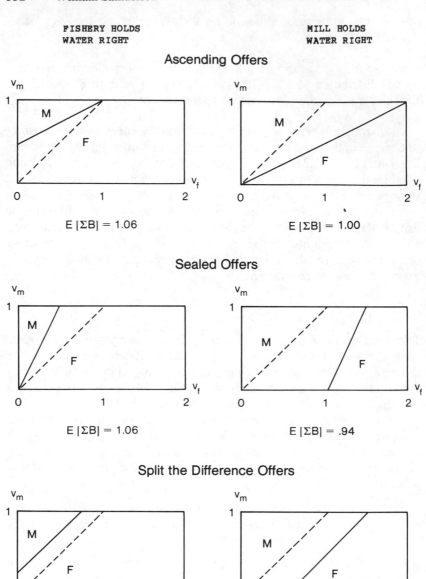

Figure 15.2 Bargaining outcomes

Bids

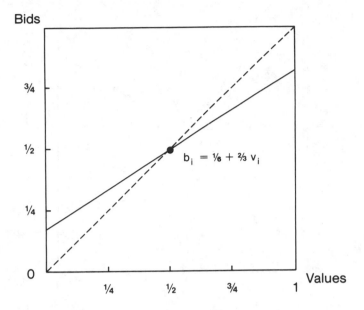

Figure 15.3 Split-the-difference bidding

Suppose that this bidding procedure is adopted and that the agents' values are drawn independently from the same distribution (i.e., $G_f(\ \ ) = G_m(\ \ )$). Then, it is straightforward to show that the split-the-difference bidding scheme is ex post efficient. The reasoning is simple. In equilibrium, each agent will use the same bidding strategy that is strictly increasing in his value. Consequently, $b_f \geq b_m$ if and only if $v_f \geq v_m$.

Example 2'. Suppose that the values are independently and uniformly distributed on the interval $[0,1]$, and that the right is assigned by competitive bid. Then, the equilibrium bid function is $b(v) = \frac{1}{6} + \frac{2}{3}v$, as graphed in Figure 15.3. At the mean value $v = \frac{1}{2}$, an agent makes a "truthful" bid $b = \frac{1}{2}$. For larger values, he shades his bid $b(v) < v$, and for smaller values, he marks up his bid $b(v) > v$.

The intuition behind this behavior should be clear. For $v > \frac{1}{2}$, the agent is more likely than not to obtain the right. Thus, as a potential buyer, he has an incentive to shade his bid and so pay a lower price. For $v < \frac{1}{2}$, on the other hand, the likelihood is that he will be outbid for the right. Consequently, he exaggerates the value of the right in order to raise his monetary receipt. At $v = \frac{1}{2}$, these incentives to shade and to mark up balance out,

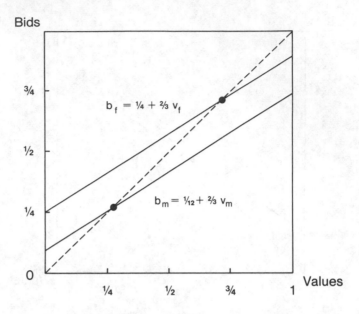

Figure 15.4 Split-the-difference bargaining

and so he bids $b = v = \frac{1}{2}$. Furthermore, it is easy to check that the bidding is profitable for both the winner and the loser of the right. Even a player holding $v = 0$ profits. Although he is always outbid for the right, his receipt is $(b_f + b_m)/4$ or $(\frac{1}{6} + \frac{1}{2})/4 = \frac{1}{6}$ on average (where $\frac{1}{2}$ is the average winning bid). In the example, the expected profit of each player conditional on his own value increases quadratically according to $\frac{1}{6} + v^2/2$.

Although bids differ from agent values, the allocation of the right is efficient (since the agent bidding strategies are identical). Figure 15.4 displays and compares the agent strategies under split-the-difference *bargaining*. Even though this bargaining behavior bears a superficial resemblance to split-the-difference bidding (both involve shading and markups), there is a crucial difference. The bidding procedure ensures ex post efficiency; the bargaining procedure cannot. Once a rights assignment is made, there is an inevitable divergence between the bargaining strategies of the agents – that is, the fishery and mill offers, respectively, overstate and understate true values.

The same point can be made in a slightly different way by showing that there is no bidding procedure that is ex post efficient and that compensates the holder for relinquishing his right. For instance, suppose that the bidding procedure in example 2′ is modified in order to provide additional compensation to the fishery (the would-be right holder). One simple means is via a lump-sum payment between the parties prior to the bidding. Under the requirement that the mill obtain a nonnegative profit (for all v_m), the largest possible lump-sum payment is $\frac{1}{6}$. With this payment, the conditional expected profits of the bidders become $\pi_m(v_m) = v_m^2/2$ and $\pi_f(v_f) = \frac{1}{3} + v_f^2/2$. If the fishery is to be compensated for giving up the right, it must be the case that $\pi_f(v_f) \geq v_f$ for all v_f. However, it is easy to check that this constraint is violated for $v_f > 1 - \sqrt{\frac{1}{3}}$. In short, there is no allocation mechanism that is both efficient and guarantees that $\pi_m(v_m) \geq 0$ and $\pi_f(v_f) \geq v_f$ for all v_m and v_f. However, if the last constraint is weakened to $\pi_f(v_f) \geq 0$, efficient outcomes are attainable via competitive bids.[6]

The lesson of this simple example holds more generally. Because of the rights assignment, the bargaining solution to the externality problem introduces a constraint that (in general) prohibits an ex post-efficient transfer of the right. By foregoing an initial rights assignment, the bidding solution relaxes this constraint. (The only "individual-rationality" constraint implicit in the bidding solution is that agents who forego the right should not be made to pay.) As a result, efficiency increases. This result is summarized in the following proposition.

Proposition 3.   Efficiency can be increased by allocating the property right via competitive bid, rather than relying on some preassignment.

15.4   Siting hazardous-waste facilities

The preceding sections have compared the alternatives of bargaining and bidding in determining rights assignments in the presence of externalities. The important point is that foregoing a rights assignment can be crucial for efficiency.

Many of the differences between the bargaining and bidding remedies for externalities can be illustrated by the process used in the state of Massachusetts for siting hazardous-waste facilities. As outlined in 1980 legislation, the siting process relies on developers (waste-management companies) and local communities to negotiate siting agreements beneficial to both, subject to certain safety and environmental standards enforced by state agencies. Besides safety and mitigation measures, the negotiation agenda includes issues of compensation, both monetary (taxes, service fees) and nonmonetary (jobs, payments in kind). Thus, in contrast to practices in many other states, the siting process is intended to be voluntary, providing neither state override of local decisions nor local veto of development proposals. (These aspirations notwithstanding, to date none of the half-dozen or so proposals for which the siting process has been initiated have resulted in a negotiated siting agreement.)

No short summary can do justice to the many complex issues inherent in the siting legislation. However, the main economic objectives underlying the legislation are not difficult to ascertain and appear to be twofold. First, a facility should be sited where it generates the greatest net social benefit (an efficiency objective). Second, the siting process should be voluntary, that is, mutually beneficial to all affected parties (an equity objective). A short list of these affected parties would include (most obviously) the developer, the potential host community, neighboring communities possibly affected by the facility, and in-state business and consumers that benefit directly or indirectly from the provision of disposal services. (In terms of aggregate net benefit, this last, general-interest group may be the most important.) Of course, the precise magnitudes of the benefits and costs accruing to affected groups remain private information. Thus, the siting process occurs in a setting of imperfect information.

In light of the arguments presented herein, and based on the experience to date with the siting process, one can identify several obstacles to the attainment of the efficiency and equity goals.

1. The exchange of information between prospective developers and potential host communities is severely limited. With few exceptions, individual developers have considered (and subsequently pursued) a limited number of sites based solely on their own costs and profits. (This is due in no small part to the significant transaction cost, in time and money, of the siting process itself.) Often, a developer's least costly site lies in a community with high cost burdens, for instance centrally located, high-density areas. In short, sites with the highest net benefits (or, conversely, lowest total costs) may not be uncovered.
2. The negotiations between the developer and the local community necessarily fail to take into account the external benefits (consumer surplus) conferred on businesses and consumers in-state. Consequently, it may be impossible for the bargaining parties to conclude a mutually beneficial agreement (i.e., the potential developer profit is insufficient to compensate the community for its costs) even when the site is socially beneficial. (Reports of the Massachusetts regulatory agencies stress repeatedly these social benefits but fail to supply a serious benefit–cost confirmation.) Of course, the presence of third-party effects is the standard problem posed by externalities.
3. Even if a mutually beneficial agreement between the developer and local community is possible, the parties may fail to attain it under incomplete information (e.g., when the local community exaggerates its cost burden and the developer downplays his potential profit for strategic reasons).
4. Under the siting act, the assignment of the property right is ambiguous.

The local community cannot unilaterally refuse to negotiate, and if after sixty days the talks are at an impasse, an arbitration board is convened to resolve the dispute. (According to the legislative mandate, the board should seek a settlement that conforms as closely as possible to the final positions of both parties.) Thus, the local community does not have the right to deny the facility under any circumstances. Furthermore, the very ambiguity surrounding the holding of the property right may deter negotiated agreements (e.g., when each side is optimistic about the merits of its case and therefore prefers arbitration).

As an alternative to the negotiation mechanism, a system of competitive bids could be used to establish the location of the facility and to determine the compensation to be paid to the host community. Such a procedure would change the property-right focus by requiring the communities to give up the local veto right but to share the responsibility for paying compensation to the host location. To illustrate, suppose that each community is asked to submit a self-assessed estimate of the cost burden of a local site. At the same time, the developer submits a list of cost estimates for the possible sites. Based on these submissions, the site with the least total cost is selected and appropriate compensation is paid. The source of this compensation includes a sum comprising the expected statewide benefits generated by the facility, a sum paid by the developer, and pro rata shares contributed by the other communities. In practice, a workable system might simply compensate the host community an amount corresponding to its bid.

Beyond the political and institutional obstacles, in order for a bidding system to work, each community must be willing to put a dollar value on its cost of hosting the facility. Indeed, one might expect communities to overstate the burden of the facility for strategic reasons or simply to avoid it. Nonetheless, as long as these overstatements arc anticipated and a common bidding strategy is used, an efficient (i.e., least-cost) assignment of the facility will be maintained. By paying compensation based on bids, the mechanism increases the chances that the host community will accept the facility voluntarily. At the same time, one would expect that the pro rata contributions of the other communities would not be burdensome.

15.5   Concluding remarks

The present discussion has examined bargaining remedies to the externality problem in the presence of incomplete information and found that, in contrast to the usual Coase result, private bargaining cannot guarantee efficient solutions to the externality. Under these circumstances, the choice of rights assignment is not simply a question of equity. Rather, the

assignment influences the efficiency of ultimate negotiated outcomes in conjunction with the bargaining method used. Indeed, foregoing a rights assignment altogether can increase efficiency. In this case, a system of competitive bids – not bargaining – determines the allocation of the right.

In actual practice, a number of other issues may play an important role in the choice of rights assignment, and in determining whether a rights assignment should be made. In many cases, the rights assignment embodied in the status quo is adopted. As we saw, a chief intent of the Massachusetts siting legislation was that developer and community preferences should count – in particular, that community preferences should not be overruled by state-government fiat. In practice, however, granting this right to communities (even in its present ambiguous form) has prevented the siting of any facility in the state. An alternative is for communities to give up this veto right but to share in the responsibility of paying compensation to the community within which the site is built.

In addition, it is important that the rights allocation be responsive to changes in relevant benefits and costs that may occur over time. Although it is true that bargainers can renegotiate agreements in response to such changes, the fact of bargaining inertia suggests that such negotiations may well fail the test of dynamic efficiency. By contrast, intertemporal efficiency can be maintained in principle (and approximated in practice) by the simple expedient of assigning rights (via competitive bid) for limited periods only and reauctioning the rights at frequent intervals.

Finally, although the focus here has been on two-party bargaining, the general results extend to multiagent settings. With large numbers of agents, the bidding procedure resembles a quasi-market in which competitive bids determine an ex post-efficient allocation of rights (e.g., in the case of pollution permits). Alternatively, if a preassignment of rights is made, the players in the "bargaining" market would include numerous competing right holders facing numerous would-be acquirers. It remains the case that under uncertainty, an ex post-efficient allocation cannot be guaranteed. However, it can be shown that the bargaining market approaches full efficiency as the number of participants on both sides of the market approach infinity. Thus, so far as efficiency is concerned, the key issue in the large-numbers case is the creation and institution of the market; the rights assignment is of secondary importance.

NOTES

1. For a succinct discussion, see Arrow (1979).
2. Crawford (1982) presents an interesting model in which precommitments lead to bargaining impasses.
3. The first proposition also holds in the case where bargaining extends over time

and involves transaction or time-related costs. Here, it is possible to achieve ex post-efficient assignment of the right but only at a bargaining cost that exceeds the additional efficiency gains. For an analysis of bargaining over time, see Chapter 8 in this volume.

4. A complete analysis of this example is found in Samuelson (1984).
5. Myerson and Satterthwaite (1982) show that of all of the possible bargaining methods, the split-the-difference procedure achieves the greatest expected group benefit.
6. The efficiency of allocation by competitive bid (as illustrated in this example) is a special case of general results proved by d'Aspremont and Gerard-Varet (1979) and Laffont and Maskin (1979). In the case of identical distributions, the split-the-difference scheme is just one of many fully efficient bidding procedures. An alternative well-known scheme requires each player to pay the expected externality associated with his bid. In our examples, firm i submits bid b_i and pays $t_i = \int_{v_j}^{b_i} v_j g_i(v_j)\, dv_j$ to the other firm, and the right is awarded to the firm making the highest bid. When $b_i \geq b_j$, agent j is outbid for the right and suffers an economic cost v_j. Consequently, t_i represents the expected cost, by agent i's reckoning, suffered by agent j. By internalizing the expected externality, this bidding scheme induces each agent to make an equilibrium bid $b_i = v_i$, and therefore ensures an ex post-efficient assignment of the right.

REFERENCES

Arrow, K. (1979): The Property Rights Doctrine and Demand Revelation under Incomplete Information. In M. Boskin (ed.), *Essays in Honor of Tibor Scitovsky.* New York: Academic Press.

Chatterjee, K. and W. Samuelson (1983): Bargaining under Incomplete Information. *Operations Research, 31,* 835–51.

Coase, R. H. (1960): The Problem of Social Cost. *Journal of Law and Economics, 3,* 1–31.

Crawford, V. C. (1982): A Theory of Disagreement in Bargaining. *Econometrica, 50,* 607–37.

d'Aspremont, C., and L. Gerard-Varet (1979): Incentives and Incomplete Information. *Journal of Public Economics, 11,* 25–45.

Harris, M., and R. Townsend (1981): Resource Allocation under Asymmetric Information. *Econometrica, 49,* 33–64.

Harsanyi, J. C. (1967, 1968): Games with Incomplete Information Played by Bayesian Players. *Management Science, 14,* 159–82, 321–34, 486–502.

Laffont, J.-J., and E. Maskin (1979): A Differential Approach to Expected Utility Maximizing Mechanisms. In J.-J. Laffont (ed.), *Aggregation and Revelation of Preferences.* Amsterdam: North-Holland.

Myerson, R. B. (1979): Incentive Compatibility and the Bargaining Problem. *Econometrica, 49,* 61–73.

Myerson, R. B., and M. Satterthwaite (1983): Efficient Mechanisms for Bilateral Trading. *Journal of Economic Theory, 29,* 265–81.

Samuelson, W. (1980): First-Offer Bargains. *Management Science, 26,* 155–64.
(1984): Bargaining under Asymmetric Information. *Econometrica, 52,* 995–1005.

CHAPTER 16

Disclosure of evidence and resolution of disputes: Who should bear the burden of proof?

Joel Sobel
UNIVERSITY OF CALIFORNIA AT SAN DIEGO

16.1 Introduction

This chapter discusses the role of a third party in settling disputes. A judge is responsible for deciding which of two bargainers should win a dispute. There is a social value associated with giving the disputed item to a particular bargainer. This is the bargainer's claim to the item. Each bargainer knows the strength of his claim and can provide evidence that proves his claim to the judge. Presenting proof is costly and distortion is impossible. However, it is possible to refuse to present evidence. The judge has a prior distribution about the strength of the claims, but does not know them exactly. The judge uses the information provided by the bargainers' disclosures (or decision not to provide evidence) and then rules in favor of the bargainer who has the best expected claim. When the bargainers must decide whether to provide evidence simultaneously, there are typically two types of equilibria. In one, each bargainer has a positive probability of winning if he does not provide evidence. In the other, one of the bargainers wins only if he proves his claim. Thus, rules about which bargainer has the burden of proof, that is, who must provide evidence in order to win the dispute, serve to select an equilibrium outcome. This discussion compares the welfare obtainable from different rules. The results are ambiguous. In general, the costs of providing evidence are smallest if the burden of proof is placed on the bargainer who has the lower cost of proving his claim, provided that this bargainer has a stronger expected claim. However, to maximize the social value of the settlement, excluding disclosure costs, it is best to place the burden of

I received helpful comments from several conference participants as well as from Steve Bundy, Joe Farrell, Lewis Kornhauser, and Craig Weinstein. NSF provided funding through SES-82-04038.

proof on the higher-cost bargainer. In this way, bargainers present more evidence and the judge makes better decisions.

My model differs from standard models of bargaining. Bargainers are not allowed to misrepresent their private information. This assumption is justified if the information revealed is verifiable, so that misrepresentation can be identified and punished. Also, if well-informed attorneys represent the bargainers, then requiring all information disclosed to be accurate is consistent with the view that an advocate should make the best possible case for his client without telling lies.

There is an explicit distinction between private and social valuations in my model. This makes the role of the judge differ from his role in other models of arbitration. Here, the judge selects a winner on the basis of the quality of a bargainer's claim, which I assume to be verifiable. Although a bargainer's private valuation influences his decision to present evidence, his preferences do not directly enter the utility function of the judge.

Ordover and Rubinstein (1983), P'ng (1983), and Samuelson (1983) present game-theoretic models of the legal process. They discuss how incomplete information affects the decision to settle a dispute. The judge is not an active player in these models. In market settings, Grossman (1981), Milgrom (1981), and Farrell and Sobel (1983) study situations in which agents may disclose information, but cannot distort it.

16.2   The model

There are two bargainers and a judge. For $i = 0$ and $i = 1$, bargainer i is characterized by $x_i \in [0, x_i^T]$, which is his claim to the disputed item. His strategy is a function s_i defined on $[0, x_i^T]$. For fixed x_i, either $s_i(x_i) = x_i$ or $s_i(x_i) = n$. If $s_i(x_i) = x_i$, then the bargainer proves that his claim is x_i (presents evidence) and incurs the nonnegative cost $c_i(x_i)$. If $s_i(x_i) = n$, then the bargainer does not prove his claim and incurs no cost.[1] Because $s_i(x_i)$ can take on only two values, distortion is impossible; bargainers either truthfully reveal x_i or disclose no information. I assume that bargainer i's von Neumann–Morgenstern utility function U_i takes the form

$$U_i(x_i, s_i) \equiv v_i(x_i) - c_i(s_i(x_i)),$$

where $v_i(x_i) > 0$ is the private value he places on winning, $c_i(x_i) \in (0, v_i(x_i))$ is the cost of proving that his claim is x_i (when his claim is, in fact, equal to x_i), and $c_i(n) = 0$. Without further loss of generality, I normalize the utility function by taking $v_i(x_i) \equiv 1$. Thus, $c_i(x_i) \in (0,1)$ is the cost of providing evidence relative to the private value of winning. It follows that if p_i is the probability that bargainer i expects to win given s_i and x_i, then his expected utility is $p_i - c_i(s_i(x_i))$.

The judge chooses the probability p_i that bargainer i wins the dispute. Thus, the judge's strategies consist of pairs of functions (p_0, p_1) such that $p_0 + p_1 \leq 1$ and $p_0, p_1 \geq 0$. These functions depend on whatever information the judge has when he makes his decision. The judge tries to maximize expected social welfare, which I take to be a weighted average of the social value of assigning the object to a particular bargainer net of the costs of providing evidence, if any. Thus,

$$U_J(p, x_0, x_1, s_1) = p_0 x_0 + p_1 x_1 - k[c_0(s_0(x_0)) + c_1(s_1(x_1))], \quad (16.1)$$

where $k \geq 0$. Equation (16.1) assumes that the social value of not assigning the item is zero.

The judge does not know the values of x_0 and x_1; a probability distribution function F summarizes his information. Here, $F(y_0, y_1)$ is the probability that $(x_0, x_1) \in [0, y_0] \times [0, y_1]$. I assume that F has a continuous, positive density function f on $[0, x_0^T] \times [0, x_1^T]$. The conditional distribution of x_i given x_{1-i} describes bargainer i's beliefs about his opponent's case. The functions F, U_0, U_1, and U_J are common knowledge, and so the only uncertainty concerns the values x_0 and x_1.

I assume that the bargainers learn the value of their claim simultaneously, and then prove their case to the judge (or decline to provide evidence). At this point, the judge, knowing what the bargainers have disclosed, decides which bargainer should win. The strategy for the judge is an allocation rule, which selects the winner. I allow the judge to use mixed strategies and, if he prefers, to select no winner. In addition, the judge is able to condition his action on the signals of the bargainers. Therefore, I represent the judge's strategy by functions $p_i(y_i, y_{1-i})$ defined for

$$(y_0, y_1) \in (n \cup [0, x_0^T]) \times (n \cup [0, x_1^T])$$

so that $p_i(y_i, y_{1-i})$ is the probability that bargainer i wins given the signals y_0 and y_1. This describes the game. Before I describe the equilibrium, I introduce some notation.

Let $F_i(x_i \mid x_{1-i})$ be the conditional probability that bargainer i's claim is less than or equal to x_i given x_{1-i}, so, for example,

$$F_0(x_0 \mid x_1) = \frac{\displaystyle\int_0^{x_0} f(x_1, t)\, dt}{\displaystyle\int_0^{x_0^T} f(x_1, t)\, dt}.$$

Let $f_i(x_i \mid x_{1-i})$ be the associated density function, and let $\mu_i(N_i, N_{1-i})$ be the expected value of x_i given that $x_i \in N_i$ and $x_{1-i} \in N_{1-i}$. Finally, let

$$V_i(x_i; p_i, s_{1-i}) \equiv \int_0^{x_{1-i}^T} [p_i(x_i, s_{1-i}(x_{1-i})) - p_i(n, s_{1-i}(x_{1-i}))] f_{1-i}(x_{1-i} \mid x_i) \, dx_{1-i}$$

be the expected change in utility associated with revealing x_i rather than not revealing x_i (excluding costs), when the strategies of the other players are fixed.

In this setting, an equilibrium consists of strategies $s_i(x_i)$ defined on $[0, x_i^T]$ for $i = 0$ and $i = 1$ and probabilities $p_i(y_i, y_{i-1})$ defined for $(y_0, y_1) \in (n \cup [0, x_0^T]) \times (n \cup [0, x_1^T])$ such that

   E1. If $V_i(x_i; p_i, s_{1-i}) > c_i(x_i)$, then $s_i(x_i) = x_i$,
       If $V_i(x_i; p_i, s_{1-i}) < c_i(x_i)$, then $s_i(x_i) = n$.
   E2a. For all (y_0, y_1), $p_i(y_i, y_{1-i}) \geq 0$ and $p_0(y_0, y_1) + p_1(y_1, y_0) \leq 1$.
   E2b. For any y_0 and y_1, $p_0(y_0, y_1)$ and $p_1(y_1, y_0)$ maximize the expected value of
       U_J. Thus, if $N_i = \{x_i \in [0, x_i^T]: s_i(x_i) = n\}$, then
       $p_i(n, n) = 1$ if $\mu_i(N_i, N_{1-i}) > \mu_{1-i}(N_{1-i}, N_i)$,
       $p_i(x_i, n) = 1$ if $\mu_i(x_i, N_{1-i}) > \mu_{1-i}(N_{1-i}, x_i)$,
       $p_i(x_i, x_{1-i}) = 1$ if $x_i > x_{1-i}$.

These conditions guarantee that players best respond to their opponents' strategies. E1 states that a bargainer proves his claim exactly when it improves his probability of winning enough to compensate for the cost of providing evidence. E2a states that the judge's strategy choice must be a probability distribution. In particular, since the only way to obtain positive value from the item is to award it to one of the bargainers, the judge cannot be best responding if $p_0 + p_1 < 1$. The conditions in E2b follow from the form of the judge's utility function. When the judge makes his decision, he either knows the value of bargainer i's claim or knows that $x_i \in N_i$. Consequently, he maximizes his expected utility by awarding the item to the bargainer who has the greater claim (in expected value). Since the judge makes his decision after the bargainers have incurred the costs of providing evidence, his decision must be based only on the quality of evidence. In order for the strategies to constitute a Nash equilibrium, the judge's strategies must satisfy E2b only for (x_0, x_1) in the range of (s_0, s_1). I require that E2b holds for all (x_0, x_1); that is, I require the judge to best respond to all signals, not just those used in equilibrium.

The analysis in Section 16.3 applies only to equilibria in which $s_i(x_i) = x_i$ if and only if $x_i > \bar{x}_i$ so that only bargainers with good claims present evidence. Therefore, equilibrium is characterized by cutoff values

$\bar{x}_0$ and $\bar{x}_1$. If $x_i > \bar{x}_i$ for $i = 0$ and $i = 1$, then the judge awards the item to the bargainer with the greater claim. Otherwise, the judge must weigh the expected claim of one bargainer against what he knows about the other bargainer's claim.

16.3   Characterization of equilibria

This section characterizes the equilibria of the model when $c_i(x_i) \equiv c_i$ is independent of x_i for $x_i \in [0,x_i^T]$ and the social values of the bargainers are independently distributed. Thus, $F(x_0,x_1) = F_0(x_0)F_1(x_1)$, the conditional distributions are independent of private information, and the mean of bargainer i's claim does not depend on x_{1-i}. Keeping these facts in mind, I write $F_i(x_i)$ for $F_i(x_i \mid x_{1-i})$ and let

$$
\mu_i(\bar{x}_i) = \begin{cases} \displaystyle\int_0^{\bar{x}_i} \frac{x_i f_i(x_i)\, dx_i}{F_i(\bar{x}_i)} & \text{if } \bar{x}_i > 0, \\[2mm] 0 & \text{if } \bar{x}_i = 0 \end{cases}
$$

be the expected value of bargainer i's claim given that it is no greater than $\bar{x}_i$. Here, f_i is the density of F_i.

When the social values are independent, the expected gain from disclosing x_i is increasing in x_i, whereas the gain from not disclosing x_i is independent of x_i. Thus, $V_i(\,\cdot\,)$ is increasing in x_i, and when the costs of providing evidence are constant, equilibrium strategies are characterized by cutoff values $\bar{x}_0$ and $\bar{x}_1$.

The results of this section continue to hold if x_0 and x_1 are stochastically dependent provided that increasing x_i induces a leftward shift in the distribution of x_{1-i}. This guarantees that $V_i(\,\cdot\,)$ is increasing in x_i, and that if disclosing x_i wins if bargainer $1-i$ does not disclose, then disclosing $y_i > x_i$ also wins if the other bargainer does not disclose. If $c_i(x_i)$ is increasing, then the results do not change provided that $V_i(\,\cdot\,)$ increases more rapidly than $c_i(\,\cdot\,)$. These cases add little insight, but much notation, so I assume them away.

The nature of equilibrium depends on whether or not $\mu_0(\bar{x}_0) = \mu_1(\bar{x}_1)$. If $\mu_0(\bar{x}_0) = \mu_1(\bar{x}_1)$, then I call the equilibrium symmetric. If $\mu_i(\bar{x}_i) > \mu_{1-i}(\bar{x}_{1-i})$, then it is an asymmetric equilibrium with the burden of proof on bargainer $1 - i$. I discuss the case in which $\mu_0(\bar{x}_0) \neq \mu_1(\bar{x}_1)$ first. If $\mu_0(\bar{x}_0) \neq \mu_1(\bar{x}_1)$, then the burden of proof is on bargainer i if $\mu_i(\bar{x}_i) < \mu_{1-i}(\bar{x}_{1-i})$ because he must provide evidence in order to win the dispute.

Let $\hat{x}_i = F_i^{-1}(c_{1-i})$.

Theorem 1. An equilibrium characterized by cutoff values $\bar{x}_0$ and $\bar{x}_1$ with $\mu_i(\bar{x}_i) > \mu_{1-i}(\bar{x}_{1-i})$ exists if

$$F_{1-i}(\hat{x}_i) - c_i - F_{1-i}(\mu_i(\hat{x}_i)) \leqq 0. \tag{16.2}$$

If (16.2) holds, then $\bar{x}_0$ and $\bar{x}_1$ are equilibrium cutoff values if and only if $\bar{x}_{1-i} = \mu_i(\bar{x}_i)$ and $\bar{x}_i$ satisfies

$$F_{1-i}(\bar{x}_i) - c_i - F_{1-i}(\mu_i(\bar{x}_i)) = 0 \text{ and } \bar{x}_i \geqq \hat{x}_i \tag{16.3}$$

or $\bar{x}_i = x_i^T$ and

$$F_{1-i}(x_i^T) - c_i - F_{1-i}(\mu_i(x_i^T)) \leqq 0. \tag{16.4}$$

Proof. If (16.2) holds, then there exists an $\bar{x}_i$ that satisfies (16.3) whenever (16.4) does not hold. This follows from the continuity of F_{1-i}. Let $\bar{x}_i$ satisfy (16.3) if a solution exists or let $\bar{x}_i = x_i^T$ if (16.4) holds and let $\bar{x}_{1-i} = \mu_i(\bar{x}_i)$. It follows that bargainer $1 - i$ receives $-c_{1-i}$ if he reveals $x_{1-i} < \bar{x}_{1-i}$, and at least $F_i(\bar{x}_i) - c_{1-i}$ if he reveals $x_{1-i} > \bar{x}_{1-i}$, because, if $x_{1-i} > \bar{x}_{1-i} = \mu_i(\bar{x}_i)$, then bargainer $1 - i$ wins whenever bargainer i does not provide evidence. Since $\bar{x}_i \geqq \hat{x}_i$,

$$F_i(\bar{x}_i) \geqq F_i(\hat{x}_i) = c_{1-i}$$

so that, given $\bar{x}_i$, bargainer $1 - i$ optimizes by using the strategy characterized by $\bar{x}_{1-i}$. Similarly, given that bargainer $1 - i$ is proving his case if and only if $x_{1-i} > \bar{x}_{1-i}$, and therefore the judge awards the item to bargainer i if $x_{1-i} \leqq \bar{x}_{1-i}$ or if bargainer i discloses $x_i > x_{1-i}$, bargainer i receives $F_{1-i}(\bar{x}_{1-i})$ if he does not present evidence and $F_{1-i}(x_i)$ if he discloses a claim of $x_i > \bar{x}_{1-i}$. Since $\bar{x}_i > \mu_i(\bar{x}_i) = \bar{x}_{1-i}$, the definition of $\bar{x}_i$ guarantees that bargainer i optimizes by revealing $\bar{x}_i$ if and only if $x_i > \bar{x}_i$. Finally, if $\bar{x}_{1-i} \neq \mu_i(\bar{x}_i)$ or if (16.3) or (16.4) does not hold, then $\bar{x}_0$ and $\bar{x}_1$ could not be cutoff values for an equilibrium with $\mu_i(\bar{x}_i) > \mu_{1-i}(\bar{x}_{1-i})$.

Note that in an asymmetric equilibrium, it is possible for one or both bargainers to provide no evidence. If the bargainer who does not bear the burden of proof never provides evidence, then he wins if and only if the other bargainer does not prove his claim. If the bargainer who bears the burden of proof never provides evidence, then he never wins, and the other bargainer never proves his claim. This happens, for example, if $x_1^T < \mu_0(x_0^T)$, and so bargainer 1's strongest claim cannot win against bargainer 0 when bargainer 0 never proves his claim.

Corollary 1. There exists an asymmetric equilibrium. If $F_i \geqq F_{1-i}$ and $c_i \geqq c_{1-i}$, then there exists an equilibrium with $\mu_i(\bar{x}_i) > \mu_{1-i}(\bar{x}_{1-i})$.

Proof. From theorem 1, it follows that an equilibrium with $\mu_i(\bar{x}_i) > \mu_{1-i}(\bar{x}_{1-i})$ exists if

$$F_{1-i}(F_i^{-1}(c_{1-i})) \leqq c_i \quad \text{or} \quad F_i^{-1}(c_{1-i}) \leqq F_{1-i}^{-1}(c_i). \tag{16.5}$$

If (16.5) does not hold for $i = 0$, then it must hold when $i = 1$. This establishes the first part of the corollary. Since $F_i \geqq F_{1-i}$ implies that $F_{1-i}^{-1} \leqq F_i^{-1}$, the remainder of the corollary follows from (16.5).

There may be multiple equilibria in which one bargainer has the burden of proof. However, if $F_{1-i}(x) - F_{1-i}(\mu_i(x))$ is strictly increasing, then (16.2) is necessary as well as sufficient for the existence of this type of equilibrium, and if (16.2) is satisfied, then the equilibrium is unique. This results because any equilibrium with $\mu_i(\bar{x}_i) > \mu_{1-i}(\bar{x}_{1-i})$ must satisfy (16.3) or $\bar{x}_i = x_i^T$ and (16.4).

Corollary 1 establishes that there always exists an equilibrium in which the burden of proof is on one bargainer. Moreover, it suggests that the burden of proof is likely to be placed on the bargainer with lower costs or a stronger (in the sense of first-order stochastic dominance) claim. However, there are many situations in which the burden of proof can be placed on either bargainer in equilibrium. For example, let $F_i(x_i) = b_i x_i$ for $x_i \in [0, b_i^{-1}]$ for $i = 0$ and $i = 1$. From theorem 1, there exists an equilibrium with the burden of proof on bargainer $1 - i$ provided that

$$b_{1-i} c_{1-i} \leqq 2 b_i c_i.$$

Therefore, if $b_{1-i} c_{1-i} \in [b_i c_i / 2, 2 b_i c_i]$, then an equilibrium in which the burden of proof is on bargainer i exists for $i = 0$ and $i = 1$. A straightforward computation reveals that these equilibria, when they exist, are unique, and that $\bar{x}_{1-i} = \min[2 c_i b_{1-i}^{-1}, b_i^{-1}]$ and $\bar{x}_i = \bar{x}_{1-i}/2$.

In an asymmetric equilibrium, the probability that the judge is indifferent about who should receive the item is zero, and specification of his behavior in these situations does not change the nature of equilibrium. If $\mu_0(\bar{x}_0) = \mu_1(\bar{x}_1)$, then the judge is indifferent whenever neither party provides evidence. Unless $\bar{x}_0$ or $\bar{x}_1$ is equal to zero, this event occurs with positive probability. In order to support an equilibrium, the judge must randomize in a particular way when neither party provides evidence.

Suppose, for definiteness, that $\mu_0(x_0^T) \geqq \mu_1(x_1^T)$ and define $\ell(x_1)$ to satisfy $\mu_0(\ell(x_1)) \equiv \mu_1(x_1)$ for all $x_1 \in [0, x_1^T]$. It follows that if $\mu_0(\bar{x}_0) = \mu_1(\bar{x}_1)$, then $\bar{x}_0 = \ell(\bar{x}_1)$. Further, if $a_i = p_i(n, n)$ is the probability that bargainer i wins if neither bargainer presents proof, then

$$a_0 + a_1 = 1, \qquad a_0, a_1 \geqq 0, \qquad \text{and} \tag{16.6}$$

$$F_{1-i}(\max[\bar{x}_0, \bar{x}_1]) - c_i \leqq a_i F_{1-i}(\bar{x}_{1-i}) \text{ with equality if } \bar{x}_i < x_i^T. \tag{16.7}$$

The right-hand side of (16.7) is the probability that bargainer i wins if he does not provide evidence; he wins precisely when $x_{1-i} \leq \bar{x}_{1-i}$ and the judge rules in his favor, which occurs with probability a_i. The left-hand side of (16.7) is the payoff to revealing $x_i = \bar{x}_i$. If $x_i \leq \bar{x}_{1-i}$, then bargainer i wins whenever his opponent does not prove his claim, since $x_i > \mu_i(x_i)$. However, he never wins if bargainer $1-i$ presents proof. If $x_i > \bar{x}_{i-1}$, then bargainer i wins whenever $x_i > x_{1-i}$. When (16.7) holds, bargainer i best responds if he discloses x_i if and only if $x_i > \bar{x}_i$. This follows because the right-hand side of (16.7) is independent of x_i whereas the left-hand side is increasing in x_i. Furthermore, if $\mu_0(x_0^T) \geq \mu_1(x_1^T)$, then if there exists a symmetric equilibrium, there exists a symmetric equilibrium with

$$F_1(\max[\bar{x}_0, \bar{x}_1]) - c_0 = a_0 F_1(\bar{x}_1).$$

This follows directly from (16.7) if $\mu_0(x_0^T) > \mu_1(x_1^T)$ or if $\bar{x}_1 < x_1^T$. If $\mu_0(x_0^T) = \mu_1(x_1^T)$ and $\bar{x}_1 = x_1^T$, then $\bar{x}_0 = x_0^T$ and

$$F_{1-i}(\max[\bar{x}_0, \bar{x}_1]) - c_i = 1 - c_i > 0,$$

and thus (16.7) reduces to

$$1 - c_i \leq a_i. \tag{16.8}$$

But there exist a_0 and a_1 that satisfy (16.6) and (16.8) if and only if

$$1 \leq c_0 + c_1,$$

and in this case $a_0 = 1 - c_0 \leq c_1 < 1$ and $a_1 = c_0 \geq 1 - c_1$ also satisfy (16.6) and (16.8). Hence, symmetric equilibria exist if and only if there exist $a_1 \in [0,1]$ and $\bar{x}_1 \in [0, x_1^T]$ such that

$$F_1(\max[\ell(\bar{x}_1), \bar{x}_1]) - c_0 = (1 - a_1)F_1(\bar{x}_1) \qquad \text{and} \tag{16.9}$$

$$F_0(\max[\ell(\bar{x}_1), \bar{x}_1]) - c_1 \leq a_1 F_0(\ell(\bar{x}_1)) \text{ with equality if } \bar{x}_1 < x_1^T. \tag{16.10}$$

In order to characterize the equilibrium, I must describe the cutoff levels for the bargainers. If bargainer 1 proves his claim whenever it exceeds x, then in a symmetric equilibrium the other bargainer presents proof whenever his claim exceeds $\ell(x)$. If both bargainers present evidence with positive probability, then the cutoff value x must satisfy

$$F_i(\max[\ell(x), x]) - c_{1-i} \geq 0$$

for $i = 0$ and $i = 1$.

Let

$$X = \{x \in [0, x_1^T]: \min_{i=0,1}[F_i(\max[\ell(x), x]) - c_{1-i}] \geq 0\}$$

and let

$$\tilde{x} = \begin{cases} \inf X & \text{if } X \neq \phi, \\ x_1^T & \text{if } X = \phi. \end{cases}$$

If $\bar{x}_1 \in X$ and $\bar{x}_0 = \ell(\bar{x}_1)$, then bargainer i receives positive expected utility if he reveals $x_i \geq \bar{x}_i$. Therefore, in any symmetric equilibrium, bargainer 1's cutoff value must be at least $\tilde{x}$. From (16.9) and (16.10), it follows that if $\bar{x}_1$ is an equilibrium cutoff value for bargainer 1, then

$$\frac{F_1(\max[\ell(\bar{x}_1),\bar{x}_1]) - c_0}{F_1(\bar{x}_1)} + \frac{F_0(\max[\ell(\bar{x}_1),\bar{x}_1]) - c_1}{F_0(\ell(\bar{x}_1))} \leq 1. \quad (16.11)$$

The next theorem states that if (16.11) is satisfied for $\tilde{x}$, then a symmetric equilibrium exists. To demonstrate this, it is convenient to define the function G by

$$G(x_1) \equiv F_0(\max[\ell(x_1),x_1]) - c_1 -$$
$$\frac{[F_1(x_1) - F_1(\max[\ell(x_1),x_1]) + c_0]F_0(\ell(x_1))}{F_1(x_1)}.$$

Theorem 2.   If $G(\tilde{x}) \leq 0$, then there exists a symmetric equilibrium. If a symmetric equilibrium exists, then the cutoff values $\bar{x}_0$ and $\bar{x}_1$ satisfy $\bar{x}_0 = \ell(\bar{x}_1)$, and either $G(\bar{x}_1) = 0$ with $\bar{x}_1 \geq \tilde{x}$ or $G(\bar{x}_1) \leq 0$ and $\bar{x}_1 = x_1^T$.

Proof.   If $\tilde{x} = x_1^T$, then there exists an equilibrium with $\bar{x}_0 = \ell(x_1^T)$, $\bar{x}_1 = x_1^T$, $a_0 = 1 - c_1$, and $a_1 = c_1$. This follows since, in this case, (16.9) becomes $1 - c_0 = 1 - a_1$ and (16.10) is always satisfied because $\tilde{x} = x_1^T$ implies that $F_0(\max[\ell(x_1^T),x_1^T]) - c_1 \leq 0$. If $\tilde{x} > x_1$, then the left-hand side of (16.9) or (16.10) is negative for $\bar{x}_1 = x_1$, and so no symmetric equilibrium exists with this cutoff value. Thus, if $\tilde{x} < x_1^T$, then a symmetric equilibrium exists if and only if (16.9) and (16.10) can be satisfied for some $\bar{x}_1 \in [\tilde{x},x_1^T]$. Since the left-hand sides of (16.9) and (16.10) are non-negative for $\bar{x}_1 \in [\tilde{x},x_1^T]$, any a_1 that satisfies (16.9) and (16.10) for $\bar{x}_1 \in [\tilde{x},x_1^T]$ must also satisfy $a_1 \in [0,1]$. It follows that a symmetric equilibrium exists with

$$a_1 = \frac{F_1(\bar{x}_1) - F_1(\max[\ell(\bar{x}_1),\bar{x}_1]) + c_0}{F_1(\bar{x}_1)} \quad (16.12)$$

and $\bar{x}_0 = \ell(\bar{x}_1)$ provided that

$$G(\bar{x}_1) = 0 \quad \text{and} \quad \bar{x}_1 \geq \tilde{x}$$

or

$$G(\bar{x}_1) \leq 0 \quad \text{and} \quad \bar{x}_1 = x_1^T.$$

This results because (16.12) comes from solving (16.9) for a_1 and G is the difference between the left- and right-hand sides of (16.10), when the expression for a_1 in (16.12) is used. By the continuity of G, a sufficient condition for an equilibrium of this type to exist is $G(\check{x}) \leq 0$.

Symmetric equilibria need not exist. For example, if $c_0 > c_1 = 0$ and $\ell(x_1) < x_1$ for $x_1 > 0$, then bargainer 1 always wants to prove his claim, and so $\bar{x}_1 = 0$. But if $\bar{x}_1 = 0$, then $\bar{x}_0 = 0$ in a symmetric equilibrium. Hence, (16.9) is not satisfied and therefore this type of equilibrium cannot exist.

Corollary 2. If $\mu_0(x_0^T) \geq \mu_1(x_1^T)$, then there exists a symmetric equilibrium if $F_1(x) - c_0 \geq F_0(x) - c_1$.

Proof. If $F_1(x) - c_0 \geq F_0(x) - c_1$, then $F_0(\check{x}) - c_1 = 0$, and hence $G(\check{x}) \leq 0$. The corollary now follows from theorem 2.

As with asymmetric equilibria, there may be multiple symmetric equilibria. However, if G is strictly increasing, then the condition $G(\check{x}) \leq 0$ is necessary and sufficient for the existence of a symmetric equilibrium and, if it exists, then the cutoff values are unique. The judge's strategy when neither bargainer proves his claim is uniquely determined by (16.9) and (16.10) when $\bar{x}_1 < x_1^T$. Otherwise, a range of values for a_1 may support the equilibrium.

The condition in corollary 2 is sufficient, but not necessary, for the existence of a symmetric equilibrium. A straightforward argument shows that if $F_i(x_i) = b_i x_i$ for $x_i \in [0, b_i^{-1}]$, then there exists a unique symmetric equilibrium. If $b_1 \geq b_0$, then the equilibrium cutoff values satisfy

$$\bar{x}_0 = \bar{x}_1 = \min[(b_0 c_0 + b_1 c_1)/(b_0 b_1)^{-1}, b_1^{-1}].$$

Therefore, for this example, there are three equilibria for a broad range of parameter values.

The analysis of this section suggests that there are frequently multiple equilibria in this model. The equilibria can be classified according to what happens when neither bargainer proves his claim. There always exists an equilibrium in which one bargainer can win only if he proves his claim. However, there may also exist equilibria in which the other bargainer has the burden of proof, and in which both bargainers have a positive probability of winning if they do not present proof. The example with $F_i(x_i) =$

$b_i x_i$ shows that all three types of equilibria may exist simultaneously.

The multiple-equilibrium problem suggests that there is a role for the judge in selecting equilibria. This role may be viewed in two ways. First, by custom or tradition, players may learn to coordinate on a particular equilibrium if it has attractive features. Second, the judge (or someone else) may have a more tangible role in designing the rules of evidence. For example, the formal game may be modified to include a move by the judge that is made before the bargainers learn their x_i. In this move, the judge commits himself to a future strategy when neither bargainer presents evidence. Assuming that commitment only to a pure strategy is possible, this game has no more equilibria than the game analyzed in this section. Moreover, if the judge prefers one of the equilibria in which the burden of proof lies on a particular bargainer, then he is able to select it. To see this, note that if the judge has committed himself to $p_i(n,n) = 0$ for $i = 0$ or $i = 1$, then it is a best response for the bargainers to play according to the equilibrium selected in the continuation and, if they do this, then the judge actually prefers to use the strategy he is committed to use. Therefore, the judge is able to select an equilibrium with the burden of proof on a particular bargainer (if that equilibrium is unique). Note also that there can be no equilibrium to the modified game with the judge committing to $p_i(n,n) = 0$ unless an equilibrium in which bargainer i bears the burden of proof exists. Therefore, at least in those situations where there is no more than one equilibrium of each type, the judge can select explicitly the asymmetric equilibrium he prefers by committing to a rule of evidence. If the judge does not commit to a rule of evidence, then there is a suggestion that the symmetric equilibrium is salient, because the judge could have picked either of the other equilibria if he wished. This argument might have sufficient force to help the bargainers coordinate on the symmetric equilibrium.

If the judge is able to make a selection from the equilibrium set, then the welfare properties of the equilibria should be compared. This is the subject of the next section.

16.4 Welfare comparisons

In this section, I compare the costs and benefits of the asymmetric equilibria characterized in Section 16.3. Although I have no general results comparing the costs and benefits of asymmetric equilibria to those of symmetric equilibria, I discuss an example in which these costs and benefits are comparable at the end of the section. The analysis suggests that an asymmetric equilibrium with the burden of proof on the bargainer with the stronger claim or lower costs minimizes the expected cost of providing evidence whereas the most efficient allocations are obtained when the burden of proof is placed on the higher-cost bargainer.

If cutoff values $\bar{x}_0$ and $\bar{x}_1$ determine an equilibrium, then the expected cost of providing evidence is

$$c_0(1 - F_0(\bar{x}_0)) + c_1(1 - F_1(\bar{x}_1)).$$

The next theorem states that placing the burden of proof on the bargainer with the lower costs minimizes the costs of providing evidence among asymmetric equilibria.

Theorem 3. If $c_1 \leqq c_0$, and for all $x \in [0, x_0^T]$, $F_1(x) \leqq F_0(x)$ and $F_1(x) - F_1(\mu_0(x)) \leqq F_0(x) - F_0(\mu_1(x))$, and there exists an equilibrium with cutoff values $\bar{x}_0$ and $\bar{x}_1$ that places the burden of proof on bargainer 0, then there exists an equilibrium with cutoff values $\bar{y}_0$ and $\bar{y}_1$ that places the burden of proof on bargainer 1 in which

$$c_0(1 - F_0(\bar{x}_0)) + c_1(1 - F_1(\bar{x}_1))$$
$$\geqq c_0(1 - F_0(\bar{y}_0)) + c_1(1 - F_1(\bar{y}_1)). \quad \textbf{(16.13)}$$

Proof. By theorem 1, $\bar{x}_1 \geqq \hat{x}_1$ and

$$F_0(\bar{x}_1) - F_0(\mu_1(\bar{x}_1)) \leqq c_1 \text{ with equality if } \bar{x}_1 < x_1^T. \quad \textbf{(16.14)}$$

Also, $F_1(x) \leqq F_0(x)$ and $c_1 \leqq c_0$ imply that $\hat{x}_1 = F_1^{-1}(c_0) \geqq F_0^{-1}(c_1) \geqq \hat{x}_0$. Therefore, $F_1(\bar{x}_1) - F_1(\mu_0(\bar{x}_1)) \leqq F_0(\bar{x}_1) - F_0(\mu_1(\bar{x}_1)) \leqq c_1 \leqq c_0$ implies that there exists a $\bar{y}_0 \geqq \bar{x}_1$ such that

$$F_1(\bar{y}_0) - F_1(\mu_0(\bar{y}_0)) \leqq c_0 \text{ with equality if } \bar{y}_0 < x_0^T. \quad \textbf{(16.5)}$$

Thus, if $\bar{y}_1 = \mu_0(\bar{y}_0)$, then $\bar{y}_0$ and $\bar{y}_1$ are cutoff values for an asymmetric equilibrium with the burden of proof on bargainer 1. If $\bar{x}_1 < x_1^T$, then algebraic manipulation using (16.14) and (16.15) shows that (16.13) holds whenever

$$(F_1(\bar{y}_0) - F_1(\bar{x}_1))(F_0(\bar{x}_1) - F_0(\bar{x}_0)) + (F_0(\bar{y}_0)$$
$$- F_0(\bar{x}_1))(F_1(\bar{y}_0) - F_1(\bar{y}_1)) \geqq 0. \quad \textbf{(16.16)}$$

However, (16.16) holds because $\bar{y}_0 \geqq \bar{x}_1$, $\bar{x}_1 \geqq \bar{x}_0$, and $\bar{y}_0 \geqq \bar{y}_1$, and so all of the factors on the left-hand side of (16.16) are nonnegative. If $\bar{x}_1 = x_1^T$, then (16.13) holds whenever

$$c_0(F_0(\bar{y}_0) - F_0(\bar{x}_0)) \geqq c_1(F_1(\bar{x}_1) - F_1(\bar{y}_1)).$$

The theorem follows because

$$c_0(F_0(\bar{y}_0) - F_0(\bar{x}_0)) = c_0[F_0(\bar{y}_0) - F_0(\mu_1(\bar{x}_1))]$$
$$\geq c_0[F_0(\bar{y}_0) - F_0(\mu_1(\bar{y}_0))]$$
$$\geq c_1[F_0(\bar{y}_0) - F_0(\mu_1(\bar{y}_0))]$$
$$\geq c_1[F_1(\bar{y}_0) - F_1(\mu_0(\bar{y}_0))]$$
$$\geq c_1[F_1(\bar{y}_0) - F_1(\bar{y}_1)]$$
$$\geq c_1[F_1(\bar{x}_1) - F_1(\bar{y}_1)],$$

where the steps follow because $\bar{x}_0 = \mu_1(\bar{x}_1), \bar{y}_0 \geq \bar{x}_1$, $c_0 \geq c_1$, $F_0(x) - F_0(\mu_1(x)) \geq F_1(x) - F_1(\mu_0(x))$, $\bar{y}_1 = \mu_0(\bar{y}_0)$, and $\bar{y}_0 \geq \bar{x}_1$.

The assumption that

$$F_1(x) - F_1(\mu_0(x)) \leq F_0(x) - F_0(\mu_1(x))$$

is satisfied whenever bargainer 1 has a stronger claim than bargainer 0 in the following sense. I will say that bargainer 1 has a stronger claim than bargainer 0 if there exists a probability distribution function H with $H(x_0^T) = 0$ and $\lambda \in (0,1)$ such that

$$F_1(x) = \lambda F_0(x) + (1 - \lambda)H(x).$$

If bargainer 1 has a stronger claim than bargainer 0, then for $x \in [0, x_0^T]$,

$$F_1(x) - F_1(\mu_0(x)) = \lambda[F_0(x) - F_0(\mu_1(x))]$$

and

$$F_1(x) = \lambda F_0(x),$$

so that the restrictions on F_0 and F_1 in theorem 3 are satisfied. If F_1 takes this form, bargainer 1's claim is drawn from the same distribution as bargainer 0's claim with probability λ; otherwise, it is strictly larger. Thus, the conditions in theorem 3 combine to state that in order to minimize the costs of providing evidence, the judge should place the burden of proof on the bargainer (if one exists) who is able to prove his claim for less and who has the stronger claim.

However, there is a tension between reducing the costs of providing evidence and obtaining information needed to make better judgments. The next theorem gives conditions under which the expected social value of the claim is greater in the equilibrium in which the burden of proof is placed on the higher-cost bargainer.

Theorem 4. If $c_1 \leq c_0$, bargainer 1 has a stronger claim than bargainer 0, and there is an equilibrium that places the burden of proof on bargainer 0, then there is an equilibrium that places the burden of proof on bargainer 1 that yields a lower expected social value.

Proof. If $\bar{y}_0$ and $\bar{y}_1$ are the cutoff values for an equilibrium that places the burden of proof on bargainer 1, then the expected social value is

$$\int\limits_0^{x_1^T}\int\limits_0^{x_0^T} x_0 f_0(x_0)f_1(x_1)\,dx_0\,dx_1 + \int\limits_{\substack{\bar{y}_1\\\bar{y}_0}}^{x_1^T}\int\limits_{\substack{0\\\bar{y}_0}}^{x_1} (x_1 - x_0)f_0(x_0)f_1(x_1)\,dx_0\,dx_1$$

$$+ \int\limits_{\bar{y}_1}^{x_1^T}\int\limits_{x_1}^{x_1} (x_1 - x_0)f_0(x_0)f_1(x_1)\,dx_0\,dx_1. \tag{16.17}$$

Expression (16.17) reflects the fact that bargainer 0 wins unless $x_1 \geqq \bar{y}_0$ and $x_1 \geqq x_0$ (so that bargainer 1 presents proof and his claim is better than his opponent's claim) or $\bar{y}_0 \geqq x_1 \geqq \bar{y}_1$ and $\bar{y}_0 \geqq x_0 \geqq x_1$ (so that bargainer 1 presents proof and bargainer 0 does not prove a claim that would have won). Similarly, the expected social value of an equilibrium with the burden of proof on bargainer 0 and cutoff values $\bar{x}_0$ and $\bar{x}_1$ is

$$\int\limits_0^{x_0^T}\int\limits_0^{x_1^T} x_1 f_1(x_1)f_0(x_0)\,dx_1\,dx_0 + \int\limits_{\substack{\bar{x}_0\\\bar{x}_1}}^{x_0^T}\int\limits_{\substack{0\\\bar{x}_1}}^{x_0} (x_0 - x_1)f_1(x_1)f_0(x_0)\,dx_1\,dx_0$$

$$+ \int\limits_{\bar{x}_0}^{x_1} \int\limits_{x_0}^{x_1} (x_0 - x_1)f_1(x_1)f_0(x_0)\,dx_1\,dx_0. \tag{16.18}$$

However,

$$\int\limits_{\bar{y}_1}^{x_1^T}\int\limits_0^{x_1} (x_1 - x_0)f_0(x_0)f_1(x_1)\,dx_0\,dx_1$$

$$= \int\limits_{\bar{y}_1}^{x_1^T} F_0(x_1)(x_1 - \mu_0(x_1))f_1(x_1)\,dx_1$$

$$= \int\limits_{\bar{y}_1}^{x_0^T} F_0(x_1)(x_1 - \mu_0(x_1))f_1(x_1)\,dx_1 + \int\limits_{x_0^T}^{x_1^T} (x_1 - \mu_0(x_0^T))f_1(x_1)\,dx_1$$

$$\tag{16.19}$$

$$
= \int_{\bar{y}_1}^{x_0^T} F_0(x_1)(x_1 - \mu_0(x_1))f_1(x_1)\, dx_1
$$

$$
+ \mu_1(x_1^T) - \mu_1(x_0^T)F_1(x_0^T) - \mu_0(x_0^T)(1 - F_1(x_0^T))
$$

$$
= \int_{\bar{y}_1}^{x_1^T}\int_0^{x_1} (x_1 - x_0)f_0(x_0)f_1(x_1)\, dx_0\, dx_1 + \mu_1(x_0^T),
$$

where the equations follow, respectively, from the definition of μ_0; the definition of x_1^T; the definition of μ_1; and the definition of μ_0 and the fact that $\mu_1(x_0^T) = \mu_0(x_0^T)$, which follows because bargainer 1 has a stronger claim than bargainer 0. Substituting (16.19) into (16.17) and comparing the result with (16.18) reveals that if $\bar{x}_0$ and $\bar{x}_1$ are cutoff values for an equilibrium that puts the burden of proof on bargainer i, then the expected social value is

$$
\mu_1(x_1^T) + \int_{\bar{x}_i}^{x_1^T} F_{1-i}(x_i)(x_i - \mu_{1-i}(x_i))f_i(x_i)\, dx_i
$$

$$
\tag{16.20}
$$

$$
+ \int_{\bar{x}_i}^{\bar{x}_{1-i}}\int_{x_i}^{\bar{x}_{1-i}} (x_i - x_{1-i})f_{1-i}(x_{1-i})f_1(x_i)\, dx_{1-i}\, dx_i.
$$

Because bargainer 1 has a stronger claim than bargainer 0, (16.20) depends only on the cutoff values, not on which bargainer bears the burden of proof. Moreover, (16.20) is decreasing in $\bar{x}_{1-i}$. To show this, we differentiate (16.20) to obtain

$$
\int_{\bar{x}_i}^{\bar{x}_{1-i}} (x_i - \bar{x}_{1-i})f_{1-i}(\bar{x}_{1-i})f_i(x_i)\, dx_i
$$

$$
- \frac{d\bar{x}_i}{d\bar{x}_{1-i}}\Big[F_{1-i}(\bar{x}_i)(\bar{x}_i - \mu_{1-i}(\bar{x}_i))f_i(\bar{x}_i)
$$

$$
\tag{16.21}
$$

$$
+ \int_{\bar{x}_i}^{\bar{x}_{1-i}} (\bar{x}_i - \bar{x}_{1-i})f_{1-i}(x_{1-i})f_i(\bar{x}_i)\, dx_{1-i}\Big].
$$

The first term in (16.21) is negative, and the bracketed term reduces to

$$-F_{1-i}(\bar{x}_{1-i})(\bar{x}_i - \mu_{1-i}(\bar{x}_{1-i}))f_i(\bar{x}_i) = 0$$

since $\bar{x}_i = \mu_{1-i}(\bar{x}_{1-i})$.

I have shown that the expected social value is decreasing in the cutoff value of the bargainer who does not bear the burden of proof. Therefore, to prove the theorem, I need only show that if $\bar{x}_0$ is a cutoff value in an equilibrium that places the burden of proof on bargainer 0, then there is a cutoff value $\bar{y}_0 \geq \bar{x}_1$ in an equilibrium that places the burden of proof on bargainer 1. However, the assumptions of the theorem guarantee that for $x \in [0, x_0^T]$,

$$F_1(x) - c_0 - F_1(\mu_0(x)) \leq F_0(x) - c_1 - F_0(\mu_1(x)).$$

Thus, the theorem follows from theorem 1.

As a special case, theorem 4 implies that if there exists a unique asymmetric equilibrium that places the burden of proof on the lower-cost (or stronger-claim) bargainer, then it generates less social value than any asymmetric equilibrium that places the burden of proof on the other bargainer.

Theorems 3 and 4 indicate that the two kinds of asymmetric equilibrium have different advantages. A bargainer who must present evidence in order to win proves his claim relatively more often than a bargainer who can win with positive probability even if he does not provide evidence. Thus, when the burden of proof is on the lower-cost bargainer, less is spent on providing evidence. Also, asymmetric equilibria are characterized by the cutoff value of the bargainer who does not bear the burden of proof. The better this bargainer's claim or the lower his costs, the more often he will present evidence. Thus, less evidence is provided when the bargainer with the stronger claim bears the burden of proof. This is why the cost of providing evidence falls if the stronger bargainer must prove his claim to win.

Theorem 4 demonstrates that placing the burden of proof on the higher-cost bargainer tends to increase social value. The proof really does two things. First, I show that higher equilibrium cutoff values reduce the expected social value regardless of who has the burden of proof. This follows because the more evidence provided, the more accurate the judge's decisions. However, in order to show that the result holds independently of which bargainer has the burden of proof, I need to assume that the distribution functions are related. (That one bargainer has a stronger claim is sufficient.) Second, I show that more evidence is provided when the weaker bargainer bears the burden of proof.

Theorems 3 and 4 suggest that the judge's most preferred outcome cannot be identified without knowing more about the tradeoff between costs and benefits. Also, I have been unable to obtain general results comparing asymmetric equilibria to symmetric equilibria. To give an idea about what the tradeoffs look like, I conclude this section by discussing an example.

Let $F_i(x_i) \equiv b_i x_i$ on $[0, b_i^{-1}]$ and let $b_0 \geq b_1$. If $2b_i c_i < b_{1-i}$, and $b_{1-i} c_{1-i} \in [b_i c_i / 2, 2b_i c_i]$ for $i = 0$ and $i = 1$, then there exist three equilibria: a symmetric equilibrium and two assymmetric equilibria, one where bargainer 0 bears the burden of proof and the other where bargainer 1 bears the burden of proof. Table 16.1 summarizes the properties of the equilibria.

Several comparative statics results follow easily. In all of the equilibria, bargainer i's payoff improves if his claim improves (b_i decreases) or if his opponent's claim worsens. Similarly, increasing c_i harms bargainer i and helps bargainer $1 - i$ in the symmetric equilibrium. This result holds in the asymmetric equilibria as well, with one exception. When the burden of proof is on bargainer i, changing c_i does not affect bargainer $1 - i$, and increasing c_{1-i} may make bargainer $1 - i$ better off – by reducing the probability that he must prove his claim – if c_{1-i} is large. Increasing c_i increases the expected costs when the burden of proof is on bargainer i, but may reduce costs if the burden of proof is on bargainer $1 - i$. Also, increasing c_i may reduce the expected costs in the symmetric equilibrium. This results because the change reduces the probability that evidence is provided in equilibrium as well as increases the cost of providing that evidence. The first effect dominates when costs are high. If the claim of the bargainer who bears the burden of proof improves, then bargainers disclose evidence less frequently, and so the costs decrease. If the other bargainer's claim improves, then he proves his claim more often and costs rise. The same arguments explain why social value (measured as the fraction of the maximum available value obtained in equilibrium) rises when b_0 rises or when b_1 falls if bargainer 0 has the burden of proof. The effects of changes in b_0 and b_1 on the social value and the expected cost in the symmetric equilibrium are ambiguous. However, if $c_0 \geq c_1$, so that bargainer 1 has a stronger claim and lower costs, then increasing b_1 or reducing b_0 (i.e., making the distributions more similar) increases welfare and costs by increasing the probability of disclosure. In all cases, increasing costs reduce the fraction of social value obtained in equilibrium (although changing c_i has no effect on social value when bargainer i bears the burden of proof).

A comparison of the equilibrium outcomes verifies theorems 3 and 4 for the example. Also, it shows that the asymmetric-equilibrium values of

Table 16.1. Description of equilibria when $F_i(x_i) \equiv b_i x_i$ for $x_i \in [0, b_i^{-1}]$

Equilibrium	Cutoff values		Expected social value	Expected utility to bargainer 0	Expected utility to bargainer 1
	$\bar{x}_0$	$\bar{x}_1$			
Symmetric	$\dfrac{b_0 c_0 + b_1 c_1}{b_0 b_1}$	$\dfrac{b_0 c_0 + b_1 c_1}{b_0 b_1}$	$\dfrac{M - b_0 b_1 \bar{x}_0^3}{6}$	$\dfrac{b_0^{-1} b_1 - 2c_0 + b_0 b_1 \bar{x}_0^2}{2}$	$\dfrac{2 - b_0^{-1} b_1 - 2c_1 + b_0 b_1 \bar{x}_1^2}{2}$
Asymmetric, burden on 0	$\dfrac{c_1}{b_0}$	$\dfrac{2c_1}{b_0}$	$\dfrac{M - b_0 b_1 \bar{x}_0^2 \bar{x}_1}{6}$	$\dfrac{b_0^{-1} b_1}{2 - c_0 + c_0 c_1}$	$\dfrac{2 - b_0^{-1} b_1 - 2c_1 + b_0 b_1 \bar{x}_1^2}{2}$
Asymmetric, burden on 1	$\dfrac{2c_0}{b_1}$	$\dfrac{c_0}{b_1}$	$\dfrac{M - b_0 b_1 \bar{x}_0 \bar{x}_1^2}{6}$	$\dfrac{b_0^{-1} b_1 - 2c_0 + b_0 b_1 \bar{x}_0^2}{2}$	$\dfrac{1 - b_0^{-1} b_1}{2 - c_1 + c_0 c_1}$

In all cases, expected costs are $c_0(1 - b_0 \bar{x}_0) + c_1(1 - b_1 \bar{x}_1)$, and $M = (b_1^2 + 3b_0^2)/(6b_0^2 b_1)$ is the maximum social value.

costs and social value are between those of the asymmetric equilibria. Simple computations show that the symmetric equilibrium never maximizes social value nor minimizes costs over the three equilibria. Finally, in the example, each bargainer prefers that the burden of proof fall on his opponent. This suggests that it might be in the interest of a bargainer to increase his cost, if by doing so he can shift the burden of proof to his opponent.

16.5   Alternative notions of proof

The basic model assumes that proof can be presented conclusively by paying a fee. Other formulations are possible. This section describes two and discusses their implications.

Proof allows the judge to have more precise information about what the bargainers know. The greater the effort the bargainers make in preparing and presenting their claim, the more accurate the judge's view of the claim's true value. Assume that the bargainers observe their claim; for concreteness take this to be a real number m. Proof could be identified with selecting an effort level v. The quality of the claim and the effort level combine to give the judge a "reading" of the bargainer's true claim; take this reading to be generated by a normally distributed random variable with mean m and variance v^2. Here, it is natural to assume that a bargainer's utility is decreasing in v so that providing more accurate information is more costly. If higher readings suggest stronger claims, then a bargainer will try to maximize the probability that the reading he generates exceeds that of his opponent. In this framework, bargainers with poor claims gain nothing from providing evidence. Their main hope of winning comes from the judge misinterpreting vague evidence in their favor. Increasing the effort spent on providing proof reduces this possibility. On the other hand, bargainers with strong positions may be able to establish their claims with little effort. Thus, in this setting, the most effort may be made by bargainers with evidence of intermediate quality who have the most to gain from minimizing the probability and magnitude of a misinterpretation.

Another variation is to let effort augment the true information to form the signal on which the judge bases his settlement. If the effort needed to induce a certain signal decreases with a bargainer's social value, then a standard signaling model results. In such a model, there will typically be an equilibrium in which the judge can invert the bargainers' signals to learn their true information. In addition, there will be other equilibria in which discrete threshold levels of evidence are needed to achieve certain probabilities of winning. These equilibria may be preferred by the judge if he is willing to trade off reduced signaling costs against increased probabilities of misallocation.

16.6   Conclusion and extensions

In this chapter, I have discussed the role that different rules of evidence have on disclosure and on the quality of settlements. Even in symmetric situations, it is often in the interest of the judge to assign the burden of proof to one of the bargaining parties.

The essential features of the model are the existence of a third party in charge of setting disputes and the restrictions that bargainers cannot misrepresent their information. In this model, the judge must be uncertain about the bargainers' evidence. Otherwise, he could make the correct decision without hearing the arguments of bargainers. In addition, there must be restrictions on how much bargainers can misrepresent their claims. If bargainers could make any statement without cost, then both would make only the most extravagant claims and these claims would be meaningless.

The nature of proof and evidence can be modified. I suggested two possible variations in Section 16.5. In the first, providing evidence makes a bargainer's true information clearer to the judge. In the second, the amount of evidence presented combines with the quality of the claim to make a claim convincing. Both of these modifications, and possibly others in which the decision to prove is not binary, have a feature that is qualitatively different from the basic model: Bargainers with better claims do not necessarily provide more evidence since their claim may be good enough to be convincing without the proof. Finally, if the judge was uncertain about what information the bargainers have or about their costs of proving their claims, then I could better characterize which pieces of evidence are omitted and which are emphasized.

The extensive form of the game could be changed. There are two notable possibilities. My model assumes that the judge cannot commit himself to a decision rule. Thus, he must award the item to the bargainer who has the better claim. However, if the judge could commit himself to a decision rule, then he might increase his utility by making allocations that are not optimal ex post. For example, to reduce the costs of providing evidence, the judge might bias his decisions in favor of a bargainer who does not attempt to prove his claim.

The other possibility is to allow bargainers to present evidence in sequence. In such a model, the judge can decide which bargainer must present evidence first in order to have an opportunity to win. The bargainer who does not bear the burden of going forward need pay the cost of presenting evidence only if the other bargainer goes forward. It is not difficult to show that the judge can induce any cutoff values that are in equilibrium for the simultaneous-disclosure model by picking the bargainer who must go forward first and selecting a probability that the other bargainer will be required to prove his claim to win even if the first bargainer does not come forward. These equilibria will have lower expected costs of providing evidence, since typically no more than one bargainer will provide evidence. For this reason, they are attractive. On the other hand, if preparing a case takes time and a bargainer must respond to the other bargainer's evidence immediately, then the simultaneous-disclosure model of this chapter seems to be appropriate.

In my model, no settlement can be made without the judge. This assumes implicitly that neither party has property rights to the disputed object. Taking this as given, third-party settlements arise naturally, provided that both bargainers expect to make a positive surplus from the judgment. On the other hand, the question of who should bear the burden of proof would have a different answer if one side has rights to the disputed object, unless the judge decides otherwise or the parties are able to make a settlement without the judge. An appropriate modification of the model would answer questions about which cases should be brought before the judge and who should bear the burden of proof.

NOTES

1. I ignore mixed strategies for the bargainers. Because I assume that x_0 and x_1 are continuously distributed, mixed strategies for the bargainers add nothing essential to the analysis. I allow the judge to use a mixed strategy.

REFERENCES

Farrell, J., and J. Sobel (1983): Voluntary Disclosure of Information. Draft.
Grossman, S. (1981): The Information Role of Warranties and Private Disclosure about Product Quality. *Journal of Law and Economics,* 24, 461–83.
Milgrom, P. R. (1981): Good News and Bad News: Representation Theorems and Applications. *Bell Journal of Economics,* 12, 380–91.
Ordover, J. A., and A. Rubinstein (1983): *On Bargaining, Settling, and Litigating: A Problem in Multistage Games with Imperfect Information.* Technical Report 83-07, New York University, April.
P'ng, I. P. L. (1983): Strategic Behavior in Suit, Settlement, and Trial. *Bell Journal of Economics,* 14, 539–50.
Samuelson, W. (1983): *Negotiation vs. Litigation.* Discussion Paper, Boston University School of Management, April.

CHAPTER 17

The role of arbitration and the theory
of incentives

Vincent P. Crawford
UNIVERSITY OF CALIFORNIA AT SAN DIEGO

17.1   Introduction

Recent years have seen the parallel but largely independent development
of two literatures with closely related concerns: the theory of arbitration
and the theory of incentives. Most of the theoretical arbitration literature
seeks to predict and compare the allocative effects of the simple compulsory-arbitration schemes frequently used to resolve public-sector bargaining disputes in practice. Crawford (1981) provides a general introduction and a brief survey of this area. Sample references include Donn
(1977), Crawford (1979, 1982*a*, 1982*b*), Farber and Katz (1979), Farber
(1980), Bloom (1981), Hirsch and Donn (1982), Brams and Merrill
(1983), and Donn and Hirsch (1983). These papers draw on, and give
some references to, the large empirical and institutional arbitration literature. The incentives literature concerned directly with bargaining focuses
instead on the theoretical limits of mechanism design in environments
with asymmetric information. The papers by Kalai and Rosenthal (1978),
Rosenthal (1978), Myerson (1979, 1983), Holmström (1982), Holm-

This paper was written in part while I enjoyed the hospitality of the Department of
Economics at Harvard University. My understanding of this subject has been
enhanced greatly by years of argument with Clifford Donn, whose work led to my
interest in arbitration. Special thanks are due him and Theodore Groves, both of
whom carefully read the manuscript and provided valuable comments. I am also
grateful for helpful conversations with David Bloom, Bengt Holmström, William
Samuelson, Joel Sobel, and Richard Zeckhauser; for the comments of participants in seminar presentations at Harvard and Northwestern universities; to
Merton Miller for calling my attention to the work of Carliss Baldwin; and to the
NSF for financial support provided through grants SES-81-06912 to Harvard and
SES-82-04038 to the University of California, San Diego. Finally, only reading
Schelling's *The Strategy of Conflict* (1963) can make clear the extent of my
intellectual debt to his thoughts on the role of arbitration.

363

ström and Myerson (1983), Myerson and Satterthwaite (1983), Samuelson (1984), and Crawford (1985), are a representative sample.

Although both literatures have the same goal – achieving better bargaining outcomes – this difference in focus, together with differences in style and analytical technique, has almost completely shut down communication between them, with discernible adverse effects on both. On the one hand, a large body of ad hoc, application-oriented analysis and measurement has developed in arbitration without recourse to carefully specified and worked-out models. This precludes a serious analysis of the strategic interactions that necessarily influence how bargainers respond to arbitration and, in particular, rules out a credible discussion of the incentive problems caused by asymmetric information, which is probably essential even to a complete understanding of the purpose of arbitration.

The dangers of overspecialization are most strikingly illustrated by the history of Carl Stevens's (1966) proposal to replace, in the arbitration statutes that frequently govern public-sector bargaining, a widely used scheme that I shall call "conventional" compulsory arbitration, with what is now called "final-offer" arbitration. Stevens's analysis is persuasive, respects existing institutions, and is sensitive to the goals of policy makers. However, it contains very little that is both correct in theory and germane to the question of which scheme is likely to perform better, even when all that is sought is a clear statement of the role of arbitration and how it is served by the two schemes. (Crawford (1979) provides background and discusses this point in detail; see also Crawford (1981).) Despite this, and some other serious drawbacks, Stevens's suggestion has been adopted in a large minority of states, and in some settings outside the public sector (e.g., professional baseball) as well. It has, in other words, enjoyed an influence on policy much greater than that of most microeconomic policy proposals based on sound analysis.

Even when based on incompletely specified and incorrectly analyzed models, arbitration studies that are sensitive to institutional detail and the practical concerns of policy makers guide empirical work and influence policy, because they have little competition. A reorientation of mechanism-design theory to provide this competition would yield obvious direct benefits. It may be less clear that it would also help to resolve open questions and suggest fruitful new directions for research in the theory of mechanism design. Arbitration, in its several forms, has survived in environments where there are real penalties for poor performance. Although the competition that imposes these penalties is less rigorous than some forms of market competition, I believe that surviving it still conveys useful information; this information is a large fraction of all we have about how best to resolve bargaining disputes. It seems likely that many of the mechanisms taken seriously in the incentives literature would *not* survive, even in simplified form. Trying to understand why, or whether, this is so, and trying to design workable mechanisms, should serve as a useful discipline in the theory of mechanism design.

This chapter attempts to support these views by examining several potential points of contact between arbitration theory and the theory of incentive schemes, with the goal of seeing whether the techniques and behavioral assumptions of the latter can resolve the problems considered most important in the former. The discussion will be organized around a particular problem – the role of arbitration – which is of primary importance and has not, to my knowledge, been treated adequately. Section 17.2 defines terms, introduces the model, and considers the correspondence between concepts in the two literatures. Section 17.3 discusses the link between actual and potential roles of arbitration: whether it is reasonable to predict that bargainers who could benefit from arbitration, will. Sections 17.4, 17.5, and 17.6 examine potential roles for arbitration that are consistent with the assumptions maintained in the incentives literature, under the headings "Contract completion," "Safety net," and (discussed together) "Information buffering and Coordination."

17.2   Definitions, assumptions, and correspondence between concepts

This section outlines the approach to be followed in the present discussion and attempts to identify correspondences between concepts used in the two literatures. Attention will be restricted to *interest* arbitration (i.e., the arbitration of disputes over new agreements), as opposed to *grievance* arbitration (i.e., the resolution of disputes about the interpretation of existing agreements). Many of my observations carry over to grievance arbitration, but interest arbitration corresponds most closely to the situations considered in mechanism design. Except where noted, the discussion will apply both to legally imposed compulsory arbitration and to binding arbitration agreed upon in collective bargaining. Examples of the former are easily found in bargaining between public-sector unions and the jurisdictions that employ them. The most important example of the latter arose in the U.S. steel industry, which in 1974 negotiated the Experimental Negotiating Agreement (recently ended) with the United Steelworkers, prohibiting strikes and providing for binding interest arbitration as a substitute.

For my purposes, *arbitration* can be defined by the presence of an arbitrator who is empowered (possibly with constraints, as in final-offer arbitration) to impose a settlement when bargainers cannot agree on one.

(*Mediation*, on the other hand, typically refers to the presence of a third party who can make suggestions but has no power to impose settlements. What power to influence bargaining outcomes this leaves a mediator is an interesting theoretical question, not considered here.)

For simplicity, unions and managements will be treated as single bargainers with coherent goals, even though they really represent overlapping generations of workers or managers with different goals. Arbitration practice suggests a model with the following general structure. First, the arbitrator (or each potential arbitrator) commits himself to a mechanism (defined later), respecting any constraints that exist, and announces his commitment to bargainers. Then, the arbitrator (or the procedure for selecting an arbitrator) is imposed or agreed upon by bargainers, depending on the context. Whether this step occurs before or after bargainers observe any private information relevant to the negotiations in question is specified where pertinent. Finally, bargainers negotiate, with the arbitrator's mechanism being imposed if they fail to reach an agreement.

Several comments on this specification are in order. First, it presupposes that bargainers always have the right to negotiate their own settlement rather than accept an arbitral settlement. Arbitral settlements can occur only by agreement, by "accident," or default. This assumption reflects the almost universal recognition in practice of bargainers' right to negotiate their own agreements; this right is often treated as inalienable. The belief that arbitration may interfere with the right to bargain seems to account for much of the opposition to it. Limiting consideration to schemes that allow bargainers to negotiate "around" arbitration may help to defuse this objection, and turns out to restrict the role of arbitration less than one might expect. Recognizing the right to bargain, however, may be costly when there is a significant public interest in the agreement reached (and not just in avoiding strikes) that is not adequately represented by one of the bargainers. In extreme cases (e.g., price fixing), these external effects may be handled adequately by legal fiat. But in other cases (e.g., "inflationary" wage settlements), the public interest seems to depend on more subtle tradeoffs among the issues resolved in bargaining, and it might therefore be helpful to have a more direct influence on negotiations. I do not consider such roles for arbitration further, because the incentives approach seems to add little to understanding them, and because it is difficult in such cases to justify intervention *only* when impasses occur, whereas this restricted intervention is all that is considered in the arbitration literature.

Second, I have assumed that the arbitrator selects and enforces a mechanism, rather than a settlement. A *mechanism,* as the term is used in the incentives literature, is simply a set of rules used to determine outcomes and, thereby, control agents' incentives. For example, each agent might be asked to report his private information, and these reports used to determine the outcome in some prespecified way. (There need be no presumption that the reports are truthful, although the mechanism can be designed so that truthful reporting is a rational response to the incentives it creates.) This specification may appear to be in conflict with the arbitration literature, where it is almost universally assumed that the arbitrator imposes a *settlement* if negotiations break down. In fact, the two notions are essentially equivalent in the absence of uncertainty, which is rarely considered explicitly in the arbitration literature. Thus, the assumptions maintained by writers on arbitration need not be viewed as carefully considered positions on this point. In practice, the arbitrator, quite sensibly, solicits information about bargainers' preferences and what is feasible before fashioning a settlement. The closest analog to this in the incentives literature is choosing a mechanism, rather than choosing a settlement.

Third, I have assumed that the arbitrator has powers of commitment that bargainers do not possess. Although ideally this might be explained rather than assumed, it appears quite realistic and follows naturally from institutional and reputational considerations. "Track records" and, to a lesser extent, long-term relationships between bargainers and arbitrators, are considered to be of paramount importance in arbitration practice. These powers of commitment give the arbitrator the power to override his personal preferences, transforming himself into an instrument for improving bargaining outcomes. This is the primary difference between the arbitrator and bargainers, and between bargaining under arbitration and in more general social institutions. The arbitrator's commitment need not be explicit for this model to be appropriate. It entails only that an arbitrator's intention and ability to fashion a fair and efficient settlement can be credibly communicated, before he is selected, to the agent or agents responsible for selection, and that the arbitrator does not engage in negotiations with bargainers about his standards of fairness and efficiency.

To close the model, it is necessary to specify how agents' behavior is determined, and to describe the bargaining environment. Given the rules specified previously, all parties are assumed to pursue their goals rationally, in the sense of playing strategies that are in Bayesian Nash equilibrium. An additional requirement that the equilibrium be perfect or sequential (see Kreps and Wilson (1982); the distinction is not important for my purposes) is imposed to ensure equilibrium play in every stage of the game. This specification is compatible with a wide range of noncooperative models of bargaining; some samples of such models are described in Crawford (1981, 1982c). It specializes to the ordinary (subgame perfect) Nash equilibrium when information is perfect or symmetric.

My observations do not depend on precise specifications of bargainers' or the arbitrator's preferences. However, it is useful, for definiteness, to think of bargainers as "selfish," whereas the arbitrator may be thought of as seeking to maximize the quality of bargaining outcomes according to some criterion. (An alternative view, that this desire is coupled with a desire to maximize fees from clients, is used in Section 17.6 to describe the implications of arbitrators' having to compete for clients. Because bargainers' views of the quality of outcomes may resemble closely those of arbitrators, and an arbitrator with no clients can have only a weak, indirect effect on outcomes, these two goals need not be in sharp conflict.)

The physical aspects of the bargaining environment are assumed to be independent of the presence of an arbitrator. This assumption rules out several phenomena that are important in practice but do not help to explain the role of arbitration. In particular, it implies that arbitrators have no advantage over bargainers in identifying feasible agreements; and it rules out the so-called narcotic effect, whereby bargainers rely excessively on arbitration because it is (physically or politically) easier than bargaining. Also ruled out is the symmetric possibility that arbitral settlements are distasteful to bargainers per se, or that a given agreement is more likely to enlist the allegiance of bargainers in trying to make it work if they have fashioned it themselves. This seems to be the main reason why the narcotic effect, as its pejorative connotation suggests, is considered a bad thing.

Finally, this assumption prevents arbitrators from administering incentive schemes that might violate the physical constraints that bind bargainers when they form a closed system. In theory, there might easily be a potential role for the arbitrator in allowing commitment to such schemes, because in some cases they allow a more effective response to bargainers' incentive problems. This possibility is discussed by Myerson and Satterthwaite (1983) and, in a different context, by Holmström (1982). I do not consider it here mainly because it is apparently never done in practice, which suggests – but does not prove – that it is not truly helpful in arbitration. There may be sound theoretical reasons for this. In the simple bargaining environments studied by Myerson and Satterthwaite, only *subsidies* to bargainers are helpful in increasing efficiency. (When their assumption that bargainers' valuations of the object they seek to exchange are independent is relaxed, roles for arbitration that do not depend on subsidization may appear; see Samuelson 1984.) These subsidies would need to be very large, some of the time, in significant applications of Myerson and Satterthwaite's schemes. Distributional considerations aside, the moral-hazard and collusion considerations associated with this kind of administration of funds, public or private, are disturbing to contemplate.

To complete the specification of the bargaining environment, I assume that all aspects of it are common knowledge, making one exception when discussing roles of arbitration that depend on informational asymmetries. In those cases, it is assumed that an agent privately observes an information variable, called his *type*, which can be thought of as reflecting other parties' uncertainty about his preferences or information. In most cases, only bargainers are assumed to have private information, so that the arbitrator knows exactly what is common knowledge to bargainers.

These strong restrictions on the information structure are convenient for the purpose of identifying potential roles of arbitration for several reasons. First, the case where some private information becomes common knowledge ex post, and it is possible to make contracts contingent on this information, is easily fitted into this framework by reinterpreting preferences and the set of feasible mechanisms. Second, given the arbitrator's powers of commitment and that I will follow the incentives literature in allowing him to use randomization if this is helpful,[1] allowing him private information would not contribute to the goal of identifying potential roles of arbitration. Neither, of course, would putting him at an informational disadvantage relative to bargainers' common knowledge. It is interesting to note, however, that informational disadvantages of this type might not impair the arbitrator's ability to achieve his goals, either. As suggested by Kalai and Rosenthal (1978), and by Rosenthal (1978), the arbitrator can ask bargainers to submit independent reports of their common-knowledge information, punishing them severely for any discrepancies and treating their reports, when there are no discrepancies, as the truth. This makes truthful reporting uniquely salient among a continuum of equilibria. As Kalai and Rosenthal are aware, this result takes full advantage of assumptions (in particular, exact knowledge of the information structure) not usually taken literally, so that practical application would be premature. Applicable schemes might be sought, however, by considering whether theoretical performance can be made less sensitive to unrealistic assumptions and trying to explain why it is considered so important in practice for the arbitrator to begin with as much information as possible about bargainers and their environment, even when that information is common knowledge to bargainers.[2]

With asymmetric information, the natural objects of choice are relationships between the environment and agents' types, and the final outcome. I will follow Holmström and Myerson (1983) in calling these relationships *decision rules*. (A mechanism, together with agents' responses to the incentives it creates, induces a decision rule.) My assumptions imply that bargainers, taken together, and the arbitrator face the same menu of physically feasible decision rules. When the arbitrator has no private information (or, more generally, when he needs no incentives to reveal any private information he has), bargainers and the arbitrator face the same incentive problems as well. It follows that any role for arbitration that emerges under my assumptions must stem from the effect of arbitration on the set of decision rules that can arise in bargaining equilibrium.

17.3   Actual and potential roles of arbitration

In Sections 17.4 through 17.6, several potential roles of arbitration that are compatible with the model outlined in Section 17.2 will be discussed. I will argue that there are several ways in which arbitration could improve the quality of bargaining outcomes. These roles of arbitration are potential, in the sense that they indicate the possibility of welfare gains but do not establish how, or whether, those gains will be realized in practice.

In applications where arbitration is imposed from outside the bargaining relationship, this creates no new conceptual difficulties in evaluating its actual impact. One simply concludes that if arbitration is used skillfully when it is needed, it will help bargainers; otherwise, it will not. (It is worth noting that the impact of arbitration on the bargaining environment, even when there are no arbitral settlements, means that there is no guarantee that unskillful use of arbitration will not hurt bargainers.) Even if bargainers can influence the choice of arbitrator, but their influence is conveyed through a procedure that results in a selection even if they cannot agree, no conceptual difficulties arise. The analysis of the choice of arbitrator in these procedures, which typically begin with each side making several proposals and end with a series of alternating, limited vetoes, is an interesting problem in applied social-choice theory, on which Moulin (1981) and others have made some progress.

The real puzzle arises when binding interest arbitration must be negotiated by bargainers themselves, within the collective-bargaining agreement.[3] (Such applications are growing in importance. A leading example is discussed in Section 17.4.) Then, a subtle question arises in evaluating the actual role of arbitration. It might be expressed as follows:

> Arbitration's only direct influence on outcomes occurs when bargainers cannot reach an agreement on their own. But choosing an arbitrator is itself a bargaining problem: If bargainers can predict arbitrators' intentions without bias, choosing an arbitrator amounts to choosing a settlement to be imposed if bargainers cannot reach one. An actual role of privately agreed-upon arbitration therefore depends on the assumption that bargainers can reach an agreement, in one guise, that matters only when they are unable to reach the same agreement in another guise.

This view, although stated strongly to provide a clear target, is widely held, and deserves to be taken seriously. It can be answered in at least three ways. All three answers rest on differences between bargaining over arbitrators and bargaining over settlements that arise even when bargainers can predict what settlements arbitrators will impose. All three answers also need to be backed up by more theoretical, experimental, or empirical work before they can be viewed as full explanations.

First, notions of "fairness" play a crucial role in determining what offers bargainers will accept. This is particularly apparent if bargaining is modeled as a noncooperative coordination game (see Schelling (1963) for the leading development of this view), since then fairness notions provide important clues to help bargainers select one of the many possible equilibria. It seems unlikely that bargainers' notions of fairness are exclusively, or even mostly, "end-state" notions. It is easy to imagine someone agreeing to follow the dictates of a *procedure* he perceives as fair, even when its outcome is predictable and violates the end-state notion of fairness he would apply if it had been suggested in isolation. Arbitration may therefore be agreed upon simply because it is more nearly congruent to bargainers' notions of fairness.

In repeated bargaining, our prevalent procedural notions of fairness may even enjoy significant efficiency advantages. When impasses are costly and cannot always be avoided in bargaining without arbitration (see Section 17.5), bargainers might benefit by being constrained for several bargains in a way that avoids impasses, even though these constraints sometimes lead to settlements that would be "unacceptable" in isolation. Section 17.6 considers how such constraints might help bargainers deal more effectively with incentive problems. Since the constraints must be imposed before the particulars of each application are known, they tend to be "procedural." Arbitration mandated by law or social custom might be the easiest way to impose and enforce them.

Finally, even when the preceding arguments do not apply, the choice of arbitrator is still a different bargaining problem than the choice of a settlement. It is resolved earlier, when bargainers may have less information. And, particularly if bargainers eschew explicit randomization, its apparently simpler set of feasible agreements might facilitate coordination. Although arbitral settlements occur only as a result of bargaining impasses, arbitration can have a significant indirect effect on outcomes even when impasses never occur (see Crawford (1982a)). This implies that bargainers' negotiating strategies will generally differ in the two problems. It follows that there is no necessary link between the occurrence of impasses in bargaining over settlements and in bargaining over arbitrators. Bargainers might easily have better luck in agreeing on an arbitrator than in agreeing on a settlement.

In summary, the potential roles of arbitration identified in Sections 17.4–17.6 should also convey some useful information about how arbitration is used in practice, even when such use requires that bargainers bind themselves to follow the dictates of an arbitrator. The associated opportunities for potential gain should thus be realized some, if not all, of the time.

17.4   Contract completion

This section discusses the role of interest arbitration as a substitute for complete contracts. The role of grievance arbitration in collective bargaining, and of arbitration in commercial contract disputes, is commonly considered to be contract completion in legal theory, where it is taken for granted that dealing by contract with every contingency, no matter how unlikely ex ante, is impractical (see Fuller (1963), for example). But contract completion may be a somewhat novel view of the role of interest arbitration, which by definition deals with contracts not yet made.

This role is possible because many important economic relationships, particularly employment relationships, extend over long periods and involve important intertemporal allocation decisions, but are governed by contracts or agreements shorter than their anticipated lives. Although the use of short-term contracts economizes on contracting costs and provides valuable flexibility, it also means that some decisions about the organization of the relationship have consequences that extend beyond the horizon of any single contract. This partial loss of control over incentives, even when it is the only imperfection in the model, can cause inefficiency in some settings. In the remainder of this section, I will describe a model, originally presented in Crawford (1983), that supports this claim, and then show how the appropriate use of binding interest arbitration can restore efficiency while allowing bargainers always to negotiate their own settlements. The section concludes with a discussion of two important applications of binding interest arbitration that seem to be well explained by these results.

In the model of Crawford (1983), it is assumed that there are two bargainers, each with perfect information and perfect foresight, who always negotiate agreements that are efficient relative to their contracting possibilities. There are two periods, and two contracting regimes are compared. In one regime, complete, long-term (two-period) contracts are possible; in the other, contracting is complete within each period, but must be done period by period, so that only current-period actions can be enforceably agreed upon in a given period. Bargainers decide, for each period, whether to cooperate in production, how to share the resulting output, and how much (if any) current output to set aside as an investment in the relationship. (Such investments are assumed to raise the relationship's productivity in the future, but not in the current period; thus, in the two-period model being considered, they make sense only in the first period.) Two different kinds of investment are compared, which differ according to whether the capital they create, once invested, can later be economically withdrawn from the relationship. A *sunk-cost* investment in the relationship is one whose returns depend on the bargainers' continued cooperation in production, and which are otherwise irrecoverable. A *reversible* investment is one whose capital can later be withdrawn and either consumed or reinvested in another relationship.

When long-term contracts are possible, the assumption that parties always negotiate efficiently, relative to the contracting possibilities, immediately implies that the level of investment in the relationship is chosen efficiently, no matter what combination of sunk-cost and reversible investment efficiency happens to require. When only period-by-period contracts are possible, however, the efficiency of investment may depend crucially on whether costs must be sunk for efficient organization of the relationship. Inefficiency can arise, in abstract terms, because of the time-consistency constraints that must be satisfied by bargainers' contracts when long-term contracts are unenforceable. To see this more concretely, consider the extreme case where only sunk-cost investment is required for efficiency, and assume that bargainers' efficient agreements result in cooperation in each period. The sunk-cost character of the investment may seem unlikely to cause problems under these circumstances. However, any returns that a bargainer anticipates from such an investment after the current contract expires must be negotiated in bargaining environments that are completely independent of which bargainer sunk the associated costs. Thus, to the extent that a bargainer pays for such an investment by foregoing his own current consumption, his position resembles that of a private provider of public goods: He pays full cost but can rationally expect to receive only part of the benefit. This analogy suggests strongly that sunk-cost investments will not be undertaken to the full extent required for efficiency under period-by-period contracting.

As it happens, this intuition is not fully borne out by analysis of the model, but it does contain an important kernel of truth. There are two things wrong with it. First, in the pure sunk-cost case, a bargainer who bears (part of) the cost of the investment can expect no return for doing so beyond the period covered by the current contract, but nothing prevents him from being compensated in the current contract. In some environments, this kind of compensation at the time of the investment is costless, in the sense that it is consistent with some fully efficient plan with the distribution of surplus that bargainers would negotiate under long-term contracting. This is the case, for example, if bargainers have access to a perfect capital market, or if their preferences make them indifferent about the time pattern of compensation. But more generally, and more realistically, this kind of compensation, although it can be used to restore the incentives for efficient sunk-cost investment under period-by-period contracting, itself has costs. Bargainers' best response to these costs is a second-best-efficient compromise between efficient investment and efficient patterns of compensation. It turns out that these compromises generally involve some of each kind of inefficiency, but that standard assumptions about preferences, technology, and surplus-sharing rules do not necessarily support the intuition that the bias in sunk-cost investment is toward too little investment. There is, however, some basis for belief that this direction of bias is more likely than the reverse direction.

The second flaw involves the extreme assumption that efficiency requires only sunk-cost investment. One might suspect that, normally, some reversible investment is also required or, more generally, that efficiency also requires some investment with technologically linked sunk-cost and reversible components. It turns out that if the preponderance of reversible investment in the efficient plan is sufficiently great, the inefficiencies associated with sunk-cost investment in its pure form can be eliminated, even under period-by-period contracting.

To see this, it is helpful to begin with an analysis of the case where only reversible investment is required for efficiency. The crucial feature of reversible investment is that its absence of sunk costs implies the existence of costlessly enforceable property rights in the capital created by it, with equal value inside and outside the relationship. (If property rights were costly, or uneconomic, to enforce, then the costs of enforcement, up to the external value of the investment, would by definition be sunk at the time of investment.) It follows that if the property rights that reversibility entails are costlessly transferable and perfectly divisible, they allow bargainers costlessly to guarantee future compensation, and thereby provide, within a sequence of short-term contracts, the incentives for efficient investment even when it has long-term consequences. This is done by assigning property rights in the reversible capital, in each period's contract, in such a way that the next period's negotiations yield the pattern of compensation associated with the fully efficient plan. Bargainers' rational anticipations of the outcomes of future bargains make the current-period part of the efficient plan efficient relative to current-period contracting possibilities. It is not hard to see that this argument remains valid so long as there is not "too much" sunk-cost investment in the efficient plan, where what is too much, of course, depends in a complex way on preferences and technology, and on bargainers' relative bargaining powers.

I will now consider two applications of binding interest arbitration, one in the public sector, and one in the private sector, that seem to be explained, in part, by considerations like those just outlined. In each case, efficient organization of the relationship in question requires irreversible actions that resemble (but are more complex than) sunk-cost investment decisions. In each case, the role of the arbitrator is, in effect, to remember who sunk costs in the past, and to ensure that future compensation is paid in a way that creates the "correct" incentives to make such investments. It is important that he can do this without infringing on the right to bargain, simply by "threatening," in each period, an arbitral settlement that leads bargainers to negotiate, for themselves, the appropriate agreement. The fact that arbitration can solve this kind of problem so well without infringing on the right to bargain may account for the empirical importance of this kind of application.

My public-sector illustration is an explanation of the pattern of use of compulsory interest arbitration in dealing with local public-sector employees. (Long-term labor contracts are, by law, not binding on workers, and only partly binding on firms in practice.) Here, applications commonly occur in conjunction with a strike prohibition, and cover police officers and fire fighters much more often than most other types of public employees. This raises the question, Why police officers and fire fighters, and not, say, librarians? On a common-sense level, the answer is clear: It is difficult, on short notice, to find trained replacements for employees like police officers and fire fighters, and extremely costly to do without them, even for a short time. Thus, once a particular group of such employees has been hired and trained, it enjoys a great deal of monopoly power in the short run. The right to strike would make it difficult for the employing jurisdiction to resist attempts to exploit this monopoly power.

It is important to note that this difference between police officers and fire fighters and most other workers arises purely because efficient organization of the employment relationship (e.g., training the workers, but not training substitutes just as a bargaining chip) causes large variations in relative bargaining power over its lifetime. Before a police officer is hired, his bargaining position with respect to his employer is not radically different from that of a librarian. Losing the opportunity to hire a particular police officer would be costly, but not especially costly. Thus, if the relationship could be governed by a single, costlessly enforceable, long-term contract, the difference would be irrelevant. Employees who are expected to acquire excessive monopoly power could simply agree never to strike, and be compensated in the agreement for this concession according to their ex ante bargaining power. There would remain a "safety-net" role for arbitration, as discussed in Section 17.5, in limiting the costs of bargaining impasses in the initial negotiations, but this role would emerge with roughly equal force for all types of employees.

It is also possible, in principle, for unions and employers simply to recognize that the union will acquire and exploit monopoly power in the course of the relationship, and to adjust the pattern of compensation in anticipation of this. This would, no doubt, require workers to post a large bond when hired, or at least to undergo a long apprenticeship without pay. This is unthinkable in real labor relations, of course, for reasons that are obvious (but not correspondingly easy to model). The use of arbitration allows a solution of the problem without incurring the costs of such distortions in the pattern of compensation over time. I interpret the widespread adoption of compulsory interest arbitration for this kind of application as powerful evidence in favor of the model proposed in Crawford (1983).

The second illustration of the contract-completion role is the most important instance, to date, of voluntarily agreed-upon compulsory interest arbitration in the private sector. (The qualification is necessary to rule out the National War Labor Board in World War II, which of course did not rely on the consent of firms and workers.) From 1974 until early 1983, new contracts in the American steel industry were negotiated under the Experimental Negotiating Agreement, which substituted binding interest arbitration for the right to strike. Baldwin (1983) gives an explanation of this partly in contract-completion terms, using a model similar in spirit to but different in substance from the model just described.

Two parts of Baldwin's argument are directly relevant to the role of arbitration. First, stability of steel supply over time is very valuable to customers. As a result, steel suppliers engage in a great deal of costly stockpiling, both to reduce the costs of strikes when they occur and to enhance their bargaining positions by reducing their vulnerability to strike threats. The first of these motives leads to a safety-net role for arbitration, discussed in Section 17.5; the second creates a contract-completion role similar to that just outlined, in allowing the industry to avoid the costs of stockpiling that takes place just to enhance firms' bargaining positions.

Second, new investment in steel capacity has a particularly large sunk-cost component. The U.S. steel industry has long experienced difficulty competing with foreign suppliers because its plant and equipment are old and inefficient. Baldwin explains this by suggesting that new investment is weak because investors are reluctant to invest in "hostage capital," whose rents are vulnerable to expropriation by unions once investment costs are sunk.

The Experimental Negotiating Agreement ended in early 1983, to mixed reviews, with the U.S. steel industry still facing great difficulties. It will be of great interest to watch the postmortems for clues to the uses and limitations of arbitration.

17.5   Safety net

This section discusses the safety-net role of arbitration in reducing the expected costs of bargaining impasses. I assume in this section that bargainers can make complete contracts (except as limited by informational asymmetries; see Myerson (1979) for a good discussion of how to incorporate incentive constraints). Under my assumptions, the effect of arbitration on bargaining is transmitted entirely through the substitution of an arbitral settlement for the status-quo impasse outcome. A safety-net role exists only when there is some chance that bargainers will fail to reach an agreement on their own, and so I shall begin with a critical discussion of the explanations of the occurrence of impasses that are used in the two literatures.

The kinds of environments in which the bargaining impasses that lead to arbitral settlements will occur is a central question in the arbitration literature. The law and economics literature faces analytically equivalent problems in explaining, for example, why not all civil suits are settled out of court. Despite the importance of these questions, both of these literatures suffer greatly from a failure to give a serious explanation of bargaining impasses.

This failure seems due in part to the technical difficulties involved, but it also seems to stem from an honest distrust of the strong rationality assumptions necessary to make strategic interactions with asymmetric information analytically tractable. This distrust deserves some sympathy, because real bargainers undeniably behave irrationally much of the time, and even a fully rational bargainer would need to take this into account. However, game-theoretic rationality, with simple rules to govern the making of agreements and informational asymmetries introduced in a controlled way, is the only mode of analysis yet proposed that is parsimonious enough to yield strong, but not arbitrary, predictions about the influence of the bargaining environment on outcomes. I therefore maintain these rationality assumptions, which are standard in the incentives literature, with a clear conscience.

In view of these difficulties and the absence of convincing competitors to the game-theoretic approach, one might expect writers on arbitration to be circumspect about bargaining impasses. Boldness rather than caution has been the rule, however. Several views of how the frequency of impasses is related to the bargaining environment, of varying levels of sophistication, have emerged. All are based on a flawed analogy between bargaining and individual decision making, where large costs, taking uncertainty and the difficulty of decision making into account, are more likely to be avoided than small costs, other things being equal. The flaw is, of course, that bargaining is one of the most interactive of all economic situations, so that there is no reason to expect bargainers' collective behavior to resemble individual decision making. (This is why there is an important distinction between actual and potential roles of arbitration.)

I now summarize the most common views of why arbitral settlements occur, in increasing order of sophistication, and then explain what I think is wrong with the most sophisticated one, which rests on a relatively subtle logical error. The simplest view is that bargaining outcomes are always efficient, taking into account bargainers' beliefs and the costs of bargaining. Impasses can occur only when they are efficient, in the sense just defined. This view becomes both more prevalent and more tautological the nearer one approaches Chicago (in the intellectual sense), where bargaining costs are sometimes even defined as anything that stands in the way of efficiency. This theory could, of course, be made operational by appending a specification of what observable variables determine bargaining costs.

The limitations of this view have been recognized by some arbitration writers, who have modified it by assuming that the probability of impasses is a decreasing function of the size of the *contract zone* – the set of feasible agreements preferred by both bargainers to the prospect of an impasse. This is less extreme than the first view, but it does not represent a real improvement. Some attempts to justify it refer to the difficulties of identifying agreements in the contract zone. In fact, in simple bargaining experiments, Malouf and Roth (1981) found that the size of the contract zone was a good predictor of how long it took bargainers who eventually reached an agreement to do so, but a poor predictor of how often an agreement was reached. Further, bargaining impasses seem intuitively likely to occur not when competition shrinks the contract zone to a point, but when there is enough surplus to be worth fighting over. Thus, it would be somewhat surprising if the frequency of impasses were always inversely related to the size of the contract zone.

The third view rests on bargainers' optimism about the impasse outcome. If bargainers have identical probabilistic beliefs about the consequences of an impasse, it is evident (and sometimes recognized in the literature) that bargainers can always duplicate by agreement the prospect of an impasse. (There is no reason to rule out random agreements if they appear mutually beneficial.) Bargainers who can negotiate efficient agreements will therefore never have a positive interest in allowing an impasse to occur, and in general the prospect of an impasse will actually be inefficient in the set of feasible agreements. It is argued in response to this that bargainers are commonly quite uncertain about the impasse outcome. This tends to make impasses still worse for risk-averse bargainers, but it also has the advantage of making it more plausible to assume that bargainers' beliefs about the impasse outcome are significantly different. If their beliefs are relatively *optimistic,* in the sense of being better for both bargainers than some efficient agreements, an impasse is perceived as efficient, and assumed to occur. (What happens when some feasible agreements also remain efficient is not discussed.) Under this assumption, a modeler who could observe everything but bargainers' beliefs would observe a negative correlation between the estimated size of the contract zone and the frequency of impasses.

This view has been taken still further; see Farber (1980) for the clearest statement. It is recognized as a flaw that bargainers have unexplained differences in their perceptions of the arbitrator's intentions. Farber explains these differences by assuming that bargainers start with a common prior, but receive different observations relevant to the arbitrator's behavior. Some of the time, *rational optimism* (the term is mine, not Farber's) results, and an impasse occurs. There are two problems with this explanation. First, many factors handicap arbitrators in fashioning settlements. Also, arbitrators' track records are almost public knowledge, and there are other reasons to believe that an arbitrator's intentions are not wildly unpredictable (see Crawford (1979, Section I)). I will argue later that, in reasonable models of bargaining, many feasible agreements (defined taking into account incentive constraints, if any) are not really available, with certainty, to bargainers, because bargaining outcomes must arise as equilibria under the rules of the bargaining game. If all feasible agreements were available to bargainers, with no risk of impasses, it would take quite a bit of optimism to prevent all of the available agreements from being better for both bargainers than the prospect of an arbitral settlement. It is only human for a bargainer to see the merits of his own arguments and goals more clearly than those of the other bargainer. But I cannot believe that there is enough optimism in this and in differences in information to explain anything like the large number of arbitral settlements that occur.[4]

The second problem concerns the logical underpinnings of the rational-optimism theory. If bargainers could be sure of reaching an efficient agreement on their own, then an arbitral settlement could not truly be better for both bargainers than all of the agreements available by negotiation. Thus, the rational-optimism theory raises the difficult question of whether such rationally misguided bargainers should be allowed to "hang themselves" when society knows better, or if the paternalism needed to prevent this would be a still greater evil. Fortunately, what I have called rational optimism is not truly rational, so that theorists, at least, can avoid this dilemma. To see this, suppose that bargainers have identical priors and that all aspects of the bargaining environment are common knowledge except for some private information that is relevant to the arbitrator's behavior. (This is true to the spirit of Farber's (1980) arguments.) Suppose further that any outcome the arbitrator can achieve is also a potential negotiated settlement. Then, an argument like that used to establish Milgrom and Stokey's (1982) "no-trade" theorem shows that it can never be common knowledge that both prefer the prospect of an arbitral settlement to an efficient negotiated settlement. (See Holmström and Myerson (1983) [Sections 4 and 5] for a simple proof, and Milgrom and Stokey for a good exposition of the argument and its implications in a market setting.) It follows that if bargainers could be sure of reaching an efficient agreement, they could never rationally agree to rely on arbitration, since that agreement would make their mutual preference for the arbitral settlement common knowledge, contradicting efficiency.

The intuitive reason for this is that it is common knowledge that any feasible change from efficient outcome must be to the detriment of at least one party. That one bargainer is willing to approve such a change is therefore proof that he knows something that means the other should not. The result has been called the Groucho Marx theorem, because it is reminiscent of his remark that he would never join a club willing to accept him as a member. (This characterization is attributed to Milton Harris by Milgrom and Stokey.) As Marx's remark suggests, the no-trade argument, although it requires some effort to formalize, has a powerful, common-sense element one would expect bargainers to appreciate. I therefore view it not as a technical quibble, but as a serious criticism of the rational-optimism theory. Like its less sophisticated predecessors, this theory can explain impasses only by assuming that bargainers do not fully understand their situation.

These arguments establish that a "fully rational" explanation for the occurrence of arbitral settlements, and therefore for the safety-net role of arbitration, must rest on bargainers' inability always to realize all physically feasible gains from trade. There are two different types of rationalization for this. The first assumes implicitly that bargainers can reach any incentive-compatible outcome. Impasses arise because in some environments a positive probability of impasse is an efficient way to achieve incentive compatibility. Efficiency is defined here taking into account incentive-compatibility constraints. From now on, I will use Holmström and Myerson's (1983) term *incentive efficiency* to express this qualification when necessary. (This general approach to bargaining is outlined in Myerson (1979). Further developments, for particular specifications of the bargaining environment, have been given by Myerson and Satterthwaite (1983) and Samuelson (1984).)

This explanation of impasses is of interest and, in my opinion, vastly superior to those criticized earlier. It also has an important element of realism. Indeed, the earliest recorded example of arbitration of which I am aware, in which King Solomon identified the true mother of a baby by threatening to resolve a maternity dispute via equal division in a highly nonconvex environment, can be interpreted in this way. Even the possibility that Solomon fooled the women about his true intentions could be accommodated in this explanation.

One reservation should be recorded, however, as a suggestion for future research along these lines. To date, almost all of the models in which incentive compatibility has been shown to require a positive probability of impasse are ones in which that is the only possible failure of full efficiency. (Some exceptions are given in Samuelson (1984).) These models therefore contain little to suggest that risking an impasse, as opposed to other forms of inefficiency, is the most efficient way to ensure incentive compatibility. Studying static models in which the physical environment is richer than a single, indivisible good, and further study of dynamic models in which waiting costs can serve as a sorting device, should help to resolve these doubts. It should be noted, however, that the common use of discrete sets of feasible outcomes, or risk-neutrality, may obscure some realistic features that bear on this question.

The second type of rationalization focuses on the effect of the rules of bargaining on which incentive-compatible outcomes bargainers can achieve. Here, impasses sometimes occur because the rules create incentives for bargainers to risk them, in an attempt to capture a larger share of the gains from trade. Examples of this approach are Chatterjee and Samuelson (1983) and Crawford (1982c), which are discussed elsewhere in this volume. For reasonable specifications of the rules of bargaining, equilibrium relationships between agents' types and the final outcome are in general not incentive-efficient decision rules.

The two kinds of explanation of the occurrence of impasses just described have very different implications for the role of arbitration, under the assumptions outlined in Section 17.2. If bargainers could achieve any incentive-compatible outcome, with impasses occurring solely to guarantee incentive-compatibility, then arbitration would be irrelevant. The entire bargaining game, with arbitration replacing the status-quo impasse outcome, is itself a mechanism, and bargainers could duplicate its effects by explicit agreement. In general, of course, they could do even better when not constrained by a particular set of bargaining rules. If, on the other hand, impasses occur in part because of the incentives created by the rules of bargaining, and bargaining outcomes (broadly construed to reflect whatever risk is inherent in the bargaining process) are not always incentive-efficient, there may be a safety-net role.

To understand this role, recall that there are three channels through which arbitration can influence bargaining outcomes. First, arbitration has an obvious direct effect on the impasse outcome. Second, it has an indirect effect (called *bias* in the arbitration literature) on negotiated settlements. Finally, it affects the probability of impasse. It is natural to think of evaluating the total effect through a simple expected-welfare calculation, with the welfare criterion possibly reflecting how well bargainers could do outside the relationship, as in most normative bargaining solutions.

If arbitral settlements could be made efficient, in the sense appropriate to the environment, then rational bargainers would always rely on arbitral settlements, and this would be an efficient social arrangement. The question becomes more interesting if one assumes, realistically, that arbitral settlements cannot always be made fully efficient, for the reasons discussed in Section 17.2. Then, it is no longer clear a priori that the arbitral settlement *should* be made as efficient as feasible: Even if this could be done without affecting bias, it might raise the probability of impasse and reduce welfare, on balance. However, some changes in the impasse outcome that could be brought about by arbitration would normally be beneficial. And it seems quite likely that improving the efficiency of the impasse outcome is the direction in which to find welfare gains, as my term "safety net" suggests.

I emphasize this last point because it runs counter to the conventional wisdom in the arbitration literature, where the role of arbitration is almost universally viewed as lowering the probability of impasse by making impasses more costly to bargainers (see Stevens (1966), Donn (1977), Farber and Katz (1979), Farber (1980), and Bloom (1981)). Although it is possible in theory for increasing the cost of an impasse to benefit bargainers by reducing the probability of impasse, this seems unlikely in practice. Much more information, theoretical and empirical, about what determines the probability of impasse is needed to resolve this question.

In conclusion, it may be worth noting that this confusion in the arbitration literature seems to stem from reasoning about bargaining by analogy with individual decision making. This conditions authors to accept, uncritically, simplistic assumptions about how the probability of impasse is related to the bargaining environment. Further, it leads to a misinterpretation of the bargaining problems that originally led to public-sector compulsory arbitration. The need for prohibiting costly strikes by police officers and fire fighters is accepted on common-sense grounds. Then, it is observed that employers who can no longer lose anything by intransigence are unlikely to bargain seriously. The final leap, to assuming the problem is that impasses are sufficiently costly for *both* bargainers, is made by false analogy. The end result is a serious misinterpretation of the role of arbitration.

17.6   Information buffering and coordination

The last roles of arbitration that I consider are information buffering and coordination. *Information buffering* refers to the arbitrator's role in enforcing mechanisms that deal efficiently with incentive problems but cannot be implemented by bargainers unaided. *Coordination* refers to the role of arbitrators and mediators in solving multiple-equilibrium problems. These two roles are discussed together because they are linked in my main illustrations.

Although the information-buffering and safety-net roles overlap somewhat, there is a significant distinction between them. The safety-net role discussed in Section 17.5 can arise even when the set of fully efficient agreements is common knowledge, provided that there is a positive probability that bargaining will end in an impasse. Examples where this happens can be found in Crawford (1982c), where the rules of bargaining create incentives for bargainers to "burn their bridges" to an uncertain extent, thereby risking an impasse, in attempts to capture a larger share of the gains from cooperation; in Chatterjee and Samuelson (1983), where impasses can occur in equilibrium even when the supports of the distributions of bargainers' reservation prices do not overlap; and in Nash's (1953) "demand game," which has perfect, mixed-strategy equilibria with a positive probability of impasse even with complete information. Although, in the examples analyzed to date, incentive-inefficiency always appears in the form of a positive probability of impasse (no trade, when trade is efficient, in the language of Chatterjee and Samuelson (1983), Myerson and Satterthwaite (1983), and Samuelson (1984)), this form is by no means inevitable in more general, multi-issue models of bargaining. For these more general models, an information-buffering role may emerge even when bargainers, in isolation, would always reach some sort of agreement.

Information buffering allows bargainers, by tacitly agreeing to rely on an arbitral settlement, to override the rules of bargaining and replace them with an alternative mechanism. Although examples are known where simple, realistic bargaining rules are an incentive-efficient mechanism,[5] this is unlikely to be true in any reasonably general environment. (One possible reason for this is that incentive-efficient mechanisms typically depend sensitively on the details of the environment, whereas perhaps only simple bargaining institutions can enjoy an evolutionary advantage over other mechanisms.) When bargaining is not incentive-efficient, it may be possible for an arbitrator to commit himself to a mechanism that is better for each type of each bargainer than the anticipated bargaining equilibrium. If there is only one possible arbitrator, he will have some incentive to make such a commitment, since this maximizes the number of his clients. If he does so, bargainers can rely on an arbitral settlement without leaking any of their private information, because it is already common knowledge that the arbitral settlement is better for both bargainers. Since this ensures that the arbitrator's mechanism will operate as intended, it is rational for bargainers, who can each insist on an arbitral settlement, to do so.

Here, the arbitrator may play a coordination role as well, in ensuring, by suggestion, that the desired mechanism equilibrium is played. This may overcome multiple-equilibrium selection problems that are assumed away in the standard use of the revelation principle to characterize incentive constraints.

The argument just outlined depends on several assumptions. First, it is important that the arbitrator can commit to a mechanism that is known to be better for both bargainers, independent of their private information. Otherwise, the tacit decision to rely on arbitration may leak some of their private information, altering the incentives created by the arbitrator's mechanism. This is not certain to cause problems, but the associated partial loss of control over incentives may prevent the arbitrator from improving on the bargaining outcome.

Second, it is important that either there be only one sensible choice of arbitrator, or that bargainers can commit themselves to an arbitrator (who has, by assumption, first committed himself to a mechanism) before observing their private information. To see why competition among arbitrators that takes place after bargainers have observed their private information may cause problems, it is helpful to model the process of choosing among arbitrators as the application of a bargaining solution to the set of possible arbitrators (evaluated by the anticipated effects of their mechanisms). With symmetric information, a solution like Nash's (1950) might be used; the generalization to asymmetric information might use the Harsanyi–Selten (1972) solution.

This model of competition among arbitrators has several interesting features. If arbitrators commit themselves to mechanisms simultaneously, it is analogous to the Rothschild – Stiglitz – Wilson model of competitive insurance markets (Rothschild and Stiglitz (1976) and Wilson (1977)); the analogy suggests that neither pure-strategy equilibria nor pooling equilibria (where all arbitrators propose the same mechanism) are likely to exist in general. In a nonpooling equilibrium, the choice of arbitrator, if it takes place after bargainers have observed their private information, will generally leak information, causing problems similar to those described earlier. (Since there are fewer arbitrators than mechanisms, partial information buffering, which may still be beneficial, will occur.) This suggests that arbitration may have elements of natural monopoly, for novel, informational reasons. It also underscores the benefits of long-term commitments between arbitrators and clients, which, interestingly (although mainly for other reasons), are often thought to give arbitration an "unfair" advantage over bargaining (e.g., see Fuller (1963)). Finally, the demand for a particular arbitrator's services responds favorably to the equity as well as the efficiency of his settlements, if one accepts the equity notion built into the bargaining solution. (This is natural if one views the bargaining solution as a focal-point resolution of the multiple-equilibrium problems in bargaining; see Schelling (1963).) Thus, the model provides a framework in which to evaluate Landes and Posner's (1979) claim that competition will eliminate bias in the analogous setting of private adjudication. This claim seems unlikely to be valid under realistic assumptions about the joint distribution of arbitrators' skills and their preferences for bias, or about the information structure.

Perhaps somewhat surprisingly, there may exist an information-buffering role even if bargainers can make binding agreements about the mechanism that will be used to control their incentives. The implications of this possibility were first discussed formally by Holmström and Myerson (1983), and are the subject of Crawford (1985), whose arguments are summarized here.

When bargainers can bind themselves to a mechanism, it is natural to assume that they evaluate possible mechanism agreements according to their rational expectations of the effect of the incentives they create, taking into account any information that is leaked in the process of selecting a mechanism. Given this, the choice of a mechanism becomes analogous to the choice of an allocation in "ordinary" bargaining theory, which suggests natural models of the process of agreeing on a mechanism.

Two cases can be distinguished. In the first, agents can bind themselves to a mechanism before observing their private information, and standard arguments suggest that they can agree on a mechanism whose ultimate effect will be an incentive-efficient allocation, evaluated according to bargainers' ex ante preferences (*ex ante incentive-efficient,* in Holmström and Myerson's terminology). This immediately implies that there is no information-buffering role for arbitration.

In the second case, where agents observe their private information before they can agree on a mechanism, it turns out that reasonable specifications of the rules for bargaining over mechanisms imply that bargainers cannot generally achieve incentive-efficiency. (Here, the appropriate notion of incentive-efficiency treats each possible realization of an agent's private-information variable as a separate person; I will use Holmström and Myerson's term *interim incentive-efficiency* to refer to this concept. Roughly speaking, an allocation is interim incentive-efficient if there is no other attainable allocation, taking into account incentive constraints, as well as physical constraints, that is better for all agents independent of their private information.) The problem is that the process of mechanism design, to yield good results, must aggregate information about bargainers' preferences over mechanisms. Because these preferences generally depend on bargainers' types, mechanism design in this case may leak some of their private information, altering the incentives created by the mechanism that is chosen. Even if the effects of this information leakage are rationally anticipated, they can make it impossible for bargainers to achieve a result that is interim incentive-efficient.

Since, under my assumptions, an arbitrator is simply a predictable and enforceable choice of mechanism, there remains in this case no role for arbitration as defined so far. If, however, the arbitrator's powers are expanded somewhat, to allow him to enforce the rules of a particular mechanism-design process, a striking result emerges. With these expanded powers, the arbitrator can make it possible for bargainers to achieve, after they have observed their private information, any desired interim incentive-efficient outcome. (As before, this need not be in conflict with the right to bargain, although information-leakage problems may arise.) Since these are the best outcomes attainable when mechanism design can take place before agents observe their types – or in any case – this form of arbitration can be said to allow bargainers to retreat behind the veil of ignorance to bargain over mechanisms, even when they are no longer truly ignorant. This is accomplished by using rules for bargaining over mechanisms that allow bargainers endogenously to restrict the language they use to bargain over mechanisms, in a way that permits aggregation of their preferences, but prevents them from encoding their private information in their mechanism proposals. I will now briefly describe these rules, and conclude by discussing the nature of the expansion of the arbitrator's powers, and his role as coordinator.

The mechanism-design process in Crawford (1985) is a generalization of Nash's (1953) demand game, modified to allow for bargainers' private information. It is assumed, for simplicity only, that there is a common-knowledge normalization of each bargainer's types' von Neumann–Morgenstern utility functions, with no agreement on a mechanism, and no information leakage, yielding zero utility for each type. Bargainers, after learning their types, simultaneously announce *demands* and *weights*. A bargainer's demand specifies a utility level for each of his types. His weights are nonnegative real numbers, one for each type of the other bargainer. If each bargainer's demand is proportional to his opponent's weights, and if bargainers' demands are *compatible,* in the sense that the demanded type-contingent utility levels are realized in equilibrium by some mechanism, then such a mechanism is implemented. (There is a common-knowledge "tie-breaking" rule, and the mechanism is imple-mented whether or not bargainers learn about each other's types in the process.) If not, the underlying game is played with no agreement, hence noncooperatively.

It is not difficult to show that for this mechanism-design process, any interim incentive-efficient outcome can be achieved as a "reasonable" equilibrium. A partial converse, using strong restrictions on equilibria, singles out these interim incentive-efficient outcomes as especially rea-sonable, in a weak but not implausible sense. Thus, an arbitrator whose suggestions are taken seriously (as they might well be in a game with such formidable multiple-equilibrium problems) might be able to use this mechanism-design process to get around the difficulties associated with bargainers already knowing their private information. This is accom-plished by creating incentives for each bargainer to ignore proposals by the other bargainer that favor one or more of his types more (or less) than the arbitrator has suggested is appropriate. Although the rules of this mechanism-design process can be specified using only bargainers' common-knowledge information, they are highly sensitive to the details of the environment, and are quite complex. Even though this sensitivity may be necessary to achieve interim incentive-efficiency when mecha-nism design takes place after bargainers have already observed their types, the associated complexity makes it clear that this process is far removed from anything that could be taken literally as a solution to the problem. (Crawford (1985) discusses some recent work that may make it possible to achieve good results in a more decentralized way.) However, the part of the arbitrator's task that involves figuring out how to reconcile bargainers' demands with their incentives appears quite realistic. This suggests that further analysis of the process of mechanism design might lead to a deeper understanding of what arbitrators actually do.

NOTES

1. Explicit randomization would be considered bizarre in arbitration circles, but uncertainty about the arbitrator's intentions has been deemed vital to the effectiveness of arbitration since the time of King Solomon, albeit for reasons I consider misguided (see Section 17.5). In practice, one would expect to see randomization only in "purified" form, based on private information possessed by the arbitrator, which in his opinion is not relevant to finding the best settlement.

2. Access to bargainers' *private* information would, of course, help the arbitrator mitigate incentive problems. But access to their common-knowledge information would be important only if information-gathering difficulties are much greater than is usually assumed in the incentives literature.

   The most striking evidence of the importance of information-gathering costs is implicit in Stevens's (1966) proposal to replace conventional compulsory arbitration with final-offer arbitration, and its subsequent widespread adoption. Recall that in conventional arbitration, the arbitrator is permitted to impose an unrestricted settlement if negotiations break down, whereas in the simplest form of final-offer arbitration, he is required to choose without compromise between bargainers' final offers. Stevens's proposal was motivated by the common belief that, in rendering their decisions, arbitrators tend to split the difference between bargainers' final positions. This makes concessions in bargaining doubly costly to a bargainer, since they then reduce the value of the arbitral settlement, if one occurs, as well as the negotiated settlement. The resulting distortion of bargainers' concession decisions is known as the *chilling effect*. Final-offer arbitration presumably weakens the chilling effect by making it possible for concessions to improve the arbitral settlement for the bargainer who makes them, by raising the probability that his final offer will be selected.

   Stevens viewed final-offer arbitration as a way of intimidating bargainers into negotiating their own agreements (thought desirable both intrinsically and for efficiency reasons) without undermining their ability to do so by the traditional series of gradual concessions. He did not notice that if intimidation was the true function of arbitration, it would be better accomplished in a nondissipative way (e.g., by fines) than by threatening bargainers with a risky settlement that might not reflect their preferences as efficiently as possible. (This has been suggested, more recently, by Hirsch and Donn (1982), for example.) It is significant that Stevens did not suggest (or apparently even consider) eliminating the chilling effect by sealing the bargaining record and requiring the arbitrator, when he is called upon to render a judgment, to gather his own information. This is now done sometimes, and has been discussed, for example, by Wheeler (1977). However, despite great dissatisfaction with both forms of arbitration, it is far from universal. I conclude from this that information-gathering costs are probably of much greater significance than the focus of research in mechanism design would suggest.

3. It is amusing that one of the most hotly contested issues in collective bargaining

is whether such an arbitrator can award, as part of his settlement, binding interest arbitration as the impasse procedure in the next negotiations.

4. This issue is misperceived in the arbitration literature partly because of excessive reliance on one-issue models of bargaining, in which inefficiency arises solely from the interaction of risk aversion and arbitral risk. This elimination from consideration of the most important sources of inefficiency overstates the case for the rational-optimism explanation. See Crawford (1981) for an elaboration of this point.

5. Myerson and Satterthwaite (1983), for example, demonstrate that this is true, in a class of examples, for the bargaining rules studied by Chatterjee and Samuelson (1983). This is no longer the case, however, as demonstrated by Samuelson (1984), when Myerson and Satterthwaite's assumption that bargainers' valuations of the object to be traded are independent is relaxed.

REFERENCES

Baldwin, C.: Productivity and Labor Unions: An Application of the Theory of Self-Enforcing Contracts. *Journal of Business 56* (1983), 155–85.

Bloom, D.: Is Arbitration Really Compatible with Bargaining? *Industrial Relations 20* (1981), 233–44.

Brams, S., and S. Merrill, III: Equilibrium Strategies for Final-Offer Arbitration: There Is No Median Convergence. *Management Science 29* (1983), 927–41.

Chatterjee, K., and W. Samuelson: Bargaining under Incomplete Information. *Operations Research 31* (1983), 835–51.

Crawford, V. P.: On Compulsory-Arbitration Schemes. *Journal of Political Economy 87* (1979), 131–59.

Arbitration and Conflict Resolution in Labor–Management Bargaining. *American Economic Review Papers and Proceedings 71* (1981), 205–210.

Compulsory Arbitration, Arbitral Risk, and Negotiated Settlements: A Case Study in Bargaining under Imperfect Information. *Review of Economic Studies 49* (1982a), 69–82.

A Comment on Farber's Analysis of Final-Offer Arbitration. *Journal of Conflict Resolution 26* (1982b), 157–60.

A Theory of Disagreement in Bargaining. *Econometrica 50* (1982c), 607–37.

Dynamic Bargaining: Long-Term Relationships Governed by Short-Term Contracts. University of California, San Diego, Discussion Paper No. 83-13 (1983), revised May.

Efficient and Durable Decision Rules: A Reformulation. *Econometrica 53* (1985), in press.

Donn, C.: Games Final-Offer Arbitrators Might Play. *Industrial Relations 16* (1977), 306–14.

Donn, C., and B. Hirsch: Making Interest Arbitration Costly: A Policy Proposal. *Journal of Collective Negotiations 12* (1983), 21–32.

Farber, H.: An Analysis of Final-Offer Arbitration. *Journal of Conflict Resolution 24* (1980), 683–705.

Farber, H., and H. Katz: Interest Arbitration, Outcomes, and the Incentive To Bargain. *Industrial and Labor Relations Review 33* (1979), 55–63.

Fuller, L.: Collective Bargaining and the Arbitrator. *Wisconsin Law Review 1963* (1963), 3–46.

Harsanyi, J., and R. Selten: A Generalized Nash Solution for Two-Person Bargaining Games with Incomplete Information. *Management Science 18* (1972), P80–P106.

Hirsch, B., and C. Donn: Arbitration and the Incentive To Bargain: The Role of Expectations and Costs. *Journal of Labor Research 3* (1982), 55–68.

Holmström, B.: Moral Hazard in Teams. *Bell Journal of Economics 13* (1982), 324–40.

Holmström, B., and R. Myerson: Efficient and Durable Decision Rules with Incomplete Information. *Econometrica 51* (1983), 1799–1819.

Kalai, E., and R. Rosenthal: Arbitration of Two-Party Disputes under Ignorance. *International Journal of Game Theory 7* (1978), 65–72.

Kreps, D., and R. Wilson: Sequential Equilibria. *Econometrica 50* (1982), 863–94.

Landes, W., and R. Posner: Adjudication as a Private Good. *Journal of Legal Studies 8* (1979), 235–84.

Malouf, M., and A. Roth: Disagreement in Bargaining: An Experimental Study. *Journal of Conflict Resolution 25* (1981), 329–48.

Milgrom, P., and N. Stokey: Information, Trade, and Common Knowledge. *Journal of Economic Theory 26* (1982), 17–27.

Moulin, H.: Prudence versus Sophistication in Voting Strategy. *Journal of Economic Theory 24* (1981), 398–412.

Myerson, R.: Incentive Compatibility and the Bargaining Problem. *Econometrica 47* (1979), 61–73.

Mechanism Design by an Informed Principal. *Econometrica 51* (1983), 1767–97.

Myerson, R., and M. Satterthwaite: Efficient Mechanisms for Bilateral Trading. *Journal of Economic Theory 29* (1983), 265–81.

Nash, J.: The Bargaining Problem. *Econometrica 18* (1950), 155–62.

Two-Person Cooperative Games. *Econometrica 21* (1953), 128–40.

Rosenthal, R.: Arbitration of Two-Party Disputes under Uncertainty. *Review of Economic Studies 45* (1978), 595–604.

Rothschild, M., and J. Stiglitz: Equilibrium in Competitive Insurance Markets: An Essay on the Economics of Imperfect Information. *Quarterly Journal of Economics 90* (1976), 629–49.

Samuelson, W.: Bargaining under Asymmetric Information. *Econometrica 52* (1984), 995–1005.

Schelling, T.: *The Strategy of Conflict.* London and New York: Oxford University Press, 1963.

Stevens, C.: Is Compulsory Arbitration Compatible with Bargaining? *Industrial Relations 5* (1966), 38–52.

Wheeler, H.: Closed Offer: Alternative to Final Offer. *Industrial Relations 16* (1977), 298–305.

Wilson, C.: A Model of Insurance Markets with Incomplete Information. *Journal of Economic Theory 16* (1977), 167–207.